The Cat
ENCYCLOPEDIA

ANIWA PUBLISHING

ROYAL CANIN

Adaptations:

German :
  Translations   K. Ayche, C. Belakhdar, B. Janka, A. Lucke, V. Matyssek, E. Moser, M. Neumann, B. Sallegger, S. Schmidt-Wussow, U. Wapler, P. Warnier-Kofler, R. Xanthopoulos.
  Layout   Magali Barrailler, Vania Soraru, Nathalie Courdent, Irina Azvedo-Tadieu, Joël Chapuis, Sabrina Monchi
  Rewriting   Kathrin Busch-Kschiewan, Nadja Hultsch, Sonja Zabel, Ursula Zabel
English :
  Translations   Diane Dinsmore, Julie Plounick, Chart Voss, Andrene Everson.
  Layout   Catherine Naas
  Rewriting   Roy Herridge, Emmanuel Pacitto, Anne Karpoff
Brazilian :
  Translations   S. Artamonoff, B. Delevallee, M. D'Orey de Faria, L. Goncalves, B. Magne, E. Rio Branco, M. Rosemberg, Madame Antunes.
  Layout   Florbela Lourenço Pires, Joël Chapuis, Irina Azvedo-Tadieu, Nathalie Courdent, Sabrina Monchi
  Rewriting   Claude Mouette, Yves Micelli, Valeria Cardoso de Melo Carvalho
Chinese :   Royal Canin Chine / François Gergaud
Spanish :
  Translations   Maria-Claudia Filgueira, Carles Sanchez
  Layout   Isabelle Riener
  Rewriting   Marie-Pierre Ellie, Maria-Claudia Filgueira
Italian :
  Translations   B. Baldi, D. Benigni, G. Conollo, D. De Leo, L. De Berardinis, L. Desotgiu, V. Fucci, C. Galimberti, S. Guazzoni, R. Kohn, P. Mequin, A.-M. Negrerte, A. Sudano, C. Torossi Bovo.
  Layout   Sabrina Monchi, Vania Soraru, Irina Azvedo-Tadieu, Nathalie Courdent, Joël Chapuis
  Rewriting   Franco Rapetti, Luca Bussolati
Netherlands :
  Translations   C. Boerhigter, K. Desmarsevers, A. Detelder, C. Dijkman, A. Frehen-Asures, B. Raemaekers, A. Scherpbier, P. Smift, M. Van Den Berg, B. Van Oosterhout, M. Van Zanten.
  Layout   Nathalie Courdent.
  Rewriting   Muriel Jacqmin, Cécile Devroy, Bastiaan Rohrer & The team Royal Canin Nederland b.v.
Swedish :
  Translations   A. Brantley, H. Hellberg, M. Jarvelin, R. Johansson, S. Jonsson, H. Karlson, J. Lindberg, U. Lundquist, M. Persson, S. Petersson, B. Sandstrom, C. Wallen, M. Vikberg.
  Layout   Joël Chapuis, Irina Azvedo-Tadieu.
  Rewriting   Bo Edoff, Anne-Catherine Edoff, Susanne Hellman, Ronan Mage, Hanna Edoff, Maud Dickson, Elisabeth Raab-Alvarson, Carin Lyrholm, Leg. Vet. Katarina Bewig, Wilhelm Dufwa, Ninni Hjortvall, Siw & Charles de Windle, Leg. Vet. Monica Stavenborn

This book is also available in French.

Coordination Royal Canin:	Catherine Legros
Project Editors:	Diffomédia / Paris
Art Director:	Guy Rolland
Coordination:	Béatrice Fortamps, Marie-Édith Baret
Illustrations:	Agnès Pezon
Cover:	Somali - © Hermeline/Cogis

© 2000 First edition in French

© 2005 Aniwa SA

Publisher: Aniwa Publishing
10, rue du Colisée - F.-75008 - Paris
Tél. : + 33 (0) 1 44 95 02 20 Fax : + 33 (0) 1 44 95 02 22
www.aniwa.com

Printed in EEC by Spada

NOTICE

The purpose of this work is to better inform the reader. It is not intended to be used as a medical guide in place of visits to and intervention by veterinary medical practitioners, who should in all cases be consulted on a regular basis.

Photo credits

All photos in this work are from the Cogis agency's photographic archives:
Francais, Garguil, Gauzargues, Gehlmar, Gelhar, Gengoux, Grissey, Hermeline, Ingeborg, Labat, Lanceau, Lepage, Lili, Nicaise, Potier, Remy, Rocher, Schwartz, Seitre, Varin, Vedie, Vidal, Willy's, Zizola.

Except:
- photos by Yann Arthus-Bertrand on the following pages: 58, 60-61, 62, 70, 95, 120, 122, 298

- illustrations from museums or agencies specializing in art or history photos, as referenced explicitly in the captions of these illustrations:

> Dagli-Orti, Paris – 261, 267, 272, 275, 278, 283, 284, 285
> National Veterinary School of Alfort – 410, 412, 414
> F. Gourdon, Paris – 266, 268, 282
> Giraudon, Paris – 286
> J. L. Charmet Collection, Paris – 262, 265, 269, 273, 280, 288, 290, 293
> Laboratoire Mérial– 411 (2 photos)
> Museum of Natural History, Paris – 5, 6
> Photographie Selva, Paris – 270, 276, 289, 291, 295, 297

- photos from the Royal Canin archives: Philippe Psaïla, Jean-Pierre Lenfant, and Yves Renner

Contributors

SCIENTIFIC ADVISORS

PROFESSOR BERNARD-MARIE PARAGON,
National Veterinary School of Alfort,
President, French Society of Feline Science

JEAN-PIERRE VAISSAIRE,
Doctor of Veterinary Medicine

And in alphabetical order:

Bacqué	Hélène	UMES – National Veterinary School of Alfort
Beugnet	Frédéric	Lecturer – National Veterinary School of Alfort
Biourge	Vincent	D.V.M. – Royal Canin Research Center
Blanchard	Géraldine	D.V.M. – National Veterinary School of Alfort
Bossé	Philippe	Professor – National Veterinary School of Alfort
Bullard-Cordeau	Brigitte	Editor-in-chief – Animal Junior
Casteran	Martine	Editor-in-chief – Atout Chat
Chatelain	Éliane	Professor – National Veterinary School of Lyon
Chaurand	Jean-Paul	D.V.M. – National Veterinary School of Alfort
Crépin	Fabrice	D.V.M. – Royal Canin
Déboise	Mikael	Researcher – Royal Canin Research Center
Fortamps	Béatrice	Editorial Coordinator – Diffomédia
Fradin-Ferme	Michèle	D.V.M. – Clinical Practitioner
Gagnon	Anne-Claire	D.V.M. – Vice President, French Society of Feline Science
Ganivet	Alain	D.V.M. – Clinical Practitioner
Garcia	Catherine	Training Director, Feline Science – Royal Canin
Gogny	Marc	Professor – National Veterinary School of Nantes
Grandjean	Dominique	Lecturer – National Veterinary School of Alfort
Guillot	Jacques	Lecturer – National Veterinary School of Alfort
Hugues	François	D.V.M. – Journalist, Europe 1
Kretz	Catherine	D.V.M. – Secretary, French Society of Feline Science
Lagarde	Henri	Chief Executive Officer – Royal Canin
Levesque	Anne	Research Center – Royal Canin
Moraillon	Anne	D.V.M. – National Veterinary School of Alfort
Morris	James G.	Professor – University of California, Davis
Pibot	Pascale	D.V.M. – Royal Canin Research Center
Pierson	Philippe	D.V.M. – Royal Canin
Samaille	Jean-Pierre	D.V.M. – Journalist, L'Action Vétérinaire
Soriano	Bruno	Journalist – Chat magazine
Vaissaire	Josée	D.V.M. – Member, Veterinary Academy of France

Publishing Managment
BERNARDO GALLITELLI,
Chief Executive Officer
Aniwa S.A.

GUY ROLLAND
Aniwa Publishing

IV

"The smallest feline is a masterpiece."

An Invitation to the World of the Cat

The cat, master of the house, so close yet so distant, so familiar yet so mysterious, has always fascinated humans with its looks and behavior.

Long-time inhabitants of the desert and savanna, cats still carry their biological needs and character within, as part of their physiology. Their character, like that of their distant ancestors, is a subtle combination of nonchalance and adventurousness.

From the deserts of yore to the countryside and cities of today, the feline world has changed rapidly:

- in thirty years, the number of feline breeds resulting from planned hybridization conducted by humans has virtually tripled, from some twenty in 1960 to over fifty at the end of the century.
- spectacular scientific knowledge has been acquired recently.

A specialist in premium feline nutrition, Royal Canin has long followed the tracks of this ancient solitary hunter. Major scientific advances of the past few years have brought us beyond the two traditional roles of nutrition (to build and maintain the organism, and to provide energy) and added a third: prevention. The notion of feline nutrition for health has been born.

Because humans domesticated cats, our primary task is to respect cats as animals, to feed them, and to ensure their health and well-being in accordance with their true specific needs, rather than based on our own human projections.
This is the approach of Royal Canin, a manufacturer specializing in premium feline nutrition which has always followed this ethic of true respect for the animal.

We hope this encyclopedia will help you discover a fascinating world rich with a long history and enhanced by the most recent scientific findings.

Thank you to all who contributed to creating this work: researchers at veterinary schools in France and abroad, as well as at the Royal Canin Research Center, under the direction of Professor Paragon and Dr. Vaissaire.

I invite you to explore these pages brimming with images and information and let yourself be swept away by the magical world of the cat, an intermingling of science and fantasy the cat offers us without restraint.

Henri LAGARDE,
Chief Executive Officer
Groupe Royal Canin

Foreword

Cats are not small dogs! Shameless hunters, cats have retained their original characteristics as strict carnivores from their hunting days. This explains why many of us are drawn to this exceptional companion and requires a careful respect for the cat's specific features, which each owner must know. This book is intended to reveal the big and small secrets that make up the cat.

The cohabitation of humans and cats, though it long remained distant, reaches back into the mists of time. The hunting skill of these small felines made them the natural protectors of granaries and kitchens. For this they were truly venerated in ancient Egypt. However, the cat's independence—sometimes bordering on disrespect—and the pagan practices with which cats were associated in the Middle Ages tarnished their image for a long time. Not until the literary salons of the 19th century and the world of artists did the cat come back into fashion. But this comeback was often at the price of the castration of males, a practice considered a means of re-entering the intelligentsia and acquiring a sort of perfection.

In our urban world, domestic cats carry a bit of the magic of the big cats, in their supple back, noble gait, and luminous gaze. We enjoy this and would hate to lose this pleasure. In France, one of every four households has at least one cat. Over eight million little felines will move in with us in the 21st century and, although most of this population might be considered "mixed breed cats," the fascination continues.

Yet another book on cats . . . but a book in which we aimed to combine knowledge, culture, and beauty; a book for an animal food manufacturer with contributions by scientists, writers, breeders, and enlightened cat fanciers. Because scientists are qualified to satisfy the natural curiosity of cat owners, we chose the best scientists for this project so that the basic knowledge gathered up to now could be made accessible to all in simple, precise terms. Because cats have been omnipresent in the world of humans throughout history, we sought proof of this presence in all forms of art and media. Because cats and beauty are closely intertwined, we aimed to gather the most beautiful illustrations in this book.

Sincere thanks to all who contributed to the technical, scientific, and aesthetic success of this work, particularly to my colleagues from the French Society of Feline Science. Our best reward will be the pleasure you find in exploring these pages and extracting the information that will help you better understand—and better love—your feline companion.

Professor B.-M. PARAGON,
President, French Society of Feline Science

Preface

Over eight million cats currently live in France. In the past decade, we made significant strides in our knowledge of this companion. For this reason, the project of making all the basic facts about this species accessible to the public, in an educational manner, is especially welcome.

By studying the origins and evolution of domestic cats, we can situate them within the Felids, of which the original type was the wild cat (Felis silvestris) that inhabited the large, Old World forests. Our Felis catus, represented by the many breeds described in the Cat Encyclopedia, is thought to have originated in Egypt from a wild felid living in Libya or eastern Africa.

Egyptian civilization gave the cat a privileged place among the gods. Bastet, the cat goddess of music, dance, and motherhood, appeared in the twenty-second dynasty, during the golden age of Pharaonic civilization.

Today, there are still many cat worshippers. Cat fanciers gather together in associations to work for the greater glory of the cat, although not always in perfect harmony. The merit of the Cat Encyclopedia is that it sums up the growing diversity of breeds and the ever-changing world of cat fancy.

Brought to France in the Middle Ages, the cat has remained highly present in art and the media. The appearance of cats in both pictorial works of the classical period and in works of animal artists of the 19th and 20th centuries shows that artists used these subjects to convey their anguish, joy, and fantasies.

The chapters covering the various aspects of daily life with a cat are of great practical value to the reader. Feline physiology and pathology are now much better understood, thanks to original work demonstrating that, contrary to an opinion long considered dogma, cats cannot be put in the same category as dogs. Cats have different nutritional needs, very different behavior, and, quite often, specific illnesses.

The Cat Encyclopedia, under the talented direction of Professor Bernard-Marie Paragon, brings together contributors who are the authority in their respective fields. They made often complex notions accessible to the general public. There is no doubt that cat lovers—I hesitate to write "owners," so true is it that, while you can own a dog, you instead live in your cat's home, with the cat always retaining a certain degree of independence—will find in this work the information they seek on their favorite animal.

Professor Robert MORAILLON,
Director, National Veterinary School of Alfort

Summary

THE BREEDS

Abyssinian
African Shorthair
American Bobtail
American Curl
American Shorthair
American Wirehair
Balinese
Bengal
Russian Blue
Birman
Bombay
British Shorthair
Burmese
Burmilla
California Spangled
Ceylon
Chartreux
Cornish Rex
Cymric
Devon Rex
Domestic Lynx
Egyptian Mau
European Shorthair
Exotic Shorthair
German Rex
Havana

Japanese Bobtail
Javanese
Kora
La Perm
Maine Coon
Manx
Munchk
Norwegian Forest Cat
Ocicat
Ojos Azules
Oriental Longhair
Oriental Shorthair
Persian
Pixie Bob
Ragdoll
Scottisch Fold
Selkirk Rex
Siamese
Siberian Cat
Singapura
Snowshoe
Somali
Sphynx
Tonkinese
Turkish Van
York Chocolate

True
respect
of the
Cat

As forgivable as it may be, treating the cat as if it were a little human being is a biological mistake that may prove to be dangerous for the animal.

Respecting the cat for what it gives us and represents to us should not consist of developing an anthropomorphic approach aiming to make the cat, as we often hear, "a child, if only it could speak". Biology is such that it preferred the earthly diversity of living creatures, making each one of them the complement of the others so as to tend towards a delicate balance that Man may not alter in any way.

This anthropomorphic reflex, as forgivable as it may be, given the sometimes powerful emotions that we all feel towards our cats, must therefore be shunned as being disrespectful of their biological and physiological functioning and, consequently, may prove to be dangerous to them.

The best examples of this reality may be found in the daily diet

• Man can change his diet at each mealtime without problems … but, if his digestive system were designed like that of the cat, such continuous dietary variation would give him constant problems with diarrhoea.

• Man needs cooked food, salt, sugar, appetizing smells and presentation of the food on his plate in order to enjoy his meal, but, if his senses were those of the cat, he would need only the merest hint of the latter to appreciate it completely …

• For thousands of years, man has been able to take his time to eat his meals, without the risk of becoming the prey of a wild predator but, if he were a cat, evolution would have left him with more of

that reflex of rapid consumption imprinted in the genes of all animals likely to have their food stolen by a member of its own species or be attacked by a predator …

• Man takes his meals at regular intervals (morning, midday, evening), but the cat is originally a lone hunter of desert lands who provides for his dietary needs by a succession of small meals, morning, noon and night (up to 16 a day).

So, with all due deference; cats are cats. They must be appreciated, treated and respected as such. And, if we consider the examples already mentioned, science and observation will only support these facts.
The digestion is a typical example of the reactions and mechanisms proper to each species, any assimilation may prove to be dangerous for the cat (or for humans), the differences being so obvious and the behaviour patterns so dissimilar.

The passage of food in the organism allows a better understanding of these key notions.
Generally speaking, the human digestive system represents 11% of the body weight, compared with only 2.8% to 3.5% for the cat. Hardly surprising to hear that Man is better able to digest the most varied elements.

Food appreciation: *smell and taste differently involved*

The cat, unlike human beings, appreciates its food first and foremost by smell. The surface of its nasal mucus is 10 times greater than that of humans. A cat's nose contains up to 67 million olfactory receptors, while the most sensitive human nose has no more than 20 million. Taste, however, despite the received wisdom, is only very marginally involved in the cat's food preferences. While humans have some 9 000 "taste buds" (the cells that receive and analyse the taste of food), the cat has 19 times fewer and, once in its mouth, the food does not linger on the tongue but is sent very quickly towards the stomach. The cat, which does not respond particularly to sweet tastes, is a strict carnivore that does not "synthetise" taurine, but finds it exclusively in the flesh of the animals it hunts or in prepared croquettes.

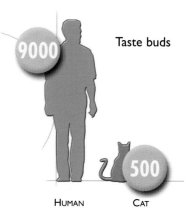

9000   Taste buds

500

HUMAN   CAT

Predigestion: *from the oral cavity to the stomach*

The cat spends very little of its time chewing its food. It eats hastily, whereas humans ready their food for digestion by prolonged chewing, finding pleasure by releasing flavours and, by grinding the food down and mixing it with saliva, and begins the first stage of digestion via the enzymes contained in the latter. For the cat, however, the stomach is the chief location where the processes of digestion are started.

Scientific reality shows us once again: the stomach represents more than 60% of the total weight of the digestive system of the feline species compared with only 11% for humans.

The very acid stomach pH, plus the large amounts of hydrochloric acid (6 times greater than in humans), equips the cat's stomach admirably for its function as a purifier, providing it with an extraordinarily efficient natural barrier against digestive infections.

Weight of digestive tract as percentage of body weight	**11%**	**2,8% to 3,5%**
Surface of nasal mucus	2 à 3 cm^2	20 cm^2
Olfactory cells	5 to 20 million	60 to 65 million
Taste buds	9 000 buds	500 buds
Dentition	32 teeth	30 teeth
Mastication	prolonged	no chewing
Salivary digestive enzymes	YES	NO
Duration of food intake	1 hour	multiple meals
Stomach capacity	1,3 l	0,3 l
Stomach pH	2 to 4	1 to 2
Length of small intestine	6 to 6,5 m	1 to 1,7 m
Length of large intestine	1,5 m	0,3 to 0,4 m
Density of intestinal flora	10 000 000 bacteria/g	10 000 bacteria/g
Duration of intestinal transit	30 hours to 5 days	12 to 24 hours
Adult glucid requirement	60 to 65% of the dry matter	low
Adult protein requirement	8 to 12% of the dry matter	25 to 40% of the dry matter
Adult lipid requirement	25 to 30% of the dry matter	15 to 45% of the dry matter
Dietary habit	**omnivore**	**carnivore**

Digestive performance: *inherited in the genes*

Originally, the cat is a "nibbler". In fact, if food is left out for it, the cat will make between 10 and 16 snacks a day. The cat also drinks about 10 times a day. Meals last only 2 to 3 minutes. These small quantities spread throughout the day explain why the digestive transit is very rapid in the cat compared with that of humans (12 to 24 hours compared with 30 to 48 hours).

To understand these elements, which may also be considered in other biological functional aspects, is to understand the cat, and above all to accept that the cat is very different to the human, not only in its appearance or in the fact that it cannot "speak". The sometimes-extreme anthropomorphism touted in certain films, for instance, is not only scientifically regrettable, but is actually very harmful and may even reduce the life expectancy of the animal.

The differences between man and cat

*Physiological differences
and differences in basic dietary habit mean
that each has specific nutritional needs.*

Failure to recognize the real needs of the animal, combined with every owner's natural desire to "do the best", may represent a danger to our animals by projecting on to them our wishes, our lifestyles, without taking account of the essential: their animal nature.

Responsible for the domestication of the cat, man has the duty of feeding it according to its true specific needs, and not according to any human projections. The animal is an animal, and in no way a human being as regards its biology. This is the first rule of true respect of the animal. The choice of food best adapted to one's animal must therefore be guided by a dietary approach that is not influenced by one's own eating habits.

Since the dawn of time Man has been an omnivore, blessed with a sense of taste and enjoying variety to dispel boredom, whereas the organism of the cat, a strict carnivore, is adapted to one particular type of food. Although it is sometimes tempting to

apply the rule of diversity to your cat and serve it food more closely resembling a human meal, this would be ill-adapted to its condition or its morphology. Nearly 5 000 years of domestication of the feline race have not succeeded in transforming these strict carnivores into omnivores.

The same applies to all those little pleasures we offer them in the image of those we treat ourselves to. Butter, a spoonful of yoghurt, fish, cheese ... all these little "extras" disturb the perfectly balanced ration calculated by a nutritionist. Such imbalances may result in intestinal problems and slowly but surely debilitate the animal. We must remain on our guard and curb our anthropomorphic instincts that may harm the good health of our animals.

From "feeding" to "Health Nutrition"

*To enjoy life
as long as possible*

Although death is, and will remain, an inescapable biological process, it is also true that immense progress has been made in medical science, especially on the preventive side of the equation, now ensuring our feline friends a steadily increasing life expectancy.

An extraordinary improvement in nutrition:

In the past 30 years, the foods prepared by animal feed manufacturers for domestic pets have brought about a revolutionary change in the conditions of life of our cats, formerly fed on scraps and leftovers. It has been estimated that cats have acquired nearly 5 years of additional life expectancy in the past 15 years alone.

It is quite probable that the years to come will bring even higher figures, since three major advances have been made in the past 30 years:

• until 1980, a cat was simply "fed" to stop it feeling hungry,

• after 1980, Health Nutrition took its first steps by allowing for 2 parameters: the Age of the animal and its Level of Activity,

• 1997 to 2000 marks the arrival of Health Nutrition with two new dimensions: Prevention and type of Breed. Four parameters were now taken into account: not only Age and Activity, but also Breed and Physiological Condition of the animal.

The four objectives of health nutrition

1 - To build up/sustain the organism
2 - To provide energy
3 - To nourish and to prevent
4 - To nourish and to treat

It is now possible to formulate feeds in the light of clearly identified requirements, according to known and indexed deficiencies that have to be combated, and to specificities discovered along the way as research moves onwards. Scientists now realise that cats do not have to be fed the same way regardless of whether they are kittens, adults, elderly, pregnant or neutered … all of which are elements to take into account in their daily diet.

This realisation is growing daily and allows the development of the simple Feed (feeding to sustain the animal), and the Basic

Nutrition (meeting the nutritional needs of the organism), then going on to Health Nutrition, where a distinction is made between two complementary approaches: "Nourish and Prevent" and "Nourish and Treat".

So, driven by scientific research in veterinary medicine, the traditional concept of nutrition, namely building up/sustaining the organism and providing energy, has transformed in a matter of years to include the dimensions of prevention and, under certain conditions, treatment.

Basic Nutrition (Nutritional Needs of the Organism)

1 - Building up/sustaining the organism:
Amino acids, minerals, trace elements, vitamins, proteins and certain lipids meet the minimum nutritional need to build up and sustain the organism.

Growth, reproduction, muscles, coat...: proteins
Nervous system, skeleton, teeth, blood...: minerals and trace elements
Sight, reproduction, skeleton, cells ...: vitamins
Cell membranes: lipids

2 - Providing energy:
Lipids, carbohydrates and, to a lesser extent, proteins give the animal the necessary energy.

Energy, appetite: lipids
Energy, digestion: carbohydrates
Non-essential amino acids

Health Nutrition

Nutrition is now - and this is at least one point of convergence between man and catkind - a key aspect of prevention, probably even the most important; this accounts for its being considered as the

first among medicines (as did Hippocrates in antiquity) … and no doubt the gentlest of them all.

3 - Nourish and prevent:
Certain nutrients are integrated in the prevention of risks such as kidney diseases, digestive problems or the effects of old age …

Bone condition: calcium, excess fatty deposits
Kidney problems: reduced phosphorus levels
Digestive problems: addition of "prebiotics", fermentable fibres encouraging good balance of the intestinal flora, proteins
Premature ageing: vitamins E-C, essential fatty acids, grape and green-tea polyphenols

4 - Nourish and treat:
To aid recovery from certain illnesses, highly specific nutrients will be included in or left out of the food as part of the therapeutic and convalescent processes.

Kidneys, allergies, heart, obesity, intestines

"Nutrients" approach
and "Ingredients" approach

*The **"Nutrients"** approach:*
a "nutritional jigsaw puzzle"
with fifty pieces.

This presentation of the concept of nutrition in general and health nutrition in particular thus reinforces the distinction between two approaches with regard to the formulation of products for use in animal feeding: the "Nutrients" approach and the "Ingredients" approach.

The **"Nutrients" approach** allows the formulation of a balanced feed by the putting together of a veritable "jigsaw puzzle" of some fifty "nutrients". Each one of them is indispensable for the health of the animal. In the right proportions, the nutrients represent a more of less large part of each piece of the puzzle. This composition makes possible the accomplishment of the four main objectives of Health Nutrition (building up and sustaining the organism,

providing energy, nourishing and preventing, nourishing and treating), taking account of the parameters of Age, Level of Activity, Breed and Physiological Condition. It also meets the real precise and specific needs of each animal.

The **"Ingredients" approach**, on the other hand, is no more than a simple list of standardised elements (or primary alimentary materials if you will) used in the composition of a food preparation, sometimes even with a simple anthropomorphic vision, as if the animal had the palate and the digestive system of a human. It therefore proves to be less precise, and above all disregards the real needs of the animal.

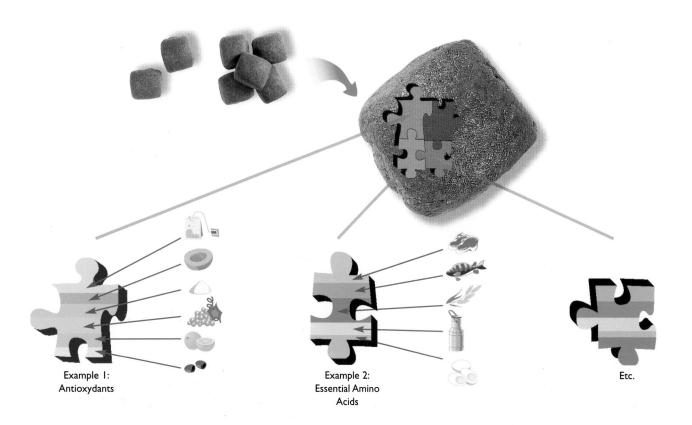

Example 1:
Antioxydants

Example 2:
Essential Amino
Acids

Etc.

Nutrients or ingredients? The "Ingredients" trap

25% fresh meat ▬▬ 4 à 5% de proteins

How does a feed containing 25% of fresh meat in fact contribute only 4% to 5% of the proteins originating in the fresh meat?

Nourishing a cat properly is therefore a 2-stage operation:

1ˢᵗ stage: a genuine understanding of the animal, its physiology, its biology, its behaviour and, therefore, the real needs of its organism.

2ⁿᵈ stage: an equally scientific approach not only to the nutrients intended to cover these needs, but also to those intended to generate the preventive side - or, as the case may be, the curative side - of the prepared animal feed.

A genuinely nutritional feed is therefore most often a veritable jigsaw puzzle of 50 or 60 essential nutrients (proteins, minerals, vitamins, trace elements, lipids, carbohydrates, …), whereas the seduction of an eye-catching list of "Ingredients" is only very anthropomorphic and serves no real purpose beyond that of flattering the master ("chicken flavour", "lamb", "salmon").

As surprising as it may seem, the protein content of a feed claiming "25% fresh meat" is only between 4% and 5% of the total weight on the dry matter. In fact, the regulations require the pet food manufacturers to list the ingredients by descending order of weight, before cooking. Fresh meat or certain ingredients containing large amounts of water may therefore be placed at the top of the list, creating the illusion of their being the main source of nutrition.

In the case of a feed claiming to contain 25% lamb, the dry croquette will therefore contain only 4% to 5% of lamb proteins after cooking. Suppose this feed also contains 20% maize, 20% rice, 15% dried fish, 10% poultry fat and 10% vegetable oil. The manufacturer can write "Lamb" in large characters as the main ingredient but, in reality, there is only 4% to 5% lamb proteins, while the cereals are the main ingredients in the finished feed in terms of quantity.

One feed, three different descriptions!

"with beef"	minimum 4% of beef
"with lamb"	minimum 4% of lamb
"with chicken"	minimum 4% of chicken
"rich in beef"	minimum 14% of beef
"rich in lamb"	minimum 14% of lamb

Dry cat food "with beef" 4% beef

=

Dry cat food "with lamb" 4% lamb

=

Dry cat food "with chicken" 4% chicken

The same ingredients... the same foodstuffs... but 3 different names and 3 different packs

Another example: the same feed containing, among other ingredients, 4% chicken, 4% lamb and 4% beef may be labelled under three different descriptions: "chicken", "lamb" or "beef". And there will always be someone there to tell you that his animal prefers the lamb version, despite the fact that the actual lamb content is exactly the same as that of the chicken version.

However, this "Ingredients" approach, which has deceived more than one owner, fails to take account of the dosage, quantity, or quality, and of the variety of origins of nutrients - essential to life and adapted to the specific needs of cats - that ensure the quality of a balanced feed. A "standard" feed may, for instance, contain some fifteen nutrients, whereas a "pedigree" or "nutritional" feed will usually contain up to fifty.

Royal Canin, undisputed precursor of feline health nutrition

*Royal Canin: a nutrition concept
that wins the day by uncompromising
fidelity to its roots: "Knowledge and Respect".*

Since its creation, the veterinarians and nutritional experts at Royal Canin have directed their constant efforts towards achieving major advances in terms of canine and feline nutrition. Each year brings its crop of new nutritional programmes and new nutritional formulas that, besides the nutrients essential for maintaining healthy life, also incorporate natural elements to prevent certain diseases and to protect the animal.

1997
First world launch: a new generation of nutritional cat food products (RCFI range), targeted according to the age and physiological condition of the cat (Kitten, Fit , Sensible, Slim, Senior). This new generation resolutely abandoned the traditional anthropomorphic approach based on ingredients ("salmon", "chicken", …). The RCFI range was an immediate spectacular world-wide success.

1998
First feed developed specifically for castrated males and spayed females at veterinary clinics: Vet Cat, to Nourish and Prevent.

1999
Persian 30: result of the co-operation between R&D and the breeders, the first feed adapted to the physiognomy and the specific nutritional needs of Persian cats:
- development of the Almond 11 croquette,
- Derm system (for a healthy coat and skin care),
- Hairball Transit System (to help eliminate hairballs in the stomach).

2001
World launch of Indoor 27 ®, 1st feed formulated for indoor cats (hairballs, obesity, smell).

2001
V-Diet, to Nourish and Treat, the development of 6 dietary products for cats in particular:
- the hydrolysate for the Hypoallergenic Program,
- the hyperprotein diet for the Obesity Program.

2002
Launch of 4 big world firsts with the new Feline Nutrition range with cats in mind:
- Reinforcement of natural defences (Immunity Program),
- Campaign against cellular ageing (Anti-ageing Complex),
- Regeneration of coat and skin,
- Specially textured croquettes.

2002
Vet Cat Neutered: the first-ever nutritional super-prevention range to cater for the physiological specificities of cats, spayed females and castrated males.

Familiarity breeds respect

To define its products, Royal Canin does not conduct market research or consumer polls, but places the cat, its "one true client", at the centre of operations.
Knowledge of the real nutritional needs of the cat is derived from the daily experience of the partner breeders and the veterinary nutritionists and from the first-hand scientific observations of the Royal Canin Research and Development experts.

An original method allows Royal Canin, more than any other Brand, to be genuinely in the vanguard of innovation and nutritional precision.
A philosophy also based on the sharing of knowledge of the cat through reference works, such as guides to breeding and training and, of course, this Encyclopaedia of the Cat.

KNOWLEDGE AND RESPECT

Part 1

CATS, YESTERDAY TO TODAY

1

FELIDS OF THE WORLD

The Prehistory of the Cat

*The cat as we know it today is the result of at least forty million years of evolution. Thanks
to numerous fossils, we are able to establish the gradual evolution of the wild felids,
the cousins of the cat.*

*The wild felids are a very homogenous family. Females and males are similar, with males
simply being larger and heavier. Only the lion, with his mane, is an exception.*

*The wild felids are fully carnivorous and the best adapted of all animals to capturing live prey.
They are present in most of the world except for Antarctica, Australia, Madagascar, the Antilles,
and a few other islands.*

*The Felidae family includes three subfamilies: the now extinct Nimravinae, the Acinonychinae,
including the cheetahs, and the Felinae, with two groups of species: Big Cats (Panthera genus)
and Small Cats (Felis genus), which gave rise to the domestic cat.*

The Origin Cats

Eusmilus, an early Felid of the Tertiary period, inhabited Eurasia and North America. About the size of a Puma, it had two enormous canine teeth in its upper jaw and walked fairly plantigrade, or flat-footed. The Fossa is an animal endemic to the island of Madagascar. Grouped in the early Viverridae family, it weighs approximately 10 kg and resembles a Puma. It is the largest meat-eater indigenous to the island.

As the dinosaurs were going extinct in the late Mesozoic era, the first Mammals appeared. In fact the survivors of these early Mammals, which were the insectivores, were during the late Cretaceous period, some seventy million years ago, thought to have given rise to the Carnivores and Primates. In the Paleocene epoch, Mammals included the Creodonts, an order of small, heavy-boned animals no taller than 30 cm that stood low to the ground and walked semi-plantigrade, but were already equipped with claws. They were the precursors of the Carnivores. The earliest known Carnivores of this epoch had a completely different anatomy from modern Carnivores. They went extinct in the Eocene epoch and were replaced by the fissiped Carnivores, which had larger, more developed carnassial teeth than the Creodonts.

The Fissipeds

Then, the canines and carnassials developed significantly, especially in the Eucreodonts. These descendents of the Procreodonts of the Paleocene epoch were the forerunners of modern-day carnivores. One of the first named was Miacis (*Miacoidea*), a type of tree-dwelling genet (an animal in the civet family) of the Americas and Eurasia which had a longer body and legs than the Creodonts.

Miacis gave rise to the Miacidae, an intermediate family between the Creodonts and the Fissipeds. The Miacidae were small in size and

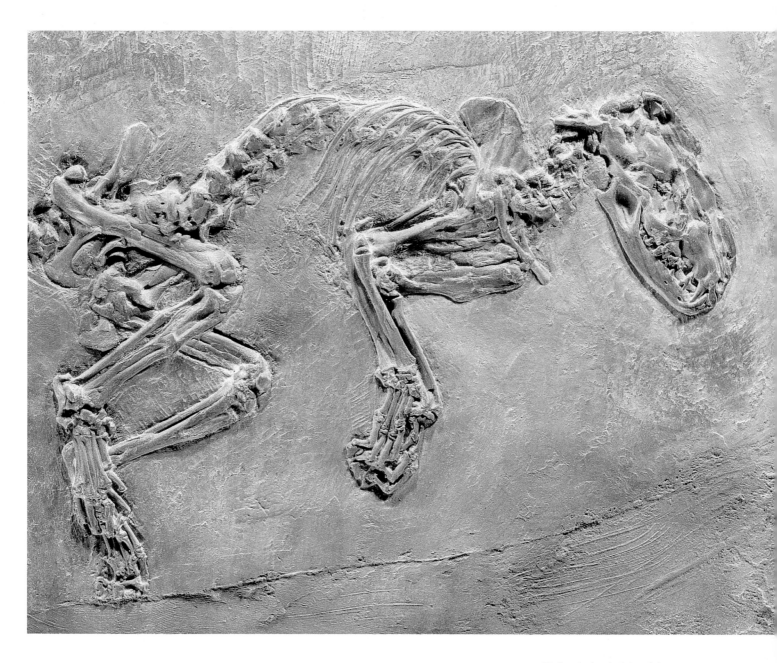

probably forest dwelling. They went extinct in the late Eocene epoch.

In addition, by the late Eocene epoch, in Eurasia and the Americas, certain descendants of the Miacids appeared, namely representatives of modern Canids (dogs and wolves), Mustelids (polecats, weasels, etc.), Ursids (bears), and Procyonids (raccoons, etc.). The Viverrids (mongooses) and later the Felids and Hyenids are thought to have descended from animals very similar to the Miacids. The Miacids are certainly the most likely ancestors of the Fissipeds, the distant ancestors of Felines.

The Early Felids

Next, during the Oligocene epoch, the Felids showed a clear tendency leading to individualization of two different branches of Felines. On the one hand, large and hardy but slow animals with enormous saberlike canines: Eusmilus; and on the other hand, large, more flexible, and faster Cats with teeth similar to those of modern-day Felids: Proailurus, and

Tailless body of a Miacid dating approximately 45 million years ago (Eocene epoch) from the Messel site in Germany. National Museum of Natural History, Paris. The body of this Miacid measures 24 cm.

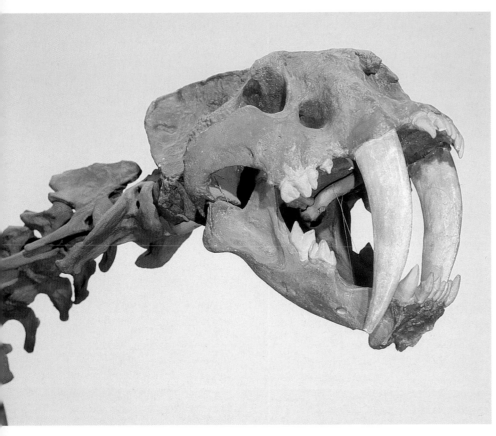

later *Pseudailurus*, whose gait resembled that of the Viverrids. For example, today's Fossa (*Crytoprocta ferox*) is a true living fossil of this animal.

Pseudailurus is thought to be the first member of the modern cat family, of which, in America, Smilodon was a spectacular representative. The Small Felines then adapted to diverse terrain, including deserts, forests, steppes, and swamps.

After, at the time of the Miocene epoch, *Felis zitteli* inhabited France. This animal was very similar to the modern-day Wild Cat that now lives in our countries. Next, during the *Pleistocene* epoch of the Quaternary period, the genus Felis appeared, and the early Cats - Smilodons and Machairodus, types of saber-toothed tigers - went extinct.

The First Wild Cats

During the Quaternary period, the first modern-day Wild Cats appeared. Probably dating from the early Pleistocene epoch (1.8 million years ago), Martelli's Wild Cat (*Felis lunensis*) can be considered one of the direct ancestors of our modern-day cats. This Feline is thought to have given rise to the Wild Cat (*Felis silvestris*), which appeared at the end of the second glacial epoch.

Smilodon: skull from Rancho La Brea, California, United States, dating approximately one million years ago. National Museum of Natural History, Paris.
Its saberlike canines measure 20 cm long. Smilodon had the stature of a tiger, with stocky limbs and a short tail. It is the most recent saber-toothed Feline and was probably encountered by the first humans. In the United States, hundreds of Smilodons were discovered in a tar depositary, where they became trapped while hunting mammoths. Its the Rancho La Brea pit.

THE CREODONTS
This order of carnivores had massive bodies, stood low to the ground, walked semi-plantigrade, and had a relatively large skull for their body, with an imposing massif facial. The tympanic bulla was not rigid. The primitive brain had large olfactory centers and nearly smooth hemispheres, leaving the cerebellum exposed. The dentition was complete and typical of a carnivore. The earliest Creodonts were the Procreodonts, which lived at the dawn of the Tertiary period in North America and Europe. The dentition of this group, which lacked distinct carnassials, was similar to that of the insectivores. The more highly developed Eucreodonts gradually developed into today's carnivores. Some of their teeth evolved into carnassials. In the Oligocene epoch, the Creodonts evolved into the Fissipeds.

THE FISSIPEDS
This order of land-dwelling carnivores had limbs well spaced from their body, unjoined fingers equipped with claws, a rigid tympanic bulla, a reduced or nonexistent pollex (thumb) and hallux (big toe), and a temporal fossa with a wide passage to the orbital cavity in most species. Some species were omnivorous or frugivorous. Young Fissipeds were altricial (born helpless).

THE FELIDS
The Felid family marked the end of carnassial evolution. They had a fairly globe-shaped skull and very pronounced zygomatic arches providing an insertion point and space for strong masticatory muscles. The mandibular joint allowed only vertical movement. The Felids walked digitigrade, or on the tips of the toes, and had retractile claws and vertical pupils.

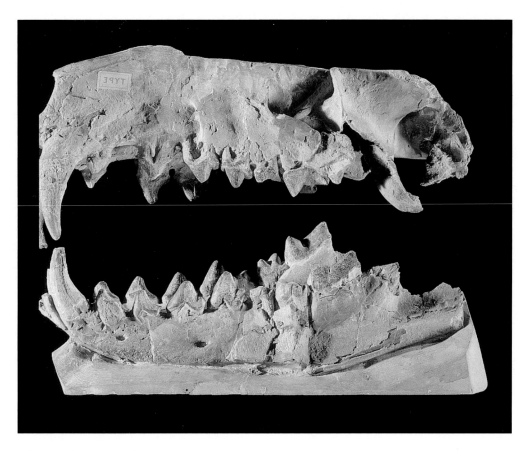

Jaws of a Creodont of the genus Hyaenodon dating approximately 35 million years ago (early Oligocene epoch). They were found at the Ronzon site in France's upper Loire Valley. National Museum of Natural History, Paris. The carnassials are already highly pronounced.

The Wild Cat rapidly spread throughout Europe, Asia, and Africa, evolving into three main types: the European Wild Cat (*Felis silvestris silvestris*), the African Wild Cat (*Felis silvestris lybica*), and the Asian or Indian Desert Cat (*Felis silvestris ornata*). Some believe that the distinct separation between European and African Wild Cats occurred approximately 20,000 years ago.

From Wild Cats to Domestic Cats

Our domestic cat (*Felis silvestris catus*, formerly *Felis catus*) appears to have descended from the African Wild Cat. In fact, it is thought to have evolved from several wild species, including the Asian Desert Cat (*Felis silvestris ornata*) of Iran, Pakistan, and India. This animal, which will naturally approach humans, has a yellowish-gray coat with round black spots and a long, ringed tail with a black tip. The African Wild Cat (*Felis silvestris lybica*), which interbred with the Asian Desert Cat and was

domesticated in Egypt in 2500 B.C., has features similar to the tiger cat: short, fawn gray or brownish-gray hair, transversal stripes on the flanks, transversal black stripes on the legs, and a ringed tail with a black tip. The African Wild Cat is easily tamed. These animals are likely ancestors of our cat. As for Felis silvestris, it is a resolutely wild, virtually untamable animal.

The Dawn of Domestication

The domestication of the cat remains rather mysterious and has not been pinned down with certainty. According to the traditional belief, cats were domesticated in Egypt, where the earliest proof of domestication around 4500 B.C. has been found. This Egyptian Cat probably descended from one of the subspecies of *Felis silvestris lybica*. Initially, it probably lived alongside humans, sharing food; then a greater degree of closeness was established between humans and the animal that became first a "familiar" and then a "companion."

Domestication is the transformation of a wild animal species into a species that can be used by humans for the purpose of providing products or services. Today, a new degree of closeness exists between Cats and Humans: Indeed, Cats now live in close contact with us, and our relations with them engender a strong emotional attachment.

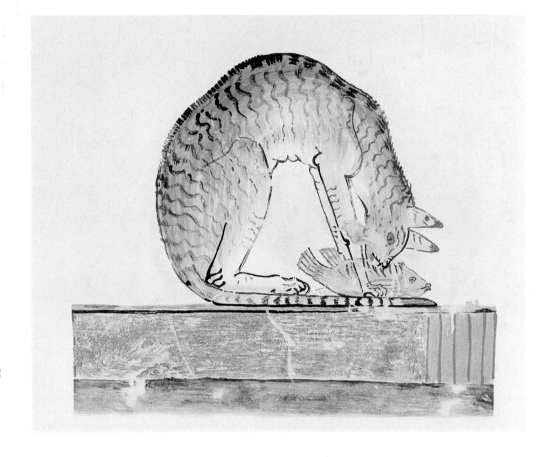

Fresco from the Tomb of Nakht. Detail: Cat eating a fish. Valley of the Kings in Thebes, Egypt. Eighteenth Dynasty. From the watercolor by Nina Davier. National Museum of Natural History, Paris.
The tomb of the scribe Nakht, dating to approximately 1425 B.C., contained a fresco depicting a banquet scene with a tiger cat eating a fish under a chair.
This cat certainly appears to have been a familiar, fed by its owners.

Throughout the New Empire (approximately 1580 - 1070 B.C.) and until the Ptolemaic periods (300 - 30 B.C.), the Egyptians must have permitted the Wild Cats to approach and therefore must have tamed them, later mummifying these Cats like those that had long been domesticated.

However, some researchers believe that cats were domesticated independently in several different areas, including Pakistan, where the small-skulled Asian Desert Cat still lives in the wild (this is the cat that might have gone to Egypt), Libya, home of the Libyan Cat with a greater skull capacity, and perhaps also the southern Far East, which would explain the separate origin of the European Shorthair.

The Egyptians' worship of Cats might have begun with a breed of domestic cats of Indian origin, but the Domestic Cat's Asian origin is still debated.

Archaeologists have used several methods to measure the degree of domestication of the Cat, including Schauenberg's cranial index, or the ratio of skull length to cranial capacity. This index is lowest in the Domestic Cat and closer to that of the Desert Cat of Afghanistan, Pakistan, and Iran than to that of the Libyan Desert Cat. According to Schauenberg, the Cat probably arrived in Egypt from Iran already domesticated or in the process of being domesticated.
This hypothesis based on cranial volume links the Domestic Cat to the Wild Cat of India and Pakistan. In fact, Schauenberg demonstrated that this Wild Cat had a cranial capacity inferior to that of the African Wild Cat and of mummified Cats from Egypt but close to that of the Domestic Cat. Domestication therefore appears to be linked to cranial capacity or brain size: the lower the capacity, the more "domesticated" the animal.

The Origin of Felids and Cats

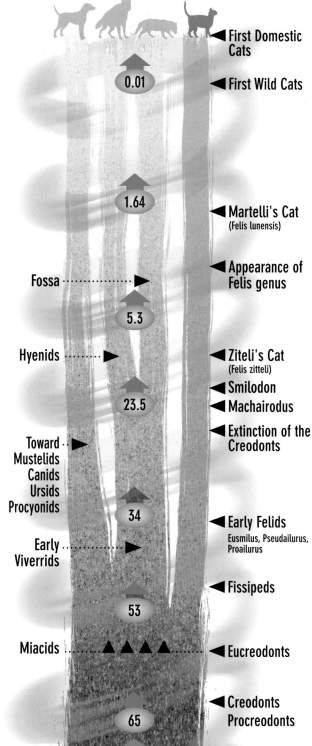

Geological Times

QUATERNARY

Holocene
Late Quaternary, approximately 10,000 years in duration.

Pleistocene

TERTIARY

Pliocene

Miocene
Appearance of highly evolved Mammals, extinction of the Creodonts.

Oligocene

Eocene
Period of differentiation of Mammals and the beginning of Alpine formation.

Paleocene

MESOZOIC

Cretaceous

First Domestic Cats

First Wild Cats

0.01

1.64

Martelli's Cat
(Felis lunensis)

Appearance of Felis genus

Fossa

5.3

Hyenids

Ziteli's Cat
(Felis zitteli)

Smilodon

Machairodus

23.5

Extinction of the Creodonts

Toward
Mustelids
Canids
Ursids
Procyonids

34

Early Felids
Eusmilus, Pseudailurus, Proailurus

Early
Viverrids

Fissipeds

53

Miacids

Eucreodonts

Creodonts
Procreodonts

65

Millions of years

Insectivores

DNA 3.5 billion years.
Deoxyribonucleic acid: a nucleic acid that is the main component of the chromosomes in the cell nucleus and is the material of heredity.

Big Bang
15 billion years.
Explosion thought to have marked the beginning of the expansion of the universe.

Earth
4.6 billion years. Estimated age of Earth, a planet in the solar system inhabited by humans.

9

The Small Cats

Unlike the Big Cats, the Small Cats have a completely rigid hyoid bone that prevents them from roaring. The Small Cats purr during inhalation and exhalation, whereas the Big Cats purr only during exhalation. All Small Cats belong to the same group, of which the Puma, similar in size to a Panther, is a member.

Felis silvestris.

Felis silvestris. Anonymous etching.
Late 19th century.
Private collection.

The Cats of Europe

The European Wild Cat (Felis silvestris silvestris) has a powerful-looking stature. It is found primarily in Scotland, Germany, eastern France, and the Pyrenees. It frequents forests and rocky areas and does not like snow. A solitary animal, it is active at dusk and nighttime. Its mating season is from January to March. In April or May, after a gestation period of slightly over two months, the female gives birth to two to four kittens born blind and with hair. The European Wild Cat never hunts in trees and feeds mainly on rodents, rabbits, ground-nesting birds, cockchafers, and grasshoppers. The European Wild Cat was long considered a pest and therefore destroyed. Its very discreet behavior has enabled the species to survive in certain regions. However, few purebred European Wild Cats are left today, since these animals often mate with feral Cats. The species is protected.

Together with the wolf and the brown bear, the Eurasian Lynx is one of Europe's three main predators and the only Big Cat living wild on the European continent.

A solitary animal inhabiting wide-open spaces, the Eurasian Lynx is a nocturnal hunter with no permanent home. With its short tail and black spotted coat, the Eurasian Lynx blends perfectly with its natural environment, making it very difficult to detect. It is carnivorous and feeds on the prey it captures, including essentially roe deer and chamois, or rodents, birds, and even insects. Once each year, by december, males and females meet for mating. After a seventy-day gestation period, the female finds shelter in an area with enough game to feed her young and gives birth to an average of two to three kittens that remain with her for a year.

The Spanish Lynx, which lives only in Spain and Portugal, resembles the Eurasian Lynx so closely that it was often considered a sub-

Lynx

Sand Cat.

*Jungle Cat. Anonymous etching.
Late 19th century. Private collection.*

The Chinese Desert Cat (*Felis bieti*) lives in the mountains of northern and central China at altitudes up to 3,000 meters. This rare and little known Feline resembles the European Wild Cat.

The Black-Footed Cat (*Felis nigripes*) is found in the arid regions of South Africa. It is the smallest Wild Felid, weighing no more than 2 kg. Its yellowish-brown coat is covered with black stripes and spots.

The Jungle Cat (*Felis chaus*) was long called the Swamp Lynx because of the tuft of hair on the tips of its ears, its long limbs, its relatively short tail, and its imposing size. Its range extends from Egypt to India and southwest Asia. This Cat frequents damp areas on the banks of rivers and streams, as well as drier wooded land.

Pallas' Cat (*Felis manul*) is adapted to a harsh climate, living at altitudes up to 4,000 meters in the low and high steppes of central Asia, Iran, and Afghanistan. Its long hair is reddish-brown and yellowish-gray.
Solitary and diurnal (active during the day), it feeds mainly on rodents.

The Serval (*Felis serval*), a fairly large cat weighing approximately 15 kg, lives in the steppes, shrub-covered terrains, and savannas of Africa and the southern Sahara. It stands tall on its long legs, has characteristically large ears, and a sandy yellow coat sprinkled with black spots and stripes.
The Serval does not fear water and is an excellent swimmer. It feeds on small rodents, hares, and birds.

species. But the Spanish Lynx is smaller and has more spots on its coat, with very distinct black markings. With fewer than 1,000 specimens, the species is highly endangered.

The Bobcat is the smallest of the Lynxes. Its range extends from southern and central North America to Canada. Its habitat consists of swamps, mountains, forests, and deserts.

Felis lynx canadensis is the only member of the Feline family that lives on both sides of the Atlantic.

The Cats of Africa and Asia

The Sand Cat (*Felis margarita*) wears a sand-colored coat and weighs no more than 3 kg. It lives on the arid terrain and sand dunes of Saudi Arabia, Pakistan, and the Sahara. It feeds on rodents, lizards, and large insects. With thick hair lining the pads of its feet, it can move easily over the burning sand.

There are two subspecies of Wild Cat, based on their range: *Felis silvestris silvestris*, which inhabits Europe and Asia Minor, and *Felis silvestris lybica*, which inhabits Africa, southwest Asia, and northern India. The Asian group is sometimes divided into a third subspecies, Felis silvestris ornata.
According to some studies, two distinct Lynx species currently exist in Europe: the Eurasian Lynx (*Lynx lynx*) and the Spanish Lynx (*Lynx pardina*), a highly endangered species found on the Iberian Peninsula.
Two other types of Lynx live in North America, particularly in Canada: the bobcat (*Lynx rufus*) and the Canadian Lynx (*Lynx canadensis*).

African Golden Cat. Anonymous etching. Late 19th century. Private collection.

Fishing Cat. Anonymous etching. Late 19th century. Private collection.

The Caracal (*Felis caracal*) is a sedentary animal inhabiting the open expanses of Africa's savannas and deserts. It is also found in Saudi Arabia and northwest India. It was long associated with the Lynx because of the tufts of hair on its ears and its relatively short tail, but its yellowish-brown coat is never spotted. It was once used by humans, like the cheetah in India and the Near East, for hunting antelope, hare, and birds.

The solitary, nocturnal African Golden Cat (*Felis aurata*) has a coat color that varies according to the region in which it lives: spotted in western Africa, and solid in central and eastern Africa. This long-limbed forest-dweller hunts primarily on the ground, but the habits of this small, fairly rare carnivore are little known.

The Asian Golden Cat (*Felis temminckii*), also known as Temminck's Golden Cat, is larger than its African cousin. Its head has black and white stripes, and its coat color varies according to region. This solitary Cat inhabits the woodlands of Asia, feeding mainly on rodents.

The Cats of the Far East

The Asian Leopard Cat (*Felis bengalensis*) is one of the most widely distributed Felids, inhabiting Southeast Asia, Indonesia, the Philippines, and Manchuria. It lives in forested regions at altitudes up to 3,000 meters and is the size of a domestic cat. The coat is more pigmented in animals inhabiting warm regions (ocher yellow or brownish-yellow) than in those inhabiting cold regions (yellowish-gray, almost silver).

The Fishing Cat (*Felis viverrinus*) is slightly larger than the Asian Leopard Cat. A fan of water, it lives in vast, swampy forests, mangroves, and estuaries from India and southern China to Southeast Asia and Sumatra. Walking with its toes spread, it moves easily over swampy land. It devours freshwater mollusks, crustaceans, frogs, and fish, as well as some Mammals and birds.

The Flat-Headed Cat (*Felis planiceps*) is a small feline weighing 2 kg and characterized by a long muzzle and flattened cranial vault, small, round ears set laterally, and short limbs. It lives on the banks of rivers and swamps and in flooded areas of Southeast Asia, Malaysia, Borneo, and Sumatra. Like the Cheetah, its claws are not completely retractile, making it better equipped to hunt frogs, fish, and crustaceans.

The Marbled Cat (*Felis marmorata*) is found from Nepal to Southeast Asia, as well as in Borneo and Sumatra. Its coat color ranges from brownish-gray to yellowish-brown and chestnut, with black spots on the flanks. This cat has become very rare.

The Rusty Spotted Cat (*Felis rubiginosus*) is a small cat weighing less than 2 kg and wearing a gray or brown coat with chestnut-colored spots. It hunts at night and feeds on birds and small Mammals. It lives in forests and scrub regions in the Indies.

The Clouded Leopard (*Neofelis nebulosa*) is a medium-sized, tree-dwelling Feline weighing 15 to 25 kg. It is named for its coat pattern of wide, dark spots distributed over a yellowish

Rusty Spotted Cat. Anonymous etching. Late 19th century. Private collection.

background. It inhabits the forests of India, Indochina, Sumatra, and Borneo. It often sleeps in trees.

It is active especially in the early morning and from late afternoon to nighttime. The Clouded Leopard is the link between the small and big cats. It belongs to a special genus within the Felid family and is a species threatened by a vanishing habitat.

The Cats of North, Central, and South America

The Ocelot (*Felis pardalis*) was once very common throughout South and Central America. Weighing 12 to 15 kg, it is an excellent climber that hunts rodents, porcupines, monkeys, small deer, and birds at night. Its reproduction seems linked to the rainy season. After a gestation period of seventy days, the female gives birth to an average of two young.

The Ocelot is the best-known American species after the Puma. Before the Ocelot was registered in 1989 under the Washington Convention on endangered species, it was hunted for its fur.

The Margay (*Felis wiedii*) is a miniature Ocelot found from Mexico to Argentina. It is an arboreal animal that climbs trees and descends headfirst. The Margay captures its prey, including small birds, rodents, and lizards, in the branches of trees. It is anatomically adapted to climbing trees: Its metatarsals, or toe bones, are mobile, and its feet rotate 180 degrees.

The Tiger Cat (*Felis tigrinus*) is a small, tree-dwelling, forest species that is now protected. It is found in Central and South America. It does not reproduce as prolifically as the other Felines, and its young develop more slowly.

Geoffroy's Cat (*Felis geoffroyi*) lives primarily in rocky regions with bushes and thickets in southern Brazil and Bolivia and as far south as Patagonia, but it avoids dense forests and open grassland.

The Kodkot (*Felis guigna*) is a small cat found in South American forests and open expanses with sufficient thickets and bushes. Although it can climb, it is primarily ground dwelling. Its ocher brown coat is sprinkled with small, blackish spots. Melanic specimens are common.

The Pampas Cat (*Felis colocolo*), also called the gato pajero (Grass Cat), inhabits prairies and forests, even in mountainous areas, from Ecuador and Brazil to Chile and Patagonia. The color and patterns of its long, silky coat are highly variable. It is nocturnal and hunts rodents, birds, and large insects. Unprotected, it is hunted for its fur.

The Mountain Cat (*Felis jacobita*), which is adapted to high altitudes (up to 5,000 meters) and a cold climate, is found in the Andes in southern Peru, southwestern Bolivia, northern Chile, and Argentina. Its silvery gray coat is marked with brown or orange spots and stripes.

The Jaguarundi (*Felis jagouarundi*), found from southeastern North America to Central America and southern Paraguay, is solitary and active primarily during the day. Humans welcome its presence in rice paddies, since it feeds on rodents that destroy crops and often carry disease. Weighing 5 to 10 kg, the Jaguarundi's long, slender body, short limbs, small, round ears, and long tail make it resemble a mongoose.

The Puma (*Felis concolor*), also called the cougar, or mountain lion, is the largest of the small cats. It is now absent from a large part of America due to the pitiless war waged against it by livestock farmers. Its range extends from the southern United States to Central and South America. Mating can occur at any time of year. After a gestation period of approximately 100 days, the female gives birth to two to four young that remain with her, sometimes up to two years.

The Puma is an extraordinary jumper. From a standing position, it can leap to a branch 6 meters off the ground. It can run very fast over short distances.

The Big Cats

One characteristic particular to the big cats is the ability to roar, thanks to a hyoid bone that is not completely rigid. The Panthera genus includes four species (Panther, Jaguar, Lion, and Tiger). Added to these is one species, the Snow Leopard, which cannot roar and was long grouped in its own genus before being associated with the four big cats.

Leopards in Kenya

The Snow Leopard (*Panthera uncia*) is found in regions extending from China's southwestern to northern borders and lives in eight countries. It is adapted to Asia's harsh mountain climate. In the summer, its range extends up to the perpetual snow line, and in winter, its range recedes to the forest. Slightly smaller than the Leopard (Panthera pardus), the Snow Leopard has a thick, pale gray coat with black spots on the head, neck, and legs, with rosette markings on the flanks and back. Mating occurs early in the year. After a gestation period of approximately 100 days, the female finds a rocky shelter in which she gives birth to two to five young that spend the first winter with her. In some regions, the Snow Leopard attacks livestock. Despite protective measures, it is still hunted in some countries. Its worldwide population is estimated at 4,000, but the species is endangered.

Of all the big cats, the Leopard (*Panthera pardus*) is the most widely distributed. Currently, it is found in Africa (it still inhabits the High Atlas mountains of Morocco in northern Africa), Asia (from Siberia to Korea), Sri Lanka, and Java.

The Leopard is highly adaptable. Mating can occur all year, except in regions with distinct seasons. After a three-month gestation period, the female gives birth to one to five young that remain with her for two years but it is at the age of three that the young will reach sexual maturity. The Leopard has a characteristic spotted coat: black spots on a light background. Variations occur according to the population and habitat: Leopards in dry areas have lighter coats with less spotting than Leopards in the tropical rain forest. Black Panthers are simply a variation in the skin pigmentation of the species. Once hunted for its fur, the Leopard is currently protected, but its population is now declining due to its vanishing habitat.

The Jaguar (*Panthera onca*) is similar to the Leopard but heavier and larger, with more powerful limbs and a shorter tail. It has a coat pattern consisting of black spots forming polygons with smaller black spots in the center. It has full spots on its head, belly, and legs. The background of the coat is chestnut yellow. Melanic Jaguars do exist, but their spots are still visible.

The Jaguar's range covers a large part of South America, with a smaller population in Central America.

Jaguars live in virgin forests and brush land, as well as regions with few thickets, as long as tall grasses and rocks provide sufficient cover.

Adult males and females are found together only when the female is in heat. In tropical regions, births can be observed at any time of year. The young remain with their mother for two years while she protects them from danger, particularly from adult male Jaguars that may attack young, especially in densely populated regions.

The Lion (*Panthera leo*) is the only Cat that lives in social groups. Generally, lionesses remain in the same group for their entire life, unlike male lions, who leave the pride as soon as they reach sexual maturity, at three or four years of age. Lionesses go into heat several times a year. After a gestation period of approximately 100 days, the female isolates herself from the group to give birth to two to five cubs in a thicket or rocky shelter. By fourteen weeks of age, lion cubs follow the Lionesses in the hunt. At one year old, they take down prey, and at two years old, they hunt alone. An exceptional phenomenon in Mammals, the female lion can nurse young from other litters and will even adopt young orphans. One hundred years ago, the Lion

Jaguars hunt primarily on the ground and will also attack terrapins when they leave the water to lay eggs on the bank.

Lion in Tanzania.

An excellent swimmer, the Tiger is also a fine jumper able to clear obstacles 1.8 m high.

White Tigers are simply a variety of the Bengal Tiger. Their white coloring is caused by a mutation in the gene for color. They live in the wild in many parts of India.

inhabited virtually all of Africa, Saudi Arabia, and Asia Minor to the Himalayas. Today, apart from the remaining Asian Lions (an estimated population of 200), the Lion population subsists in Africa primarily in animal reserves (Kenya, Tanzania), with a few groups in South and West Africa.

The Tiger (*Panthera tigris*) is the second biggest predator after the bear. It is one of the animals responsible for the greatest number of human deaths. "Man-eating" tigers are often injured or handicapped animals that can no longer hunt. In addition, habitat destruction due to the growing presence of humans has forced tigers into unexpected confrontations. Tigers and tigresses meet only to mate. The Tiger population has a low reproductive rate, due to the animal's late sexual maturity (three to four years of age for females, and four to five years for males), the fact that 50% of young do not live beyond the age of two, and an average birth rate per female of two young every two years.

The Cheetah (*Acinonyx jubatus*) is unique among the Felines. Everything about its anatomy predisposes it to running: its long limbs, body, and tail, as well as its deep chest which facilitates breathing. All this enables the Cheetah to reach speeds of 75 km/h in two seconds from a standstill and up to 115 km/h over short distances.

The Cheetah's permanently extended claws give it excellent footing, and its flexibility enables it to pivot immediately in any direction while running. For these reasons, Cheetahs can attack prey larger than them-

Once present in most of Asia, the Tiger is now confined to limited areas. The species Panthera tigris is currently divided into five geographic breeds:

- Bengal Tiger (Panthera tigris tigris), population: 5,000;
- Indo-Chinese Tiger (Panthera tigris corbetti), population: less than 2,000;
- Sumatran Tiger (Panthera tigris sumatra), population: 600 to 800;
- Siberian Tiger (Panthera tigris altai), population: approximately 350;
- South China Tiger (Panthera tigris amoyensi), population: some 30 specimens.
Today, approximately 8,000 tigers live in Asia, while there were 100,000 at the beginning of the 20th century.

selves. Male and female cheetahs remain together only one or two days to mate. After a gestation period of approximately 100 days, the female gives birth to three or four young that she raises alone for two years. With a mane of long, silvery hair, baby cheetahs are different from other Felids. Cheetahs do not have a true territory and move based on the migration of their prey. This Feline shares the thinly wooded African savanna with the Lion and Leopard but is less successful than its cousins at adapting to environmental disturbances caused by the presence of humans.

Cheetahs in the African savanna.

The Cheetah's range has been decreasing for several decades. Currently, there are two subspecies: the African Cheetah (*Acinonyx jubatus jubatus*) and the Asian Cheetah (*Acinonyx jubatus venaticus*). The last Asian Cheetah population lives in Iran. The population density of the African Cheetah remains fairly normal in eastern and southern Africa, with a estimated population of 25,000.

Domestic Cats Today

Cats brushed shoulders with prehistoric humans. From the first traces of their domestication until the 18th century, cats adapted to living with humans and were alternately loved, destroyed, hunted, and worshipped. The cat has often been considered the wildest of the tame animals. After all, cats can return to the wild, and aren't mixed breeds the freest of all cats? The domestic cat's history is interwoven in the history of the Feline species over the centuries until today.

If "tame" means "less wild, less dangerous," and "domesticated" means, with respect to a wild animal, "having long been tame, living alongside humans for their aid or pleasure and belonging to a species that reproduces in conditions controlled by humans," then cats became truly domesticated when humans became involved in their selective breeding and reproduction. Indeed, despite the cat's long history alongside humans, the pedigreed cat was not born until the late 19th century. Since then, cats have slowly and majestically entered the world and the environment of their owners.

Stray Cats in Venice.

Successful Integration

Now truly tame and familiar, the domestic cat's status reflects its official recognition as an individual. Tattooed and vaccinated, the cat is tracked by the administration that keeps its papers up to date. Recorded and monitored, the cat, whether purebred or not, has acquired a certain importance for its owner and has made a place for itself in the regulated world of humans.

The more we observe the cat's behavior and reactions, the better we understand and respect the cat for its true self. In the 20th century, the areas of veterinary practice and Feline nutrition were marked by innovations in diet and in preventive and curative medicine. Better cared for, the cat can now escape illness.

Blue and white Persian together.

The cat's resulting well-being has made it calmer, gentler, and more pleasant to live with. Over the past century, a new relationship was established between cats and humans. Cats developed loyalty to humans, bridging the gap that once separated them from us. Cats have come to trust us.

Once used to the half-sleep of a hunter, the cat is much less on the alert now and can relax its attention and let go. Released from the preoccupation with survival, the cat has more energy for humans and can therefore devote more time to companionship, petting, cuddling, and cajoling. Cats may have accepted humans as their friends, but they are still troubled by solitude. This is a sad situation that must be avoided for today's cat.

Cats may have accepted humans as their friends, but they are still troubled by solitude. This is a sad situation that must be avoided for today's cat.

Cats have invented a new dialog. Once content to simply respond to cuddling, they now call their owner, demand food, and request that the door be opened. Their repertoire is expanding, and they vary their intonation as if to make themselves better understood. We can tell what they are feeling from the way they move their ears. We now have cat flaps, harnesses, travel bags, scratching posts, cathouses, automatic feeders, and so on. These inventions for the small feline prove that we have studied its behavior and requirements in an effort to enhance its daily life.

Diversification of Breeds and Feline Standards

Whether the result of mating or of spontaneous mutation, the cat breeds would not be what they are today without human intervention. In 1871 at the first cat show in London's Crystal Palace, twenty-five classes of cats (not yet actual breeds) were presented to the public, including European Shorthairs and Persians with various coats. In the early 19th century, sixteen breeds were officially recognized. Since then, great changes have occurred.

There are now fifty-four registered cat breeds, and dozens of Persian and Oriental varieties. The broad range of Feline breeds throughout the world reflects physical as well as behavioral diversity.

Organized breeding has increased the number of breeds and distinct traits.

Shapes and Colors

A round or triangular head, a slender or stocky body . . . Feline morphology has changed gradually. The standard describes five body types, ranging from cobby, or short and stocky (like the Persian, Himalayan, Manx, Burmese, and Cymric), to semi-cobby, or with a longer body and limbs (like the Norwegian Forest Cat and the Ragdoll). Additional types include the long-limbed foreign (like the Abyssinian), the semi-foreign, with fairly long limbs but a relatively heavy bone structure (like the Devon Rex, Egyptian Mau, and Singapura), and the very long-limbed and slender Oriental (like the Siamese).

Head shape is also part of the description (round in the European Shorthair, triangular in the Siamese), as are eye color and tail size (long in the Norwegian Forest Cat, absent in the Manx), not to mention the coat.

The hair can be up to 15 cm long (Persian, Himalayan), semilong (Turkish Angora), or short (European Shorthair, Chartreux). The

A child and his cat.

ACTIVE, CALM, PLAYFUL: WHICH TO CHOOSE?

The following cat breeds are considered active, meaning they are rambunctious and outgoing, love to run around the house or fenced yard, and never miss a chance to hunt: American Bobtail, American Shorthair, American Wirehair, Bengal, Bombay, British Shorthair, Chartreux, Himalayan, La Perm, Manx, Munchkin, Ocicat, Oriental Shorthair, Cornish Rex, Singapura, Selkirk Rex, and Snowshoe.

This dynamic category also includes playful cats that are naturally lively and will play with children or invent their own games: Turkish Angora, shorthaired American Curl, shorthaired Japanese Bobtail, Bombay, Burmese, Siberian, Exotic Shorthair, Ocicat, Chinchilla Persian, Devon Rex, Cornish Rex, and Scottish Fold. Independent cats also fit in this category. These Cats set their schedule as they please, but once their nap is over, they never slow down: California Spangled, Siberian, Cymric, and European Shorthair.

At the opposite end of the spectrum are dependent, possessive Cats that are extremely attached and deeply devoted to their owner: Abyssinian, Turkish Angora, Russian Blue Havana Brown, Korat, Manx, Russian Black, Ojos Azules, Oriental Shorthair, Chinchilla Persian, Selkirk Rex, Somali, Sphynx, and Tonkinese.

Other Cats will expand their entourage to include the entire household, both humans and other animals: Balinese, Burmese, Cymric, Maine Coon, Scottish Fold, Norwegian Forest Cat, and Snowshoe. These highly sociable. Cats often express themselves vocally, calling their owners simply to start a conversation. The most talkative Felines are the Balinese, Burmilla, Oriental Longhair, Oriental Shorthair, Siamese, and Norwegian Forest Cat.

Still other Cats prefer to keep to themselves and plunge into deep meditation, which only makes them more mysterious: Abyssinian, longhaired American Curl, Egyptian Mau, and Somali.

Finally, some Cats despise conflict, preferring to live in peace, away free from any disturbances: Birman, longhaired Japanese Bobtail, Russian Black, and Persian. Still other Feline features could be mentioned, including agility, curiosity, mellowness, mischievousness, adventurousness, attentiveness, and so on.

colors allowed for each breed are specified. The palette is vast: solid-color, bicolor, parti-color (tortoiseshell, smoke), and silver (like the Chinchilla Persian), as well as patterned coats, including colorpoint like the Siamese, tabby like the European Shorthair, and marked with patches, spots, or thick or thin stripes.

Breed Promotion and Cat Behavior

Breed promotion, a concept that appeared fairly late in the history of domestication, is linked to a behavioral change in the Small Feline. While character may not be included in the standards established by Cat associations, it is not just a simple detail. During competition, a Cat's behavior may be grounds for disqualification. If a Feline candidate is intractable or aggressive, it has little chance of earning an award. In everyday life, a Cat's behavior is just as essential as its looks. Behavior is thus a truly important criterion in choosing a Cat.

Towards Behavior Classification

There is a certain tendency to classify breeds in terms of behavior, although such a classification remains somewhat controversial in the world of Cat fancy. Still, this sort of classification can help owners better select a Cat, based on the desired character type. The criteria vary and reflect specific Feline characteristics that are more or less pronounced. Often, sociability is included in this classification, as is the degree of activity or calmness.

Expert opinion is divided on the question of breed and character type. This is due to the fact that Feline breeds are perceived not as genetic specificities but as the result of selective breeding by breeders.

For example, we cannot deny that the Siamese has a specific character. Its extreme talkativeness and coarse voice make it perfect for an outgoing owner. It is also a good conversational partner for the elderly and for people who live alone. The refined and hardy Norwegian Forest Cat awakens the love of nature and is appreciated by city-dwellers lucky enough to have yards. The calm Ragdoll, a wonderful playmate for children, is especially popular with calm people who detest chaos.

Cats Choose Their Owners

Cats, too, have a say. They play favorites within the family. At the cattery, a kitten may approach its future owner and refuse to leave his side. This demonstrates that absolutely perfect cat-human pairs do exist, with complete understanding between Cat and owner. Very intuitive, a Cat can figure a person out and detect any affinity between itself and its protector. Cats can exert a certain influence over humans and sometimes guide humans into their domain.

Contrary to the saying "like owner, like dog," we could say "like cat, like owner."

A Complete Individual

Elegant and subdued, purebred cats compel admiration and enjoy their owner's respect. With a pedigree and a unique and imposing name, they are destined to frequent the stage alongside the champions of Feline society.

We can tell that cats can be trained, retain lessons well, and are fascinated by human activities. They love music and even have their own CDs that induce "interactive" hunting sequences, as if to awaken their predatory instinct.

A large portion of the mixed breed cat population belongs to no one and receives support only from protection association volunteers. They form the bulk of the stray cat population.

The purebred cat, symbol of a certain financial value, is kept inside, protected from all danger, and treated with consideration. With a well-groomed coat and healthy body, it enjoys a specially adapted diet. For this cat, nothing is too good, and love and petting make it blossom. The cat is king, worthy of all honors. However, unlike dogs, cats make allowances. Their freedom - through escape to an imaginary world - remains intact, allowing them to keep their distance without offending their protector.

Mixed Breed Cats, Always and Forever

The mixed breed Cat is the most popular and widespread: Of the estimated eight million cats in France, for example, only 2 to 3% – approximately 200,000 – are purebred (Persians, Siamese, Birmans, etc.). Mixed breed cats claim the lion's share of the domestic cat population. But the large number of mixed breed cats does not necessary mean that humans give them special attention; quite the contrary.

The mixed breed cat owes its primacy to its incredible resistance - it has had to face many hardships over its history, and still does today - and especially to the near absence of control over its birth rate.

Free and Free Roaming . . .

The mixed breed cat may be the freest of the cats, but this freedom is not without a price. Overall and in comparison to purebred cats, mixed breed cats also have the hardest life, due to owners (to use the term loosely) who care little about their cats' absence and advances in veterinary research, whether in Feline health or diet. After all, haven't cats gotten along for centuries on their own or on leftovers?

Mixed breed cats are also "free" in the financial sense. They are not bought; they are given or adopted, or the cat itself may simply choose to take up residence in someone's home. For many owners, the mixed breed cat represents no financial responsibility. These owners care little about getting their cat vaccinated, tattooed, or even properly cared for, let alone neutering a male or spaying a female.

. . . But Still Loved

Strangely enough, mixed breed cats inspire an often-exclusive passion in true owners. "I prefer mixed breeds to purebred cats, because I prefer normal people to Chanel models," joked the French writer Rémo Forlani. And he's not alone!

Having a mixed breed Cat in the home is a

family tradition some people cannot forego. They love their Cat's sense of independence, legendary resourcefulness, and hardy, vigorous good looks. They also appreciate its uniqueness, as no two mixed breed Cats are exactly the same. The mixed breed is the Cat par excellence, with no frills or fakeness, either physical or moral. If these people ever lose their companion, they will automatically look for a replacement among others of similar breeding.

A Forgotten Ancestor?

The mentality changed slightly in the late 19th century, with the first cat shows in Great Britain and then in France featuring primarily Persians (they had stolen the spotlight from Angoras), Siamese, and some wild species like the margay, as well as domestic cats chosen for their beauty. Still, it must be noted that only a few upper-class people took pleasure in showing their cat in public.

Then the domestic cat, with no known origin and therefore no pedigree, was gradually excluded from these fashionable activities to make room for new breeds that were much more exotic and valuable. But did you know that if we could climb back to the top of the family tree of these noble little felines, or even to a few intermediate branches, we would find lowly mixed breeds from which these "fancy"

breeds borrowed sometimes a color, sometimes a coat?

Breeds as odd as the Rex and Scottish Fold were born in litters of mixed breed country cats, and the coat of "tabby point" Siamese and Birmans is derived from the mixed breed. The lovely tortoiseshell coat worn by Persians also comes from the "commoners," as does the bicolor coat. What, then, is specific to the mixed breed cat? The insufficiently recognized honor of having contributed to the creation or improvement of most cat breeds, especially the breed directly descended from it: the European Shorthair.

Disabuse yourself of one important point: The European breed, the European Shorthair, is not a mixed breed cat. It is therefore incorrect

WHAT A CHARACTER!
It's hard to pinpoint a mixed breed cat's temperament, which may be as quirky as its looks. Some are calm, others more outgoing; some are silent, others talkative, friendly, ferocious, or more or less affectionate. Their motto is, "Love me as I am, because I'm unpredictable!" One thing you can be sure of is that mixed breeds love to hunt, in true cat nature. Some people think that mixed breed cats are not suited to living in an apartment, but they are, in fact, no less suited to apartment life than a cat of another breed if they have never known anything different. Make sure to arrange your interior to meet your cat's needs: Cats love to climb, so protect your furniture by providing a scratching post and ample playtime with you.

SHOWING YOUR MIXED BREED
Why not show your mixed breed alongside its noble cousins? There is even a class especially for it: "housecat class." To participate in competition, the cat must be neutered (castrated or spayed), in good health, easy to handle (with a pleasant character), and good looking. Give it a try-with your mixed breed, you can enjoy the excitement of the stage just as much as with a fancier cat!

ITS TIME OF GLORY
In 1935, a veterinarian from Le Havre, France, named Adrien Loir founded the Rat-Hunting Cat Club of Normandy in order to improve and maintain the characteristics of the Cat of France, also called the French Cat at the time. This feline ratter was renowned for its ferocity in eliminating vermin from the docks of the port of Le Havre, helping to save a great deal of money. Other institutions, including the French rail network, department stores, silk factories in Lyon, the Palais-Bourbon in Paris, and the Natural History Museum in Le Havre, also used these ratters with great success. Dr. Loir hoped these cats would be honored for their wonderful deeds. He wrote: "Doesn't the cat deserve to be recognized today for its public service?" Unfortunately, his dream never came true.

Wearing all kinds of coats in all kinds of colors, the mixed breed is true tolerance. Anything goes: solid (black, white, chestnut, blue, tortoiseshell, etc.), bicolor with random white markings, Tiger, shorthaired or longhaired, a round head or a tapered muzzle, teddy bear or TV antenna ears, a stocky build or a gazelle's body, and so on. Everything suits the mixed breed, who has no dress code, unlike purebred cats.

to call the mixed breed a European Shorthair.

The European Shorthair and the Mixed Breed Cat

Of course, the standard for the European Shorthair was developed based on the most common characteristics of domestic cats. The standard of the Fédération Internationale Féline d'Europe (FIFe) [International Feline Federation of Europe] specifies, in particular: "The ideal European Shorthair is assumed to have never been crossed with another breed. It must be bred as a hardy, flexible cat with no anatomical differences from the European domestic cat." The mixed breed, unlike the European Shorthair, has no standard and is not required to meet any specific criteria. Its pureness is difficult to demonstrate, especially now, when the number of breeds is so great. For this reason, an owner may be led to believe that his semilonghaired cat is a Norwegian Forest Cat or Maine Coon, especially when the cat has tiger markings, or a Turkish Angora when it is self-colored. In the mixed breed cat

population, the Siamese pattern is common (often combined with white markings). This is plausible if the two parents are themselves descended from Siamese cats, but it does not make their offspring Siamese.

The World's Oldest Breed

Isn't there any value in simply being a perfectly good mixed breed cat? After all, it is the oldest breed in the world.

The Americans and the British have succeeded in resolving this issue. The American counterpart of the European Shorthair is called the American Shorthair, and the British counterpart is the British Shorthair. Both these breeds, like the European Shorthair (a rather vague term, in the end), are descended from the mixed breed cat.

But the Americans and the British have succeeded in breeding these two kinds of cat without creating as much confusion as in France. It is true that the current American Shorthair and British Shorthair really have nothing to do with the basic model. The problem with the European Shorthair is probably that it has remained much too close to its ancestor. Perhaps we could imagine, then, that the European Shorthair, finally free from any hybridization with new breeds, might help us travel back in time to the original mixed breed when it was the one and only, highly useful representative of the feline species.

2

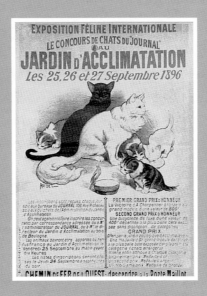

CAT FANCY

Cat Fancy and Current Breeds

The first cat fanciers, or ailurophiles, appeared in Europe. They brought together the first cat breeders and created the first cat shows. The first federation of cat clubs, the Governing Council of the Cat Fancy, was established in Great Britain in 1910. In 1949, the Fédération Internationale Féline d'Europe (FIFe) [International Feline Federation of Europe] was created. Today, a number of national and international organizations monitor the development of cat breeds and their numerous varieties.

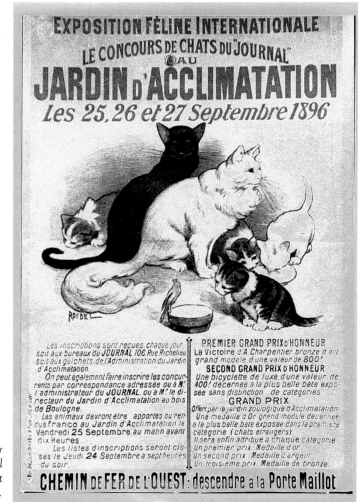

EXPOSITION FÉLINE INTERNATIONALE
LE CONCOURS DE CHATS DU "JOURNAL"
AU
JARDIN D'ACCLIMATATION
Les 25, 26 et 27 Septembre 1896

Poster by Roedel for an international Cat show, Viollet collection, Paris.

Main Cat Organizations of the World

Created in 1949, the Fédération Internationale Féline d'Europe initially included France, Belgium, the Netherlands, Switzerland, Denmark, Sweden, Norway, Italy, Austria, and Germany. Today, it is present in forty countries and includes some thirty-member countries. Its primary missions are the establishment of consistent show regulations, the adoption of unique standards, the management of studbooks, and the training of judges. Other federations have been founded, including the World Cat Federation of Europe (WCFE). Founded in 1906, the Cat Fanciers' Association (CFA) is the largest association in the United States and possibly the world. The International Cat Association (TICA), another American association, was founded in 1979.

While there are over forty million cats in Europe, purebred cats represent only an estimated 8% of this population.

Cats in Competitions

The first cat show was held in London in 1871. Slightly over 300 cats were shown, primarily Persians, Siamese, and Birmans. The Cat Club of Paris, affiliated with the FIFe, held the first cat show in France in 1946. Showing a cat or cats in a competition entails preparing the cat through grooming (related mainly to the cat's health and daily care) and completing various administrative and veterinary formalities prior to the actual competition (such as registering and paying fees). When a cat first arrives at the show site, a veterinarian checks its identity and health against its tattoo record and vaccination record, respectively. Then the veterinarian inspects the animal itself. Cats may not be shown or placed in a cage if they do not undergo this veterinary inspection.

The organization running the show provides a cage to each participant. Owners often decorate these cages to highlight their cat.

The Ideal Cat

The cat must meet certain requirements. According to the Fédération Internationale Féline, these are the following:
- The cat must exhibit the characteristics specific to its breed. Its health and well-being must be apparent.
- The cat must be in excellent physical condition, with no anatomical or postural faults.
- The cat must be able to be judged without showing anxiety or aggression. The judge must be able to evaluate the size and shape of its skeleton and feel its muscles. The basic characteristics must be apparent.
- The cat must be well groomed and show no signs of dandruff, dirt, or parasites. Its feet must be spotless, and it is recommended that the claws be clipped.
- For cats with white markings, there should be no trace of soiling. The grooming must highlight the features of the cat and its breed.
- With regard to the head, the skull must be slightly rounded, to an extent depending on the breed. The jaws must be well set and the teeth sharp, with the upper and lower jaws aligned, equal in length, and free of deformity. The upper external surface of the lower incisors must touch the lower internal surface of the upper incisors. The canines should meet in a scissor bite. Ideally, all the teeth should be present, of normal size, set evenly in the mouth without overlapping, and properly aligned.

Judging

There are two styles of judging - traditional judging and American judging (TICA or CFA).

One of the main differences between these two styles of judging involves the number of judges that rate each animal. In American judging, each cat in the show must be evaluated by each judge, no matter the number. Each judge therefore sees each competitor, regardless of its sex, age, and breed.

Another aspect of American judging is that judging is not public, and each judge gives comments on his or her choice, whereas traditional judging is conducted with greater discretion.

In American judging, cats are shown in six categories:
1 - Adults (male and female),
2 - Kittens (male and female),
3 - Neutered,
4 - Adult HHP (household pets), former mixed breeds (male and female),
5 - Kitten HHP (household pets, male and female),
6 - NBC, or new breeds and colors.

Everything is important to the judge: the morphology, type, and presentation of the cat, all of which is judged against the breed standard. Breed by breed, the cats are judged on their color. The various competitors of a single color receive a "flat," or a small colored card attached to their cage to indicate their ranking: blue for first, red for second, yellow for third, green for fourth, and white for fifth. In breed judging, Cats are always ranked by divisions: the three best self-colored Cats, the three best tabbies, the three best tortoiseshells, etc.

The purpose of the veterinary inspection conducted before the show is opened to the public is to ensure that only healthy animals enter the show, to prevent any infection. The vaccination record and tattoo record are two essential documents. Vaccinations against rabies, typhus, and Feline respiratory disease complex are required. It is suggested that Cats also be vaccinated against Feline leukemia. The veterinarian makes sure the animal is free of any skin disease (ear mange, ringworm) and that the eyes, nose, and hindquarters are clean.

The main Cat fancy associations are listed by country in the index of this book.

Finally, the three Best of Breed are chosen for each breed. Each judge selects the ten best in each of the six categories (all breeds combined). The winning animals receive ribbons.

In American judging, cats earn points. Each judge records his or her results in a judging book that is then sent to the United States so that the points accumulated from May to May can be recorded. The twenty best cats in each category, all breeds and countries combined, receive awards in an annual show.

Breeders record the points received in competition in their catalog.

In traditional judging, the cat is shown in order to obtain a title based on conformity to the standard. The cat goes before a single judge, and all the results of judging are submitted to the breeder.

The judge begins by examining the body, color, and condition of the cat, often beginning with the head (shape, nose, eyes, ears, chin) then moving to the body and tail. Then the judge studies the coat and the quality and distribution of color. Finally, the judge gives his or her general impression of the cat.

With regard to mixed breeds or household cats, the judge's work is slightly different, since there is no actual standard. In this case, the judge's impression is what makes the difference. The judge may award a title or not, based on the quality of the animals presented for judging.

Cups and ribbons are awarded, but never sums of money.

THE VARIOUS FIFE TITLES ARE:

CAC: Certificate of Aptitude for Standard Champion.
Three are required to qualify for champion.
CACIB: Certificate of Aptitude for International Beauty Champion.
Three are required to qualify for champion, including one obtained abroad.
CAGCIB: Certificate of Aptitude for International Beauty Grand Champion.
Three are required, including two obtained abroad and awarded by different judges.
CACE: Certificate of Aptitude for European Champion. Three are required, awarded in three different countries and by three different judges.
Honors class: After obtaining all these titles, cats can still compete for this honorific distinction and continue to win awards, while making room for newcomers.
In addition, the cats shown can receive other awards, including Best Variety (best color of breed) and Best in Show (best in each category). From the winners of Best in Show, the Best of Best is chosen in the following three categories: shorthair, semilonghair, and longhair.

Point Score

The point score is a numbered rating of the various morphological features of a cat for evaluating or judging it in a competition or show. The breed standards include a point score. A perfect score is 100. Each area of the body is assigned a number of points based on significance.
Point scores vary not only by breed, but also by each cat association for the same breed.
The table below gives an idea of the differences in rating for the breeds described in this book.

Breeds	Head	Ears	Eyes	Neck	Body	Legs Feet	Tail	COAT			Condition
								Texture	Color	Pattern	Balance
Abyssin	25				30			10	35		
	30				35			10	25		
	15		10		20			10	25	15	5
American Bobtail	25				25		20	15	5		10
American Curl	25	5	5		25	5	5	20			10
	20	30	10		25			15			
	15	30	10		30			15			
American Shorthair	15	30	10	2	18	5	5	13	2		
	30		10		25			15	20		
	45				20	10	5	10	10		
American Wirehair	25	5	10	5	20	10	5	10	10		
	25				20			45	10		
	25				20			45	10		
Turkish Angora	25	5	10	5	20	10	5	10	10		
	20	12	6	6	20	8	8	10	5		5
	25		10		30		15	15			5
Balinese	20	12	6	6	20	8	8	10	5		5
	20		5		30			20	25		
	25		10		25			25	10		5
Bengal	25		15		25			10	20		5
	10	10	5	5	10	10		10	10	30	
	10	10	5	5	10	5	5	10	10	30	
Russian Blue	25		15		20			20	20		
	15	5	10	3	15	7	5	20	20		
	25		10		30			20	10		5
Bombay	25		5		20			20	30		
	30		20		30			20			
British Shorthair	25	5	20		20	5	5	15	5		
	25				35			20	20		
	20	5	5	5	20	5	5	15	10		10
Burmese	30		10		20			10	25		5
	30				30			10	30		
	25		10		25			10	25		
Burmilla	25		20		20			15	15		5
	20	10	20		25			10	10		5
	19	6	10		15	5	5	15	25		
California Spangled	20	5	5	5	20	11	6	8		20	
Ceylon	20	15	15		25			10	10		5
Chartreux	35				30			20	15		
	15	10	10	4	20	8	4	14	15		
	35				25		10	25			5
Cornish Rex	25				30			40	5		
	12	5	5	4	15	5	4	36	5		9
	25		5		30			35			5
Cymric	25		10		30	15		15	5		
Devon Rex	35				30			30	5		
	30				30			35	5		
	25				20			40			5
European Shorthair	35				25			10	25		5
Exotic Shorthair	30		10		20			10	20		10
	30		10		25		5	10	20		10
Norwegian Forest Cat	50				30			5	5		10
	20	5	5		20		10	20	5		15
	20	5	5		10	10	10	20	5		15
German Rex	15	5	10		20		5	40			5
	10	5	10		15		5	40	10		5
Havana	33		10		15		5	5	10	22	
	15	5	10		20	10	5	9	10		16
	15	5	10		20	10	5	10	10		15

C.F.A.   T.I.C.A.   F.I.Fe   S.C.F.F.
S.C.F.F. = now L.O.O.F.

Breeds	Head	Ears	Eyes	Neck	Body	Legs Feet	Tail	Texture	Color	Pattern	Balance
Japanese Bobtail	20				30		20	10	20		
	20				30		20	10	20		
	20						20	10	20		30
Javanese	20		5		30			20	25		
	25		10		25			25	10		5
	25		15		25			10	20		5
Korat	25		15		25			10	25		
	18	7	18	2	15	4	3	13	20		
	20		20		25			10	20		5
Laperm	20	5	5		25			35	10		
	20	5	5	5	10	5	5	35	10		
Domestic Lynx	20	5	5		15	10	15	10	10		10
Maine Coon	30				35			20	15		
	20	10	5		20	10	10	20	5		
	25	10	5		25		10	20			5
Mandarin	18	7	13		17	5	8	20	7		5
Manx	25		5		25	15	5	20	5		
	25		10		30	15		15	5		
	15		5		25		35	15			5
Egyptian Mau	20				25			5	25	25	
	10	5	10		15	5		10	15	25	
	10	5	15		10		5	5	15	25	5
Munchkin	25				50			10	5		10
	15	5	5	5	10	30	5	10	5		10
Ocicat	25				25				25	25	
	20				30		5	20		25	
	15	5	10		10	5	5	15	5	25	5
Ojos Azules	15		15		20	10	5	10	15		10
	15		15		10	10	5	10	15		20
Oriental Shorthair	20		10		30			10	30		
	15	5	15	2	15	5	3	10	10		20
	25		15		25			10	20		5
Persian	30				30			40			
	30		10		25		5	10	10	10	
	30		15		20				30		5
Ragdoll	30		15		30	5		10	20		5
	20		5		20	5	5	10	25		5
	30				35			10	20		5
Birman	30				30			10	30		
	20				20	20	10	10	15		5
Scottish Fold	55				40				5		
	15	30	15		10		20		10		
	15	30	15		10		20		10		
Selkirk Rex	24	4	7		10	10	5	25	5		10
Siamese	20		10		30			10	30		
	24		10		40			10	16		
	25		15		25			10	10	10	5
Siberian	30				35	5		10	10		10
	21	4	5	5	30	5		10	10		10
Singapura	25		10		20			15	15	15	
	20		10		20			10	40		
	9	8	13	4	10	4	2	10	4	0	
Snowshoe	20				30			5	35		10
	13	3	4	2	14	10	4	5	35		10
African Shorthair	15		10		25			15	30		5
	10	5	10		15	5	5	15	30		5
Somali	25				25			20	30		
	30				35			10	25		
	15		10		20			25	15	10	5
Sphynx	35				35				25	5	
	23	7	5	5	20	5	5		25	5	
Tonkinese	25				30			10	35		
	27				27			9	27		10
	14	5	16		14	7	6	10	18		10
Turkish Van	30				35				15	20	
	15	7	8		20	10	10		15	15	
	25	10	10		25				2	5	5
York Chocolate	15	5	5		15	5	5	20	20		10

C.F.A.   T.I.C.A.   F.I.Fe   S.C.F.F.
S.C.F.F. = now L.O.O.F.

3

CAT BREEDS

The breeds

The breeds in this book are listed in alphabetical order. Nearly all recognized breeds as of this writing are included in this encyclopedia, whether breeds only recently recognized or long-established breeds, including breeds currently being developed. A brief history of the origin of the breed is followed by information on its personality, characteristics, and a lengthy discussion of the current standard (description of the ideal specimen) as defined by the primary international cat associations, including two American organizations, T.I.C.A. (The International Cat Association), the C.F.A. (Cat Fanciers' Association), as well as the F.I.Fe. (Fédération Internationale Féline) and the L.O.O.F. (Livre Officiel des Origines Félines). Standards for the same breed often vary from one association to the next. These differences, when significant, are noted and indicated with a symbol identifying the specific association, particularly with regard to varieties. Personality traits, weight (according to B. Fogle), and breed characteristics are presented as a general description of each breed. Since all cats are unique individuals, no one description will fit every cat.

A glossary is provided to help you understand the definitions and information contained in the standards. This glossary contains terms relating to the External Cat, Body Types, Colors, and Coat Patterns.

General morphology

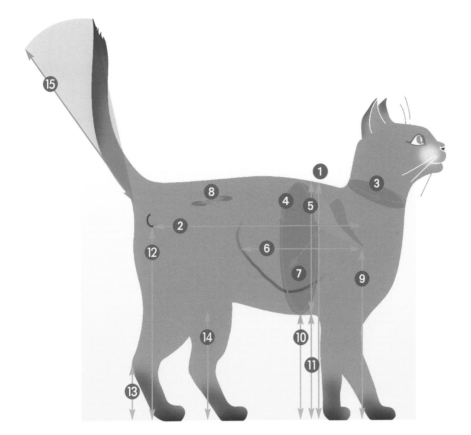

The primary body measurements of the cat

1. Size: Height at the withers
2. Length of body
3. Diameter of neck
4. Diameter of chest
5. Height of chest
6. Depth of chest
7. Width of chest
8. Depth of flank
9. Height of shoulder
10. Height of elbow
11. Distance from ground to sternum
12. Height at top of thigh
13. Height at hock
14. Height at stifle
15. Length of tail

From Horchois (J.P.), thesis Alfort, 1974)

Generally, cats have a rather elongated body and relatively short legs. The head can be round, with a broad, short face, or triangular. The average cat has short ears and a long, flexible tail carried low or upright. The loose skin on the short neck allows the cat to easily extend his neck, facilitating capture of prey. The abdominal walls are thick and meaty. The abdominal cavity is longer than wide. The croup and thigh form a large, rounded area.

1. Ticking
2. Chinchilla
3. Shaded
4. Smoke
5. Self
6. Tabby

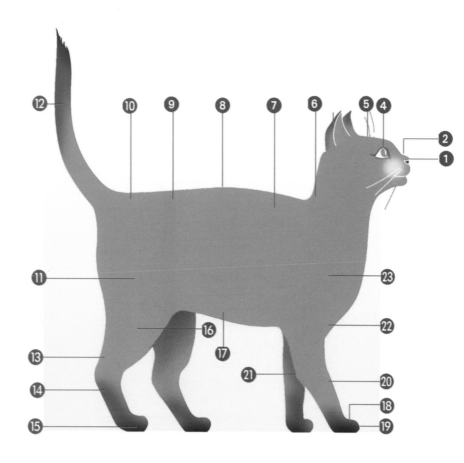

Body parts of the cat

1. Nose
2. Nose bridge
3. Eye
4. Brow
5. Ear
6. Neck
7. Interscapular region
8. Back
9. Loin
10. Croup
11. Thigh
12. Tail
13. Hock (tarsal)
14. Metatarsal
15. Phalanges (toes) of the hind paw
16. Leg
17. Belly
18. Metacarpal
19. Phalanges (toes) of the forepaw
20. Forearm
21. Elbow
22. Arm
23. Shoulder

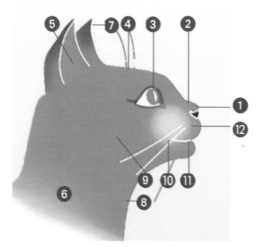

Lateral view of the head

1. Nose
2. Nose bridge
3. Eye
4. Skull
5. Auricle
6. Neck
7. Ear
8. Throat
9. Cheek
10. Lips
11. Canthus of the lips

Glossary

Accepted

Said of a characteristic accepted in a breed standard, although not necessarily sought in breeding

Active

Term describing an animal in action, moving, always alert.

Agouti

Said of a hair exhibiting alternate light and dark areas. Agouti gene A produces striping in the fur.

Barring

Stripes associated with tabby markings.

Bib

The part of the body including the lower chin and the chest (said of the frill of Persians).

Bicolor

Cat with a coat consisting of white and another color.

Blaze

A marking, often white in color, running from the middle of the forehead to the nose.

Blotched (Classic Tabby)

A term indicating the classic, marbled tabby coat.

Blue Point

In the Siamese, Colorpoint, and Birman, a term indicating the slate blue-gray color of the points (mask, ears, legs, and tail).

Blue

Coat color ranging from blue-gray to slate gray. Chartreux cats are blue.

Blue-cream

The colors blue and cream must be present in equal proportions and perfectly mixed, as in the Blue Tortie, a variety with even patches of blue and cream. Blue Torties are almost always female.

Full cheeks.

Blue Point (Siamese).

Break or Stop

The well-pronounced angle between the nose and forehead (see Break, Stop).

Break

The sharp angle formed where the bridge of the nose meets the lower forehead.

Breed

A subdivision of the species consisting of individuals with common hereditary characteristics. These characteristics can be morphological and physiological. Individuals are said to be purebred if they descend from parents belonging to the same breed. There are relatively few feline breeds but endless varieties. Differences between breeds of cats are morphological and, more specifically, related to coat. New breeds often arise from genetic mutations (sudden modifications that can be transmitted genetically, as in the American Curl, the Sphynx, etc.). However, many breeds would have disappeared if not for the hard work of dedicated breeders (for example, the Chartreux).

Brindling

White, lighter, or depigmented hairs in a color, design, or pattern. Traces of color that contrast with the base color of the coat.

Britches or Breeches

In longhaired or semilonghaired cats, the longer, denser hair on the back of the thighs.

Brush or Plume

A thick covering of hair on the tail typical of longhaired, Persian-type cats.

Calico

An American term indicating the tortoiseshell and white variety (white coloring on the underparts).

Cameo

• Silvery cats in which the tips of the hairs are reddish-brown or cream (tipping).
• Silvery reddish-brown or cream ticked variety.

Break (Exotic).

Chocolate Tortie Colorpoint.

Champagne

The American term for the Chocolate Burmese and Lilac Tonkinese (see Honey Mink in breed section).

Chinchilla

A coat in which the tip of the hair is black, with the rest being silvery white. This is the lightest degree of tipping.
• Original Persian, with black markings, surely the result of a cross between a Silver Tabby Persian and a Smoke. Very stocky body with short legs. Round, wide head with very pronounced stop. Round green or bluish-green eyes. Long hair. Chinchilla coat: pure white undercoat. Black tipping distributed evenly over the back, flanks, head, ears, and tail and covering approximately 1/8 the length of each hair. Brick nose with black outline. Black or seal pads. In the Silver Shaded Persian, which is darker than the Chinchilla, the black tipping covers approximately 1/3 the length of each hair.

Frill (Birman).

Chocolate

A fairly light chestnut-brown color common in Oriental breeds.

Cinnamon

A honey or reddish-brown coat color.

Colorpoint.

Classic Tabby or Blotched Tabby

The rings on the tail and legs are wide and well-spaced. The "M" on the forehead, the parallel stripes on the skull, and the stripes on the neck are wide. The shoulders have bull's eye or oyster-shaped designs. Three wide bands run parallel to the spine, from neck to tail. The flanks have wide markings resembling butterflies with outstretched wings. The stomach is blotched.

Coat

All the hair of a mammal, considered in its external aspect (color, smoothness, softness to the touch, thickness, length, etc.). Felids usually have a thick, soft, supple coat. It is either solid yellowish or grayish in color, light or dark, sometimes black, sometimes spotted, striped, or marbled with a darker color on a light background.

Coat

The characteristics of the coat include the hair (texture, length, etc.), the color of the hair, and the placement of colored and colorless areas.

Wedge-shaped head.

Cobby

A massive, stocky, short, muscular body with a wide chest and hips (Persian).

Colorpoint

A cat with a light-colored body and darker "points" (markings) of color on the mask (face), ears, legs, and tail. All Siamese varieties are colorpoints.

Convex

Term describing a domed forehead.

Cream

A very pale shade of buff, fairly common in the Persian.

Curly-coated

A term describing the hair found in the American Wirehair and the Rex.

Dilution

A paler version of a basic color: lilac, cream, etc.

Disqualification

Elimination for a fault serious enough to deny a cat a title in a show (for example, if the animal has a dyed or shaved coat or an abnormal number of toes, is aggressive, unclean, overweight, underweight, cryptorchid, etc.).

Ears

• Medium-sized, erect (European Shorthair, etc.);
• Very large (Devon Rex);
• Folded back (American Curl);
• Set in a caplike fashion, flat against the head (Scottish Fold).

Tortoiseshell.

Eyes

Oriental eyes: almond-shaped eyes set at a slant.
• White cats with orange or copper-colored eyes are not deaf.
• White cats with heterochromatic eyes (one blue eye and one orange eye) are deaf only in one ear.

Fault

Any significant imperfection with relation to the breed standard and its specific features.

Fawn

A buff color in the black range. Delicate, pale

color. Dilution of cinnamon, pale buff, light sand, slightly pinkish-gray.
- Fawn Point: pinkish-buff extremities.
- Fawn Tortie: ranging from cinnamon to golden honey and from reddish-brown to cream.

Feral
A term describing a domestic cat that has reverted to a wild state and subsists on game.

Foreign
A term describing a fine-boned, long-limbed, elegant cat, such as the Abyssinian, Siamese, and Somali.
- Oriental shorthair, self-colored coat.

Frill or Ruff
A mass of long, dense hair around the neck.

Full Cheeks
Term describing the cheeks, particularly in the standard of the Chartreux.

Gauntlets
White markings on the hind paws of a colored or bicolored cat, ending below or above the hock. Also called "boots."

Ghost Markings
Tabby markings visible in young cats that are genetically self-colored. These markings fade as the cat reaches adulthood and sheds.

Gloves
Pure white areas of fur on the back of the feet in the Birman and Ragdoll.

Gold or Golden
A golden apricot color. Among rare colors:
- Golden Shaded: a dark apricot background with no trace of gray and with black tipping.
- Golden Chinchilla: a very warm apricot background with no trace of gray. Only the tip of the hair is black, on 1/8 of the lenght

Guard Hair
One of the three types of hair in a cat's coat. Guard hairs provide insulation of a certain thickness (see Hair).

Hair
There are several categories of hair (grouped according to the author):

- Outer coat or guard hairs (primary hairs): long, thick, straight, pigmented, spatulate at the distal end. Protective element of the coat, abundant in the upper parts of the body.
- Awn hairs (also for protection): bent at the end and pointed at the tip, giving them a club-like appearance.
- Undercoat, down hair, underfur: thin, wavy, very dense hairs, for thermal insulation. A coat is called "double" when it consists of an outer coat (guard hairs) and an undercoat. Down hair is abundant in the Persian, is the only covering in the Sphynx, and is absent in the Balinese:
- Tactile hairs (called "antenna" by French writer Colette. Whiskers, vibrissae).

Hairless
Hereditary alopecia is rare in cats. Mexican hairless cats, a breed created by the Aztecs, were described in 1924 as follows: skin slightly wrinkled, bluish on the back, and lighter on the belly. Well-developed whiskers and light winter coat on the back and tip of the tail. In 1930, Létard studied a pair of hairless cats, describing them as having fleshy, very wrinkled, piebald slate skin. A hairless cat brought back from India was observed in 1930. In 1935, Letard studied two male hairless kittens from a litter of Siamese. He demonstrated the recessive autosomal nature of genetic transmission (hr) in this case. In 1966 in Canada, crosses in a litter of hairless cats produced only hairless cats that gave rise to the Sphynx (Canadian Hairless) breed.

Havana
A warm chestnut color.

Heterochromatic
Said of eyes of two different colors, for example, one blue eye and one gold eye in white Persians (see Odd-eyed).

Himalayan
Another name for the Colorpoint Persian. A Persian with Siamese markings. The Himalayan is a lovely cat with large blue eyes and a coat with a distinctive contrast between the points and the body.

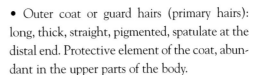

Tortoiseshell.

Foreign.

Gloves.

Golden

Lilac Point.

Inbreeding

The mating of related individuals (from the same family). A cross between a brother and sister can reveal defects carried by the parents but can also help to rapidly establish the characteristics of a new breed.

Jowls

Cheek folds prominent in unaltered, adult male cats.

Laces

A white area running from the foot to the hocks, particularly in Birmans and Snowshoes ("boots" on the back of the leg, to the hock) (see Gauntlets, Gloves).

Lavender or Lilac

A light pinkish-buff coat color with no markings.

Length, texture

- Short hair (outer coat): 4.5 cm (European Shorthair, Chartreux),
- Long hair (outer coat): 15 to 20 cm (Persian),
- Diameter of guard hair (Persian): 40 to 80 microns,
- Diameter of down hair (Persian): 10 to 35 microns.

Lilac

A light pinkish-buff color (see Lavender). Rare color. Taupe gray or even, extremely light pinkish-buff with no ghost markings. Platinum (Burmese and Tonkinese). Lilac Persians are very light in color on the entire belly, frill, and tail. Lilac Cream: a combination of cream and lilac. Lilac Point: the extremities are pinkish-buff, the body varies from off-white to extremely light antique ivory, with eyes as dark as possible.

Lynx Point or Tabby Point

Said of a cat with a colored coat in which the extremities (or points: mask, tail, legs, and ears) have tabby markings (Siamese, Himalayan, etc.).

Lynx Tip

A tuft of hair at the tip of the ear, a characteristic sought in the Maine Coon, Norwegian Forest Cat, and Himalayan, and retracted for the Persian and Exotic.

Lynx tip.

Lynx Tip

A tuft of hair on the ear tip.

Mackerel Markings

A tiger tabby design. Mackerel tabby: the legs and tail have thin, tight rings, as does the necklace. The "M" on the forehead and the lines on the skull, neck, and spine are continuous, tight, and parallel. The flanks, shoulders, and thighs have either striping in a fish bone pattern or thin, even, parallel lines. The belly is spotted.

Maltesing

A dilution of pigment in the hair follicle.

Marble

A term used exclusively for the Bengal, a breed exhibiting a classic tabby pattern with rosettes on the flanks, markings typical of wild cats. The marbled cat, a wild cat from Asia, has marbling on the back and flanks and a lighter line on the belly marked with back spots.

Marking

A tabby design or striping, called "ghost markings" when it fades with age or when the cat exhibits tabby markings but is genetically self-colored. A clearly outlined pattern on a more or less even background. The pattern is created by a group of darker or lighter hairs that form stripes, marbling, or spotting, patches on the extremities, a mask on the head, or cuffs on the feet.

Mascara Lines

Dark lines connecting to the eyes.

Mask

The darker area of the face which stops between the ears and covers the nose, whisker pads, chin, and area around the eyes. Darker parts of the face in the Siamese and Birman.

Mi-ke

Tortoiseshell and white (calico) variety of the Japanese Bobtail. Tortoiseshell, light reddish-brown, dark reddish brown, and black on a white background.

Mink

The result of the influence of point and sepia genes on the self gene. The cat has darker col-

Mask.

Mink.

oring on the points and back and lighter coloring on the body, especially the underparts, while Colorpoints have coloring only on the extremities. The eyes are blue-green, as in the Tonkinese.

Examples:
- Chocolate Mink: points resembling the Chocolate Point Siamese, light golden-brown body.
- Blue Mink: points resembling the Blue Point Siamese, very light steel blue body.
- Lilac Mink: points resembling the Lilac Point Siamese, very light rice flour or pinkish-buff body.

Mittens
White fur on the forepaws, as in the Ragdoll.

Morphological Types
Terms corresponding to body type. Three different morphological types can be distinguished:
- Medium-limbed or medium type. Balanced, harmonious proportions. Intermediate in size. Straight profile, head (face) is round or trapezoid-shaped; slight stop, medium-sized nose, ears, and eyes. Example: European Shorthair, British Shorthair, Chartreux;
- Long-limbed or Oriental type. Slender body, fine bone and muscle structure, long legs, small feet. Head fairly triangular and elongated, domed profile, no stop. Almond-shaped eyes. Large, pointed ears. Long tail. Examples: Siamese, Abyssinian, Egyptian Mau;
- Short-limbed or stocky type. Massive silhouette, compact muscle structure. Heavy bone structure. Short legs. Wide head is square-shaped. Concave profile, domed forehead, pronounced stop, short, wide nose, angular chin, full cheeks. Round eyes. Wide, short, well-spaced ears. Short, well-furnished tail. A long-haired coat enhances the short-limbed type by making the legs appear shorter. Example: Persian.

Mutations have given rise to new breeds:
- Shorthaired, wavy coat without guard hairs (Cornish Rex);
- Shorthaired, wavy coat with guard hairs (Devon Rex);
- Curly, rough coat (American Wirehair);
- Coat reduced to a fine down (Sphynx);
- Shorthaired (Russian Blue);
- Semilonghaired (Somali);
- Longhaired (Persian).
- Intermediate or heterotype hairs: wavy and thin at the base, also ending in a club. For protection.

Necklace
Continuous or broken stripes on the upper part of the chest in tabby varieties.

Non-agouti
A solid-colored coat. (agouti gene A is what produces stripes in the coat, always accompanied by a design called a tabby pattern). Non-agouti gene aa produces self colors (uniform over the entire length of the hair), except in reddish-brown, cream, and orange varieties. All cats, for example, those with reddish-brown or cream coats, exhibit the tabby pattern to a certain extent.

Nose Leather
The hairless tip of the nose and nostrils.

Odd-eyed
A cat with one blue eye and one copper eye, for example. Only possible in cats with a white coat or with a colored coat with white markings (see Heterochromatic).

Particolored
A coat consisting of two or more colors, such as tortoiseshell and white.
- A coat consisting of several colors, for example, reddish-brown, white, and black.

Patched Tabby
A tabby coat with superimposed tortoiseshell coloring. Also called tortie tabby (see Torbie).

Pattern
A design characterizing the coat.

Pewter
The coat color of the Silver Shaded cat with orange or copper-colored eyes.

Point Score
A numbered rating of the various elements involved in evaluating a cat. A perfect score is

Erect ears.

Large ears (Devon Rex).

Folded ears.

Ears set in a caplike fashion, flat against the head.

Plume (Turkish Angora).

Particolored cat.

one hundred. Each region of the body is assigned a number of points based on significance, in order to achieve an accurate rating. Point scores vary by breed (see point score table in Cat Fancy section).

Points

Colored extremities that are darker than the body, including the mask, ears, legs, and tail. A characteristic of the Siamese.
• Colorpoint: colored at the extremities. The contrast is variable in density and less pronounced in the Burmese pattern than in the Siamese pattern.

Short hair (Russian Blue).

Long hair (Persian).

Prefix

The cattery name preceding the cat's name, indicating the breeder's cattery.

Rex

A term describing animals with a wavy, curly coat and usually curly whiskers. Actually, this term encompasses several different mutations, both in terms of genotype and phenotype. The rex trait is always a monogenetic, autosomal trait which is usually recessive. Only the Selkirk Rex and Dutch Rex traits are dominant.

Rexing

A term describing a curly coat like that of the Rex.

Roman

Said of a slightly rounded profile, especially in the Birman; the profile is arched in the Cornish Rex.

Ruddy

Term used in the United States to describe the original color of Abyssinians and Somalis. "Usual" is the British equivalent.

Ruff or Frill

A mass of longer, thicker hair around the neck.

Rumpy

A Manx with no tail. The "rumpy riser" has one to three coccygeal vertebrae covered by a tuft of hair.

Rustiness

Traces of reddish hairs in the coat of a black cat.

Points (Siamese).

Sable

A term used in the United States to describe the brown Burmese, the darkest form of the breed.

Sable

A chestnut-colored (brown, sable) variety of Burmese with a dark coat and a brown nose and pads. The Burmese, which arrived in France in 1956, was nicknamed "sable cat" due to its coat coloring.

Scarab Marking

A marking in the form of an "M" on the forehead of many foreign-type spotted tabbies. This marking is complex enough in design to evoke an ancient Egyptian scarab beetle. Also called "frown lines."

Seal Point

A coat in which the extremities are the darkest brown possible. The body ranges from eggshell white to golden. This is the best known and most appreciated Siamese color.

Seal

A dark brown coat color in the black range.

Self

Said of a coat of a single, solid color. All hairs have the same intensity and the same color.

Self

A solid-colored coat with no white.

Semi-cobby

Having a slightly longer and leaner silhouette than the cobby.

Semi-foreign

Having a fairly long-limbed silhouette but a relatively heavy bone structure.

Sepia

This color, specific essentially to the Burmese, slightly tones down the corresponding base color, making it lighter.

Shading, Shaded

A "shaded" coat falls between chinchilla and smoke (in which most of the hair is colored), with tipping covering approximately 1/3 the length of the hair and the rest white or light-

Absent tail (Manx).

Short tail (Japanese Bobta

Reddish-brown and white.

colored. Shading may appear as darker coloring only on certain areas of the coat, as the hips in Colorpoints (Siamese, Himalayan, Birman). The tone of the coat varies gradually, as in the Burmese.

Shell

In this effect, the tipping (darker marking at the hair tip) covers approximately 1/8 the length of the hair. A "shell" cat is lighter than a "shaded" cat.

Silvering

A silvery coat. A coat with colored tipping on a white background. If the term is not preceded by another color, such as blue silver, it indicates black tipping. In the Silver Egyptian Mau, the black spotting contrasts with a very pale silver background. In the Somali, silver black (black bands, white bands and underparts) and silver blue (blue bands, white bands and underparts) varieties are recognized. In Silver Tabbies, the affected hairs are confined to lighter areas placed between darker markings.

Smoke Cameo

A smoke coat in which the pigmentation is orange.

Smoke

A coat in which most of each hair is colored, with the base being white or light-colored.
• 50 to 80% of the length of each hair is colored, the rest being silver, as seen mainly in the Persian.

Seal Point Siamese.

Smoke

The effect when color covers 50 to 80% of the length of the hair (black, blue, red, cream, etc.). The rest of the hair, down to the root, is a luminous, silvery white. A lovely Smoke Persian must appear to be a solid color. If the cat is black, for example, the white background should be visible only when the cat is moving or if the hair is parted.

Sorrel

Chocolate ticked coloring in the Abyssinian and Somali.

Spectacles

A lighter area encircling the eyes in a colored mask (Siamese, Birman, Himalayan).

Spotted

"Found only in the European Shorthair, this pattern corresponds to clear, non-overlapping spots that are oval, round, or rosette-shaped and vary in color or said to be "in keeping with the background color, "in the standard" (Chaudieu, 1974). Spotted tabby: Legs and tail ringed with fairly thin, tight markings. The spine may be covered either with parallel lines or spots arranged in a line. The flanks, shoulders, and thighs have spots of varying sizes and shapes, preferably round and even (like those of the ocelot or panther). In all cases, the spots must be well-separated and distinct. The belly is spotted.

Spotted

Said of a coat having round, crisp, distinct spots. Spotted tabby: spotted or patched tabby coat consisting of spots on an agouti background.

Standard

The set of characteristics of the different parts of the body (head, ears, eyes, legs, tail, etc.) and coat (texture and length of hair, coloring, etc.) that an individual of a specific breed must exhibit.

Stocky

Having a compact body shape, as the British Shorthair.

Stop

The indentation between the forehead and nose; the separation between the top of the skull and the face. Depending on breed, the stop may be slight (British Shorthair), very pronounced (Persian), or absent (Oriental). A stop is less visible than a break.

Silver Shaded Persian.

Black smoke.

Striping

On the tabby, distinct markings resembling fish bones.

Stumpy

Term describing a Manx cat with a tail 1 to 10 cm long and consisting of one to three caudal vertebrae, often with bone defects ("knotted tail").

Suffix

The cattery name following the cat's name, indicating the cattery in which the cat resides.

Tabby

Tabby cats have a coat with striping, marbling, or dark spots on a light background, including:
• Blotched (or classic or marbled) tabby: wide, dark stripes curving over the flanks, butterfly wings on the shoulders, three large stripes running from the withers to the base of the tail.
• Mackerel (or tiger) tabby: thin, either continuous or broken stripes perpendicular to the spine.
• Spotted (or patched) tabby: round, even, distinct spots on a light background.
• Ticked tabby (Abyssinian coat): striping is almost absent and confined to the legs, necklace, or tail. Tabbies exist in all colors.

Tail

The domestic cat has a long tail (slightly shorter in the Persian, may be totally absent in the Manx) which is often abundantly furnished and naturally curves backward. The photos illustrate tail variations based on breed. Several Asian breeds have short tails or caudal defects. Corkscrew or pompom tail (Japanese Bobtail).

Spotted tabby

Ticking

Stripes of color on a single hair. Each hair has dark bands alternating with light bands. Found in ticked tabby varieties. The Abyssinian has a ticked coat.

Classic tabby

Tiger

Tiger or mackerel designs are dark markings on short or long hair that appear as:
• Rings on the legs, tail, and chest.
• A single stripe along the spine.
• Concentric, transversal stripes on the back, running from the spine to the belly. The wild cat sports this attire, which helps it blend in with its natural surroundings.

Tipped, Tipping

Only the tip of the hair is colored. The following distinctions are made, depending on the ratio of the dark part to the total length:
• Chinchilla Persian: tipping on 1/8 the length of the hair;
• Shaded Persian: tipping on 1/3 the length of the hair;
• Smoke Persian: tipping on 2/3 the hair.

Torbie

A female with both tortoiseshell (tortie) markings and tabby markings.

Tortie

A nickname for tortoiseshell, or a combination of red and black or cream and blue. In principle, this coloring exists only in females. In a Tortie Point, the coloring covers the points and must be evenly mixed.

Tortoiseshell and White

A cat with tortoiseshell coloring and white markings.

Tortoiseshell or Tortie

A coat with a combination of red and black or cream and blue. In principle, this combination exists only in females. Black and orange coat color. Also exists in dilute versions. A term describing a coat in which two colors are more or less distinctly intermingled in an even reddish-brown, cream, or apricot color. The color pairs include black, chocolate, or cinnamon with reddish-brown or lilac; fawn with cream; and caramel with apricot.

Undercoat

Fine, downy hair lying close to the body beneath the guard hairs and providing good insulation. The density depends on the breed.

Van

American van pattern: particolor variety in which the entire body is white and only the top of the head and tail are colored. European van pattern: particolor variety in which the entire body is white except for a small colored patch, and the head head and tail are colored.

Variation

Any modification affecting living beings, based on a type considered "normal" or average. In cats, variations involve head shape (round in the European Shorthair, triangular in the Siamese), tail length (ranging from long in some breeds to absent in the Manx), coat markings (tabby, etc.), and coat length and color.

Variety

A variety is a subgroup of animals of a breed that selective breeding has rendered distinct from

Medium-limbed type

Long-limbed type

Short-limbed type

other animals of the breed. In cats, varieties in coat color are the most common (see Persian in the breed section, for example).

Wedge-shaped

Said of a head characterized by a straight line running from the outer base of the ear to the side of the muzzle. Flat skull, straight nose. Narrow face with angular features.

Whip Tail

A long, thin, flexible tail tapering from the base to the tip, as in the Siamese, Sphynx, and Oriental.

Whisker Pad

The area of the upper lip on which whiskers grow; the fairly fleshy part of the muzzle on either side of the tip of the nose.

Whisker Pinch

The distinct demarcation between the cheeks and the muzzle.

White

White cats with blue irises are almost always deaf (Letard, 1925).

Whole

A queen or tom, that is, a cat that has not been spayed or neutered.

Wooly

Said of a thick undercoat on the belly, britches, or tail in Persians. The coat has the wooly appearance of the Chartreux.

Sources: P. Bossé, A. Brisson, B. Bulard-Cordeau, M. Casteran, C.F.A., J. Dutillet, F.I.Fe., M.-L. Hubert, J.-L. Klein, C. Kretz, A. Noël, C. Sacase, L.O.O.F., T.I.C.A., E.J.J. Verhoef-Verhallen.

Almond-shaped eyes

Round eyes

Coppery yellow eyes

Green eyes

Abyssinian

Country of Origin: Asia?
Other names:
Aby, Bunny Cat

The Aby, an elegant, distinguished cat with gold-flecked eyes.

The exact origins of the Abyssinian, one of the oldest cat breeds, remain a mystery. Perhaps it originated in Ethiopia, formally known as Abyssinia. Unfortunately, there is no record of agouti cats in Ethiopia. Nevertheless, since it resembles the sacred cat of Ancient Egypt, legend holds that the Abyssinian was born along the banks of the Nile. In fact, it is said that Ramses II asked the king of Abyssinia for a band of cats to take back to Egypt. Cats sporting a coat similar to the Abyssinian can also be found in Africa, Eurasia, and Asia, including Felis Libyca, the African Wild Cat or Gloved Cat, and Felis chaus, the Swamp Cat or Jungle Cat. However, the existence of cats with ticked coloring in India and Asia makes it more likely that the Abysinnian originated in Asia.

An early Abyssinian cat, a cat with a ticked coat (like that of a rabbit), was apparently brought back to Great Britain from Ethiopia by Sir Robert Napier in 1868. Named Zula, he was shown in 1871 at the Crystal Palace of London. G. Stables began a scientific study of the cat in 1874. The breed, recognized in England in 1882, was fixed and then improved by crossing it with the British Shorthair. The first standard was published in 1889 by H. Weir. Development of the breed began in the United States prior to 1910 and the C.F.A. recognized the Abyssinian in 1917.

In 1926, an Abyssinian Cat Club was formed. Two females, Aluna and Osira, born in Vienna, were brought to France in 1927. In the 1930s, European breeders focused on selection of the Abyssinian. After two world wars and a feline leukemia outbreak from 1960 to 1970, the breed almost disappeared. Today, the Abyssinian is one of the best-known and best-loved of the shorthaired breeds.

BLUE ABYSSINIAN, A NEW VARIETY. THE FIRST TICKED ABYSSINIAN
PRESENTING BLUE IN ITS COAT WAS DISCOVERED IN GREAT BRITAIN.
IN 1942.

Abyssinian

BLUE ABYSSINIAN

GENERAL

Of medium size. Weight: 4 to 7.5 kg
Regal in appearance, lithe.
Elegant, well-proportioned. Oriental body type with an elongated head (English Abyssinian), or more compact with a more rounded head (American Abyssinian). Short coat with agouti color pattern.

SILVER ABYSSINIAN

HEAD

Wedge-shaped (▼), with slightly rounded contours (◆); without flat planes (★). Arched brow. The moderately long nose bridge must never be straight; no break. The profile lines of the head show a gentle contour. Jowls are allowed in mature males (■). Muzzle not sharply pointed; no whisker pinch. Strong, well-developed, rounded chin, neither receding nor protruding.

RED (T.I.C.A.–SORREL) ABYSSINIAN NEW VARIETY.

EARS

Large, broad at the base with slightly rounded tips (▼); moderately pointed (■). Relatively wide-set, alert. Covered with short, close-lying hair. A spot on the back of the ear ("wild print" or "thumb print") is to be desired. Tufts at the tips are desirable (▼).

EYES

Large, almond-shaped, wide-set. Accentuated by a fine dark line of the base color and encircled by a light-colored area (◆). Brilliant, expressive, of one intense color. Yellow (gold), green (★), and amber (▼).

NECK

Rather long and gracefully arched.

BODY

Medium in length and build, lithe, strong, and muscular. Rounded rib cage. Slightly arched back.

LEGS AND PAWS

Long, straight, fine-boned. Small, oval, compact paws. The cat gives the impression of being on tiptoe.

TAIL

Fairly long, thick at the base and tapering to the tip.

COAT

Thick, dense, and resilient to the touch, lying close against the skin. Short in length or

medium particularly along the spine. Ticking (two or three bands of alternating dark or light color on each hair shaft) similar to the coat of a rabbit. Ticking is not present on the throat, underside, or inside of legs (▼).

Recognized colors:

Ruddy ("usual" in Great Britain): Black or dark brown ticking on a ruddy brown ground color. Tile red nose leather, black pads.

Blue: Slate blue ticking on a warm beige ground color. Dark rose nose leather, gray pads.

Sorrel: Chocolate brown ticking on rich red ground color. Rosy pink nose leather, chocolate brown pads.

Fawn: Light cocoa brown ticking on a beige ground color. Dark pink nose leather and pads.

Red: Orange-brown ticking. Pink nose leather and pads.

Silver: Sorrel, blue, or fawn ticking on silvery ground color (...).

Ticking does not appear in kittens until the sixth week.

NOTES

Allowable outcross breeds: Somali

FAULT

Long (like that of a Siamese) or round head. Small or pointed ears. Round eyes. Overly massive body. Dull, fluffy coat. Disqualify: White locket or white anywhere on the body, other than the nostrils, chin and throat (■).

RUDDY ABYSSINIAN (ORIGINAL VARIETY) KITTENS.

CHARACTERISTICS

The Abbyssinian is a very active, extroverted, playful cat that is curious about its surroundings and has a well-balanced temperament. This cat has a strong, independent personality, but is social and affectionate. Very gentle and loving, the Aby requires considerable attention, despises solitude, and is devoted exclusively to its owner. The Aby is talkative, but its voice is very quiet. The exuberance seen in young kittens mellows with age. This athlete and hunter requires exercise, and therefore space. An enclosed yard is highly desirable.
Grooming is simple. The Aby requires only weekly brushing and combing. When shedding, dead, loose hairs must be removed regularly. For a shiny coat, rub the coat with a chamois cloth. If the cat will tolerate it, bathe him with an appropriate shampoo two days prior to a show.

(▼) F.I.Fe   (■) L.O.O.F.   (★) C.F.A.   (◆) T.I.C.A.

American Bobtail

Country of Origin: United States

A shaggy little lynx with a bobbed tail originating in the Americas.

This American cat is rare outside of the United States. Around 1964, an American couple named Sanders was vacationing near an Indian reservation in Arizona when they noticed a wild-looking kitten with a short, upright tail. They adopted the kitten and named him Yodie. He was crossed with Michi, a Siamese. A kitten from this litter, crossed with a cream-colored cat, was the origin of the breed.

The Bobtail's distinguishing feature, its short tail, was the result of a mutation caused by a dominant gene. Initially, the Bobtail's coat was short. However, Himalayans (Colorpoint Persians in Britain) were introduced and resulted in a medium-length coat. The breed was recognized by T.I.C.A. in 1989.

The semi-longhair American Bobtail, the longhaired version of the American Bobtail, has the same characteristics as its cousin.

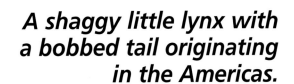

AMERICAN BOBTAIL SILVER TABBY AND WHITE.

ABOVE: BROWN TABBY AND WHITE AMERICAN BOBTAIL
RIGHT: SILVER TABBY AMERICAN BOBTAIL

American Bobtail

LONGHAIR BLACK, SMOKE AND WHITE AMERICAN BOBTAIL.

GENERAL
Medium to large. Weight: 3 to 9 kg.
Semi-cobby to cobby body, powerful, heavy,
muscular. Short tail. Medium-long, double coat.

CREAM POINT AMERICAN BOBTAIL.

HEAD
Broad with rounded contours. Slightly curved brow. Full, well-developed cheeks. The width of the muzzle is almost as great as its length. Slight nose break. The broad nose is almost straight, with a gentle concave curve between the nose and brow. Strong, firm, well-developed chin. Powerful jaws.

EARS
Medium in size; broad at the base and rounded at the tips, preferably Lynx tip. Fairly wide set. Held alert. The interior of the ear is well clad with long hairs.

EYES
Large, broad, oval, almond-shaped and angled slightly upward toward the ears. Color appropriate to coat color.

NECK
Medium in length, muscular.

BODY
Of medium size, stocky. Broad chest. Slightly arched back. Plenty of bone. Powerfully muscled.

LEGS AND PAWS
Medium length. Hind legs are slightly longer than forelegs. Powerful bone structure and musculature. Broad, round paws. Tufts of hair between the toes.

TAIL
Short (2.5 to 10 cm) and flexible; may be either knotted or slightly curled. Well clad with long, thick, shaggy hairs.

COAT
Double coat; thick and dense; medium length, rather harsh and shaggy. Abundant undercoat. Longer at the ruff and on the tail. Any color is permissible.

NOTES
Allowable outcross breeds: All breeds (■).

FAULTS
A muzzle that is too short. A nose break that is too pronounced. Tail too long or too short.
Overly fine bone structure.
Overly silky or smooth coat.
Disqualification: Tail of normal length or no tail (■).

LONGHAIR AMERICAN BOBTAIL KITTEN.

CHOCOLATE TORTOISESHELL TABBY POINT AMERICAN BOBTAIL.

CHARACTERISTICS
The American Bobtail is a calm, patient, debonair cat. He is gentle and very attached to his owner. The American Bobtail loves to be in the company of other cats and accommodates dogs. This breed does not like to be alone. The American Bobtail is also an excellent hunter. This cat does not reach full maturity until two or three years of age. Easy care.

(▼) F.I.Fe   (■) L.O.O.F.   (★) C.F.A.   (◆) T.I.C.A.

BROWN TABBY AND WHITE AMERICAN BOBTAIL.

American Curl

Country of Origin: United States

A spontaneous mutation is responsible for this breed's full crescent ear curl.

I n 1981, in Lakewood, California, the Ruga's welcomed a black, semi-longhaired stray with curled ears into their home and named her Shalamith.

At the end of the year, she gave birth to four kittens, two of which had inherited the curled ears of their mother. In 1983, Nancy Kiester, a breeder and friend of the Ruga's, successfully showed Shalamith and her offspring at a cat show in California. At the same time, she began selectively breeding this new breed.

The mutation resulting in the ear curl is caused by a dominant gene that can be transmitted by one parent. Whether sporting long or short hair, the American Curl has beautiful ears accentuated by abundant interior furnishings. The cartilage is firm to the touch. There are three degrees of curl: slight, partial, and full crescent (the most coveted).

The American Curl was recognized by T.I.C.A. in 1985, then by the C.F.A. in 1991. The fist American Curl arrived in France in 1988 (the first litter was born in 1989), and the breed was introduced in Great Britain in 1995.

The American Curl is a rare cat, especially outside of the United States.

SILVER AMERICAN CURL. THE EXPRESSION OF THE CURL GENE VARIES, RESULTING IN VARIOUS DEGREES OF EAR CURL.

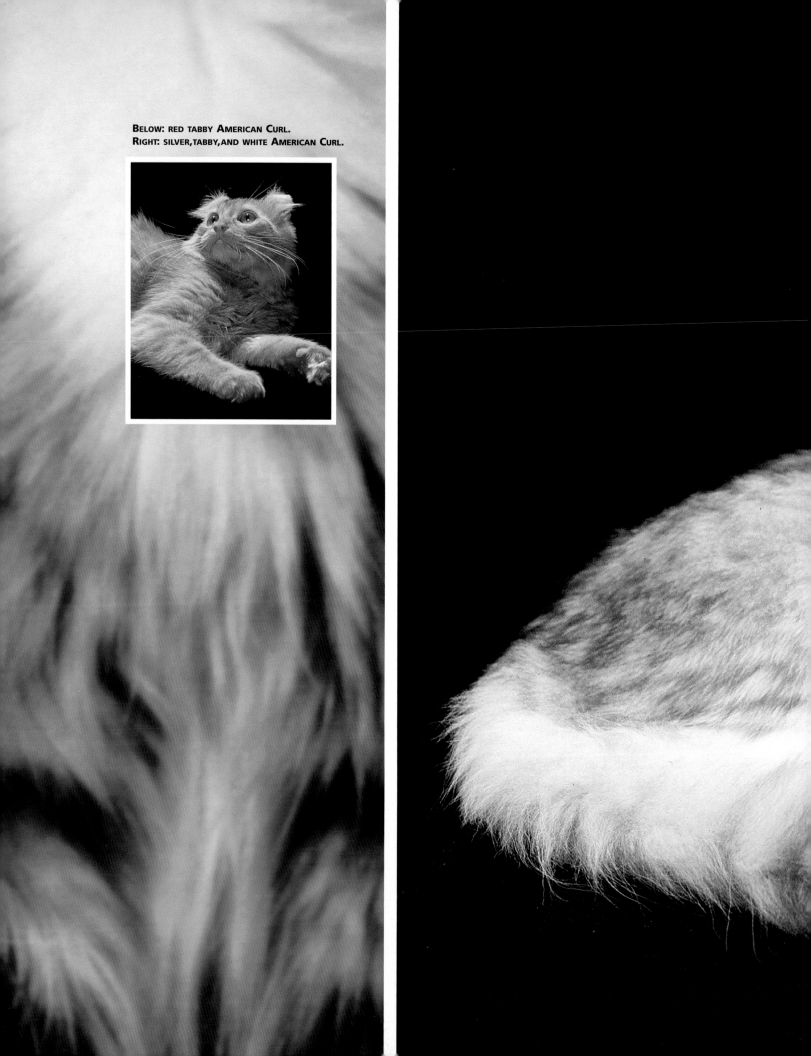

BELOW: RED TABBY AMERICAN CURL.
RIGHT: SILVER, TABBY, AND WHITE AMERICAN CURL.

American Curl

AMERICAN CURL COAT TYPES FROM LEFT TO RIGHT: BROWN TABBY, WHITE, BROWN TABBY, BROWN TABBY AND WHITE.

GENERAL
Size: Intermediate. Weight: 3 to 5 kg.
Slender, well-balanced build.
This breed's distinctive feature is its uniquely curled ears.

HEAD
Medium in size, moderately longer than wide, without flat planes. The straight nose gives way to a slight rise from the bottom of the eyes to the forehead. Muzzle is neither pointed nor square. No whisker pinch. Firm chin.

EARS
Moderately large, broad at the base, rounded tips, set very high on the skull. Ear leather curls back toward top of the head. Degree of curl ranges from 90 degrees, not to exceed 180 degrees. Furnishings and Lynx tips desirable (♦).

LONGHAIR TORTOISESHELL AMERICAN CURL.

EYES
Moderately large, walnut shape, and wide set. Color, which must be clear, brilliant, and uniform, has no relation to coat color.

NECK
Medium.

BODY
Semi-foreign, length one and one-half times height at shoulder (■). Boning and musculature neither heavy nor fine.

LEGS AND PAWS
Moderate length, in proportion to body.

Forelegs slightly shorter than hind legs. Straight with good muscle tone. Paws are medium in size and rounded.

TAIL
Length equal to body length. Broad at the base and tapering to a rounded tip.

COAT
Two varieties:
Semi-long (currently the most common) - fine, silky; sparse undercoat; no ruff, full plume on tail.
Shorthair - fine, silky, laying flat; minimal undercoat.
All colors are permissible.

NOTES
Allowable outcross breeds: None.

FAULTS
Deep nose break. Heavy, coarse coat with thick undercoat, ruff. Ears set low; extreme curl (tip of ear must not touch back of ear or back of head) (♦).

AMERICAN CURL LONGHAIR BROWN TABBY.

CHARACTERISTICS
The American Curl has a well-balanced personality and an even disposition. Mischievous, playful, and a comfortable companion, this breed talks only rarely.
The friendly, affectionate, and loving, American Curl is very attached to its owner. This breed is comfortable with other cats, dogs, and enjoys children. The American Curl is active and requires exercise, and therefore, will enjoy an enclosed yard.
The American Curl reaches full maturity around two or three years of age. The cartilage in the ears begins to curl and harden four days after birth, but the definitive curl is not set until three or four months of age.
Weekly brushing and combing is sufficient. The ears must be cleaned with a quality ear-cleaning product. A Curl should be bathed several days prior to a show.
The gene responsible for the ear curl does not carry any associated diseases. Unlike the Scottish Fold, two Curls may be mated without endangering the offspring. Curls are very rare; in order to avoid excessive inbreeding, experts recommend that they be crossed with normal-eared cats.

(▼) F.I.Fe   (■) L.O.O.F.   (★) C.F.A.   (♦) T.I.C.A.

American Shorthair

Country of Origin: United States
Other Names: Shorthair,
Domestic Shorthair

This even-tempered European immigrant is an excellent hunter.

The American Shorthair's counterpart is the British Shorthair and the European Shorthair. Early immigrants arrived in the United States with cats that adapted well to the harsh climate of the northern states.

This breed is the result of selectively breeding common "alley cats" with other imported breeds, such as the British Shorthair, Burmese, and Persian.

In 1904, the C.F.A. registered the first American Shorthair - Buster Brown, a male smoke descended from a British Shorthair.

This breed was called Domestic Shorthair until the 1960s, when the breed was officially recognized as the American Shorthair in 1966. The F.I.Fe. does not recognize the breed.

The American Shorthair is rare in Europe. The breed is highly prized in Japan and very popular in the United States.

AMERICAN SHORTHAIR BLOTCHED SILVER TABBY, A HIGHLY PRIZED VARIETY. CLOSELY RESEMBLES THE EUROPEAN SHORTHAIR.

BOTTOM LEFT: AMERICAN SHORTHAIR SILVER TABBY.
RIGHT: AMERICAN BROWN TABBY.

GENERAL
Size: Medium to large. Weight: 3.5 to 7 kg.
Powerfully built and symmetrical. Shorthaired.

YOUNG BROWN TABBY AMERICAN SHORTHAIRS.

AMERICAN SHORTHAIR RED TABBY.

HEAD
Broad and rounded; medium in size. Moderately convex rise from the bridge of the nose to the forehead. Definite jowls in mature males. Square, not overly short muzzle. Medium length nose. Square, firm chin. Strong jaws.

EARS
Medium size. Wide set and not unduly open at base. Rounded at tips.

AMERICAN SHORTHAIR BROWN TABBY.

EYES
Medium to large, round and set well apart. Outer corners set slightly higher than inner corners. Color appropriate to coat color.

NECK
Medium in length, muscular and strong.

BODY
Medium to large in size. Slightly longer than tall, not elongated. Broad chest, particularly in mature males. Well-developed shoulders. Medium boned and powerfully built.

LEGS AND PAWS
Medium in length and heavily muscled. Paws are medium in size and rounded.

TAIL
Medium in length, heavy at the base and tapering to a rounded tip. Carried nearly in line with the back.

COAT
Short, thick, and glossy, lying close to the body. Thick undercoat in winter. All colors permissible except chocolate, lilac and colorpoint (■).

NOTES
Allowable outcross breeds: American Wirehair.

FAULTS
Long, pointed, or close-set ears. Eye color not solid green in Silver Tabbies, eye color other than yellow in Brown Tabbies. Overly short, thick, long, or thin neck. Excessive cobbiness or ranginess. Overly thin or short tail. Tail carried over the back. Fine, long, silky coat. Disqualify: White lockets or buttons.

YOUNG SILVER BLACK TABBY AMERICAN SHORTHAIRS.

CHARACTERISTICS
This calm, easygoing cat adores its owner. The American Tabby is playful, athletic, and very social. This breed is made for the great outdoors, particularly since the American Tabby is an excellent hunter. However, the American Tabby can adapt to indoor living.
This hardy, solidly built cat reaches puberty early (around seven or eight months of age). Care is simple. Weekly brushing is sufficient, but should increase to daily during shedding season. An American Shorthair should be bathed three to seven days prior to a show.

(▼) F.I.Fe   (■) L.O.O.F. (★) C.F.A.   (◆) T.I.C.A.

SILVER SPOTTED TABBY AND WHITE AMERICAN SHORTHAIR.

American Wirehair

Country of Origin: United States
Other Name: Wire

The Wirehair's unusual coarse, prickly coat was caused by the spontaneous mutation of a gene.

In 1966 on a farm in Verona, New York, the American Wirehair made its debut in a litter of American Shorthairs. Its crimped, coarse coat was the result of the spontaneous mutation of a dominant gene.

The first-ever Wirehair was a red-and-white kitten named Adam. Breeder Joan O'Shea began a selective breeding program, crossing the Wirehairs with American Shorthairs to avoid excessive inbreeding and to develop the breed.

The American Wirehair was officially recognized in the United States in 1978. Wirehairs were first imported to France in 1972. Still rather uncommon in the United States, this breed is extremely rare in Europe.

BROWN TABBY AND WHITE AMERICAN WIREHAIR. EARLY WIREHAIRS WERE WHITE.

ABOVE: BROWN TABBY AMERICAN WIREHAIR
RIGHT: SILVER TABBY AMERICAN WIREHAIR

American Wirehair

BROWN D TABBY AMERICAN WIREHAIR

GENERAL
Medium size. Weight: 3.5 to 7 kg.
Except for the coat, the standard for the American Wirehair is the same as that of the American Shorthair, its ancestor.

BLACK AMERICAN KITTEN

Round, medium-sized (■) paws; small and oval (◆).

TAIL
Length in proportion to body. Heavy from the base to the rounded tip. Carried nearly in line with the back.

COAT
Short, tight, and even. Coarse and hard to the touch. Slightly crimped, ending in a slight hook.

BROWN, TABBY, AND WHITE AMERICAN WIREHAIR

FAULTS
Deep nose break. Long, pointed, or close-set ears. Color of eyes not entirely green in Silver Wirehairs, color other than yellow in Brown Wirehairs. Overly short or long neck. Overly thin or short tail. Tail carried over the back. Fine, long, silky coat. Disqualify: White lockets or buttons. (■)

HEAD
Medium in size. Broad and fairly round. Rounded skull. Prominent cheekbones. Definite jowls in mature males. Square, well-developed muzzle. Slight whisker break (◆). Moderately short nose shows a gentle, concave curve. Square, well-developed chin.

EARS
Medium in size. Set wide apart and not unduly open at base. Rounded at tips.

EYES
Large, round, expressive, and wide set. Color in harmony with coat color is preferred.

NECK
Moderately short, well-muscled.

BODY
Medium to large. Broad chest. Medium in bone. Powerfully muscled.

LEGS AND PAWS
Medium in length and bone. Well muscled.

WHITE AMERICAN WIREHAIR WITH ONE BLUE AND ONE YELLOW EYE

Whiskers and ear furnishings are also curly.
All colors permissible except chocolate, lilac, and colorpoint.

NOTES
Allowable outcross breeds: American Shorthair and British Shorthair (■).

AMERICAN WIREHAIR KITTEN

CHARACTERISTICS
This solidly built, highly active, agile, and playful cat needs exercise to burn off its abundant energy. The American Wirehair is social, affectionate, and gentle, demonstrating the same excellent character as its American Shorthair relative. Care is simple. The coat should be brushed and combed weekly.

(▼) F.I.Fe   (■) L.O.O.F.   (★) C.F.A.   (◆) T.I.C.A.

BROWN, TABBY, AND WHITE AMERICAN WIREHAIR

Turkish Angora

This elegant cat with a silky white coat was favored by the kings of France.

The Angora, which originated in Turkey, bears the name of the capital city of Turkey, formerly called Angora, but now called Ankara. This ancient breed remained true to its original type for many years. In the 17th century, Italian explorer Pietro Della Valle brought several Angoras back to his home country. This cat, with its immaculate, fluffy coat, was consider a gift "fit for a king." The European aristocracy, particularly the court of Louis XV, favored Angoras. In the 18th century, Linné renamed the breed *Cattus angorensis* to distinguish it from domestic cats and Chartreux cats. Buffon described it as the "solid white, longhaired cat of Angora."

In the 19th century, after contributing to the development of the Persian (to which the Turkish Angora transmitted the gene responsible for long hair), the breed almost disappeared as a result of the remarkable popularity of Persians. After the Second World War, the breed was on the verge of extinction. Breeders in Europe and the United States imported Angoras from Turkey, where the breed is now protected. The Torio's, American breeders, purchased Yildiz and Hildizcik from the Ankara Zoo. In 1970, the C.F.A. registered the first Turkish Angoras. The breed was officially recognized by the C.F.A. in 1973, and by the F.I.Fe in 1988. Despite its remarkable beauty, this breed is rare.

WHITE TURKISH ANGORA.

ABOVE: LILAC TURKISH ANGORA.
RIGHT: WHITE TURKISH ANGORA KITTENS.

Turkish Angora

GENERAL
Medium size. Weight: 2.5 to 5 kg. Long, lithe body. Graceful and elegant. Semilong to long coat.

WHITE TURKISH ANGORAS.

HEAD
Small to medium in size, tapering toward the chin. Moderately flat skull. Allowance for jowls in mature males.

Barely rounded, fairly long muzzle. No whisker break. Nose is straight, medium in length, and without break. Firm, gently rounded chin forms a perpendicular line with the nose.

LILAC TURKISH ANGORA.

EARS
Large, pointed, wide at the base, and set high on the head. Tufted. Lynx tip preferred.

EYES
Large, almond shaped, and set at a slight angle. All colors, in harmony with coat color, allowed.

NECK
Moderately long. Slim and graceful.

BODY
Long, lithe, and muscular. Narrow chest. Shoulders and rump of same width. Rump slightly higher than shoulders. Fine in bone.

WHITE TURKISH ANGORA ARE LIGHT BLUE, AMBER, OR ODD-EYED AND HAVE A PURE WHITE COAT.

RED TABBY TURKISH ANGORA. THIS BREED HAS A THICK COAT, PARTICULARLY IN WINTER.

LEGS AND PAWS
Long and slender. Hind legs longer than front. Small, oval paws; round ('). Tufts between toes.

TAIL
Long; length in proportion to body.

COAT
Medium long. Fine, silky texture. Minimal undercoat. Longer at ruff, on back of legs, and on the belly where the coat is slightly wavy. The ruff is not fully developed until one year of age (▼).

All colors are recognized with any amount of white, except chocolate, lilac, cinnamon, fawn, and colorpoint or Burmese color patterns. Solid white is the most prized color.

NOTES
Allowable outcross breeds: None (■).

FALTS
Heavy bone structure, Persian body type or cobbiness. Overly round head or foreign head shape. Nose break. Overly short tail. Green eyes permissible only in white, silver, or golden cats (◆).

WHITE TURKISH ANGORAS.

CHARACTERISTICS
This active, lively, well-balanced cat is playful, but easygoing.
The Turkish Angora enjoys other cats and gets along well with dogs. This breed is highly adaptable, even adjusting well to travel.
The Turkish Angora is extremely affectionate and gentle. He loves a good petting session. In fact, you may never be able to get your Turkish Angora off your lap! Though talkative, the Turkish Angora has a soft voice.
This cat is strong, athletic, and agile. He loves water and is an excellent hunter. The Turkish Angora needs room to run.

(▼) F.I.Fe   (■) L.O.O.F.   (★) C.F.A.   (◆) T.I.C.A.

Balinese

Country of Origin: United States
Original Name: Longhair Siamese

A luxuriously silky, svelte little imp with deep blue eyes.

*I*n the 1940, American breeders developed an interest in Siamese kittens born with semilong hair. They did not know if the longer hair was the result of outcrosses with Persians or spontaneous mutation.

Until that time, semilonghaired kittens had been considered undesirable. After World War II, Marion Dorsey of California began raising "Longhair Siamese," also called Balinese to reflect their Asian heritage and gracefulness. These Longhair Siamese were shown for the first time in 1955.

The C.F.A. and T.I.C.A. recognized the breed in 1970, the F.I.Fe in 1972, and France in 1983.

This breed is still uncommon in Europe.

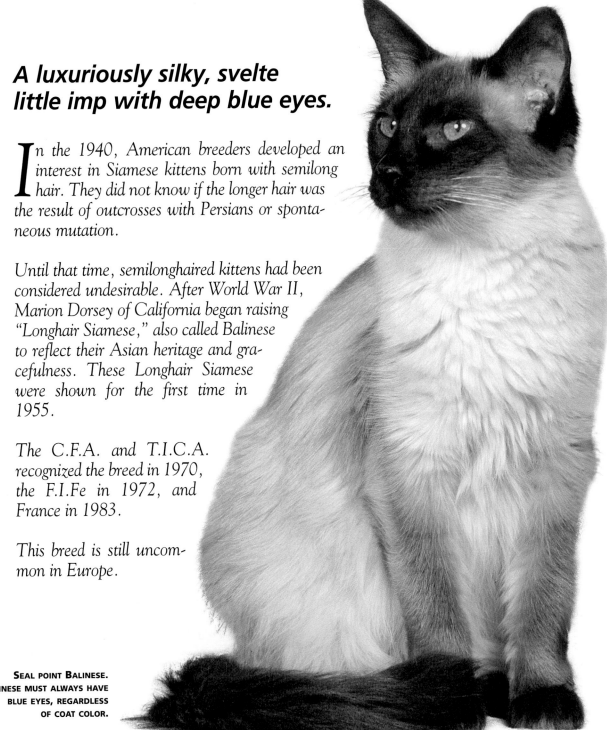

SEAL POINT BALINESE.
BALINESE MUST ALWAYS HAVE
BLUE EYES, REGARDLESS
OF COAT COLOR.

Balinese

GENERAL
Svelte, with long lines.
Elegant, lithe, and muscular.
Medium in size.
Weight: 2.5 to 5 kg.

CHOCOLATE POINT (LEFT)
AND LILAC POINT
(CENTER AND RIGHT)
BALINESE KITTENS.

HEAD
Medium size. Long and triangular with a straight profile. Slightly convex skull (▼); flat (■). Flat forehead. Fine muzzle. No nose or whisker break. Long, straight nose. Medium size chin (▼).

EYES
Of medium size, almond shape, and slanting slightly toward the nose. Color: Deep blue.

NECK
Long, slender, elegant.

BODY
Long, svelte, oriental body type. Fine bones and firm muscles.

color and body color. Kittens are born solid white. The coat does not take on its adult coloring until one year of age.
The C.F.A. recognizes only four varieties:
Seal Point: Deep seal brown points
Blue Point: Deep blue points
Chocolate Point: Milk chocolate points
Lilac Point: Frosty gray points
Cats of other colors are classified as Javanese in the United States.
In France, no distinction is made between the Balinese and the Javanese.

WHITE FOREST BALINESE.

SEAL POINT BALINESE.

NOTES
Allowable outcross breeds: Siamese and Oriental Shorthair.

FAULTS
Round or broad head. Short or broad muzzle. Nose break. Small or round eyes. Eyes not slanted. Short or massive body. Short legs. Heavy bone structure. Coat too short or too coarse.
Disqualify: Eye color other than blue.

EARS
Large and pointed, broad at the base. Wide set. Well-clad. Lynx tip desirable.

LEGS AND PAWS
Long and slim. Length in proportion to body. Small, oval paws with tufts between the toes.

TAIL
Very long and thin, tapering to the tip.

COAT
Semilong, silky, fine hair.
Longer on the body, belly, and tail (plume). Slight undercoat.
All Siamese colors are recognized. Color points must be uniform. Clear contrast between point

BICOLOR CHOCOLATE POINT BALINESE.

CHOCOLATE POINT
BALINESE KITTEN.

CHARACTERISTICS
This extroverted, active, lively cat is curious and playful, though more subdued and even-tempered than its Siamese cousin. The Balinese voice is also softer.
This cat loves company, despises solitude, and requires considerable love and affection. A Balinese will enjoy the company of another active cat or a cat-friendly dog. Devoted to his owner, the Balinese is sensitive, affectionate, and endearing. Since this breed is highly active and loves to hunt, a yard is appropriate. Maintaining the coat is easy. Weekly brushing and combing is sufficient. The Balinese does not shed much.

(▼) F.I.Fe   (■) L.O.O.F.   (★) C.F.A.   (◆) T.I.C.A.

Bengal

Country of Origin: United States
Other Names: Bengal Cat, Bengali, Leopardette

A golden, black-spotted coat like that of the Asian Leopard Cat, the Bengal Cat's wild ancestor.

In 1963, Jean Mill, a Californian breeder, purchased a wild cat, the Asian Leopard Cat, Felis prionailurus bengalensis, a miniature leopard with a spotted coat that is a strong swimmer and excellent fisher.

She crossed the cat with an American Shorthair queen, creating a breed of domestic cats presenting the physical features of wild cats. The females resulting from this cross were fertile. When crossed with the sire, they gave birth to kittens with spotted coats. Thus was the Bengal breed created.

In 1973, Dr. Centerwall of the University of California continued this crossbreeding program to determine the Asian Leopard Cat's resistance to feline leukemia. He gave eight of these hybrids to Jean Mill, who continued her selective breeding program.

Siamese, Egyptian Mau, and Burmese cats were used by breeders to create new lines.

The first specimen, "Millwood Finally Found" was registered with T.I.C.A. in 1983. The F.I.Fe only recently recognized the Bengal; the C.F.A. does not recognize the breed. The Bengal cat was introduced in France in 1991.

This breed is part of the new generation of "wild cats" and is still quite rare.

BROWN SPOTTED TABBY BENGAL. SPOTS RANGE FROM CINNAMON, TO CHOCOLATE, TO BLACK, DEPENDING ON VARIETY

ABOVE: CHOCOLATE TABBY MARBLED BENGAL.
RIGHT: BROWN SPOTTED BENGAL.

Bengal

GENERAL
Medium to large. Weight: 5.5 to 9 kg.
Long and substantial.
Robust bone structure.
Short coat.

YOUNG BROWN SPOTTED BENGAL.

BROWN SPOTTED BENGAL.

BODY
Long, large, and powerful, but not oriental. Robust bone structure and powerful musculature.

LEGS AND PAWS
Medium in length, slightly longer in the back than in front. Strong, substantial bone structure. Large, round paws. Black pads.

butterfly markings at the shoulders. The coat of the "Snow Leopard" is white with spots and marbling ranging from red to black; blue eyes.

NOTES
Allowable outcross breeds: None.

FAULTS
Spots on body running together and forming stripes. Absence of black on tip of tail. Belly not spotted. Pink pads, or pads not all of the same color.

HEAD
Rather large with rounded contours.
Slightly longer than wide. Gently curves from forehead to bridge. High, prominent cheekbones. Full, broad muzzle.Large, broad nose with very slight concave curve. Pronounced jaws (◆).

BROWN MARBLED BENGAL

BROWN SPOTTED BENGAL.

EARS
Medium small, wide at the base with rounded

tips, pointing forward. Lynx tips not desirable (▼).

EYES
Large, oval, set wide apart, slanting slightly up toward the base of the ear.
All colors permissible except blue and aquamarine (◆).
Blue in Seal Lynx Point Blues; yellow to green in Brown Tabbies; Bluegreen in Seal Mink Tabbies (▼).

NECK
Long, thick, muscular, and powerful. Length in proportion to body.

TAIL
Medium in length, thick, tapering to a rounded tip.

COAT
Short and fine. Thick, luxurious, and unusually soft to the touch. Colors and patterns include:
- Spotted Tabby, with spots being black, chocolate, or cinnamon in color. Orange ground color is preferred. Black horizontal shoulder streaks and rings on the tail, with the tip being black.
- Marbled Tabby, with broad oyster shell pattern on the flanks and

BROWN SPOTTED BENGAL.

CHARACTERISTICS
This even-tempered cat makes a pleasant companion provided it is of the fourth (■) to seventh generation following crossing of a domestic cat with an Asian Leopard Cat. Nevertheless, the Bengal's hunter instinct and energy are beyond that of most cats. Kittens tend to be destructive. The male is reputed to be more friendly than the female Bengal, who is often very independent and temperamental, strongly expressing her anger and very effusive in her displays of affection.
The Bengal gets along with other cats and dogs, but this breed's "wild" behaviors sometimes appear. The lively, active Bengal Cat loves exercise and water. He needs space. Rather exclusive with his owner, who must devote time to him, this cat can be as affectionate as any other. The Bengal has a quiet voice.
Care is easy.

(▼) F.I.Fe   (■) L.O.O.F.   (★) C.F.A.   (◆) T.I.C.A.

Russian Blue

Country of Origin: Russia
Other Names: Archangel Cat,
Spanish Blue, Chartreuse Blue,
American Blue, Russian Shorthair,
Norwegian Blue, Maltese cat.

A plush silvery blue coat, charming personality, and remarkable, vivid green eyes

The origins of this breed are disputed. Some experts believe that relatively longhaired, blue-coated cats lived along the shores of the White Sea in the Port Arkhangelsk region beginning in the 17th century.
In the 1860s, an English or Russian merchant ship may have carried these cats to Great Britain, where they were shown in London as Russian Shorthairs, Archangel Blues (after Arkhangelsk Port), and Blue Foreigns beginning in 1871.

Others theories hold that the breed originated instead in the Mediterranean region, like the Chartreux; hence the name Spanish Blue.

The breed was officially named the Russian Blue in 1939. Following World War II, Russian Blues were crossed with British Shorthair Blues and particularly with Blue Point Siamese in order to restore the breed.

Its body type is quite oriental.
In the 1960s in Europe, and more specifically England, the cat world saw a return of the Russian Blue to its original shorter body and darker coat. American breeders created a lighter cat with very fine head, body, and paws and a lighter coat color. This breed is very popular in the United States and Japan (where the Russian Blue is virtually idolized).
In the 1980s in the United States, after several outcrosses, a semilonghaired Russian Blue named Nebelung (creature of the mist) appeared. This extremely rare variety was recognized as a new breed by T.I.C.A. in 1987.

Russian Blue

RUSSIAN BLUE KITTENS. DEFINITIVE EYE COLOR IS NOT ATTAINED UNTIL QUITE LATE

GENERAL
Long, graceful body. Weight: 3 to 5.5 kg.
Short double coat.

SHADES RANGE FROM MEDIUM BLUE TO DARK BLUE

HEAD
Short, wedge-shaped, with straight lines.
Flat forehead and skull.
Medium length muzzle.
Straight nose. No nose break.
Strong chin.

EARS
Large, wide at the base, and pointing forward.
Slightly rounded tips.
Skin of the ears is thin and translucent, with little inside furnishing.

EYES
Large, fairly wide set, almond-shaped (almost

LONG, THIN TAIL OF THE RUSSIAN BLUE

BODY
Long, foreign type (■).
Fine- to medium-boned.
Muscular.

LEGS AND PAWS
Long and fine-boned.
Firm muscles. Small, round (◆), oval (▼) paws.

TAIL
Long (but in proportion to the body), straight, tapering from a moderately thick base to a thin tip.

RUSSIAN BLACK

round, barely oval), angled slightly (◆).
Color: Vivid green. Eye color in kittens ranges from yellow to green (■). Definitive color is not attained until one year of age.

TAIL
Long, slender, and straight.

COAT
Short, dense, very fine, and plush. Stands out from the body. Soft, silky feel. Double coat with a very thick undercoat. Solid, uniform blue-gray in color, with silvery sheen caused by silver tipping. Ghost tabby markings are to be tolerated in kittens. These markings disappear before the cat reaches one year of age. Slate gray nose leather and dark lavender paw pads (▼).

Prolonged exposure to sunlight tends to darken the coat.
Black and white varieties, developed in Europe and New Zealand, are recognized by the G.C.C.F., but not by the F.I.Fe and American cat associations.

NOTES
Allowable outcross breeds: Nebelung (◆), Russian Blacks and Whites (■).

FAULTS
Square, round, or Siamese-type head.
Round or yellowish eyes. Weak chin.
Massive, stocky body.
Tail overly thick at the base. Close-lying coat.
Tabby markings, white spots.

The standard for the Nebelung (more common in the United States) is the same as that of the Russian Blue, but its double coat is longer and of a lighter blue-gray shade.

Blue and White are also recognized; eye color must be green.

CHARACTERISTICS
The Russian Blue is lively, athletic, and playful, but enjoys a calm environment, since this cat dislikes noise and commotion.
This independent, cautious cat has a dominant personality, and as a result, does not like to have limits placed on him. Though fairly social, the Russian Blue is reserved and does not like strangers.
Russian Blues are sensitive and affectionate, through quite exclusive with their affections. This breed has a very soft voice.

(▼) F.I.Fe   (■) L.O.O.F.   (★) C.F.A.   (◆) T.I.C.A.

Bombay

A black panther with copper eyes

In 1958, in an attempt to create a black Burmese, Nikki Horner, an American breeder from Kentucky, crossed a sable Burmese queen with a copper-eyed black American Shorthair. The result was the creation of a "miniature black panther" (the name referring to the black panther of India). The breed was recognized by the C.F.A. in 1976 and by T.I.C.A. in 1979. The first Bombay, a female named Opium, imported to France arrived in 1989.

Though highly popular in the United States, the Bombay is almost unknown in Europe.

BOMBAY KITTEN

Bombay

GENERAL
Medium in size. Heavy bone structure, muscular. Weight: 2.5 to 5 kg.

NECK
Medium in length; thick and arched.

BODY
Medium in size, semi-cobby. Powerful shoulders and well-developed, broad chest. Heavy bone structure. Firm muscles.

LEGS AND PAWS
Medium in length, in proportion to the body. Heavy bone structure, muscular. Paws small to medium in size, round.

TAIL
Medium in length, straight, moderately thick and tapering to the tip.

HEAD
Medium in size, rounded, with no sharp angles.
Rounded forehead.
Full cheeks.
Moderately short nose.
Broad, moderately short muzzle with a slight nose break.
Firm, rounded chin.
Powerful jaws.

NOTES
Allowable outcross breeds: Sable Burmese (■) and Black American Shorthair (★).

FAULTS
Flat skull, green eyes. Overly exotic body type. Overly fine tail or bone structure. Wooly coat. Nose leather or paw pads other than black. White spots (◆).

KITTEN

EARS
Medium in size, alert, broad at the base, slightly rounded tips, set well apart. Furnishings with slight undercoat.

EYES
Large, round, set well apart. Bright, shiny gold to copper eyes (gold is preferred).

COAT
Short and very close-lying with a shimmering sheen. Almost complete absence of undercoat. Satinlike texture.
Color: Black only. Skin and pads are also black. Definitive eye color is attained by six months of age.

CHARACTERISTICS
This is a self-assured cat. Bombays are athletic, playful, curious, and remarkably agile. They are also excellent hunters. This highly social cat adapts easily to its surroundings and makes a good companion. Bombays can live with dogs, but do not always get along with other cats.
Affectionate and extremely gentle, the Bombay loves to snuggle, though often restricts his affections to its owner. This cat does adjust well to solitude. Though less talkative than the Burmese, the Bombay has a rather husky voice. Care is simple.

(▼) F.I.Fe   (■) L.O.O.F.   (★) C.F.A.   (◆) T.I.C.A.

British Shorthair

Country of Origin: Great Britain

From rags to riches

In the late 19th century, the Cheshire Cat of Lewis Carroll's (1865) *Alice in Wonderland was depicted as a British Shorthair tabby. Around the same period, English breeders, including Harrison Weir, had begun selectively breeding the most beautiful mixed breed cats, which were shown for the first time at London's Crystal Palace in 1871. These cats were called British Shorthairs to distinguish them from foreign and oriental breeds and from longhaired breeds such as the Angora. The British Shorthair is the counterpart of the European Shorthair and the American Shorthair.*

In 1901, the British Cat Club was formed. The first British Shorthairs (mostly blues) resembled the Chartreux. As a result, the two breeds were crossed, to such an extent that the F.I.Fe decided to combine the two and recognize just one breed. But, in 1977, the F.I.Fe once again separated the two breeds and prohibited crossing of the two breeds.

Following World War II, British Shorthairs were crossed with Persians to add mass and to fill out the British Shorthairs silhouette, as well as to increase the range of coat colors. New patterns, such as colorpoint, were recognized.

In the United States, where the breed was crossed with American Shorthairs, the British Shorthair was recognized by the C.F.A. in 1980. The most recent standard established by T.I.C.A. was published in 1993. The French F.F.F. recognized the breed in 1979. British Shorthairs are extremely popular.

YOUNG, BLUE CREAM BRITISH SHORTHAIR. OVER ONE HUNDRED BRITISH. SHORTHAIR VARIETIES ARE RECOGNIZED!

ABOVE: WHITE BRITISH SHORTHAIR
RIGHT: BLUE BRITISH SHORTHAIR

British Shorthair

BLUE BRITISH SHORTHAIR. THIS BREED DOES NOT REACH ITS FULL ADULT SIZE UNTIL QUITE LATE.

GENERAL
Medium to large. Weight: 4 to 8 kg.
Semi-cobby to cobby body type (compact). Powerful, muscular, well-knit.

CREAM TABBY BRITISH SHORTHAIR

NECK
Short, thick, and muscular.

BODY
Compact, well-knit. Broad chest, shoulders and rump. Muscular.

LEGS AND PAWS
Short and strong. Well boned and muscled. Round paws.

TAIL
Length is equal to 2/3 the length of the body. Thick at the base and tapering slightly to a rounded tip.

BRITISH SHORTHAIR

COAT
Short, dense, and well bodied. Firm to the touch. Plush, giving the impression of natural protection. Abundant undercoat.
British Longhairs also exist, the result of the introduction of too much Persian blood. All colors permissible. The British Blue is the most popular variety.

Oriental eyes. Fine boning. Overlong coat. No undercoat. White lockets or buttons.

HEAD
Round, broad, and massive.
Full cheeks.
Distinctive muzzle.
Short, broad, straight, nose with a gentle dip (but no nose break).
Firm chin forming a perpendicular line with the nose.

CHINCHILLA BRITISH SHORTHAIR

NOTES
Allowable outcross breeds: Scottish Fold and Manx (◆); Manx, American Wirehair, and Cymric (■).

FAULTS
Overly fine head, jaws, or skull structure.

BLUE BRITISH SHORTHAIR

EARS
Medium in size, wide at the base with rounded tips. Moderately wide set.

EYES
Large, round, and set wide apart. Color appropriate to coat color (copper, gold, blue, green, blue-green, odd eyed).

CHINCHILLA BRITISH SHORTHAIR

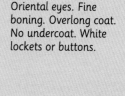

CHARACTERISTICS
This calm, good-tempered, easygoing cat looks like a teddy bear. British Shorthairs are excellent, well-balanced companions that adapt easily to life in the city or in the country (where they can act on their strong hunting instinct).
The British Shorthair gets along well with other cats and dogs. He is lively, playful, and very affectionate, but not to the point of being bothersome.
This hardy breed does not reach full maturity until two or three years of age. Onset of puberty is relatively late. Weekly brushing and combing is sufficient. During shedding season (this cat sheds a lot), daily brushing is required.

(▼) F.I.Fe   (■) L.O.O.F.   (★) C.F.A.   (◆) T.I.C.A.

90

Burmese

Country of Origin: Myanmar (Burma)

English or American: of all colours, but uniform, and with a common ancestror, the Tonkinese.

Manuscripts from Ayuthia, former capital of Siam, dating to the sixteen and seventeenth centuries depict cats that resemble today's Burmese. In the 16th century, brown cats similar to Burmese, called "Rajahs," roamed the halls of Buddhist temples in present-day Myanmar. In 1930, a military physician named J.C. Thompson was accompanied from Burma to San Francisco by a cat named Wong Mau, who was probably a Burmese/Siamese mix, what is today called a Tonkinese. Wong Mau was dark brown, almost mahogany, and had yellow eyes. Thompson mated her with Tai Mau, a Seal Point or Chocolate Point Siamese. One of the kittens (dark brown) was mated with its mother, Wong Mau. The result of that mating was a litter of solid brown kittens, the first specimens of the modern Burmese breed. The breed was recognized by the C.F.A. in 1936. The most recent T.I.C.A. standard was published in 1994.

Burmese arrived in Great Britain in 1949 and were shown for the first time in London in 1952. The G.C.C.F. recognized the breed in 1954. Though the Burmese has only recently been recognized, it is worth recalling that brown cats with yellow eyes were brought into England as early as the late 19th century.

The Burmese was officially introduced in France in 1956. The standard for the breed identifies an American version (compact, stocky, round head) and a British version (longer body and slightly triangular face). Originally, only sables were recognized. Blue was introduced in 1955, chocolate and lilac in 1959, and tortoiseshell varieties in the 1970s. The Burmese contributed to the development of the Bombay when it was crossed with the American Shorthair in 1981, the Burmilla (Persian/Burmese cross), the Tiffany (longhaired Burmese), and in the 1960s, the Tonkinese (Burmese/Siamese cross).

Though uncommon in France, this breed is popular throughout the world, particularly in Anglo-Saxon countries.

SABLE BURMESE, THE ORIGINAL BURMESE COLOR

BELOW: LILAC BURMESE
RIGHT : CHOCOLATE BURMESE

Burmese

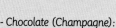
LILAC BURMESE

GENERAL
Medium size. Weight: 3.5 to 6.5 kg.
American version: Well-balanced, moderately compact body, with well-developed musculature and bone structure (★)(◆).
British version: Elegant, foreign body type; slender, but must not resemble the Siamese (elongated) nor the British Shorthair (too short) (▼).

HEAD
American version (★) (◆): Rounded and broad without flat planes. Round skull, forehead, and cheeks. Short, round muzzle. Nose break. Round, firm chin. Strong jaws.
British version: Short, blunt triangle with a broad, slightly rounded skull. Prominent cheekbones. Pronounced nose break. Jaws broad at the joint.

SABLE BURMESE

LILAC BURMESE

EARS
Medium in size, set well apart, wide at the base and rounded at the tips. Short, sparse furnishings.

EYES
Large, round, and wide set (★). Slanting upper line, with rounded lower line (▼). The darkest, most vivid colors are preferred, with gold being the most favored color.

NECK
Well-developed, short neck.

BODY
Medium in size, moderately compact and rounded. Broad, ample chest. Solid bone structure and good muscular development (★) (◆). Slender, less compact, but muscular and surprisingly heavy for its size (▼).

LEGS AND PAWS
Length in proportion to body.
Paws medium in size, round (★); small and oval (▼).

TAIL
Medium in length, straight, thick at the base (★); not thick at the base (▼), tapering slightly to a rounded tip.

CHOCOLATE BURMESE

COAT
Very short, fine, silky, glossy, and close-lying. Lustrous, satinlike texture. Almost complete absence of undercoat.
Color: As dark as possible at the points (mask, paws, tail), slightly lighter on the back and flanks, and a lighter hue still on underparts. No white or tabby markings. Definitive color appears by the age of two and a half months. The gray-blue eye color turns to yellow at the same age.

There are four main varieties:
-Sable (Brown in Great Britain): Dark brown.
-Blue: Silvery blue.

- Chocolate (Champagne): Milk chocolate color.
- Lilac (Platinum): Silvery gray, pale lavender pink.

Other more recent varieties recognized only in Europe: Red, Cream, and Tortoiseshell.
In the United States, these varieties are considered Malayan.

PHYSICAL CONDITION
Perfect physical condition with excellent muscle tone. No evidence of obesity, weakness, or apathy.

NOTES
Allowable outcross breeds: Bombay, Tonkinese, Burmilla, Siamese (◆).

FAULTS
Almond-shaped eyes. Blue or green eye color. Overly fine bone structure. Overlong or excessively oriental body type. Kinked or abnormal tail. Tabby markings or white spots.

LILAC BURMESE KITTEN

CHARACTERISTICS
This particularly extroverted, energetic, exuberant cat has a strong personality and fears nothing. This little "talker" has a loud voice, though it is less husky than that of the Siamese. The Burmese expresses dominance with other cats. A social creature, this cat loves company and detests solitude. The affectionate Burmese is a tireless playmate for children. It is so devoted to its owner that it has been nicknamed the "dog-cat". This spirited hunter loves a romp in the yard, but does adapt well to indoor living. The wildness of kittenhood diminishes over the years. Females reach puberty early (around nine months) and bear slightly more offspring than average. Care is simple. Weekly brushing is sufficient.

(▼) F.I.Fe   (■) L.O.O.F.   (★) C.F.A.   (◆) T.I.C.A.

Burmilla

Country of Origin: Great Britain
Other Names: Silver Burmese

Green eyes on a silvery white backdrop

This breed was created in Great Britain in 1981 by crossing a male Chinchilla Persian and a Lilac Burmese, resulting in a Silver, Burmese-type cat. This sort of selective breeding is a delicate process, and as a result, these cats are rare. The names Burmese and Chinchilla were combined to form the name for this breed.
The Burmilla Cat Club was founded in England in 1984. Recognized by the G.C.C.F. in 1989 and by the F.I.Fe in 1994, the breed is rare in France.

SILVER BURMILLA BLACK-RIMMED EYES ARE CHARACTERISTIC OF THIS BREED

95

Burmilla

CREAM BURMILLA

GENERAL
Medium size.
Surprisingly heavy for its size: 4 to 7 kg.
Foreign body type (▼), elegant.
Substantial bone, well-developed musculature.

SILVER BURMILLA

NECK
Short and well-developed.

BODY
Moderately compact.
Broad, rounded chest.
Shoulders and rump of same width. Higher at the rump than at the shoulders. Very solid bone structure.
Powerfully muscled.

LEGS AND PAWS
Hind legs slightly longer than forelegs. Good bone structure.
Powerfully muscled.
Paws medium in size, round (■), oval (▼).

introduced by a silvery white undercoat.
Silver or golden ground color with sable, blue, chocolate, lilac, red, cream, etc. tipping.
The back, mask, and tail are darker than the belly.

PHYSICAL CONDITION
Perfect physical condition with excellent musculature. No evidence of obesity, weakness, or apathy (■).

NOTES
Allowable outcross breeds: Burmese and Tiffany (semi-longhaired Burmese) (■).

HEAD
Medium in size and rounded. Broad face tapering to a short, blunt triangle.
Full, round cheeks.
Heavy jowls in mature males.
Broad, well-developed,

short muzzle.
Slight nose break.
Well-developed chin.
Coat slightly less thick above eyebrows (■).

EARS
Medium in size, wide at the base with rounded tips. Alert, tilted slightly forward and set well apart. Short, sparse furnishings.

EYES
Large, wide set, slightly slanted. Half-moon opening.
Rimmed with appropriate color.
All shades of green are allowed, though luminous green is preferred. A trace of yellow is to be tolerated in kittens and young cats up to two years of age.
Amber is permissible for Reds, Creams, and Tortoiseshells (▼).

SILVER BURMILLA

TAIL
Semilong to long, of moderate thickness, tapering to a rounded tip.

COAT
Short (longer than the Burmese coat), fine, very glossy, and silky, with just enough undercoat to lift hairs slightly away from the skin.
Color: Tipping (only the tip of each hair is pigmented), with nuances

FAULTS
Weak chin. Eyes almond-shaped or of wrong color. Cobby or oriental body. Overlong legs. Overlong or bristly coat. Tabby markings on the legs.

CREAM BURMILLA

SILVER BURMILLA

CHARACTERISTICS
The Burmilla combines the energy of the Burmese and the moderation of the Persian.
This rather talkative cat is gentle and makes an excellent companion.
Care is simple.

(▼) F.I.Fe   (■) L.O.O.F.   (★) C.F.A.   (◆) T.I.C.A.

California Spangled

Country of Origin: United States
Other Name: American California Spangled Cat

A small "house-leopard"

Upon his return from Tanzania, Paul Casey, a Hollywood scriptwriter, was inspired to create a cat that resembled the wild, spotted African Cats similar to leopards in appearance, but gentle... as a lamb.

In order to reach this goal, a long breeding and selection program started in the 1970s, crossing several breeds, including: Siamese, British Shorthairs, American Shorthairs, Manx, Abyssinians, and a line of Egyptian and Asian stray cats.

It took eleven generations before type was fixed. The breed was formally introduced in 1986.

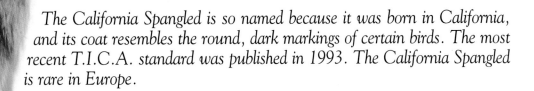

The California Spangled is so named because it was born in California, and its coat resembles the round, dark markings of certain birds. The most recent T.I.C.A. standard was published in 1993. The California Spangled is rare in Europe.

BROWN SPOTTED CALIFORNIA SPANGLED CAT. SPOTS, WHICH COVER THE ENTIRE BODY, MAY BE ROUND, TRIANGULAR, OR RECTANGULAR IN SHAPE.

ABOVE: BROWN SPOTTED CALIFORNIA SPANGLED
RIGHT: SEAL SEPPIA LYNX SPOTTED SNOW LEOPARD WITH BLUE EYES

California Spangled

GOLD SPOTTED CALIFORNIA SPANGLED

GENERAL
Wild appearance. Walks low to ground, like wildcats. Long, strong body. Short coat.
Weight: 4 to 8 kg.

CALIFORNIA SPANGLED CATS: LEFT, BLACK SPOTTED, RIGHT, GOLD SPOTTED

HEAD
Sculpted, of medium length and width. Rounded skull. Slightly domed forehead. Slight nose break. Prominent cheekbones. Full, well-developed muzzle of medium length. Strong chin. Powerfully developed jaws.

BROWN SPOTTED CALIFORNIA SPANGLED

NECK
Medium in length, cylindrical, muscular.

BODY
Muscular and moderately long. Solid thighs. Strong bone structure. Well-developed musculature.

LEGS AND PAWS
Long and strong. Hind legs form nearly a 90-degree angle, giving the appearance that the cat is sitting back on its legs and lowering the body close to the ground. Feet of medium size.

CALIFORNIA SPANGLED CATS: LEFT, GOLD SPOTTED; RIGHT, BLACK SPOTTED

EARS
Of medium length and width, rounded tips, set high on the head.

EYES
Almond-shaped, well-open, set at a slight slant and well apart. Color: Gold to brown, appropriate to coat color; blue in Snow Leopards.

TAIL
Moderately long, with thickness at the base equal to that at the tip. Tail has dark rings and

BROWN SPOTTED CALIFORNIA SPANGLED

a dark tip of the ground color. Well clad.

COAT
Short, except on the belly and tail where it is longer.
Pattern: Spotted tabby. Spots covering the back and sides of the body are round, square, or triangular in shape and must be well-defined and separate.
Stripes on the head, throat, legs, and tail.
Colors - Eight classic varieties:
Black, brown, blue, bronze, charcoal, red, gold, and silver.
The Snow Leopard has a white coat with black markings and blue eyes.

NOTES
Allowable outcross breeds: None (■).

FAULTS
Excessively massive body.
Insufficient boning or musculature.
Overly round or narrow head. Pointed ears.
Green eyes. White spots on the toes.
Overlong coat.
Absence of tabby markings, coat pattern, or contrast.
Light tail tip.

CHARACTERISTICS
The California Spangled is a lively, energetic, extremely active cat, though certainly not aggressive. This cat in an excellent hunter.
Though wild in appearance, the California Spangled is social, affectionate, and gentle. Weekly brushing is sufficient.

(▼) F.I.Fe   (■) L.O.O.F.   (★) C.F.A.   (◆) T.I.C.A.

GOLD SPOTTED CALIFORNIA SPANGLED

102

Ceylon

Country of Origin: Southeast Asia
Other Names: Gatto de Ceylon,
Sri Lankan Cat

A natural breed originating in Sri Lanka

In 1984, Dr. Paolo Pellegatta brought the first six "Gatto di Ceylon" specimens into Italy. The cats came from Sri Lanka (formerly Ceylon), an island located southeast of India.

A breeding and selection program is currently underway to fix breed type. The Ceylon has grown rapidly in popularity in Italy. A club dedicated to the Friends of the Gatto di Ceylon was formed in 1988.

CEYLON KITTENS - A NATURAL ASIAN BREED.

Ceylon

AGOUTI CEYLON

GENERAL
Compact body. Medium size. Short coat.

HEAD
Medium in size and dimensions.
Slightly rounded skull and rather flat forehead.
Gently rounded cheeks.
Moderately short nose with slight nose break.
Chin not strong.

EARS
Medium to large in size.
Set high on the head and close together.
Moderately broad at the base with rounded tips.
Lighter "thumb prints".
Lynx tips are allowed.

EYES
Rather large and set at a slight angle.
Upper line is almond-shaped and lower line is rounded.
Dark rims.
Color: Yellow-green

CEYLON KITTENS

(dark bar in shaft of agouti hair) on the chest, back, and flanks.
Two or three lines on the cheeks with a "cobra" pattern on the forehead.
Stripes on the legs and ringed tail.
Ground colors: Sable to golden.

NOTES
Allowable outcross breeds: None.

FAULTS
Ears too widely set.
Rounded eyes. Absence of tabby markings.
White spots.

BODY
Medium size, compact and muscular. Well rounded chest. Fine boning.

LEGS AND PAWS
Medium in length.
Forelegs are shorter than hind legs.
Well muscled.
Round paws.

TAIL
Moderately short, broad at the base and tapering to a rounded tip.

COAT
Short, fine, and silky. Sparse undercoat. Pronounced ticking

RED CEYLON

GOLD CEYLON

CHARACTERISTICS
This social, confident, affectionate cat readily adjusts to indoor living. Simple care.

(▼) F.I.Fe   (■) L.O.O.F.   (★) C.F.A.   (◆) T.I.C.A.

Chartreux

The blue cat of France, with golden eyes, has existed for centuries

This breed is very old. Its short, wooly coat is said to have been sold as otter fur in ancient times! The Chartreux has apparently existed in France for many centuries. In the 16th century, Joachim du Bellay mourned the death of this little gray cat, Belaud. In the 18th century, Buffon, in Natural History, refers to the Chartreux as the Cat of France, while Linné distinguished it from the Angora cat, naming it Felis cattus caeruleus, or blue cat.

There are many theories as to the origins of this breed. Legend holds that the Carthusian monks bred these cats after bringing them back to France from South Africa.

So what is the origin of this breed's name? Some believe the name describes its dense, wooly coat that resembles a Spanish wool fabric called Chartreux pile. Others, such as Fizniger, posit that the breed is a cross between the Manul cat and the Egyptian cat. In fact, its ancestors may have been born in the harsh mountainous regions of Iran, Syria, and Turkey where they would have needed their thick coat. Some Chartreux were introduced in France during the Crusades.

In the 1920s, French breeders crossed the Chartreux with Persians. A formal breeding program did not begin until 1926, when the Léger sisters began working with smoke blue cats roaming freely on Belle-Ile-sur-Mer in Morbihan, France. After defining their body features, Dr. Jumaud (1930) named these cats Felis cattus cartusinorum. The breed was shown at the Cat Club de Paris in 1931.

The first standard was published in 1939.

In the 1960s and 1970s, crossbreeding with Blue British Shorthairs was so common that the F.I.Fe decided in 1970 to combine the two breeds. So was the Chartreux destined to disappear? Indeed no. J. Simonnet, President of the Chartreux Cat Club, effectively proved the authenticity of this ancient French breed to the F.I.Fe, which then separated the two breeds and prohibited mating across the two breeds.

The first Chartreux arrived in the United States in 1970. Both the C.F.A. and T.I.C.A. recognize the breed.

THIS HIGHLY PRIZED BREED WAS CELEBRATED BY COLETTE'S *LA CHATTE* (1933) AND A CHARTREUX WAS COMPANION TO FRANCE'S GENERAL DE GAULLE.

Chartreux

General
Medium to large. Weight: 3 to 7.5 kg.
Medium long. Males are larger and more massive than females.
Robust, powerful appearance. Sweet, smiling expression.

CHARTREUX KITTENS

Head
Rounded and broad, but not a sphere, resembling an upside down trapezoid. Skull not domed (▼), slightly rounded (■), with a narrow, flat space between the ears (▼). Full, round, low-set cheeks, with mature males having larger jowls. The straight, broad nose is not turned up. Slight nose break allowed, though no nose break is preferred. Muzzle straight in relation to the head, tapered, but not pointed. Sizable whisker pads with moderately pronounced whisker pinch, giving the breed its characteristic smile (◆). Powerful jaws, particularly in males over two years of age (■).

Ears
Small to medium in size. Set high on the head. Erect with rounded tips. Narrow at the base.

Eyes
Large and round, with the outer corner slightly upturned (▼).
Color: Orange to gold. No flecks of green or washed out colors.

Neck
Short, strong, and heavyset.

Body
Robust and massive, particularly in males. Broad shoulders and deep chest. Straight back. Strong boning.

Muscle mass is solid and dense.

Legs and paws
Straight, short to medium in length, strong, and very muscular. Small, round (◆), broad (▼) paws.

Tail
Of moderate length. Thick at the back and tapering slightly to a rounded tip.

Coat
Short, thick, extremely

CHARTREUX KITTEN

dense (like an otter), glossy, slightly wooly, and water-repellant, standing away from skin due to the profuse undercoat.
Color: Any shade of blue, from ash to slate, but bright blue is preferred.
Uniformity of color is essential (▼). Slate gray nose leather and rose taupe paw pads (◆). The skin is blue.
Kittens are born with tabby markings that fade between the age of six months and one year. Orange eye color does not appear until the age of three months, replacing the typical blue-gray eyes of kittens (■).

Notes
Allowable outcross breeds: None.

Faults
Upturned nose or severe nose break. Broad, heavy muzzle. Eyes almond-shaped or set too close together.

Green eyes, dull or washed out eye color (▼). Coat: White lockets. Tipping, ghost barring, or variation in coat color. Brown or red highlights (▼).

CHARTREUX DISPLAY ALL SHADES OF BLUES, BUT BRIGHT BLUE IS THE MOST HIGHLY PRIZED.

Characteristics
This well-balanced, easygoing, independent cat has a strong personality, though it is not very vocal. Affectionate and devoted to its owner, the reserved Chartreux enjoys solitude and tranquility.
This robust, hardy, lively cat is perfectly suited to cold climates and life in the open air, which enables it to develop it hunting instincts and ensures a quality, wooly coat. However, too much time in the sun results in brown highlights in the coat.
The Chartreux does not reach maturity until two to three years of age.
A curry brush must be applied weekly to maintain the wooly coat. Heavy shedding.

(▼) F.I.Fe   (■) L.O.O.F.   (★) C.F.A.   (◆) T.I.C.A.

Norwegian Forest Cat

Country of Origin: Norway
Original Names: Skogkatt,
Skaukatt, Wegrie, Norsk Skogkatt
Other Names: Forest Cat

A peaceaful wildcat with a long, thick coat

The Norwegian Forest Cat has wandered Scandinavia for centuries. Many legends depict a large cat with a long, thick tail. According to Norse mythology, Thor, the most powerful god, was unable to lift this cat, and Freya's (the goddess of love and fertility) chariot was pulled by these cats. Though Norway is considered the country of origin of the "Fairy Cat", it is possible that the Vikings of the 13th century brought specimens back from Asia Minor (Caucus, Anatoly, etc.) to hunt the rats that infested their drakkars. Or perhaps Central European or Asian tribes traveling to Scandinavia before the Middle Ages introduced the cats. Cats brought in from other regions would have had to adapt to the extremely harsh climate of Scandinavia, and therefore, develop a thick, double, insulating, weather-proof coat. Their weight and size would have increased. Norwegian Forest Cats slowly moved from the wild to farms. Around 1930, Norwegian breeders began a selection program to preserve the breed and to combine hardiness and the beauty of its coat.

Several specimens were shown in Oslo. The breed was recognized in 1972, and the first breed club and standard appeared in 1975. The F.I.Fe recognized the Norwegian Forest Cat in 1977. An official standard was written, then modified to avoid confusion with the Maine Coon Cat. For example, the Nrcoon is a cross between a Norwegian Forest Cat and a Maine Coon.

The first Forest Cats arrived in Germany and the United States in 1979, in Great Britain in 1980, and in France in 1982. Sweden is thought to maintain the highest population of Forest Cats. This breed meets great success in cat shows. Its wild, robust appearance and natural beauty are greatly admired.

Norwegian Forest Cat

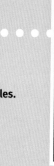

GENERAL
Large. Weight: 3 to 9 kg.
Females may be considerably smaller than males.
Long, solidly constructed body. Double coat.

HEAD
Triangular shape with equal length and width. Flat forehead. Straight nose.
The muzzle follows the line of the head; no whisker pinch.
Nose of medium length.
Strong, square rather than rounded chin; never pointed (♦).
Early Forest Cats had longer heads and their profile was not as straight as it is today.

EARS
Medium large, well open and broad at the base with slightly rounded tips. Set well apart on the sides of the head so that the base of the ear follows the line from the head to the chin. Heavy ear furnishings. Lynx tips are desirable.

EYES
Large, almond shaped,

and set at a slight angle. Any color is acceptable (▼), but preferred colors are green or gold. White cats may be copper, blue, or odd-eyed (♦).

NECK
Of medium length, muscular.

BODY
Massive, robust, with a powerful appearance. Moderately long with a broad, rounded chest. Heavily boned and muscled.

LEGS AND PAWS
Medium in length, muscular, and straight, with hind legs longer than the front legs, making the rump higher than the shoulders. Heavily muscled with

substantial bone. Large, round paws with long tufts between each toe.

TAIL
Long, shaggy, carried high. Tip of tail should reach the neck. Broad at the base and tapering to the tip.

COAT
Double coat.
Medium long, with a very thick, wooly undercoat.
The smooth, shiny, oily guard hairs are waterproof.
The coat is uneven; shorter on the shoulders and becoming progressively longer on the back and flanks.
The full ruff is comprised of the back-of the

neck ruff, side mutton chops, and a full front bib.
All colors permissible, except colorpoint, chocolate, and lilac (■), cinnamon, fawn, and Burmese patterns (▼). Any amount of white is allowed (▼).

PHYSICAL CONDITION
An alert, firm, muscular cat.

NOTES
Allowable outcross breeds: None.

FAULTS
Undersized, frail cat. Cobby or extremely long body.

Round or square head.
Nose break.
Small ears.
Small or round eyes.
Delicate bone structure.
Dry coat.

CHARACTERISTICS
This extremely self-assured cat has a well-balanced temperament. A friendly, easygoing animal, the Norwegian Forest cat is calm, though playful. It readily accepts other cats, dogs, and children, and its voice is soft.
This hardy, robust, athletic cat is remarkably supple. He is a good climber and a fearsome hunter. If a Forest Cat is to live indoors, a cat tree is a must. A large yard is preferable, particularly since its coat reaches its full beauty when it lives out of doors. Forest Cats mature slowly, not reaching full maturity until four or five years of age. Regular brushing and combing will maintain the beautiful coat and avoid snarls. During shedding season (the Forest Cat sheds heavily), daily brushing is required.

(▼)F.I.Fe   (■) L.O.O.F.   (★) C.F.A.   (♦) T.I.C.A.

Cornish Rex

Country of Origin: Great Britain

A curly-coated, playful, sociable acrobat

The first Cornish Rex was a male named Kallibunker born to Serena, a tricolor housecat, in 1950 on the Ennismore's farm near Bodmin in Cornwall, England (hence the name Cornish Rex). His curly coat resembled that of Rex rabbits discovered on a French farm in 1919. In order to preserve this recessive mutation, the breeding program combined inbreeding with outcrosses to Siamese, British Shorthairs, and Burmese. In 1967, the Cornish Rex was officially recognized in England. In 1960, Professor E. Letard brought a Rex couple from Germany to France. Only the green-eyed male, Marco, survived the trip. He was mated with a Burmese queen. The kittens were black and straight-coated, proving that the gene responsible for the Rex coat was indeed recessive. Letard inbred the mixed-breed offspring and in 1962, finally obtained a male Rex, Lisko, a descendant from the French Rex line. In the United States, a breeding program began in 1957. Crosses with Siamese and Orientals resulted in a lighter, oval-headed cat, while the English Cornish Rex was heavier and had a more triangular, rather than long, head. This breed is highly prized in the United States and Europe.

BROWN TABBY CORNISH REX

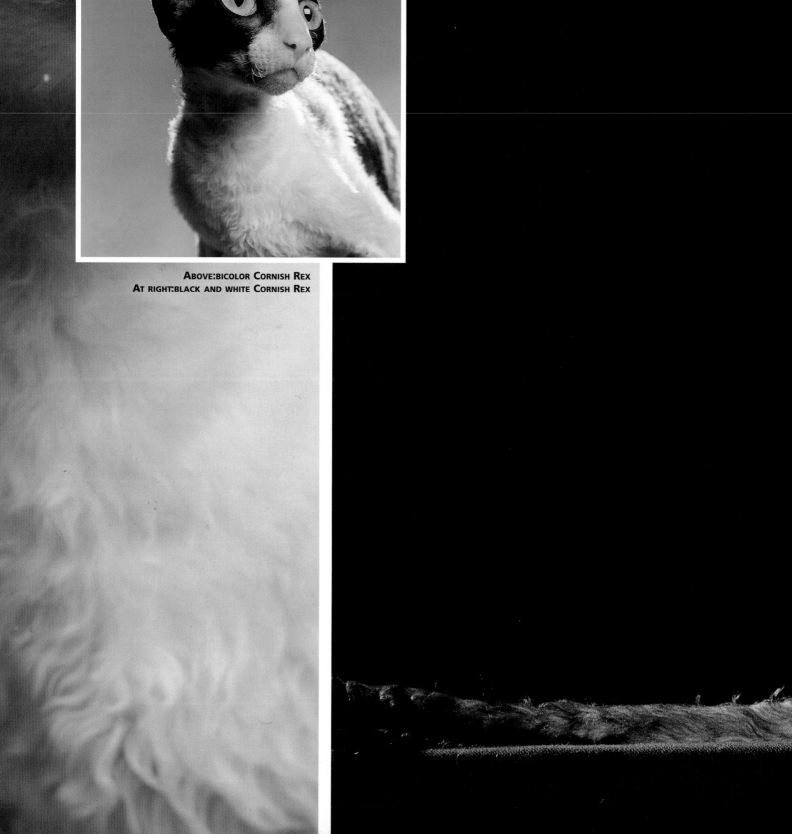

ABOVE:BICOLOR CORNISH REX
AT RIGHT:BLACK AND WHITE CORNISH REX

Cornish Rex

BICOLOR RED AND WHITE CORNISH REX KITTEN

GENERAL
Medium. Racy body type.
Weight: 2.5 to 4.5 kg. Arched back.
Fine to delicate bone structure.
Wavy coat.

BICOLOR TORTOISHELL AND WHITE CORNISH REX

EARS
Large and full. Wide at the base, set high on the head. Rounded tips. Abundantly covered with fine hairs (▼); generally lacking interior furnishings and hair on the ear leather (◆).

EYES
Medium to large in size, oval in shape, and

HEAD
Length greater than width, moderately wedge-shaped (▼).
Egg-shaped skull (◆).
Roman nose (◆).
Straight line from middle of the forehead to tip of the nose (▼).
Straight nose (▼).
Definite whisker break.
Strong chin.
Curly whiskers and eyebrows.

BODY
Small to medium, rather long.
Full, deep chest.
Very arched back.
Rounded rump. Very fine bone structure.
Firm, powerful, and long musculature.

LEGS AND PAWS
Long and straight.
Fine bone structure.

BICOLOR BLACK AND WHITE CORNISH REX

slanting slightly upward. Color, which should be clear, shiny, and intense, appropriate to coat color.

NECK
Of medium length.
Slender, but muscular.

Firm muscles.
Small, oval paws.

TAIL
Long and slender, covered with a wavy coat.

COAT
Short, dense, and wavy with uniform waves

over the entire body.
Wave effects are desirable on tail and legs.
Absence of guard hairs, resulting in an extremely soft, fine satin or silklike coat.
Coat grows slowly.
Colors: Any color.
The Siamese pattern variety is called Si-Rex.

NOTES
Allowable outcross breeds: None (◆).

FAULTS
Overly large or long head. Small ears.
Massive, stocky body.
Tail that is too thick, short, free of hair, or shaggy. Large hairless areas, except at temples and on the tail.
Coarse, straight hairs.

BICOLOR BLACK AND WHITE CORNISH REX

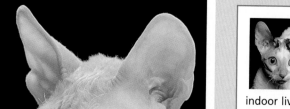

CHARACTERISTICS
This playful, lively, rather eccentric acrobat is always in motion. The good-natured Cornish Rex enjoys other cats and dogs, and dislikes solitude.
This affectionate, gentle cat makes a loving companion, albeit with a rather strident voice. The Cornish Rex enjoys indoor living, particularly since he tends to be cold-blooded. Females cycle frequently and are quite prolific. Their appetite is phenomenal, and kittens develop rapidly. Weekly brushing will help maintain the wavy coat. This breed hardly sheds.

BICOLOR TORTOISESHELL AND WHITE CORNISH REX

(▼)F.I.Fe   (■) L.O.O.F.   (★) C.F.A.   (◆) T.I.C.A.

Cymric

Country of Origin: United States
Other Names: Welsh Cat, Longhaired Manx

A longhaired, tailless cat from Ireland

A specific gene was responsible for the semilong coat of the cats living on the Isle of Man in the Irish Sea.
In the 1960s, Canadian breeder Blair Wright and American breeder Leslie Falteisek decided to fix this characteristic and thus created a new longhaired Manx breed, the Cymric (Cymru means Wales in Gaelic).
Around 1970, the Canadian Cat Association recognized the breed. Naming it Longhaired Manx, the C.F.A. recognized the breed in 1989. As of this writing, the F.I.Fe has not recognized the Cymric. This breed is almost unknown in Europe.

RED TABBY CYMRIC. ORIGINATING ON THE ISLE OF MAN, THE CYMRIC (KIM RICK) WAS SELECTIVELY BRED IN THE UNITED STATES WHERE IT WAS ALSO REFERRED TO AS LONGHAIRED MANX.

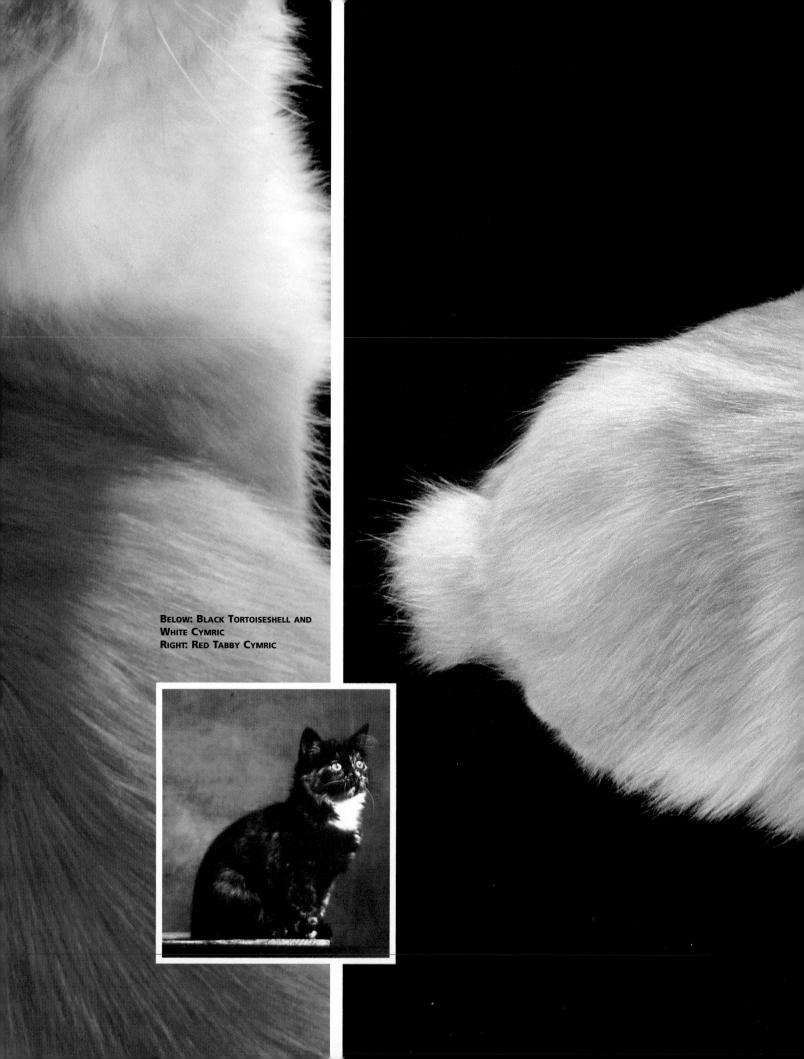

BELOW: BLACK TORTOISESHELL AND
WHITE CYMRIC
RIGHT: RED TABBY CYMRIC

Cymric

GENERAL
Manxlike. Weight: 3.5 to 5.5 kg.
Semilong to long coat.

BLACK TORTOISESHELL CYMRIC

HEAD
Of medium size, round and slightly longer than broad. Moderately rounded forehead, pronounced cheekbones, and jowliness. Nose of medium length. Muzzle slightly longer than broad. Definite whisker break. Strong chin.

EARS
Wide at the base with rounded tips. Set well apart.
Full interior furnishings.

EYES
Large and round. Color appropriate to coat color.

NECK
Short and thick.

BODY
Compact and cobby. Broad chest. Short back. Rounded rump. Robust bone structure. Solidly muscled.

LEGS AND PAWS
Hind legs are much longer than forelegs. Heavily boned. Muscular. Paws round and medium in size.

TAIL
Short or absent.

COAT
Semilong, longer on underparts.
Very silky texture.
Double coat (abundant undercoat).
Colors: Same varieties as the Manx (natural colors, tabby patterns, etc.).

RED TABBY CYMRIC

RED TABBY AND WHITE CYMRIC

WHITE TORTOISESHELL CYMRIC

CHARACTERISTICS
This is a playful, active, hardy cat. The highly social Cymric readily acceptes strangers and gets along well with other animals. It is also gentle with children.
Care is simple. Weekly brushing is sufficient.

(▼)F.I.Fe   (■) L.O.O.F.   (★) C.F.A.   (◆) T.I.C.A.

Devon Rex

Country of Origin:
Great Britain
Other Name: Poodle Cat

A *funny little creature with a lambswool coat and bat ears*

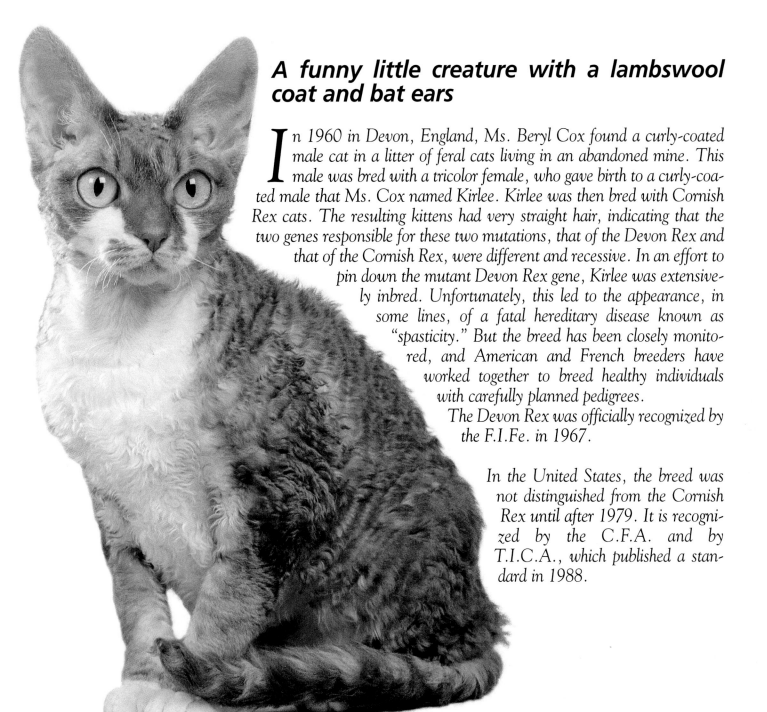

In 1960 in Devon, England, Ms. Beryl Cox found a curly-coated male cat in a litter of feral cats living in an abandoned mine. This male was bred with a tricolor female, who gave birth to a curly-coated male that Ms. Cox named Kirlee. Kirlee was then bred with Cornish Rex cats. The resulting kittens had very straight hair, indicating that the two genes responsible for these two mutations, that of the Devon Rex and that of the Cornish Rex, were different and recessive. In an effort to pin down the mutant Devon Rex gene, Kirlee was extensively inbred. Unfortunately, this led to the appearance, in some lines, of a fatal hereditary disease known as "spasticity." But the breed has been closely monitored, and American and French breeders have worked together to breed healthy individuals with carefully planned pedigrees.

The Devon Rex was officially recognized by the F.I.Fe. in 1967.

In the United States, the breed was not distinguished from the Cornish Rex until after 1979. It is recognized by the C.F.A. and by T.I.C.A., which published a standard in 1988.

BROWN TABBY AND WHITE DEVON REX

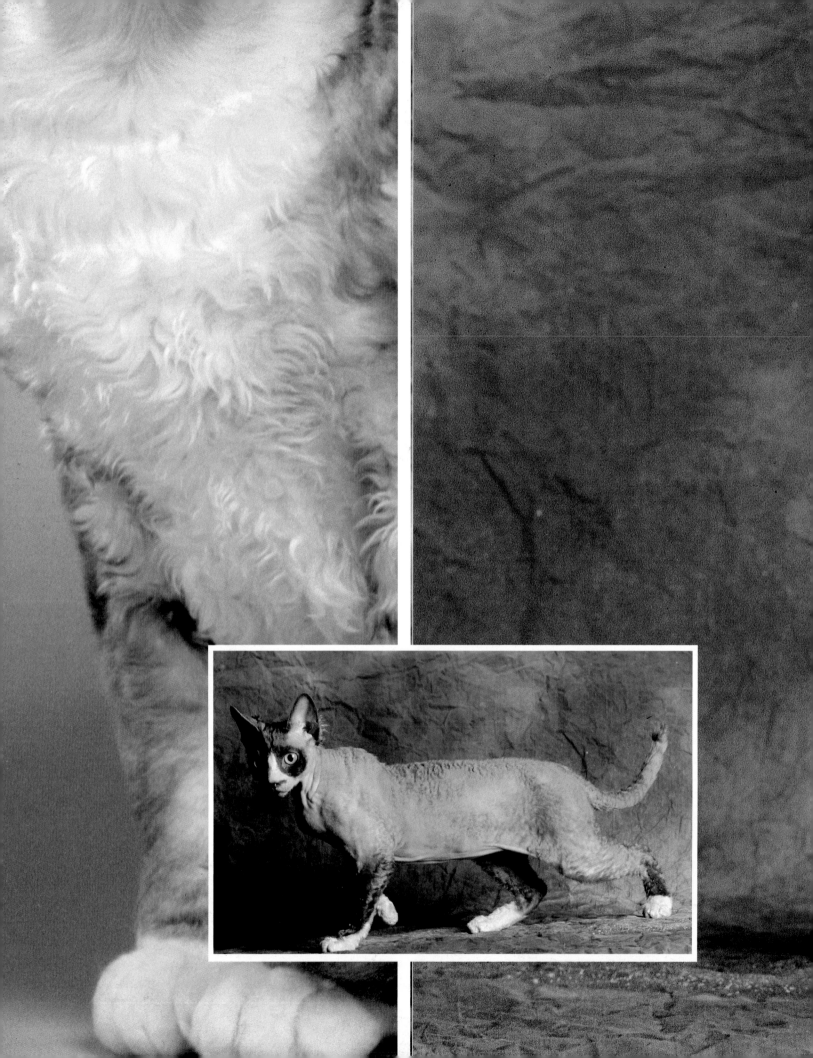

Devon Rex

BLACK SMOKE DEVON REX

WHITE DEVON REX

GENERAL
Medium sized. Medium-limbed type.
Weight: 2.5 to 4 kg.
Very large ears.
Short, curly hair.

TABBY AND WHITE CHOCOLATE DEVON REX

HEAD
Fairly small, wedge-shaped, short, angular. Flat skull, domed forehead. Full cheeks, prominent cheekbones. Short muzzle. Short nose. Well-marked stop (◆). Large chin. Well-marked whisker pinch. Curly, fairly harsh whiskers and eyebrows of medium length (▼).

EARS
Very large, very broad at the base, cone-shaped with rounded tips. Set very low, covered with fine hair. Sparse hair on the inside. Hairs on the ear tips (lynx tips).

EYES
Large, oval, well-spaced, set at an angle toward the outer edge of the ear. Luminous, clear, pure color corresponding to that of the coat.

NECK
Moderately long, thin, slightly arched.

BODY
Medium in size and length. Broad chest. Firm, strong muscles.

LEGS
Long, thin. Hind legs clearly longer than forelegs. Fine- to medium-boned. Muscular. Small, oval paws.

TAIL
Long, slender, tapering, well-furnished with short hair.

COAT
Short, fine, kinked, wavy hair with or without guard hairs. Coat not as neat as that of the Cornish Rex, but slightly wild like that of a Poodle or sheep. Some Devon Rexes have only down on the belly (▼).

As in the Cornish Rex, the hair grows slowly. All colors and patterns are allowed, with or without black.

NOTES
Allowable outcross breeds: none.

FAULTS
Narrow head like that of the Oriental Shorthair or broad head like that of the British Shorthair. Small, high-set eyes. Small eyes.

Stocky body. Short, hairless or shaggy tail. Close-lying coat. Wiry or smooth hair. Large, hairless areas.

DEVON REX KITTEN

BLUE TABBY DEVON REX

WHITE DEVON REX

CHARACTERISTICS
The Devon Rex is a lively, playful, acrobatic cat but is a bit less active than the Cornish Rex. Naturally cheerful and independent, Devon Rexes are friendly toward other cats and toward dogs. They hate being left alone.
Very affectionate and sensitive, they are pleasant companions with soft, quiet voices. They are well-suited to apartment life, as they are susceptible to cold. Kittens develop quickly. The coat does not attain its adult appearance until about 6 months.
Daily brushing is enough to maintain the Devon's coat. Devons hardly shed at all. They must be bathed regularly, since they sweat and their ears produce a great deal of wax.
The pedigree should be examined closely in order to avoid the risk of spasticity.

(▼) F.I.Fe   (■) L.O.O.F.   (★) C.F.A.   (◆) T.I.C.A.

126

European Shorthair

Country of Origin: Continental Europe
Other Name: European

A commoner with a pedigree!

The European Shorthair is the Continental European equivalent to the British Shorthair in Great Britain and the American Shorthair in the United States. The European Shorthair is derived from the common domestic cat (house cat or mixed breed cat) through selective breeding based on aesthetic criteria.

In 1925, so-called "European" cats obtained their first standard. This breed, previously grouped with the British Shorthair, was approved by the F.I.Fe. in 1982. It is not recognized by Great Britain's G.C.C.F.

127

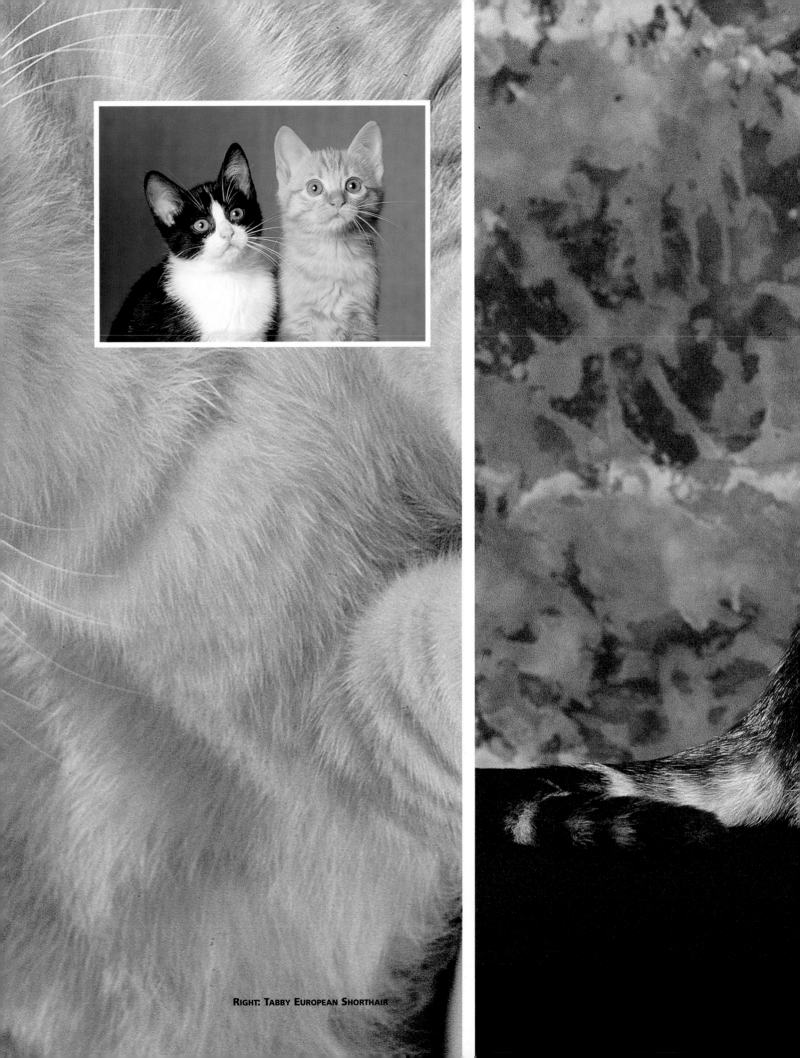

RIGHT: TABBY EUROPEAN SHORTHAIR

European Shorthair

BICOLOR

GENERAL
Medium-limbed type (the British Shorthair is shorter-limbed).
Medium to large in size. Males can reach 8 kg.
Shorthaired.

TORTOISESHELL, THREE COLORS

EARS
Medium-sized, slightly rounded at the tips, which may have lynx tips. Well-spaced and erect.

EYES
Large, round, widely spaced, set at a slight slant. Color must be clear and pure and correspond to that of the coat.

NECK
Moderately long and muscular.

BODY
Fairly long, not stout. Stocky, strong, muscular. Broad, well-developed chest.

COAT
Short, dense, close-lying, lustrous hair without undercoat. All colors except chocolate, lilac, and colorpoint.

NOTES
Allowable outcross breeds: none.

FAULTS
Body too large or too stout. Strong resemblance to British Shorthair and American Shorthair. Pendulous cheeks. Clear stop. Long, wooly fur (▼).

BICOLOR

HEAD
Fairly broad with rounded contours but a bit longer than it is wide. Slightly rounded skull and forehead. Well-developed cheeks, especially in males. Straight, moderately long nose with no stop (■) and a clearly defined base (▼). Rounded, firm chin.

LEGS AND PAWS
Moderately long, strong, solid, tapering evenly to the paws, which are round and firm.

TAIL
Moderately long, fairly thick at the base, tapering gradually to a rounded tip.

ORANGE TABBY

CHARACTERISTICS
The European Shorthair is a hardy, active, dynamic, playful cat. More easygoing in nature than the mixed breed cat, the European Shorthair is calmer and gentler.
An affectionate, pleasant companion, it is highly adaptable. A good hunter, it likes being outdoors. It is easy to groom. Weekly brushing is quite sufficient, except during shedding.

TABBY

(▼)F.I.Fe   (■) L:O.O.F.   (★) C.F.A.   (◆) T.I.C.A.

Exotic Shorthair

This feisty ball of fluff takes time to grow up

In the United States, around 1960, breeders crossed the American Shorthair with the Persian in order to improve the American's coat color and make it heavier. Thus were born shorthaired Persians, dubbed Exotic Shorthairs and recognized by the C.F.A in 1966.

During the breeding program, crosses were also made with the Russian Blue and the Burmese. Since 1987, the only allowable outcross breed is the Persian.

The F.I.Fe. recognized the Exotic Shorthair in 1986. Very common in the United States, Exotic Shorthairs are conquering Europe.

BROWN TABBY EXOTIC SHORTHAIR

Exotic Shorthair

CHINCHILLA EXOTIC SHORTHAIR

GENERAL
Shorthaired Persian.
Weight: 3 to 6.5 kg.
Medium-sized, short-limbed.

SILVER TABBY

Large, round, well-spaced. Pure, deep color corresponding to that of the coat (gold to copper in most varieties; green in the chinchilla and the golden; blue in the white and the colorpoint).

NECK
Short and thick.

BODY
Medium in size, cobby, low to the ground. Broad chest. Massive shoulders. Large-boned, powerful muscles.

LEGS AND PAWS
Short, straight, and large. Round, large paws. Tufts of hair between the toes are desirable.

TAIL
Short, thick, carried low. Rounded tip.

COAT
Shorthaired but slightly longer than that of other shorthaired breeds. Dense, fluffy,

erect hair. All Persian colors are recognized.

NOTES
Allowable outcross breed: Persian.

FAULTS
Head too long or too narrow. Nose too long or roman nose. Narrow, thin muzzle. Small, slanted, pale-colored eyes. Ears too large. Body too long or narrow. Narrow chest. Long, slender legs. Oval paws. Tail too long. Disqualify: lockets or spots (■).

BLUE CREAM TORTIE

HEAD
Round, massive. Very broad skull. Rounded forehead. Round, full cheeks. Short, broad, round muzzle. Short, broad nose with pronounced stop. Broad, open nostrils to facilitate air flow (▼). Strong chin. Broad, powerful jaws.

EARS
Small, rounded at the tip, not too open at the base. Widely spaced and well-furnished with hair on the inside.

EYES

CHARACTERISTICS
The Exotic Shorthair is a tranquil cat but a bit livelier than the Persian. Curious, playful, and even-tempered, it is friendly to other cats and to dogs. Easygoing and quiet, as it rarely meows, it does not like being left alone. It is affectionate and needs the tender presence of its owner. This sturdy cat does not reach maturity until around three years of age and enters puberty fairly late. When two Exotic Shorthairs are crossed, they may produce longhaired kittens called "Exotic Longhairs" by the C.F.A. and considered Persians in France.
Exotic Shorthairs are easy to groom. Weekly brushing and combing is sufficient. During shedding, they should be brushed and combed daily. Because of their fairly productive tear ducts, their eyes should be cleaned daily.

TORTIE

TABBY AND WHITE KITTEN

(▼) F.I.Fe   (■) L.O.O.F.   (★) C.F.A.   (◆) T.I.C.A.

134

German Rex

Wearing a full lambswool coat

The German Rex is the oldest known breed of curly-coated cat. It first appeared in 1946 in the home of Dr. Scheuer-Karpin but was actually developed from a stray adopted by breeders in 1951. Curly-coated kittens were obtained through crosses with the Cornish Rex. This proved that the two breeds had the same gene responsible for the mutation. Both the F.I.Fe. and the L.O.O.F recognize the German Rex. However, the C.F.A. does not distinguish it from the Cornish Rex and Devon Rex. The German Rex is very rare.

BROWN TABBY

135

German Rex

BLACK AND WHITE BICOLOR

GENERAL
Medium-sized, strong, muscular.

WHITE WITH ORANGE EYES

correspond to that of the coat.

BODY
Medium-sized, solid, muscular, but not mas-

COAT
Short, velvety, soft, very silky. Must be wavy or curly. Curly over the entire body, longer than that of the Cornish Rex,

more spiky. No guard hairs. Colors: all are recognized, except chocolate, lilac, and color-point.

NOTES
Allowable outcross breeds: none.

FAULTS
Head too long, too pointed. Small ears. Short, hairless tail. Shaggy coat, not wavy enough, with hairless patches (▼).

BROWN TABBY

HEAD
Rounded, very broad between the ears. Well-developed cheeks. Nose with a slight break at the base. Massive, strong chin. Curly whiskers, shorter than usual.

EARS
Medium-sized, broad at the base, with slightly rounded tips. Outside covered with fine, thick fur, inside slightly furry.

EYES
Medium-sized, well-spaced, and wide open. The color must be uniform and luminous, and must

sive or heavy. Rounded, powerful chest. The back is straight from the shoulders to the croup.

LEGS AND PAWS
Slender, moderately long. Well-developed,, slightly oval paws (✳) with a rounded shape (▼).

TAIL
Moderately long, thick at the base and tapering to a rounded tip. Thick fur.

TORTIE

CHARACTERISTICS
German Rexes are active but patient cats. They are even-tempered, friendly toward other cats, and very affectionate toward their owner. They are easy to groom.

(▼) F.I.Fe   (■) L.O.O.F.   (★) C.F.A.   (◆) T.I.C.A.

138

Havana

Country of Origin: Great Britain
Original Name: Havana Brown
Other Name(s): Chestnut Brown Foreign,
Chestnut Oriental Shorthair

Either a chestnut or lilac coat, but always green-eyed

In the early 19th century in England, a female chestnut brown cat named Granny Grump was reported. Much later, around 1880, other cats of the same color were successfully shown.

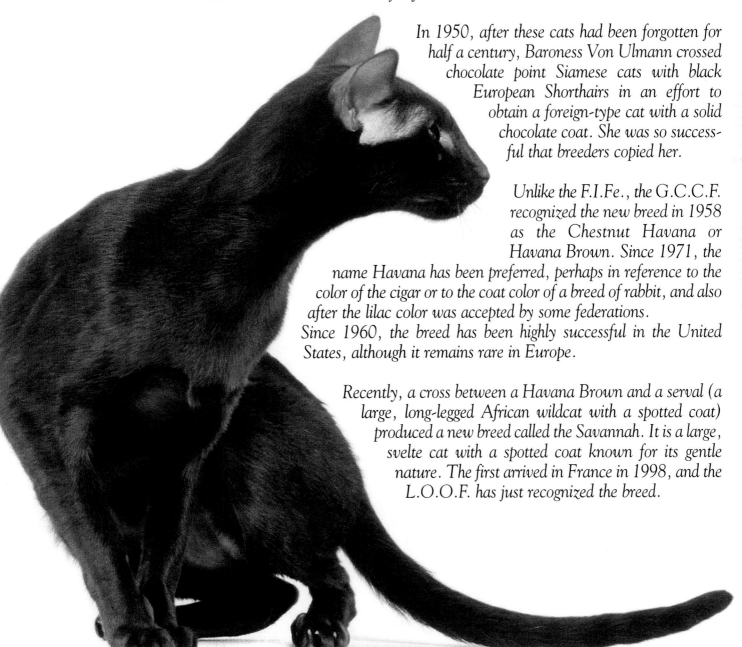

In 1950, after these cats had been forgotten for half a century, Baroness Von Ulmann crossed chocolate point Siamese cats with black European Shorthairs in an effort to obtain a foreign-type cat with a solid chocolate coat. She was so successful that breeders copied her.

Unlike the F.I.Fe., the G.C.C.F. recognized the new breed in 1958 as the Chestnut Havana or Havana Brown. Since 1971, the name Havana has been preferred, perhaps in reference to the color of the cigar or to the coat color of a breed of rabbit, and also after the lilac color was accepted by some federations.
Since 1960, the breed has been highly successful in the United States, although it remains rare in Europe.

Recently, a cross between a Havana Brown and a serval (a large, long-legged African wildcat with a spotted coat) produced a new breed called the Savannah. It is a large, svelte cat with a spotted coat known for its gentle nature. The first arrived in France in 1998, and the L.O.O.F. has just recognized the breed.

139

Havana

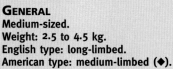

GENERAL
Medium-sized.
Weight: 2.5 to 4.5 kg.
English type: long-limbed.
American type: medium-limbed (◆).

HEAD
Longer than it is wide. English version: Oriental type without whisker pinch or stop. American version: slightly triangular with significant pinch and stop (◆). Slightly rounded skull. Jowls allowed in adult males. Long, angular muzzle. Strong, angular, firm chin.

EARS
Large, rounded at the tip, widely spaced. Pointed forward when alert. Very little fur, especially on the inside.

EYES
Large, oval, not globular, set near the bridge of the nose. Colors: all shades and intensities of green. A change in color is allowed until the age of one year.

NECK
Medium in size and length.

BODY
Medium in size and bone structure. Medium-limbed (American type) or long-limbed (English type). Firm muscles.

LEGS AND PAWS
Long, slender but not too thin. Compact, oval paws.

TAIL
Moderately long, not too thick at the base, tapering toward the tip.

COAT
Short, fine, silky, lying flat against the body. Very thick undercoat. Slightly fluffier fur allowed for lilac coats (◆). Colors:
- chocolate: chestnut brown, solid hazelnut brown. Brown whiskers and nose leather, pink paw pads. The C.F.A.

recognizes this color only.
- lilac: taupe with pink highlights. T.I.C.A. recognizes both these colors.

Kittens are born with tabby ghost markings that disappear during the first year.

NOTES
Allowable outcross breeds: none.

FAULTS
Absence of break in the muzzle. Absence of chin. Kinked tail. Disqualify: wrong eye color. White markings.

CHARACTERISTICS
Havanas are lively, active, and playful but not aggressive cats. Standoffish toward strangers, they like tranquility and comfort. Calm, affectionate, and very gentle, they adore their owner. Less talkative than the Siamese, they also have a softer voice. In terms of grooming, weekly brushing is sufficient for this breed.

(▼)F.I.Fe   (■) L.O.O.F.   (★) C.F.A.   (◆) T.I.C.A.

Japanese Bobtail

Countries of Origin: China, Japan

A pompom tail and a tricolor coat

These worshipped cats might have originated in China, then Japan, as they appear on many artifacts and prints from as early as the 11th century from several far eastern countries. In that long-ago era, only the royal family and the aristocracy owned cats of this breed. Highly honored and even venerated (especially the tricolor or "Mi-ke" variety), a symbol of luck and happiness, these cats are depicted with the front right paw raised (Maneki-neko means "waving cat") in art found in Japanese homes and temples.

The breed's bobbed tail is a characteristic determined by a recessive autosomal gene. In 1968, the first Japanese Bobtails were imported to the United States by the breeder E. Freret, who started a breeding program. The C.F.A. published a standard in 1971. The F.I.Fe. recognized the breed in 1990. In 1981, the female Sirikit and the male Aikido became the first Japanese Bobtails imported to France. Highly popular in the United States, the breed remains very rare in France.

143

Japanese Bobtail

TRICOLOR AND BICOLOR

GENERAL
Medium-sized. Well-muscled body that is long and svelte, rather than massive.
Tail curled like a pompom.
Weight: 2.5 to 4 kg.

EARS
Large, straight, well-spaced, never facing outward. At rest, appear to be slanted forward.

EYES
Large, oval, wide open. Appear clearly slanted in profile. Color corresponding to that of the coat.

BODY
Long, svelte, well-muscled without appearing heavy.

HEAD
Appears long and chiseled, shaped like an equilateral triangle with soft curves. High, prominent cheekbones. Jowls are allowed in unaltered males. Whisker pinch. Long, well-defined nose with a slight depression at or just below the eyes. Fairly broad muzzle, neither pointed nor flat, rounding in a slight break at the whiskers. Well-marked whisker pads (◆).

The tail may consist of one or more sections; if it has several sections, it is curled and angled. Hairs longer and thicker than that on the body give the tail a pompom appearance (▼).

COAT
Short or semilong, soft, silky but without a true undercoat.
Two varieties:
- shorthaired
- semilonghaired or longhaired. Possible ruff.

All colors are recognized except chocolate, lilac,

FAULTS
Short, round head. Stout, massive body. Absence of bones in the tail; tail too straight, standing out too much from the body. Absence of pompom.

LEGS AND PAWS
Long and thin but not delicate or fragile. The hind legs are clearly longer than the forelegs. Oval paws.

TAIL
Maximum tail length is 5 to 8 cm, although when fully extended it can reach 10 to 13 cm. The bones are large, rigid, virtually fused (except at the base).

and colorpoint. Tricolors and bicolors are among the preferred patterns. The Mi-ke (tricolor black, reddish-brown, and white cat that produces only females) is the most prized. Patterns should be clear and well-marked, and colors should be even.

NOTES
Allowable outcross breeds: none.

TRICOLOR, OR MI-KÉ VARIETY

CHARACTERISTICS
The lively, extraverted, independent, and curious Japanese Bobtail has a strong personality, like all Oriental-type cats. Not always friendly toward other cats, it usually ignores dogs.
The very playful Japanese Bobtail gets along well with children. It is talkative and "sings" in a soft voice. Very affectionate, it is highly attached to its owner.
Well-balanced thanks to an excellent character, Japanese Bobtails adapt well to both apartment and outdoor life. Athletic hunters, they are crazy about water.
In terms of grooming, they require only weekly brushing. They shed very little.

(▼) F.I.Fe.   (■) L.O.O.F.   (★) C.F.A.   (◆) T.I.C.A.

146

Javanese

Country of Origin: United States

Like the Oriental Shorthair or the Balinese, but with semilong hair

Despite its name, this cat did not originate in Java. During breeding programs that led to the creation of the Balinese (semilonghaired Siamese), American breeders obtained a semilonghaired Oriental called the Javanese because of its type.

Feline associations are divided on the issue of whether the Javanese is truly a new breed or simply a variety of Balinese. The F.I.Fe., for example, considers it a semilonghaired Oriental type with a solid coat and green eyes. The C.F.A. considers the Javanese simply as a Balinese with coloring other than the four recognized basic colors (seal, blue, chocolate, and lilac point). The Javanese is therefore a colorpoint with dark blue eyes like the Siamese.

The Javanese is still quite rare in Europe.

147

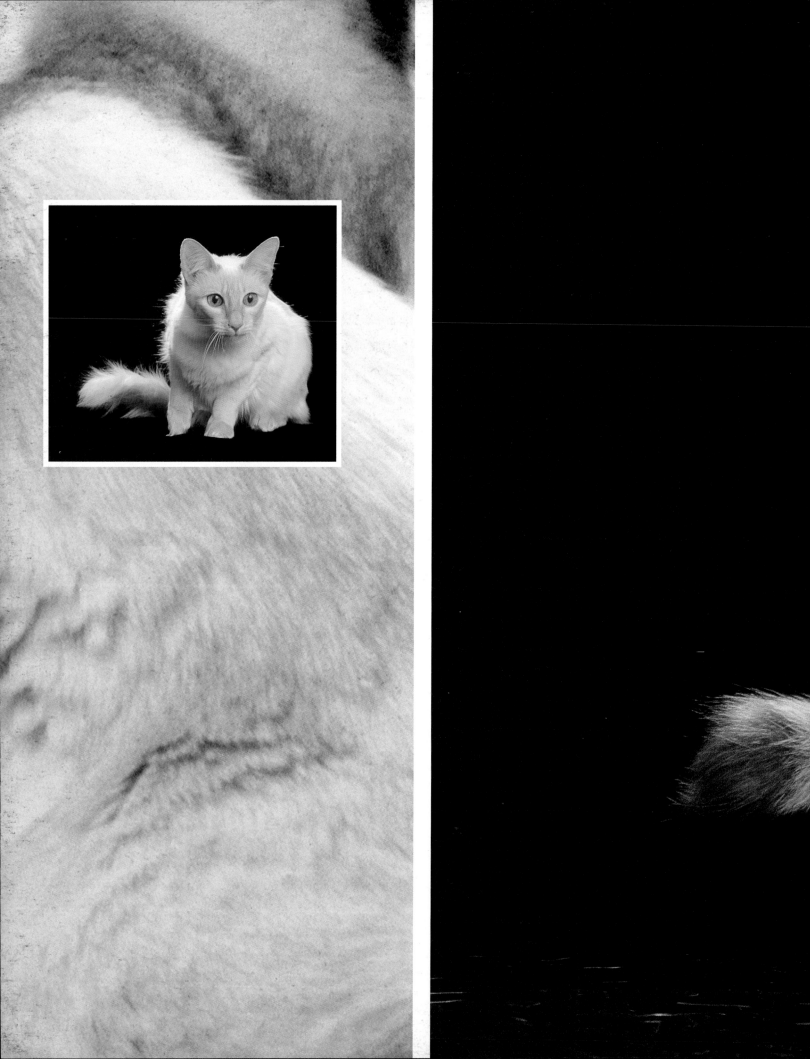

Javanese

GENERAL
Medium-sized, but heavier than the Siamese (∗).
Svelte, long-limbed, elegant but muscular cat (▼).

HEAD
Medium-sized, can be inscribed in a triangle. In profile, the skull is slightly convex. Slender muzzle. Long, straight nose continuing the line of the forehead without break. Medium-sized chin.

EARS
Large, broad at the base, pointed. They extend the sides of the triangle.

EYES
Medium-sized, almond-shaped, set slightly at a slant toward the nose. Color: luminous green (▼). Colorpoints and white-coated cats have dark blue eyes (∗).

NECK
Long and slender.

BODY
Long, svelte, graceful but muscular.

LEGS AND PAWS
Long, slender, in proportion to the body. Small, oval paws.

green, except in the white-coated Javanese, which has dark blue eyes (▼). Colorpoint with dark blue eyes, in the varieties recognized for the Siamese (∗).

FAULTS
White markings. Eyes more yellow than green (▼). Tabby markings in non-agouti varieties.

TAIL
Very long and slender, even at the base, tapering to the tip.

COAT
Thin, silky hair moderately long on the body, slightly longer on the ruff, shoulders, and tail (plume). No wooly undercoat (▼).

Even color without tabby markings or shading in non-agouti varieties. Varieties are those of the Oriental type. The eyes are

CHARACTERISTICS
The Javanese has the character and temperament of an Oriental type cat. Javanese cats are extraverted and "talk" a lot in a melodious voice.
They are possessive, following their owner like a small dog, and they know how to get all the petting they want.
They are also athletes and excellent hunters. They are easy to groom, especially since they love being brushed.

(▼) F.I.F.e   (■) L.O.O.F.   (★) C.F.A.   (◆) T.I.C.A.

Korat

This independent gray cat brings good luck

This natural breed originated in Thailand, where it was first established in the 14th century. It is named after a province in Thailand, where it is considered a bearer of good luck. In fact, its original name, Si-sawat, means culture and prosperity.

In The Cat Book of Poems of the Ayutthaya kingdom (1350-1767), this cat is said to have "eyes that shine like dewdrops on a lotus leaf."

Specimens were imported and shown in Great Britain in the late 19th century, but without success, since they were seen simply as Siamese cats with blue coats.

American breeder Jean Johnson began breeding Korats in 1959. The breed was recognized by the C.F.A. in 1966 and by T.I.C.A. in 1969.

Upon its arrival in Europe in 1972, the Korat was approved by the F.I.Fe. Well-known in the United States, the breed is quite uncommon in Europe.

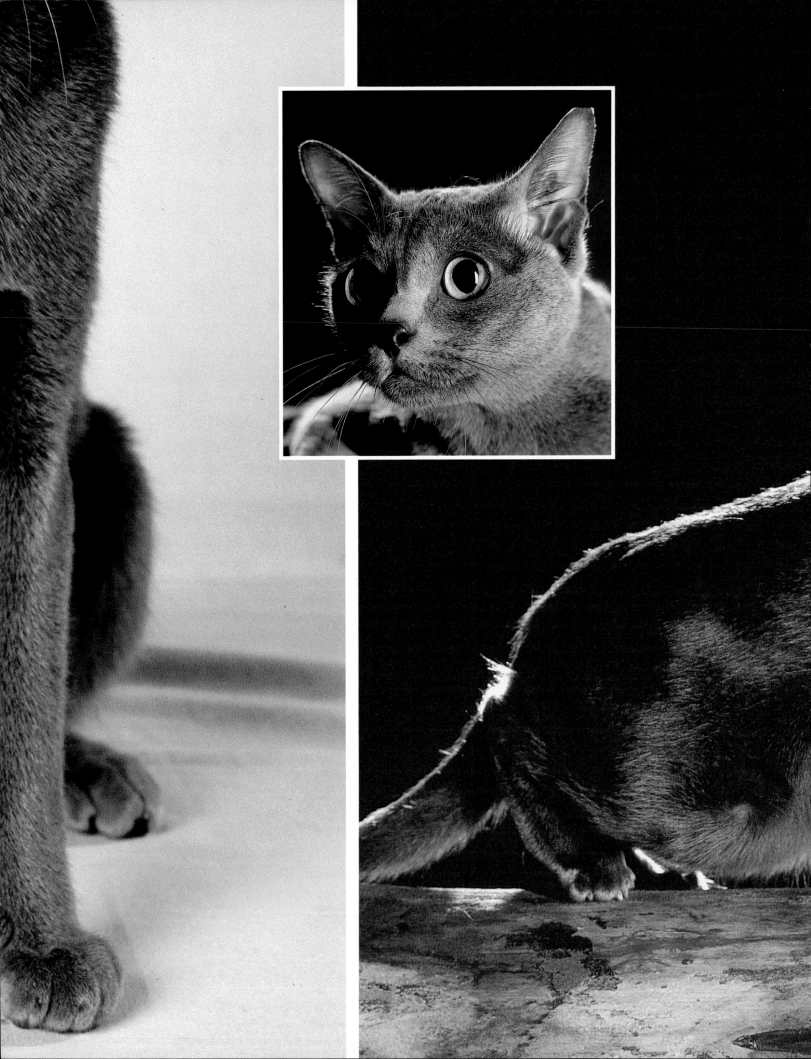

Korat

GENERAL
Medium-sized, semi-cobby body, fairly medium-limbed.
Weight: 2.5 to 4.5 kg.
Shorthaired.

SILVER BLUE

HEAD
Heart-shaped when seen from the front. Flat forehead. Slight stop between the forehead and nose. Firm, well-developed cheeks. Muzzle neither pointed nor angular. Long nose, slightly domed at the tip. Strong, well-developed chin. Strong jaws.

EARS
Large, broad at the base with slightly rounded tips. Set high on the skull, on alert. Short hair on the outside.

EYES
Large, round, well-spaced, slightly slanted. Preferably luminous green in color. Amber eyes are accepted, especially in young cats (▼). Actually, the final color is not attained before the age of two. Eyebrows form two broad curves above the eyes.

NECK
Medium-sized, long.

BODY
Medium-sized, semi-cobby, neither compact nor svelte (✳). Slightly arched back. Strong, muscular, flexible.

LEGS AND PAWS
Hind legs slightly longer than forelegs. Medium to heavy bone structure. Oval paws.

TAIL
Moderately long, thicker at the base, tapering to a rounded tip.

COAT
Short, fine, lustrous, dense hair. Simple coat (no undercoat) tending to stand erect on the spine when the cat is in motion. Even, silver blue color (✳). The tip of the hair is silver, making the coat appear frosted (◆). The nose leather is dark blue-gray. Paw pads dark blue to pinkish lavender.

NOTES
Allowable outcross breeds: none.

FAULTS
Narrow head. Small, closely spaced eyes. Yellow eyes (◆). Nose too long or too short. Pinched chin. Disqualify: any color other than blue. White markings.

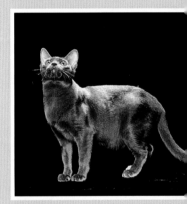

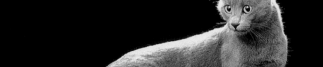

CHARACTERISTICS
The Korat is lively, active, very agile and playful but does not like agitation or noise. It needs a tranquil environment. Korats are not very friendly toward other cats and are reserved toward strangers. Gentle, very affectionate, and hypersensitive, they are highly attached to their owner. They need lots of love and attention. They have a melodious voice. They are easy to groom, as weekly brushing is sufficient.

(▼) F.I.Fe   (■) L.O.O.F.   (★) C.F.A.   (◆) T.I.C.A.

La Perm

Country of Origin: United States
Original Name: Dalles La Perm

With or without hair!

In 1982 in an orchard in The Dalles, Oregon, a cat owned by Linda Koehl had a litter of six kittens, including a female named Curly. Curly was born hairless; two months later she had a curly, silky coat.

For five years, Koehl raised many other curly-coated cats who are the ancestors of the Dalles La Perm breed, the result of a spontaneous mutation by a dominant gene.

T.I.C.A. recognized the breed and published a standard in 1996.

155

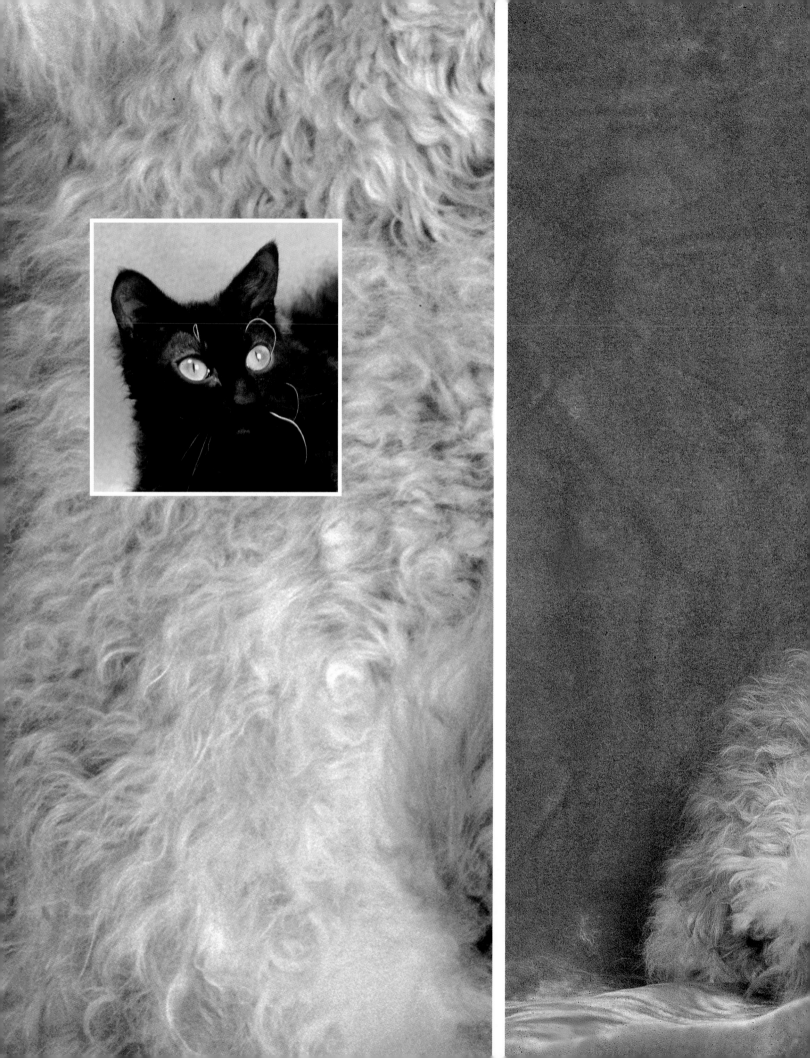

La Perm

GENERAL
Medium-sized, semi-foreign type with a curly coat.
Weight: 3.5 to 5.5 kg.

EYES
Large, almond-shaped, moderately spaced. No relationship between eye color and coat color.

NECK
Moderately long; carried high.

BODY
Semi-foreign type, medium-sized. Surprisingly heavy for its size. Medium bone structure, fairly muscular (■)(♦).

HEAD
Triangular shape with rounded contours. Rounded skull. The profile presents a slight stop. High cheeks. Moderately long nose. Moderately prominent muzzle. Full, pronounced whisker pads. Firm chin (■)(♦).

EARS
Medium-sized, broad at the base with rounded tips. The inside surface is well-furnished with curly hair at the bottom of the ear. Lynx tips are desirable (■)(♦).

LEGS AND PAWS
Moderately long. Forelegs shorter than hind legs. Medium-boned. Fairly muscular. Round paws (■)(♦).

TAIL
Long and slender. Wavy fur.

COAT
Two varieties:
- shorthaired coat: soft, silky texture, wavy on the back and belly.

the ears. Disqualify: thin, angular body. Short legs.

Moderate undercoat.
- semilonghaired or longhaired coat: soft and curly texture. Heavy undercoat. Ruff accepted in adults. Whiskers and hair inside the ears may be curly.
These cats are hairless at least once in their life, often when they are very young. The coat often grows back curly.
Colors: all are allowed.

NOTES
Outcrossing with other breeds allowed as long as the population is insufficient (■).

FAULTS
No hair in the ears. No long, curly hair below

CHARACTERISTICS
This extraverted, curious farm cat is an excellent hunter and good companion. It has a soft voice.

(▼) F.I.Fe.   (■) L.O.O.F.   (★) C.F.A.   (♦) T.I.C.A.

Domestic Lynx

Country of Origin: United States

A tame little wild cat

*T*his new breed was created in the 1980s in the United States by crossing the small bobcat and Canadian lynx with domestic cats. "The ideal in breeding is a cat as similar as possible either to the bobcat or to the Canadian lynx or jungle cat (Felis chaus), with the gentle, trusting nature of a domestic cat" (■). The Domestic Lynx is still very rare.

BROWN SPOTTED TABBY

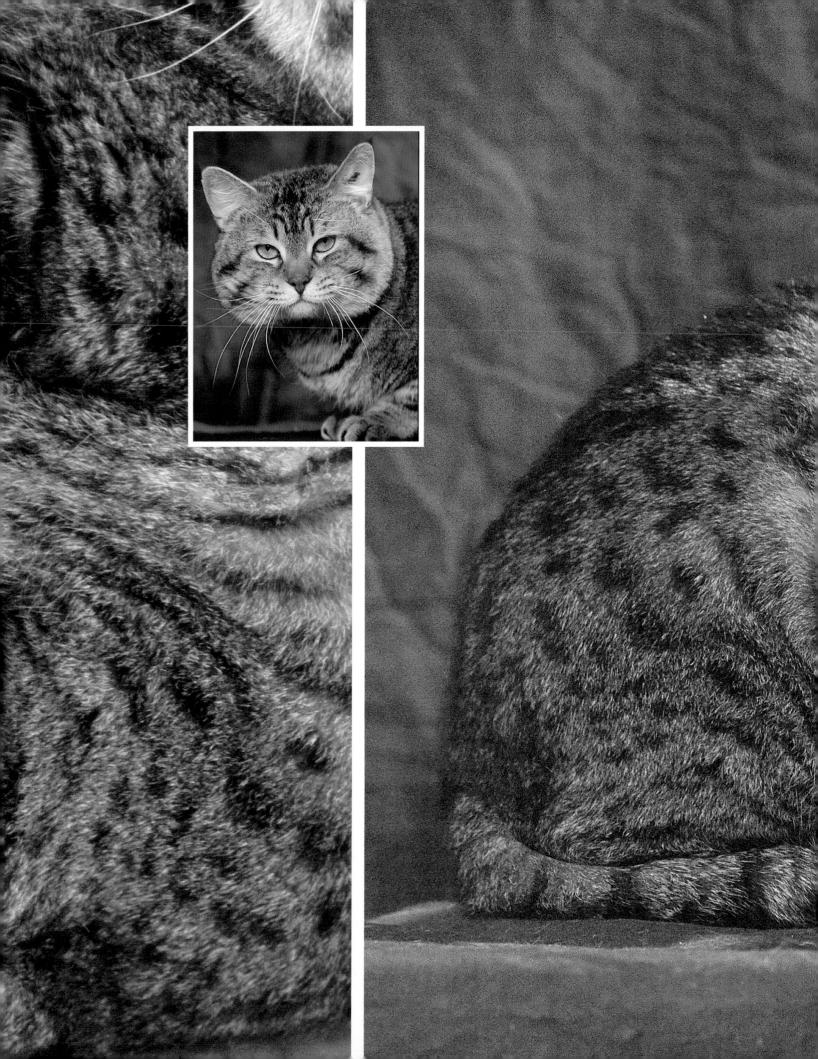

Domestic Lynx

GENERAL
Powerful, fairly long-legged cat with a heavy bone structure and well-developed muscles.
Males are much larger and stronger than females.

HEAD
Triangular in shape. Slightly concave profile without a clear break. High cheekbones. Angular muzzle. Nose moderately long and very broad. Strong chin. Relatively short, very powerful jaws (■).

EYES
Almond-shaped, slightly slanted. All colors are allowed. Blue eyes in the colorpoint (■).

BODY
Large in size, rectangular in shape. Slightly curved back.

EARS
Medium-sized, broad at the base, pointed, set high. Covered with hair and preferably having lynx tips.

LEGS AND PAWS
Long, massive. Hind legs are slightly longer than forelegs. Round paws. Hair between the paw pads.

TAIL
Short like that of the wild lynx. Its minimum length of 10 cm should not extend below the knee. It must be flexible.

COAT
Short to semilong coat. Longer on the belly and thighs. A ruff or beard is preferable. Thick, silky texture with a heavy, nearly waterproof undercoat.

All eumelanistic colors: black, blue, cinnamon, fawn, chocolate, lilac, either in a light or dark shade or in combination with the silver factor for spotted and ticked patterns only, or the above colors in a colorpoint pattern (■).
Typical agouti markings on the forehead and face. The legs are striped or, preferably, spotted. Well-defined spots on the belly. The tail is ringed with a black tip. Reddish-brown and tortoiseshell coloring do not exist in this breed. There is also a "snow" version, that is, with blue eyes and Siamese markings on a light, spotted body.

FAULTS
Disqualify: reddish-brown coloring. White markings. Tail too short or too long.

NOTES
Allowable outcross breeds: European Shorthair, Maine Coon, American Shorthair (■).

CHARACTERISTICS
This cat is gentle and sociable. It gets along well with dogs but is rather dominant toward other cats. The affectionate Domestic Lynx makes a good pet.

TABBY

(▼)F.I.Fe   (■) L.O.O.F.   (★) C.F.A.   (◆) T.I.C.A.

162

Maine Coon

Country of Origin:
United States
Other Name:
Maine Shag

An American giant and a gentle wild cat

According to legend, the Maine Coon is the result of the mating of a wild cat and a raccoon, a genetic impossibility imagined because the coat and tail of the breed resemble those of the raccoon.

The Maine Coon originated in the United States, in Maine. It is thought to have arisen from crosses between Angoras brought from the Middle East by sailors, English cats brought by the first colonists, Russian and Nordic cats, and shorthaired American farm cats. The harsh climate of this region of the United States produced this large, hardy cat which may be considered the first American feline breed. Captain Jenks, a black and white cat, was the first Maine Coon successfully shown at cat shows in Boston and New York in 1861. The breed also caused a stir in 1895 at New York's Madison Square Garden.

Persians and Siamese stole the stage from the Maine Coon for half a century. Interest in the breed was renewed around 1950 and has been growing rapidly since 1980.

A standard was published in 1960. The C.F.A. and the F.I.Fe. recognized the breed in 1976 and 1980, respectively. Although the Maine Coon is one of the world's most significant breeds, it is fairly uncommon in Europe and rare in France, where it was introduced in 1981.

The Maine Coon Feline Association breed club was created in 1987.

The breed has changed greatly in recent years. It is larger, taller, and more wild.

Maine Coon

TABBY

GENERAL
Very large in size. Weight: 4 to 10 kg.
Medium-limbed.
Very muscular body. Solid bone structure.
Appearance of power and hardiness.
Long, harsh hair.

HEAD
Medium-sized, typically wedge-shaped (◆). Slightly domed forehead. Slight concave curve in profile. High, prominent cheek bones. Angular muzzle (◆). Broad nose, sometimes slightly domed at the tip. Firm chin. Powerful, fairly long jaws (◆).

EARS
Large, broad at the base, moderately pointed, set high on the head. The inside is well-furnished with long, fine hair growing outward. Lynx tips desirable (◆).

EYES
Large, well-spaced, slightly oval but appearing round when wide open (▼).
Set at a slight slant. All colors are allowed.

NECK
Moderately long, powerful, slightly arched.

BODY
Long, rectangular, large in size. Heavy-boned. Powerful muscles.

COAT
Coat adapted to all seasons. Dense, silky, short on the head, shoulders, and legs, longer on the back and flanks, with considerable, well-furnished britches. Long hair on the belly. A ruff is desirable. The undercoat is soft, fine, and covered with smooth, waterproof, slightly oily hair (▼).

All colors are allowed, except chocolate, lilac, and colorpoint (✱), as well as cinnamon and fawn (▼). Any amount of white is accepted.

TORTOISESHELL

FAULTS
Small size, frail appearance. Round head. Straight or convex profile. Nose with a break. Round, pointed muzzle. Prominent flews. Receding chin. Ears too widely spaced, too flared. Eyes almond-shaped, too slanted. Body short, stocky. Fine, light bone structure. Short tail. Coat of equal length over entire body.

LEGS AND PAWS
Moderately long, strong. Heavy-boned and muscular.
Large, round paws. Well-furnished interdigital regions.

TAIL
Long, broad at the base, tapering toward the tip with long, abundant, fluttering hair.

The main categories of coat color are as follows:
- tabby
- solid color
- tortoiseshell
- silver
- smoke
- particolor

NOTES
Allowable outcross breeds: none.

CHARACTERISTICS
Well-balanced and calm, this "gentle giant" with quiet strength is sociable and non-aggressive, albeit dominant. He is affectionate and very attached to his owner.
Playful, athletic, and good hunters, Maine Coons need space. A large yard is better than an apartment. These hardy cats can tolerate the harshest winters. Females enter puberty late. Kittens grow slowly and do not reach adulthood until three or four years old. They are easy to groom, as a good weekly brushing is sufficient.

(▼) F.I.Fe.   (■) L.O.O.F.   (★) C.F.A.   (◆) T.I.C.A.

Oriental Longhair

A refined Oriental type with a long coat

This semilonghaired Oriental type was obtained recently by crossing Oriental Shorthairs and Balinese (longhaired Siamese). Today, American breeders continue to cross Oriental Shorthairs, Balinese, and Siamese in order to better establish the new breed's characteristics.

The Oriental Longhair received provisional recognition from the C.F.A. in 1994. T.I.C.A. published a standard in 1998.

This breed is still rare in Europe.

Oriental Longhair

GENERAL
Svelte, refined, very flexible but strong and muscular cat.
Its body is thicker than that of the Oriental Shorthair.
Weight: 4.5 to 6 kg.

EYES
Medium-sized, almond-shaped, and slanted as in Oriental types. Green or blue in white cats.

All Oriental Shorthair colors are recognized. Chocolate and lilac are the most desirable.

NOTES
Allowable outcross breeds: Oriental Shorthair, Siamese, and Balinese.

FAULTS
Round or broad head. Short or broad muzzle. Sloped nose. Small, round eyes without slant. Short body. Short coat. Absence of plume on the tail.

HEAD
Long and triangular. Flat forehead. Straight profile. Slender muzzle without break. Long, straight nose. Strong chin.

EARS
Very large but in proportion to the head.

NECK
Long, slender, and graceful.

BODY
Medium-sized and Oriental in type, that is, long and tubular. Fine-boned. Firm muscles.

LEGS AND PAWS
Long and slender. Hind legs longer than forelegs. Fine-boned. Slender, firm muscles. Small, oval paws.

TAIL
Long and well-furnished.

COAT
Semilong, fine, silky hair lying flat against the body. Thin undercoat. Shorter hair on the tops of the shoulders and head. Ruff and britches present. Plume on the tail.

TABBY

CHARACTERISTICS
These lively, energetic, playful cats with a strong personality are calmer and more even-tempered than the Oriental Shorthair.
Oriental Longhairs are sociable, getting along well with other cats, but reserved with strangers.
Very affectionate and highly attached to their owner, they are real "talkers" with a lovely voice. They do not like being left alone.
They are easy to groom.

(▼) F.I.Fe   (■) L.O.O.F.   (★) C.F.A.   (◆) T.I.C.A.

Manx

Country of Origin: Isle of Man
Original Name: Man's Cat
Other Name: Isle of Man Cat

A tailless cat that hops like a rabbit

This cat's name is derived from its native Isle of Man, off the coast of Ireland. These cats, described in China, Japan, Malaysia, and Russia, were once thought to be from the Far East. For example, they could have been brought by Spanish sailors after the wreck of a Spanish galleon in Philip II's invincible armada in 1588. Actually, the breed is the result of a spontaneous genetic mutation caused by a dominant autosomal gene (M) expressed in various ways: from tailless Manx cats (rumpies) to those with a normal tail (tailies).

Because of the high degree of inbreeding in the feline population on the small Isle of Man, the M gene was easily passed down through many generations. The Manx was very popular in England by the late 19th century. A Manx Club was created in Great Britain in 1901.

While very popular in countries including the United States and Great Britain, the Manx is quite uncommon in France.

A semilonghaired Manx called the Cymric has been selectively bred in North America.

171

TORTOISESHELL BLOTCHED TABBY

Manx

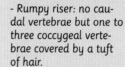

GENERAL
Medium-sized.
Weight: 3.5 to 5.5 kg.
Compact, fairly short-limbed.
Impression of roundness.

BROWN TABBY AND WHITE

HEAD
Relatively broad and round. Moderately rounded forehead. Prominent cheeks. Muzzle slightly longer than it is wide. Medium-sized nose without clear break, not turned up (▼). Well-developed, round whisker pads (◆). Strong chin. Large whiskers.

EARS
Medium-sized, broad at the base, rounded tips. Well-spaced. Sparse fur.

EYES
Large, round, slightly slanted (◆). Color corresponding to that of the coat.

NECK
Short, thick, powerful.

BODY
Medium-sized, solid, compact (cobby). Broad chest. Short, convex back. Croup very rounded and higher than shoulders. Heavy-boned. Muscular.

- Rumpy riser: no caudal vertebrae but one to three coccygeal vertebrae covered by a tuft of hair.
- Stumpy: tail several centimeters long, one to three caudal vertebrae, often with bone deformities ("kinked" tail).
- Taily: normal or kinked tail.

COAT
Short, dense, double coat (very thick undercoat). All colors and patterns are allowed, with or without white.

NOTES
Allowable outcross breeds: Cymric, British Shorthair (■).

FAULTS
Eyes not set at a slant. Long, slender body. Flat back. Short hind legs. Fine-boned. Disqualify: weakness in hindquarters (■).

CREAM AND WHITE KITTEN

RED AND WHITE KITTEN

RED BLOTCHED TABBY AND WHITE

LEGS AND PAWS
Forelegs shorter than hind legs. Heavy-boned and very muscular. Round paws. Hopping gait resembling that of a rabbit.

TAIL
Variety:
- Rumpy: tail absent (no caudal or coccygeal vertebrae). There must be a depression at the tail base.

CHARACTERISTICS
With its excellent character, this cat adapts easily to changes in lifestyle.
Manxes are sociable and accepting of other animals. Patient with children, they are affectionate toward their owner. Hardy, lively, and active, they are good hunters. Manx kittens grow slowly. Manxes are less prolific than average domestic cats, and they are difficult to breed. Homozygotic kittens (MM, carriers of two "doses" of the dominant mutant gene) die in the uterus (due to the incomplete development of the spinal cord). Thus, all Manxes are heterozygotic (Mm). Rumpies should not be bred together, due to the risk of this fatal gene combination. Instead, it is advised to breed Manxes with American Shorthairs or British Shorthairs, knowing that not all the kittens in each litter will be Manxes. Manxes are easy to groom.

(▼) F.I.Fe   (■) L.O.O.F.   (★) C.F.A.   (◆) T.I.C.A.

Egyptian Mau

This spotted cat with lovely mascara markings was deified in ancient times

Mau is the Egyptian word for cat. In fact, the ancestors of this breed were protected, worshipped, and represented on the monuments of ancient Egypt. Nathalie Troubetskoy, a Russian princess exiled in Italy, obtained Egyptian Maus from Cairo in 1953, including a female named Baba and a kitten named Lisa who were shown in Rome in 1955.

In 1956, when the princess emigrated to the United States, she brought her cats and founded the Fatima Cattery. Baba was awarded in 1957. This rapid success encouraged others to breed Egyptian Maus, and the breed was recognized by the C.F.A. and by T.I.C.A., which published a standard in 1988. That same year, the Egyptian Mau was also bred in Europe, where it is still quite uncommon. The F.I.Fe. approved the breed in 1992. The spotted tabby Oriental Shorthair, developed in Britain, is often mistaken for the Egyptian Mau.

BLACK SILVER TABBY

175

Below and facing page: BLACK SILVER SPOTTED TABBY

Egyptian Mau

GENERAL
Medium-sized, medium-limbed type, similar to the Abyssinian. Graceful body with well-developed muscles.
Weight: 2.5 to 5 kg. Spotted coat.

Short hair on the inside lying flat. Lynx tips appreciated.

EYES
Large, almond-shaped, neither round nor Oriental type, set at a slight slant. Light green, gooseberry green (▼). Amber is allowed in young adults up to 18 months.

HEAD
Wedge-shaped with slightly rounded contours and no flat surfaces. Slightly rounded forehead. Slight stop or slope between the nose and forehead. The cheeks are not full, except in adult males. Muzzle neither short nor pointed. Nose as long as it is wide.

EARS
Medium to large in size, well-spaced, broad at the base, on alert, and moderately pointed.

COAT
Short, fine, silky, resilient, lying very flat against the body. At least two bands of ticking on the ground color. Coat naturally spotted tabby. Dark, round, evenly spaced spots on the trunk and belly. Stripes on the extremities. "M" or scarab marking on the

SPOTTED TABBY

NECK
Very muscular and arched.

BODY
Moderately long, between foreign and cobby types. High, angular shoulders. Heavy-boned. Very muscular.

LEGS AND PAWS
Hind legs longer than forelegs. Muscular. Small, slightly oval paws.

TAIL
Moderately long, thick at the base, tapering slightly to the tip.

forehead, mascara lines on the cheeks, rings on the tail, broken necklace on the chest, and broken rings on the paws.

VARIETIES
- **silver:** black spots; pale silver ground color; brick red nose; black paw pads
- **bronze:** very dark browns spots; light

brown ground color; brick red nose
- **smoke or black smoke:** jet black spots; smoke gray ground color; black nose and paw pads

NOTES
Allowable outcross breeds: none.

FAULTS
Round or short head. Small ears. Full cheeks, except in adult males. Muzzle too pointed or too short. Small, round, or Oriental type eyes. Amber eyes in cats over 18 months old. Massive or Oriental type body. Spots that are touching. Continuous necklaces.

CHARACTERISTICS
Lively, playful, active, and well-balanced, Egyptian Maus are neither aggressive nor nervous. They do not like agitation. Reserved toward strangers and sociable around other cats, they are gentle and very affectionate toward their owner. They have a soft, pleasant voice.
They can adapt to apartment life but do not tolerate solitude well. A garden lets these athletic hunters blow off steam. They require only weekly brushing.

(▼) F.I.Fe   (■) L.O.O.F.   (★) C.F.A.   (◆) T.I.C.A.

BLACK SILVER SPOTTED TABBY

Munchk

Country of Origin: United States
Other Name: Munchkin Cat

A long body and short legs, like a Dachshund

In 1991 in New York's Madison Square Garden, a strange cat with short legs was shown. It was nicknamed the "Dachshund cat" or "Basset cat." Already by the 1930s, cats of the same type were reported in England but forgotten during World War II. A specimen was described in Stalingrad in 1953.

These cats are named after the inhabitants of Munchkin Land in Fleming's famous movie The Wizard of Oz (1939).

The ancestors of today's Munchkins are descended from Blackberry, a black cat found in Louisiana around 1982.

The gene responsible for short legs, the basis for this spontaneous mutation, is dominant.

T.I.C.A. recognized the breed in 1995 and published a standard the same year. The first Munchkins arrived in France in 1993.

TORTOISESHELL AND WHITE SHORTHAIR

179

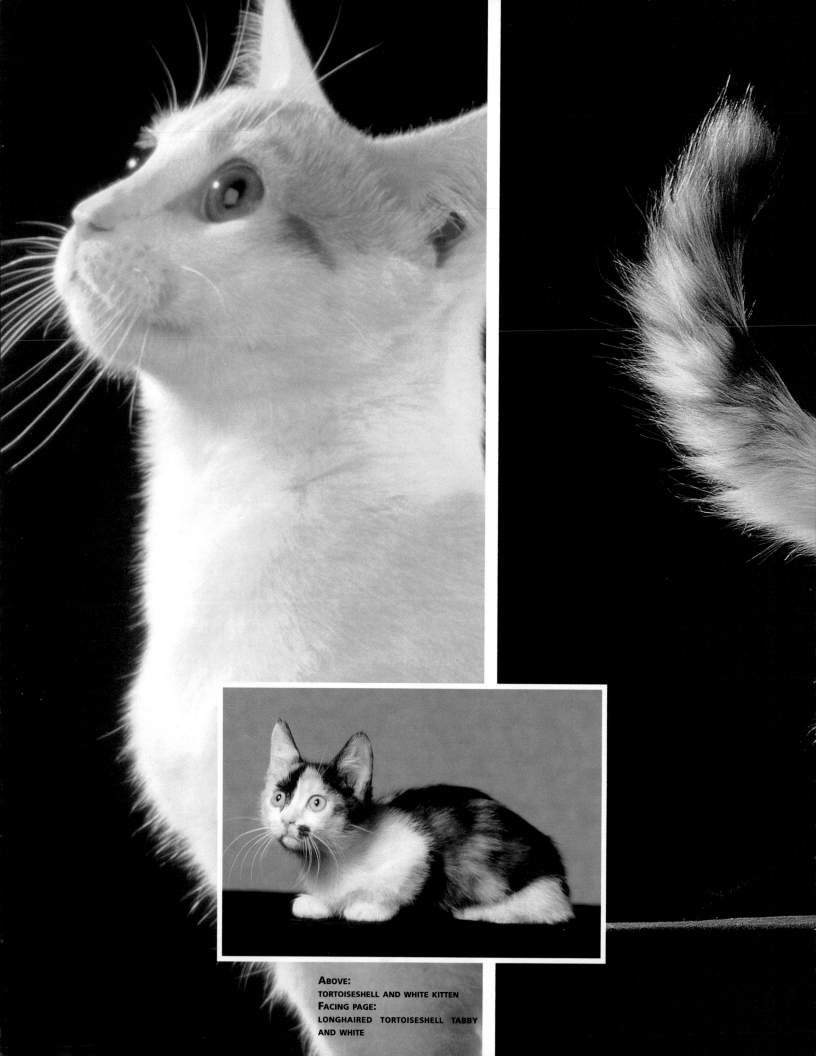

ABOVE:
TORTOISESHELL AND WHITE KITTEN
FACING PAGE:
LONGHAIRED TORTOISESHELL TABBY
AND WHITE

Munchkin

RED AND WHITE

GENERAL
Very short-limbed cat.
Weight: 2.2 to 4 kg.

EYES
Large, walnut-shaped, well-spaced, set slightly at a slant. There is no relationship between eye color and coat color (◆).

NECK
Moderately long, thick, and muscular.

BODY
Medium-sized. Round chest. Broad shoulders. Spine as flexible as in other breeds. Moderate to heavy bone and muscle structure.

FAULTS
Too stocky. Weakness in the back. Arched, too heavily boned paws. Low, prominent sternum. Lockets or white buttons (■).

HEAD
Shaped like an equilateral triangle with rounded contours. Rounded skull. Flat forehead. Cheeks can be broad, particularly in males. Slender muzzle with a slight break (◆). Moderately long nose. Firm but not prominent chin.

EARS
Triangular, moderately broad, straight.

LEGS AND PAWS
Short, medium-boned, very muscular. Medium-sized, round, compact paws.

NOTES
Allowable outcross breeds: shorthaired or longhaired cats, while avoiding heavy, massive breeds (■).

TAIL
Moderately thick, tapering to a round tip. Well-furnished, held high and very straight in motion.

COAT
Two varieties:
- shorthaired
- semilonghaired
Silky texture, moderate undercoat. All colors are recognized.

CHARACTERISTICS
While the Munchkin's short legs do not hinder the cat's mobility, they do prevent it from jumping as high as other cats.
Active, lively, and playful, Munchkins are very sociable and affectionate. They adore their owner.
They are easy to groom, especially the shorthaired variety.

(▼) F.I.Fe   (■) L.O.O.F.   (★) C.F.A.   (◆) T.I.C.A.

182

Ocicat

Country of Origin: United States
Other Name: Oci

A spotted athlete with mascara markings around her eyes

"Ocicat" is a combination of the words "ocelot" (a spotted wild cat of the Americas) and "cat." Indeed, this breed has a spotted coat that makes it resemble a small wild cat. In 1964, Virginia Daly, a breeder in Berkeley, Michigan, crossed a Siamese-Abyssinian mix with a chocolate point Siamese in an effort to obtain tabby point Siamese cats. A male in the litter named Tonga and wearing an ivory coat with gold spots was unfortunately neutered. Daly continued her work while other breeders, including Tom Brown, crossed Abyssinians, Siamese, spotted Oriental Shorthairs, Egyptian Maus, and American Shorthairs in order to obtain the Ocicat's current morphology.

The breed was officially recognized by the C.F.A. in 1986, and T.I.C.A. published a standard in 1988. Outcrosses with Abyssinians are now forbidden. In 1989, the first Ocicats were sent to France. Though popular in the United States, the Ocicat is still very rare in Europe.

**CINNAMON
SPOTTED
TABBY**

183

ABOVE AND FACING PAGE: CHOCOLATE SPOTTED TABBY

Ocicat

GENERAL
Large, medium-limbed type, powerful, very muscular, solidly built cat whose spotted coat gives it a wild appearance.
Weight: 2.5 to 6 kg.

CHOCOLATE SILVER SPOTTED TABBY

CINNAMON SPOTTED TABBY

EARS
Moderately large, alert, set at the corners of the head. Lynx tips are appreciated.

EYES
Large, almond-shaped, set slightly at a slant, separated by more than one eye-width. All colors are allowed except blue and are not related to coat color. Colorpoints

COAT
Hair is short but long enough to have several bands of color. Fine, smooth, satiny coat with shiny highlights. Spotted and agouti coat (spotted tabby coat). Each hair, except those at the tip of the tail, has several bands of color.

kings around the eyes and cheeks.

NOTES
Allowable outcross breeds: none.

FAULTS
Massive or stocky body. Blue eyes (▼). Weak and indistinct markings. White spotting or white locket.

HEAD
Slightly triangular, as long as it is wide, with rounded contours. The profile exhibits a slight inward curve. Jowls are tolerated in adult males. Well-defined, broad, slightly angular muzzle. Slight whisker pinch (▼). Slight rise from the bridge of the nose to the brow. Strong chin.

CINNAMON SPOTTED TABBY

have blue eyes (■). Even, intense color is preferred.

NECK
Arched.

BODY
Large, fairly long, semi-foreign, powerful, but never massive. Fairly deep chest. Well-developed bone and muscle structure.

LEGS AND PAWS
Moderately long, powerful, and muscular. Compact, oval paws.

TAIL
Fairly long, moderately slender, tapering slightly to a dark tip.

The recognized colors are:
- brown (or tawny)
- chocolate
- lilac
- blue
- cinnamon
- fawn

These six colors also exist in silver varieties. All colors must be clear and pleasant. The lightest coloration is normally found on the face, chin, and lower jaw. Markings consist of hairs with darker tipping. They should be clear and distinct. They are darker on the face, legs, and tail than on the body. Dark tail tip. Tabby "M" on the forehead. Mascara mar-

BLUE SILVER SPOTTED TABBY

CHARACTERISTICS
The Ocicat is very lively, highly active, curious, and playful. Despite his similarity to a small wild cat, he is very friendly, gentle, and affectionate. In fact, he will not tolerate solitude. Ocicats are loyal and exclusive like the Siamese, but they have a softer voice. They are very accepting of children but fairly dominant toward other cats. They adapt easily to new living conditions. They are easy to groom, as they simply require regular brushing.

BLACK SILVER SPOTTED TABBY

(▼) F.I.Fe   (■) L.O.O.F.   (★) C.F.A.   (◆) T.I.C.A.

186

Ojos Azules

Extraordinary dark blue eyes

This new breed is descended from *Cornflower*, a tortie female discovered in New Mexico in 1984. She had very dark blue eyes, a feature normally found only in white or colorpoint cats. The breed's Spanish name means "blue eyes." These cats have blue eyes regardless of coat color. In 1991, T.I.C.A. published a standard. The breed is very rare.

187

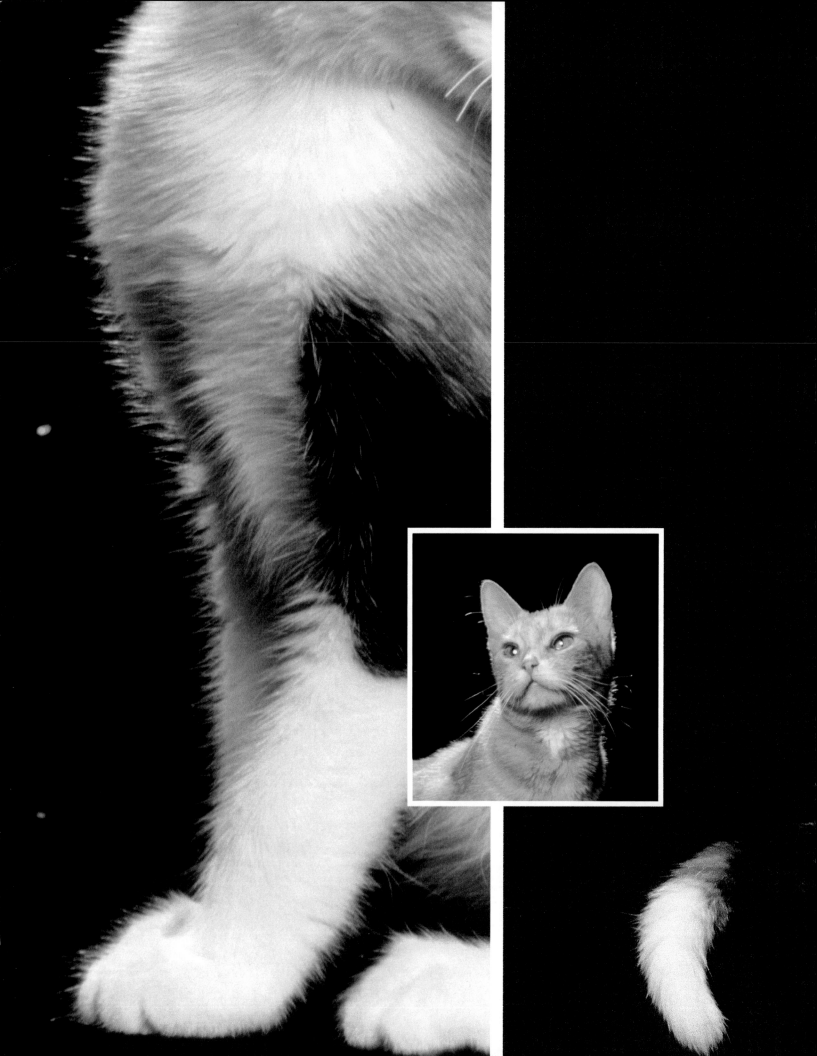

Oriental Shorthair

GENERAL
Medium-sized, long-limbed, svelte, elegant but muscular.
Long limbs. Short hair.
Weight: 4 to 6.5 kg.

HEAD
Long, can be inscribed in an isosceles triangle. Straight profile without stop. The skull, seen in profile, is slightly convex. Slender, well-formed muzzle. Long, straight nose. Medium-sized chin.

EARS
Large, well-spaced, broad at the base, pointed.

EYES
Medium-sized, almond-shaped, set at a pronounced slant.

Separated by one eye-width. Emerald green or jade except in the white Oriental Shorthair, which has blue eyes. Yellow or copper eyes are accepted for red and cream coats (◆)(▼). Note that the color may not be acquired until the cat is one year old.

NECK
Long, slender.

BODY
Long, svelte, slender, tubular. Narrow abdomen. Fine-boned. Firm, long muscles.

LEGS AND PAWS
Long, slender, proportionate to the body. Forelegs slightly shorter than hind legs. Fine-boned. Small, oval paws.

TAIL
Long and slender, even at the base, tapering to a point.

COAT
Hair is short, dense, fine, silky, lying flat.

FOUR MAIN GROUPS OF VARIETIES:

- Solid coats: solid color without stripes or tabby markings. Pure white, ebony, blue, chocolate, lilac, cinnamon, fawn.

TORTOISESHELL

- Tortoiseshell coats and variants: orange, black, and chocolate.
- Coats in which the base of the hair is diluted:
- Smoke: dilute color in a short band at the base.
- Silver: pigmentation at the hair tip (tipping).
- Tabby coats:
- Blotched: broad stripes.
- Mackerel: narrow stripes perpendicular to the spine.
- Spotted: circular, evenly distributed spots.

The spotted tabby Oriental Shorthair, also called Maus, is often

mistaken for the Egyptian Mau. Between stripes and spots, agouti-type hairs with alternating dark and light bands.

CONDITION
Very muscular, firm, but not emaciated. Neither underweight or heavy (◆).

NOTES
Allowable outcross breeds: Siamese, Balinese, Oriental Longhair.

FAULTS
Round, broad, excessively short head. Muzzle too short, too broad. Presence of a stop or whisker pinch. Receding or massive chin. Ears too small, too close together. Round, small eyes. Short, massive body. Short legs. Heavy-boned. Rough coat.

CHARACTERISTICS
Like the Siamese, Oriental Shorthairs are very lively, extraverted, proud, and captivating. They are sociable and do not like being alone. These playful cats can tolerate children.
They are affectionate and often very possessive, even tyrannical, toward their owner. Indifference is not acceptable to them. They are "talkative" and have a loud voice.
They have the temperament of a hunter.
Female cats are sexually precocious (entering puberty by 9 months) and have frequent heats. They are more prolific than average for domestic cats. They are easy to groom, as weekly.

(▼) F.I.Fe   (■) L.O.O.F.   (★) C.F.A.   (◆) T.I.C.A.

Persian

Country of Origin: Great Britain
Other Name: Longhair

The world's most famous breed

Longhaired cats were unknown in Europe until around the mid-16th century. The Persian's first ancestors were imported from Persia (now Iran) to Italy in the 17th century by Pietro della Valle. Later, Nicholas-Claude Fabri de Peiresec, an advisor to the Parliament of Aix-en-Provence, brought two cats to France from Turkey (perhaps they were Angora in type). These cats were highly prized by the European aristocracy. Louis XV had a white angora Persian. In the first half of the 19th century, some "Persians" bred in Italy and brought to France and England were crossed with "Persians" of Turkish origin. The first specimens were shown in London's Crystal Palace in 1871. At that time, British breeders organized a selective breeding program. Crosses were made with Angoras to improve the coat. In addition, a systematic effort aimed at increasing the range of colors and patterns was begun, leading to over 200 varieties today. Thus, the smoke Persian, the product of black, white, and blue Persians, was shown in Brighton in 1872. A cat named Silver was the first chinchilla Persian shown in London in 1888. Colorpoint Persians, called Himalayans in the United States and considered a separate breed by T.I.C.A. and Kmehr (or Kmer) in Germany, appeared around 1920. Tabby Persians, which appeared over a century ago, were shown in Paris in 1927 as "tigers." Also in the 19th century, British breeders selected the roundest, most massive cats. Around 1930, American breeders obtained an extremely short-limbed type called the "Peke face" (after the Pekingese dog). Possibly the world's most famous feline breed, the Persian was probably used to create the Birman and the British Shorthair.

Persian

GENERAL
Medium to large in size.
Short-limbed type with a massive body.
The limbs are short. The fur is very long. Royal, majestic bearing.
Weight: 3.5 to 7 kg.

COLORPOINT

chinchilla, silver, and golden; blue in the colorpoint; heterochromatic in some white-coated Persians, etc.).

NECK
Short, strong, very muscular.

BODY
Medium to large, massive (cobby), powerful. Broad, deep chest; shoulders and hips of equal width. Broad, short back. Short abdomen. Short, massive bones. Firm, well-developed muscles.

HEAD
Round, massive, domed. Very broad, round skull. Rounded forehead. Round, full cheeks. Strong, prominent cheekbones. Short, broad nose, sometimes slightly turned up. Marked break between the eyes. Short, broad muzzle. Strong, full, well-developed chin. Broad, powerful jaws (▼).

EARS
Small, rounded at the tip, widely spaced. Not too open at the base, well-furnished inside.

EYES
Large, round, wide open, well-spaced. The intense, deep color corresponds to that of the coat (gold to copper for all colors; green in the

LEGS AND PAWS
Short, strong, straight. Powerful bones, well-developed muscles. Broad, round, strong paws. Long tufts of hair between the toes.

TAIL
Short, in proportion to the body, well-furnished

with very long hairs forming a plume. Carried fairly low.

COAT
Very fine fur with long hair in the topcoat and undercoat. Dense, silky, long hair on the entire body (10 cm on average and up to 20 cm on the frill). All colors are recognized.

CLASSIC VARIETIES
Self-colored coats (solid with no stripes or tabby markings). All colors

(white, black, blue, red, etc.). White Persians with a pink nose and paw pads can have three eye colors:
- Light blue: the most prized and the oldest officially recognized color
- Orange or copper
- Heterochromatic ("odd-eyed"): one light blue eye and one orange eye.

- Tortoiseshell coats and variants. Combination of patches of hair with orange pigmentation and patches of black hair. Normally, only females can be tortoiseshell.

- Coats in which the base of the hair is diluted: smoke Persians. The hair root is pure white, and the tip is the darkest possible. The ideal proportion is 1/3 white and 2/3 colored. The most common colorations are black smoke, blue smoke, chocolate smoke, lilac smoke, tortie smoke, etc. Orange

coloration produces a so-called "smoke cameo" coat.

Bicolor coats with white patches. Among the recognized varieties (in combination with white) are black, blue, chocolate, lilac, red, and cream. Bicolor coats include:
• strict bicolor: white covering 1/3 to 1/2 the body
• harlequin: white covering 1/2 to 3/4 the body
• van: the entire body is white except for the tail and two spots forming a hood around the eyes and the base of the ears (cap)

- Tabby coats, including:
• blotched tabby: broad stripes, characteristic "M" on forehead, dark lines (mascara markings) on the cheeks, continuous necklaces on the upper chest, butterfly wings between the shoulders, rings around the legs and tail.

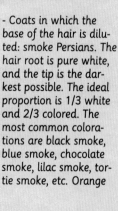

- Chinchilla Persians and variants, originating from a cross between a smoke Persian and a silver tabby Persian. General appearance of the classic Persian but often smaller in size, less short-limbed, and with a less massive head. Very light coat with silver highlights. Tipping (dark pigmentation limited to the hair tip) covers 1/8 the length of the guard hair. The base of the hair is white. Green eyes and a brick red nose with a dark outline.

VARIANTS

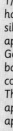

•Mackerel tabby: narrow stripes that are parallel to each other and perpendicular to a longitudinal stripe running down the spine
• spotted tabby: circular spots evenly distributed up to the belly. Hairs between spots are agouti-type (with alternating dark and light bands)

- Silver shaded Persian: base of the hair is pure white. Tipping covers 1/3 the length of the hair, producing the silver shaded appearance.
Gold shaded Persian: base of the hair is apricot, with black tipping. This gives the coat its apricot or gold shaded appearance.

- Colorpoint Persians: produced by crossing a Siamese with a Persian. Persian wearing a Siamese coat. Blue eyes.
•Seal colorpoint: buff body, dark brown markings
• Blue colorpoint: white body, blue-gray markings
• Lilac colorpoint: white body, pinkish-gray markings
• red colorpoint: cream-white body, red markings.

Colorpoint Persian kittens are born white. Markings appear by around 6 months.

- "Peke face" Persians: This supertype is not always very popular. It suffers from complications involving head deformities (overproductive tear ducts that lead to constant tearing, underbite, difficulty breathing due to a pushed-in nose, etc.).

NOTES
Allowable outcross breeds: Exotic Shorthair (shorthaired Persian).

FAULTS
Long or narrow head. Long nose, narrow muzzle, obvious underbite. Large, pointed ears that are too close together. Small, slanted eyes too pale in color. Narrow, slender, long, high-standing body. Tail too long. Oval paws, long toes. Disqualify: lockets or buttons; kink in the tail, serious jaw deformity (■).

CHARACTERISTICS
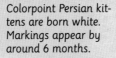
The placid, calm, phlegmatic, sedentary Persian is perfectly suited to apartment life. Sociable, peaceful, never aggressive, gentle, and very affectionate, he is very attached to his owner. Persians get along well with other cats, dogs, and children. They are more distant toward strangers. For their well-being, they need a tranquil life. They can tolerate solitude. They rarely use their soft voice.
Persians reach maturity at the age of two. They enter puberty late (at approximately 12 months). The breed is not very prolific, and birthing is difficult. Grooming (brushing, combing, and cleaning) is a considerable undertaking. The Persian's long hair is prone to the rapid formation of knots and tufts. It is therefore essential to untangle the coat every day. Persians shed in spring and summer. Their eyes, which produce tears constantly, must be cleaned regularly.

(▼) F.I.Fe.   (■) L.O.O.F.   (★) C.F.A.   (◆) T.I.C.A.

Ragdoll

Country of Origin: United States

Big and floppy, like a ragdoll

Around 1960 in Riverside, east of Los Angeles, a white Turkish Angora type female named Josephine was born in the home of Ms. Pennels. This cat was crossed with a gloved Birman type tom named Daddy Warbucks. Their litter sparked the interest of Ann Baker, who set about intense inbreeding. Thus was created the so-called Ragdoll breed, named for the way the cats typically relax completely, with low muscle tone.
The Ragdoll was approved in the United States in 1965. In 1971, Baker founded the International Ragdoll Cat Association (I.R.C.A.).

In 1969, two Ragdolls from Baker's cattery were sent to Great Britain. A British Ragdoll club was founded in 1987.

The G.C.C.G. recognized the breed in 1991, and the F.I.Fe. recognized it in 1992.

The Ragdoll arrived in Germany and France in 1985 and 1986, respectively. In 1993, a French breed club was created.

The Ragdoll is quite uncommon outside the United States.

Ragdoll

GENERAL
Large, solid, muscular, powerful.
Weight: 4.5 to 9 kg.

HEAD
Medium-sized, broad, slightly wedge-shaped with rounded contours. Skull is flat between the ears. Slightly rounded forehead. Well-developed cheeks. Rounded, moderately long, well-developed muzzle. Nose with gentle break. Well-developed chin.

EARS
Medium-sized, broad at the base, well-spaced, pointed slightly forward, rounded at the tips.

EYES
Large, oval, slightly slanted. As intense a shade of blue as possible, corresponding to coat color.

NECK
Short and strong.

BODY
Large, long, well-built. Broad, well-developed chest. Heavy, solid hindquarters. Medium-boned.

LEGS AND PAWS
Moderately long, medium-boned. Hind legs slightly longer than forelegs. Large, round, compact paws with tufts of hair between the toes.

TAIL
Long, proportionate to the body, fairly thick at the base, tapering slightly to the tip. Well-furnished and fluffy.

COAT
Semilong, soft, silky hair lying flat against the body. In motion, the hair separates into tufts. Very substantial ruff.
Four classic colors (seal, blue, chocolate, lilac). Three patterns for coats with points:
- Colorpoint: body lighter in color than extremities (points).
- Mitted or gloved: also with Siamese pattern, but with gloves on the paws. White blaze on the nose. White chin.
- Bicolor: colorpoint with white extending over the face in an inverted V; four white paws. White chest and belly.
Coloring is not complete until the cat is two years old and darkens with age.

NOTES
Allowable outcross breeds: none.

FAULTS
Narrow head. Nose with a stop (▼). Large or small, pointed ears. Almond-shaped eyes (▼). Neck too long or too slender. Stocky body. Narrow chest. Short legs. Lack of interdigital hair. Short tail. Short hair. Disqualify: white markings in the colorpoint; absence of white chin in the mitted; dark markings on the white mask in the bicolor. Eyes of a color other than blue (▼).

CHARACTERISTICS
The Ragdoll's calmness and his debonair, docile temperament make him a very pleasant companion. He does not tolerate agitation and noise. Ragdolls are sociable, getting along well with other cats and with dogs. Very affectionate and loving, they like company and despise solitude. They adapt very well to apartment life. They are not noisy.
They do not reach full size until the age of three or four. In terms of grooming, they require frequent brushing and combing.

(▼) F.I.Fe.   (■) L.O.O.F.   (★) C.F.A.   (◆) T.I.C.A.

208

Birman

Country of Origin: France
Other Name: Sacred Cat of Burma

Very impressive, with dark blue eyes and white gloves

Having appeared recently in Europe, this cat's origins are still mysterious. British travelers are thought to have brought back a pair of cats from the so-called Lao-tsun Temple in Burma. A certain Ms. Leotardi in southern France owned Poupée de Madalpour, a seal point Birman shown in Paris in 1926. This cat's parents, from Burma, were given to Leotardi by a certain Ms. Thadde-Haddish.

Actually, the first specimens resulted from a cross between a Siamese with white markings on the paws and a longhaired cat (Angora or Persian) made in the 1920s in the region of Nice, in France. By around 1930, a male seal point named Dieu d'Arakan was the star of the shows.

The breed nearly disappeared during World War II. After the war, colorpoint Persian blood was added to limit inbreeding. In 1950, the breed was named Chat Sacré de Birmanie (Birman in English) in order to avoid any confusion with "Burmese", the adjective form of the word Burma.

Introduced to the United States in 1959-1960 and to Great Britain in 1965, where it was officially recognized, this highly prized breed has become very popular.

Birman

GENERAL
Medium-sized, medium-limbed type but imposing and massive.
Weight: 4.5 to 8 kg.
Longhaired

EARS
Medium-sized with rounded tips, moderately spaced to well-spaced. Slightly slanted. Well-furnished on the inside surface.

EYES
Large, nearly round, well-spaced. Color: blue, as dark as possible.

HEAD
Large, broad, fairly round. Slightly longer than it is wide. Fairly rounded skull. Slightly domed forehead. Full cheeks, high, prominent cheekbones. Roman nose of medium length with a defined (◆) or absent (▼) stop. Well-developed muzzle. Strong. Firm chin.

TAIL
Moderately long, carried erect. Plume.

COAT
Silky hair, semilong to long on the ruff, body, flanks, and tail. Short on the face and limbs. Sparse undercoat. Coat pigmented only on the extremities or points (mask, ears, paws, and tail), as in the Siamese.

2/3 the distance between the large paw pad and the hock.
The darker markings can be seal point (dark brown), chocolate point (light brown), blue point (gray-blue), lilac point (pinkish steel gray), red point (reddish-brown), or cream point.
The rest of the coat varies from white to cream. The paw pads are pink or pink with spots of color.
Kittens are born almost entirely white. The points and gloves do not appear until around 1-2 months. The color of the body and markings is not final until adulthood. In addition, the coat darkens with age.

NOTES
Allowable outcross breeds: none.

FAULTS
White or colored markings on the chest or belly. Disqualify: a non-gloved toe. White on the points.

NECK
Medium-sized, muscular.

BODY
Fairly long, fairly heavy (semi-cobby). Strong boned; powerful, firm muscles.

LEGS AND PAWS
Moderately long, strong. Heavy-boned, muscular. Round, firm paws. Tufts of fur between the toes.

A good contrast between the color of the points and the rest of the body is required. White markings, or gloves, on the paws. These absolutely pure white gloves must stop at the joint or transition between the toes and the metacarpus, which they should not go past. On the plantar surface of the hind paws, the gloves end in a point (gauntlets) at 1/2 to

CHARACTERISTICS
Halfway between the Persian and the Siamese, the Birman is calm, well-balanced, and neither passive nor exuberant. He is friendly toward other cats and toward dogs.
Playful Birmans are good companions for children, but they also like peace and quiet. Gentle, affectionate (especially males), and often somewhat possessive, Birmans do not tolerate indifference and are even less fond of solitude. They have a soft voice. Outside, they are hardy and athletic, making excellent hunters.
They require daily brushing during the shedding season. Otherwise, weekly brushing and combing are enough.

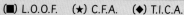

(▼) F.I.Fe.   (■) L.O.O.F.   (★) C.F.A.   (◆) T.I.C.A.

Scottish Fold

A roly-poly guy with little ears set in a caplike fashion, flat against the head

*I*n his 1897 Treatise on Animal Breeding, Professor Cornevin indicated a breed of shorthaired cat with pendulous ears that was fattened for eating in its native China. A spontaneous mutation by a dominant gene that caused the ear flap to fold forward was first observed in Scotland in 1961. William Ross, a shepherd in Tayside, and his wife Mary noticed a white female cat named Susie with folded ears who lived at the McRae family's neighboring farm. Susie gave birth to Snooks, a white female with the same type of ears. When crossed with a British Shorthair, she gave birth to a white male named Snowball. This new breed was named after the "folded ear" mutation. Unfortunately, limb, tail, and joint deformities linked to the dominant Fd gene appeared, to such an extent that the G.C.C.F. discontinued registration of the breed in 1973.

In 1971, Mary Ross sent some Scottish Folds to Neil Todd, an American geneticist in Massachusetts who set about breeding the cats again. Crosses were made with British Shorthairs, Exotic Shorthairs, and American Shorthairs in order to prevent severe joint disorders.
The C.F.A. and then T.I.C.A. recognized the breed, which was highly successful in the United States. A return to Europe began in 1980, with the first Scottish Fold born in France in 1982. Recognized neither by the F.I.Fe. nor the G.C.C.F., the Scottish Fold is relatively rare throughout Europe.

In the United States, a Scottish Fold was crossed with a Persian to produce a new, longhaired version called the Highland Fold or Longhaired Scottish Fold, which is recognized by T.I.C.A.

A cross with rexes made in Germany in 1987 gave rise to the Pudelkatze or Poodle Cat, a curly-coated feline with pendulous ears. With a very limited population, the Pudelkatze is not yet recognized as a new breed.

213

Scottish Fold

GENERAL
Short-limbed type, stout, stocky, entirely round in form.
Weight: 2.5 to 6 kg.

NECK
Short and muscular.

BODY
Medium-sized, stout, rounded, very muscular. Medium-boned.

LEGS AND PAWS
Length in proportion to the body. Medium-boned. Round, compact paws.

COAT
Two varieties:
- short, thick, tight, very dense, fluffy, resilient coat
- semilong: this variety is called the Highland Fold.
All colors are recognized. Chocolate, lilac, and Siamese markings are not allowed (*).

FAULTS
Head too slender, pointed. Stop too pronounced. Disqualify: tail too short, lacking flexibility due to abnormally thick vertebrae.

HEAD
Round. Domed forehead. Rounded cheeks. Jowls allowed in adult males. Broad, short nose. Slight stop accepted. Well-rounded muzzle. Round whisker pad. Firm chin.

EARS
Small, folded forward in a caplike fashion. Well-spaced, rounded at the tips.

EYES
Large, round, fairly well-spaced. The color corresponds to that of the coat.

TAIL
No longer than 2/3 the length of the body. Thick at the base, tapering to a rounded tip. Very supple and flexible.

NOTES
Allowable outcross breeds: British Shorthair (■), Exotic Shorthair, American Shorthair (*).

CHARACTERISTICS
Scottish Folds are especially peaceful, non-dominant, and friendly toward other cats and toward dogs. Gentle, very affectionate, loving, and very playful, they adore family life. They are discrete and have a soft voice.
Hardy and resistant, these cats are excellent hunters. In terms of grooming, they require weekly brushing. During shedding, their fluffy coat must be combed regularly. It is best to keep an eye on their ears. In order to prevent bone deformities, two cats with folded ears should not be mated together. Instead, the Scottish Fold is crossed with prick-eared cats like the British Shorthair or American Shorthair.
The "folded ear" characteristic is not visible until the third or fourth week, and the degree of folding cannot be observed until the fifth or sixth week.

(▼) F.I.Fe   (■) L.O.O.F.   (★) C.F.A.   (◆) T.I.C.A.

Selkirk Rex

Country of Origin:
United States
Other Name:
Selkirk Rex Longhair,
Sheep Cat

Curly-coated like a Poodle or sheep

I n 1987 in Wyoming, a cross between a flat-coated female and a curly-coated male produced a curly-coated female named Miss DePesto of NoFace, who was adopted by Jeri Newman, a breeder of Persians in Montana. In 1988, Miss DePesto was crossed with Photo Finish, a black Persian, and gave birth to three curly-coated kittens. Later bred to one of her kittens, she again produced three curly-coated offspring. Jeri Newman named this new breed after the nearby Selkirk Mountains.

This spontaneous mutation is caused by a new dominant gene different from other curly-coated genes.

While the Devon Rex resembles E.T., the Selkirk Rex looks more like a Poodle. Popular in the United States, the Selkirk Rex appeared in Europe in 1990 and is still rare.

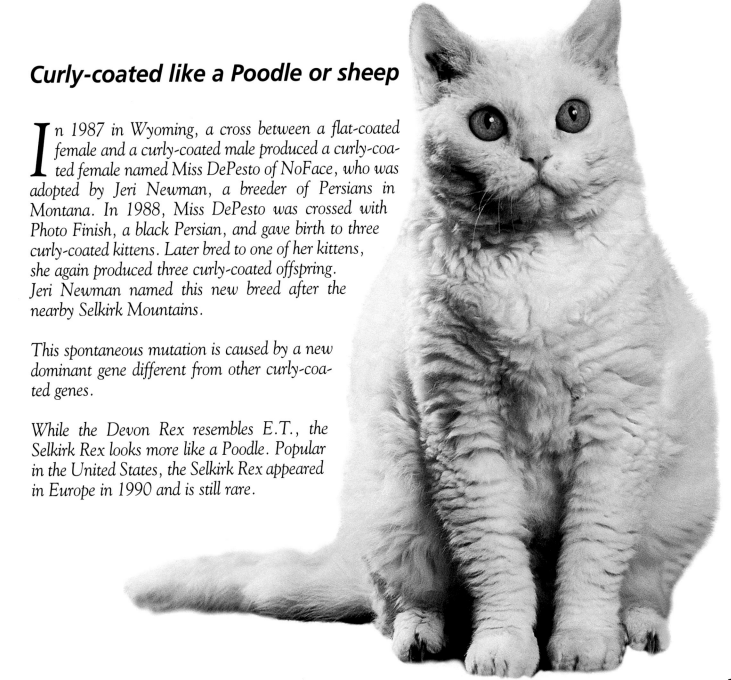

Selkirk Rex

GENERAL
Medium-sized, the largest and shaggiest of the curly-coated feline breeds.
Heavy-boned.
Weight: 3 to 5 kg.

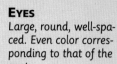

EARS
Medium-sized, well-spaced, ending in slightly rounded tips. Curly hair on the inside.

EYES
Large, round, well-spaced. Even color corresponding to that of the coat.

condition, especially in females. Kittens are born curly-coated. The curls relax and reform around 8-10 months. The coat continues to develop until the age of two. Shorthaired and longhaired varieties. All colors are recognized (■), with clearly defined shades being preferred. White lockets are allowed (◆).

NOTES
Allowable outcross breeds: none.

FAULTS
Disqualify: break in the nose. Crossed eyes. Kink in the tail (■).

BODY
Moderately long, rectangular, stout, heavy. Muscular and strong boned.

HEAD
Medium-sized, round, and broad. Skull with a gentle curve. Round forehead. Full cheeks in both sexes. Short, angular muzzle. Hooked nose, slight stop. Curly whiskers and eyebrows. Heavy jaws.

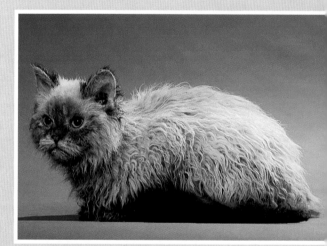

NECK
Short, thick.

LEGS AND PAWS
Moderately long. Medium to strong bone and muscle structure. Large, round paws.

TAIL
Moderately long, thick, with a rounded tip.

COAT
Thick coat with well-separated curls that are especially numerous on the neck and tail and cover the entire body. No hairless areas. Thick undercoat.
The curliness of the coat varies with the climate, seasons, and hormonal

CHARACTERISTICS
This active cat with a debonair, calm character gets along well with other cats and with dogs.
The playful Selkirk Rex is an excellent companion for children.
Gentle and affectionate, Selkirks are very pleasant to live with. They adapt well to apartment life.
They need minimal grooming. Light brushing twice a month is enough. They should be bathed several days before a show.

(▼) F.I.Fe   (■) L.O.O.F.   (★) C.F.A.   (◆) T.I.C.A.

220

Siamese

Country of Origin: Thailand
Other Name: Royal Cat of Siam

This royal cat is born all white

This very old breed is mentioned in a manuscript dated 1350 from Ayuthia, then the capital of Siam, now Thailand. Note also that in the early 19th century, German naturalist Pallas described white cats with dark extremities in central Asia. In Siam, the breed was reserved to the royal family and carefully guarded in the royal palace. However, two Siamese of unknown origin were successfully shown at London's Crystal Palace in 1871. In 1884, Sir Owen Gould, English Consul to Bangkok, obtained a pair named Pho and Mia. He brought them home and entrusted them to his sister, Ms. Veley. Pho and Mia produced the first champions awarded in 1885.

That same year, August Pavie, a French diplomat, also brought home two specimens from Bangkok. They had been presented to the Jardin des Plantes by Mr. Paire, France's resident minister in Siam.

In 1893, also in Paris, Mr. Oustalet, a professor at the Paris Museum of Natural History, drafted an article on the "Cats of Siam" brought back by the daughter-in-law of President Carnot.

In 1889, Harrison Weir published Our Cats and All About Them, including a chapter on the Siamese. The first standard was established by the G.C.C.F. in 1892. The first breed club, the Siamese Cat Club, was created in England in 1901. The "royal" Siamese thus began its rich career.

In 1890, the first Siamese cats were introduced to the United States. The Siamese has enjoyed considerable popularity since 1920. The breed's current morphology is quite different from its original type, which was rounder and more massive. Crossed eyes, a kinked tail, and even green eyes were allowed. Since then, selective breeding following a certain aesthetic has refined the breed's traits. The head is now triangular, the tail has no kinks and is therefore longer, and crossed eyes have been eliminated, in part.

Siamese

GENERAL
Medium-sized, long-limbed, Oriental type, svelte, elegant, flexible, and muscular.
Weight: 2.5 to 5.5 kg.

HEAD
Medium-sized, can be inscribed in a triangle formed by the straight lines running from the nose to the top of the ears. Equilateral triangle in the British type Siamese, isosceles in the American type. Skull slightly convex in profile. Flat cheeks, but jowls allowed in adult males. Slender muzzle. Long, straight nose without break. No whisker pinch. Firm chin in line with the tip of the nose.

EARS
Large, broad at the base, well-spaced, pointed, an extension of the sides of the triangle.

EYES
Medium-sized, almond-shaped, Oriental type, set at a slant. Color: the most intense blue possible.

NECK
Long, thin, graceful, slightly arched.

BODY
Long, svelte, tubular. Shoulders and hips of the same width. Fine-boned. Firm muscles.

LEGS AND PAWS
Long, slender. Fine bone and muscle structure. Small, oval paws.

TAIL
Long, thin, narrow at the base, tapering to a point.

COAT
- Short, fine, dense, silky, shiny, lying flat against the body. Almost no undercoat.
- Color: pigmentation on the extremities of the body (points): face (mask), ears, legs, and tail. The color of these darker areas must be as even as possible. There must be a clear contrast between the color of the points and that of the body. All Siamese are colorpoints.
The most traditional colors (recognized by the C.F.A.) are:
- seal point: dark brown markings (points); egg-shell white, light buff background
- blue point: steel blue points; cold, bluish-white background
- chocolate point: light brown points, ivory background
- lilac point: pinkish-buff points; off-white to ivory (magnolia) background
The Siamese, once called the Colorpoint Shorthair, can also be:

- red point: reddish-golden points, apricot-shaded white background
- cream point: cream points, cream-shaded white background
- tortie point (seal tortie, blue tortie, chocolate tortie, etc.): tortoise-shell markings on points
- seal tortie point: brown spots on the points, red blaze on the face, light brown background
- tabby point: stripes around the legs and tail, striped mask, etc.
- particolor: pure white spots on part of the mask, legs, and body
Siamese kittens are

born white. By the fifth day, the points start to appear. The coldest areas of the body darken; this is why a Siamese cat living outside in winter is darker than one living inside. Coloration is final at 12-15 months. In addition, the body pigmentation darkens with age. Ghost markings should fade by adulthood.

NOTES
Allowable outcross breeds: Balinese, Oriental Shorthair, Oriental Longhair, and Burmese to obtain the Tonkinese.

Today, there are several types of Siamese:
- American: head shaped like an isosceles triangle, narrow skull, eyes reduced to slits, enormous ears, spectacular neck, tubular body, endlessly long legs. This is the hypertype or supertype.
- British: intermediate between the old type and the American type. Head shaped like an equilateral triangle, large ears, body is long but not extreme. This type is more popular, especially in France.

In addition, breeders faithful to the old Siamese type have created Siamese types that do not comply with today's standards and thus have new names:
- Apple Head or Apple Face: old type with a rounder head recreated by American breeders in the Traditional Cat Association (T.C.A.) founded in 1987.
- Thai: old type obtained in Germany by crossing Siamese with British Shorthairs and self-colored European Shorthairs.

FAULTS

Eyes too pale. Obvious flaw in the tail. Imperfect coat. Disqualify: eyes another color than blue. White markings in the points except in particolors. Clear spots on the belly.

CHARACTERISTICS

This "Prince of Cats" (F. Méry) is perhaps the most extraverted of the domestic cats. With his volatile, or unpredictable, temperament, he has a very strong personality and tends toward excess in all areas. He is not peaceful or calm. If you want a cat with a true presence, the Siamese is for you. Hypersensitive and highly emotional, Siamese cats adore company. They hate solitude and cannot stand indifference. If neglected, they become depressed.

These "big mouths" will harass their owner with their often loud, raucous voice and will follow their owner everywhere to get attention. Exclusive, very possessive, and brimming with affection, they can become jealous. The sociable Siamese likes to play with children but does not always appreciate the company of other cats. Siamese cats are sensitive to cold and like comfort and thus apartment life.

They reach puberty early, as females can have their first heat by 5 months. Heats occur approximately every two weeks, with no period of sexual quiescence in fall and winter.

The Siamese is more prolific than average for domestic cats. Siamese kittens, who are obviously hyperactive and fearless, must be raised attentively.

In terms of grooming, they require brushing once or twice weekly. They should be bathed several days before a show.

(▼) F.I.Fe   (■) L.O.O.F.   (★) C.F.A.   (◆) T.I.C.A.

Siberian Cat

Countries of origin:
Russia, Ukraine
Original Name:
Sibirskaya Koshka
Other Name: Sibi

His pedigree must indicate his Russian origin

This large cat lived in the wilds of Russia for quite a while. It might be the product of crosses between domestic cats brought to Siberia and the Ukraine and local wild cats. Its thick, insulating fur is adapted to its harsh native climate.

Mussa, a female red and white tabby, and Tima, a tom, were purchased in St. Petersburg and brought to Berlin in 1987. Hans and Betti Schulz bred the first Siberians in their Newski Cattery. In 1990, some fifteen specimens were recorded in western Europe.

The Siberian has been established in France since 1991. It was recognized by the F.I.Fe. in 1997.

In 1990, Elizabeth Terrell imported the first specimens of the breed to her Starpoint Cattery in the United States. T.I.C.A. recognized the Siberian and published a standard in 1998.

The breed is quite uncommon outside eastern Europe and the United States.

Siberian Cat

GENERAL
Very large, compact, massive, heavy. Powerful, pronounced muscle structure.
Weight: 4.5 to 9 kg.
Stockier than the Maine Coon; head more rounded than that of the Norwegian Forest Cat.

HEAD
Medium-sized, broad, triangular, with rounded contours. Flat top of the head. Slightly curved forehead. Cheeks not pronounced or prominent. Rounded, moderately long muzzle. Nose broad between the eyes, receding toward the tip, with a slight curve. Round chin. Long, thick whiskers (■).

EARS
Moderately broad, rounded tips. Short hair on the backs of the ears, long on the inside. Lynx tips desirable.

EYES
Large, nearly round, well-spaced, set at a slight slant. Traditional adult color: green to yellow, but blue in colorpoints. No relationship to coat color (◆).

NECK
Moderately long, rounded, thick, very muscular.

BODY
Compact, moderately long. Long back, slightly curved or arched. Well-rounded chest.

Strong bone and muscle structure.

LEGS AND PAWS
Hind legs slightly longer than forelegs. Heavy-boned, very muscular. Large, round paws with tufts of hair between the toes. All claws but one are retractile (■).

TAIL
Moderately long, broad at the base, well-furnished, and thick.

COAT
Semilong to long hair, fluffy, oily, waterproof, effectively protecting the cat from bitter cold. Stiff guard hairs. Long hair on the belly, slightly shorter on the shoulders and part of the chest. Long, well-furnished ruff. Thick undercoat. All traditional colors and color combinations are accepted except chocolate and lilac. Colorpoint specimens are known as Neva Mascarade (■).

NOTES
Allowable outcross breeds: none.

FAULTS
Straight profile. Narrow or pointed muzzle. Almond-shaped eyes. Very long legs. Disqualify: stop on the nose (■).

CHARACTERISTICS
These large cats exude quiet strength. They are quite lively and can be highly active. Despite a strong personality and character, Siberians are very friendly toward other cats. They are playful and get along well with children. They are affectionate and very attached to their owner. They have a soft voice. These hardy, water-loving cats are good climbers and excellent jumpers. They need space for their emotional well-being, and their beautiful coat makes them well-adapted to outdoor life.
They are not fully grown until the age of five.
They are easy to groom, since their coat resists matting. Normally, weekly brushing is enough. During heavy shedding in the spring, daily brushing is required.

(▼) F.I.Fe   (■) L.O.O.F.   (★) C.F.A.   (◆) T.I.C.A.

Singapura

Country of Origin: Singapore Island

The lightest of the domestic cats

"Singapura" is the Malaysian name for Singapore Island and also designates a true common cat who walks the streets of the capital. American tourists Tommy and Hal Meadows noticed the cats in 1974. The following year, they became the first to import the breed to California. They acquired three cats (Tess, Tickle, and Puss) who were being shown by 1976. T. and S. Svenson were among the ardent supporters of the breed. In 1980, more Singapuras were brought to the United States. T.I.C.A. and then the C.F.A. recognized them in 1984 and 1988, respectively. The first specimens of the breed were reported in France and Great Britain around 1988-1989. The F.I.Fe. has not yet recognized it. Although the Singapura was developed in the United States, it is not common there. It is rare in France.

Singapura

GENERAL
Compact cat, small to medium in size.
Weight: under 3 kg (the lightest of the domestic cats).
Ticked coat.

COAT
Fine, very short hair, not fluffy, lying flat against the body. Ticking of four or more alternating on a warm antique ivory background (brown ticked tabby). Dark salmon pink nose, pinkish-brown paw

NOTES
Allowable outcross breeds: none.

FAULTS
Small ears and eyes. Muzzle too short. Fluffy coat. Cold, grayish cast. Absence of bars on the inside of the legs. Absence of necklaces and outline around the nose. Disqualify: blue eyes. Continuous necklaces, circular bracelets on legs, bars on tail. White lockets or any other markings.

HEAD
Small, round. Jowls allowed in adult males. Short, broad muzzle. Delicately domed nose with a slight stop below the line of the eyes. Well-developed, rounded chin. Well-defined whisker pads.

EARS
Large, slightly pointed, broad at the base, moderately spaced. Shiny, richly colored coat.

EYES
Large, almond-shaped, accentuated by dark outlines. Separated by one eye-width. Color: green, gold, or copper. Blue is not allowed.

NECK
Short and thick.

BODY
Small to medium-sized, moderately stocky, compact. Well-built, muscular. Rounded rib cage, slightly arched back, round croup.

LEGS AND PAWS
Muscular, fine-boned legs. Small, oval paws.

TAIL
Moderately long, fairly thin but not excessively tapered. Rounded tip.

bands of dark brown to ivory except on the belly, throat, and inside of the legs, which are antique ivory. "M" on the forehead, dark outline around nose, eyes, and paw pads. Broken bracelets on the legs. Sepia agouti coloring with dark brown ticking

pads. The inside of the ears is salmon-colored with ivory hair. Hair along the spine and on the tail tip may be dark.

CHARACTERISTICS
The Singapura is well-balanced. Into everything, sociable, very affectionate, and loving, these cats are sensitive and demand petting. They are discreet and have a very soft voice. They follow their owner everywhere.
Outside, they are excellent hunters.
Female Singapuras are known for being very loving mothers. In terms of grooming, they require weekly brushing.

(▼) F.I.Fe   (■) L.O.OF.   (★) C.F.A.   (◆) T.I.C.A.

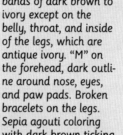

Snowshoe

Country of Origin: United States

A white-footed breed made in America

*T*his new breed resulted from a desire to combine into one cat the points of the Siamese and the gloved paws of the Birman. It was created in the United States in the 1960s by Dorothy Hinds-Daugherty, a breeder in Philadelphia, by crossing the Siamese with the bicolor American Shorthair.
The Snowshoe looks like a hefty Siamese sporting white gloves.
Recognized by T.I.C.A. in the 1980s, the breed has been somewhat successful in the United States but remains rare.

Snowshoe

GENERAL
Medium-sized.
Weight: 2.5 to 5.5 kg.
A combination of strength, grace, and elegance.
It is larger and heavier than the Siamese.

EARS
Medium to large in size, broad at the base, slightly rounded at the tips. Sparsely furnished.

HEAD
Medium-sized, shaped almost like an equilateral triangle (◆), with slightly rounded contours. Slightly flat forehead. High cheekbones. Fairly broad muzzle, neither too broad nor pointed or angular. No whisker pinch (◆). Straight nose with very slight curve at the base of the forehead. Firm chin.

Legs and paws
Proportionate to the body. Medium bone and muscle structure. Medium-sized, oval paws.

EYES
Fairly large, oval, walnut-shaped, slightly slanted. Separated by one eye-width. Color: blue, as intense as possible.

NECK
Moderately long.

BODY
Well-balanced, semi-foreign, can be inscribed in a rectangle. Croup slightly higher than shoulders. Slightly arched back. Medium-boned. Muscles powerful but not massive.

TAIL
Length in proportion to the body. Moderately thick at the base, tapering slightly to the tip.

COAT
Short, thick, shiny hair lying flat against the body. Very slight undercoat. Classic Siamese colors: seal, blue, chocolate, and lilac.
The color of the extremities (points) should contrast clearly with the body color, which is always lighter. The eyes are always blue.
Inverted V on the

forehead, white markings on the paws. Ideally, four even gloves. The nose leather may be white with no coloring, flesh colored, or multi-colored.
In the mitted variety, the white should cover no more than 1/3 the body. In the bicolor, the white should cover no more than 2/3 the body. Among the recognized varieties are:
- seal point: dark buff coat on the back, light buff on the belly and chest with brown points
- blue point: bluish-white body, with a lighter belly and chest. The points are dark bluish-gray.
Snowshoes are born all white, and the points darken with age.

NOTES
Allowable outcross breeds: none.

FAULTS
Head too long. Muzzle too broad. Small, rounded ears. Small, rounded, very slanted eyes. Body very long and frail or too short

and massive. Thin tail. Knotted, fine-boned legs. Disqualify: longhaired coat, eyes not blue. White markings covering the colored points. Fewer than four white "shoes" (■).

CHARACTERISTICS
This extremely lively cat with a strong personality is a good hunter. He is sociable and gets along well with other cats and with dogs.
Playful Snowshoes are excellent companions for children.
They are gentle and very affectionate toward their owner. Less demanding than the Siamese, they are more talkative than the American Shorthair. In terms of grooming, they require weekly brushing.

(▼)F.I.Fe   (■) L.O.O.F.   (★) C.F.A.   (◆) T.I.C.A.

African Shorthair

Country of Origin: Kenya (Africa)
Original Name: Khadzonzo
Other Name: Sokoke

From the trees of Kenya

Khadzonzos have long inhabited the forests of Kenya's Sokoke district. Spending their time in trees, they are voracious insect hunters. In the 1970s, Jeni Slater, an Englishwoman living in Kenya, adopted a female cat and her kittens, the origin of the breed. Canadian native Gloria Moldrup, a friend of Slater, first brought two kittens back to Denmark, then began importing them regularly around 1980. All her cats came from Jeni Slater's cattery. Moldrup started a breeding program with other breeders.

In 1983, the breed was named the African Shorthair. It was officially recognized first in Denmark in 1992, then in other countries. The F.I.Fe. approved it in 1993.

Internationally, it received the name Sokoke. It is still extremely rare.

African Shorthair

GENERAL
Medium-sized, svelte, with a marbled tabby coat.

HEAD
Appears small compared to body. Wedge-shaped. Nearly flat top of the skull. High, well-defined cheekbones. Nose moderately long, with a gentle concave curve. Strong, broad chin. Well-defined whisker pads. No whisker pinch.

EARS
Medium-sized, broad at the base, slightly rounded tips. Moderately spaced. Lynx tips desirable.

EYES
Large, slightly almond-shaped, moderately spaced, slightly slanted toward the nose. Amber to light green. Outlined in the same color as the solid parts of the markings.

BODY
Moderately long, svelte, very muscular. Solidly boned. Well-developed chest.

LEGS AND PAWS
Long, svelte, and very muscular. Forelegs are shorter than hind legs. Oval paws.

TAIL
Moderately long, thick at the base, tapering to the tip.

COAT
Short hair, shiny but not silky, lying flat against the body. Little or no undercoat. Recognized color: brown blotched tabby, that is, brown or black marbled tabby with a somewhat darker base. The tip of the tail is always black. Each hair has alternating light and dark bands.

NOTES
Allowable outcross breeds: none.

FAULTS
Head too Oriental in type. Stop too pronounced. Whisker pinch. Body too stocky and lacking elegance. Disqualify: white locket or white markings anywhere on the body except the nostrils, chin, and throat.

CHARACTERISTICS
This active, lively, independent cat is a very good climber and swimmer.
He is sociable with other cats and with dogs. Gentle and affectionate, he makes a good companion.
He can adapt to apartment life, but he needs space and therefore appreciates a yard.
Weekly brushing is enough to maintain his coat.

(▼) F.I.Fe   (■) L.O.O.F.   (★) C.F.A.   (◆) T.I.C.A.

Somali

A fox in the house

For a long time, kittens with semilong, soft hair appeared in litters of Abyssinians (which were actually of a much heavier type than today). But breeders were not interested in them and did not use them in reproduction. The gene responsible for semilong hair was probably introduced by crossing Abyssinians with longhaired cats (Persians or Angoras).

In Canada, it was not until the 1960s that breeders Don Richings and Mary Mailing and judge Ken MacGill became interested in these new cats. In 1967, American breeder Evelyn Mague managed to pin down the semilonghair gene in Abyssinians. The new breed was named the Somali, in reference to the neighboring country of Ethiopia, the supposed birthplace of the Abyssinian.

Mague founded the Lynn Lee Cattery and the first breed club in the United States. She showed the first Somali in 1972. The C.F.A. recognized the breed in 1978.

Lynn Lee's Picasso and Lynn Lee's Pearl, two Somalis from Mague's cattery, arrived in France in 1979.

The F.I.Fe. approved the breed in 1982. It is highly prized by more and more people.

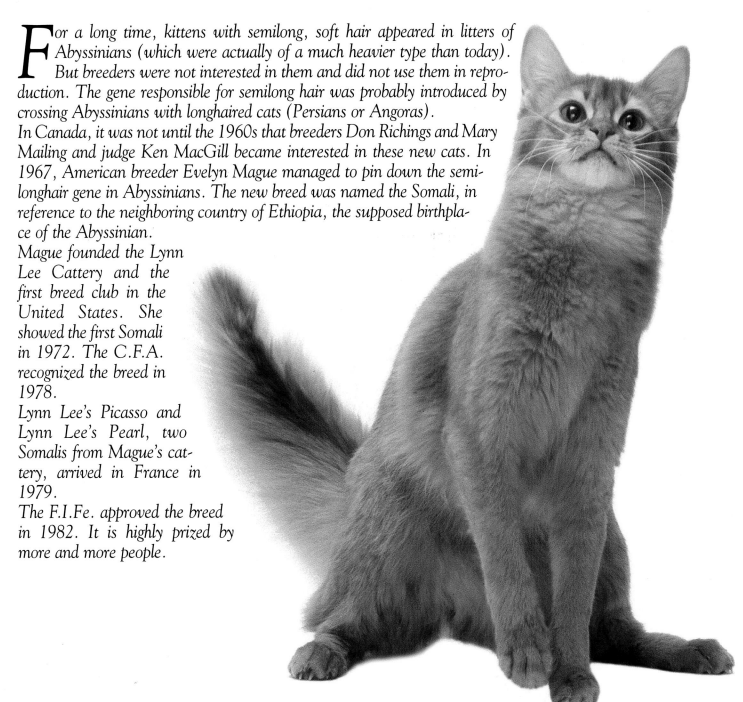

Somali

GENERAL
Medium in size and "royal" in appearance, the Somali resembles an Abyssinian but has semilong hair. Long-limbed type.
Weight: 3.5 to 5.5 kg.

EYES
Large, almond-shaped, well-spaced, with dark markings below the eyes. Above each eye is a short vertical marking (remnants of the tabby "M"). Color: amber, green, gold.

NECK
Carried gracefully.

BODY
Medium in size and length, semi-foreign

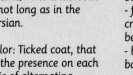

HEAD
Viewed from the front, shaped like a triangle with rounded contours. Slightly domed forehead. In profile, the head has a gentle curve. Muzzle neither small nor pointed. A whisker pinch is a fault (▼). Nose of medium length, without stop. Firm, well-developed chin.

EARS
Large, broad at the base, fairly well-spaced, with slightly rounded tips. A "thumbprint" is desirable on the back of the ear. Lynx tips are appreciated.

type, graceful. Slightly arched back. Powerful muscles.

LEGS AND PAWS
Long and thin, well-muscled. Compact, oval paws. The Somali appears to stand on tiptoe.

TAIL
Long, carried high, and well-furnished like that of a fox.

COAT
Semilong, dense, very fine, and soft hair. Short on the face, front of the legs, and shoulders; semilong on the back,

flanks, chest, and belly. It is long on the throat (ruff), behind the thighs (britches), and tail (plume). The undercoat is not long as in the Persian.

Color: Ticked coat, that is, the presence on each hair of alternating bands of dark and light coloration. At least two or three bands, up to eight banks. The tip of the hair must have a

dark band. Let us mention several varieties:
- ruddy ("usual" in Great Britain): black bands and apricot bands

- blue: slate blue bands and cream bands
- red (or sorrel): chocolate bands and apricot bands
- fawn beige: dark cream bands and dull beige bands
- black silver: black bands and white bands
- sorrel silver: chocolate bands and white bands
- blue silver: blue bands and white bands
The C.F.A. accepts the ruddy, red, blue, and fawn. A greater number of colors is accepted in Europe.

NOTES
Allowable outcross breeds: Abyssinian.

FAULTS
Round, Siamese type head. Pronounced stop. Round eyes without markings the same color as ticking. Small or pointed ears. Body too stocky. Short legs and tail. Disqualify: absence of or too little ticking. Ringed tail and legs. Whip tail. White locket, markings on the belly, etc.

CHARACTERISTICS
This very lively cat is active but not exuberant. Hardy, well-balanced, and even-tempered, he is calmer than the Abyssinian.
Somalis have a gentle temperament and are sociable toward other cats and strangers. Very playful, they get along well with children. Gentle and very affectionate, they demand lots of attention but are less possessive than the Abyssinian.
Although a bit sensitive to cold, they do not tolerate apartment life very well. They are big hunters, so a yard suits them.
In terms of grooming, they require only weekly brushing. During shedding, they should be brushed daily.
Somali kittens are born with nearly bicolor coats: dark on the back and light on the underparts. Ticking appears very gradually. Similarly, the length and final appearance of the coat are not attained until the second year.

(▼)F.I.Fe   (■) L.O.O.F.   (★) C.F.A.   (◆) T.I.C.A.

Sphynx

Countries of origin:
Canada, United States, Europe
Other Name: Canadian Hairless

A hairless cat highly sensitive to sunlight

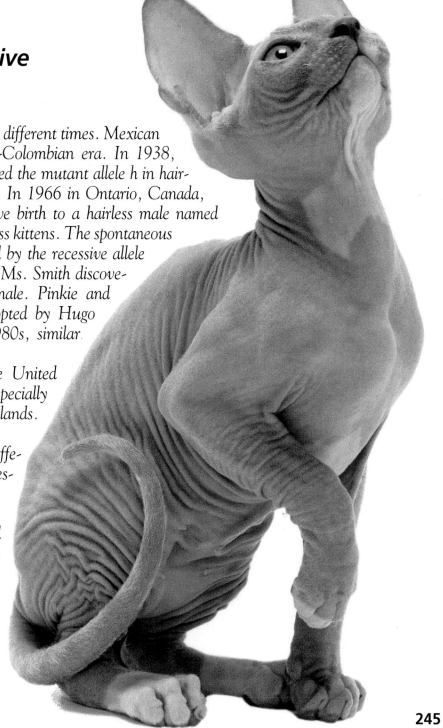

Hairless cats appeared in the world at different times. Mexican hairless cats date back to the pre-Colombian era. In 1938, French professor E. Letard described the mutant allele h in hairless kittens produced by a pair of Siamese. In 1966 in Ontario, Canada, Ms. Micalwaith's female cat Elisabeth gave birth to a hairless male named Prune. Prune and Elisabeth produced hairless kittens. The spontaneous mutation responsible for this trait is caused by the recessive allele hr. Also in Ontario and at the same time, Ms. Smith discovered Bambi, a black and white hairless male. Pinkie and Squeakie, two hairless females, were adopted by Hugo Hernandez in the Netherlands. In the 1980s, similar cases were reported in Great Britain.

As interest in these cats declined in the United States, their popularity grew in Europe, especially in France by 1983, as well as in the Netherlands.

It is true that it is impossible to remain indifferent to these cats, adored by some and detested by others.

Seeing the success of these cats in shows and the curiosity they generated, American breeders began importing Sphynxes from Europe. The breed is recognized by T.I.C.A., but the C.F.A. and the F.I.Fe. have rejected it. The Sphynx is quite rare.

Sphynx

GENERAL
Medium-sized.
Weight: 3.5 to 7 kg.
Medium-boned, fairly muscular.
Skin covered with a fine down.
Sparse hairs. Wrinkled skin.

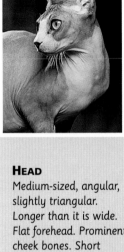

EARS
Very large, very broad at the base. The inside is totally hairless. Light down on the back of the ear is allowed

EYES
Large, lemon-shaped, upper corner pointing toward ears, well-spaced. Color corresponding to that of the coat.

HEAD
Medium-sized, angular, slightly triangular. Longer than it is wide. Flat forehead. Prominent cheek bones. Short nose, pronounced (■) or slight (◆) stop. Muzzle very rounded, broad, short. Pronounced whisker pinch. Firm chin. Whiskers sparse, short, or absent.

very broad, barrel-shaped. Rounded abdomen. Powerful loins. Fairly fine-boned (◆) to moderately boned. Well-muscled.

LEGS AND PAWS
Length proportional to that of the body. Forelegs slightly arched, slightly shorter than hind legs.

TAIL
Moderately long, slender, whip tail known as a "rat tail." It may have a tuft of hair on the tip ("lion tail").

COAT
Skin appears hairless and resembles that of a chamois in texture. Skin wrinkled on the head, body, and legs. Elsewhere, it is taut. The coat is limited to a fine down covering most of the body. A few hairs are present on the face, paws, tail, and testicles. Thus, "hairless cat" is a misnomer. All colors are recognized, as are all patterns. White looks pinkish, and black looks dark gray.

NOTES
Allowable outcross breeds: none.

FAULTS
Too frail, delicate in appearance. Too small in size. Head too narrow. Straight profile. Compact or long body. Disqualify: eyes too small. Absence of whisker pinch. Toes too small (◆). Kinky hair of Devon Rex or Cornish Rex during shedding. Obvious tweezing or shaving.

NECK
Long, arched, muscular, powerful in males.

BODY
Medium-sized. Chest

Medium-boned. Firm, well-developed muscles. Medium-sized, oval paws with long toes. Very thick paw pads.

CHARACTERISTICS
The Sphynx is lively, mischievous, playful, and independent. Friendly toward other cats and toward dogs, Sphynxes are never aggressive. Very affectionate and even possessive, they adore being doted on.
Apartment life is perfect for them, since they are sensitive to cold, heat, and humidity. In winter, they should be fed a high-calorie diet in order to keep their body temperature slightly above normal. Although they tan, they must be kept out of direct sunlight, which can lead to sunburn.
Unlike other feline breeds, Sphynxes sweat through the skin and should thus be cleaned regularly with a washcloth. Bathing is not advised. The ears must also be cleaned periodically, as they produce a great deal of wax.
Female Sphynxes have no more than two heats per year. The breed has a high rate of neonatal mortality. Sphynx kittens are born with very wrinkled skin and hair along the spine that disappears with age.

(▼)F.I.Fe   (■) L.O.O.F.   (★) C.F.A.   (◆) T.I.C.A.

248

Tonkinese

Countries of origin:
United States, Canada
Original Name: Golden Siamese

A Siamese-Burmese hybrid in a mink coat

This new breed initially called the Golden Siamese was created in North America and Canada in the 1930s by crossing the Siamese and the Burmese. At first, it was not popular at all. Note that at the time, the Siamese was larger and stockier, and the Burmese was less round than today.

Not until 1960 was this cat, renamed the Tonkinese, finally appreciated. It was recognized in 1974 by the Canadian Cat Association and in 1978 by the C.F.A.

Popular in the United States, the Tonkinese remains rare in Europe.

Tonkinese

GENERAL
Medium in size, its morphology is intermediate between that of the long-limbed Siamese and the medium-limbed Burmese.
Weight: 2.5 to 5.5 kg.

HEAD
Seen from the front, resembles an equilateral triangle with rounded contours. Medium-sized, slightly longer than it is wide. High cheekbones. Muzzle of medium length, angular with a slight break. Nose with a very slight stop. Slight whisker pinch. Chin neither prominent nor weak.

EARS
Medium in size, broad at the base, with rounded tips. Skin visible through a layer of very short hair.

EYES
Shaped like a peach pit, well-spaced, and set at a slant. Blue-green or aqua in color.

NECK
Moderately long, muscular.

BODY
Neither light nor compact. Semi-foreign type. The croup is slightly higher than the shoulders. Medium-boned. Well-developed muscles.

LEGS AND PAWS
Hind legs slightly longer than forelegs. Well-muscled. Oval paws.

TAIL
Moderately long, broad at the base but not thick, tapering slightly to the tip.

COAT
Short, fine, silky, lustrous, luxuriant, lying very flat against the body like that of the mink.
Colors: characteristic Siamese markings on a darker background close to the original color of the Burmese. These markings blend gradually into the coat with no clear contrast as in the Siamese. The Tonkinese does not attain final coloring before 16 months and tends to darken throughout life, like the Burmese and Siamese. Colors are the same as for the Burmese but slightly more subtle:

- natural mink (sable in the Burmese; seal in the Siamese): medium warm brown body and dark chocolate extremities
- champagne mink: cream chamois body, light brown extremities
- blue mink: soft blue-gray body, medium blue to slate-gray extremities
- platinum mink: very pale silver-gray body, darker silver extremities
- honey mink: apricot gold to amber body, reddish-brown extremities
The C.F.A. does not recognize the honey mink variety.

NOTES
Allowable outcross breeds: The Burmese crossed with the Siamese produces the Tonkinese in the first generation.

FAULTS
Round head, round eyes, short muzzle. Cobby or Oriental type body. Bars on the body. Bone deformities in the tail. Yellow eyes.

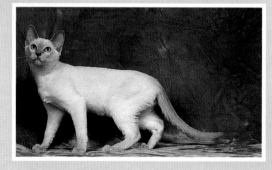

CHARACTERISTICS
Always on the alert, the Tonkinese is active and playful. As an athlete, he needs space, but he tends to run away.
Very sociable with other cats, gentle and affectionate toward his owner, the Tonkinese is less exclusive than the Siamese. Still, he requires lots of attention and despises solitude.
In terms of grooming, he requires weekly brushing.
While a Siamese-Burmese cross produces only Tonkinese kittens, it must be noted that mating two Tonkinese statistically produces 50% Tonkinese, 25% Burmese, and 25% Siamese kittens, which explains why European cat associations do not consider the Tonkinese to be a true breed.

(▼) F.I.Fe   (■) L.O.O.F.   (★) C.F.A.   (◆) T.I.C.A.

Turkish Van

Country of Origin:
Turkey
Other Name:
Turkish Swimming Cat

All white with markings on the head and a lovely colored tail

The Turkish Van is a more massive variety of Turkish Angora. It is named for the Lake Van region near Mount Ararat in eastern Turkey. This very old breed was reported as early as the 18th century, but it was not until 1955 that a British breeder named Laura Lushington imported Turkish Vans and truly began breeding them in Europe. The G.C.C.F. and the F.I.Fe. recognized the breed in 1969.

By 1982, the Turkish Van arrived in the United States, where the C.F.A. and T.I.C.A. approved it.

Nevertheless, this breed is quite uncommon in Europe.

Turkish Van

GENERAL
Medium-limbed type, solidly built, fairly massive.
Weight: 3. to 8.5 kg.

HEAD
Medium to large in size, at least as long as it is wide. Rounded contours. No angles or straight lines. High cheekbones. Full, rounded muzzle. Nose with slight stop, then delicately hooked (♦). Considerable whisker pinch. Slightly rounded chin.

EARS
Large, broad at the base, set high on the head, with slightly rounded tips.

EYES
Large, shaped like a walnut or peach pit, set slightly at a slant. Eyelids outlined in pink. Color: blue, amber, or heterochromatic. Green is allowed, but amber is preferred.

NECK
Short and strong.

BODY
Long, large, strong. Rounded rib cage. Fairly broad hips. Large-boned, well-developed muscles.

LEGS AND PAWS
Moderately long. Hind legs longer than forelegs. Medium-boned, well-muscled. Round paws. Dense tufts of hair between the toes.

TAIL
Moderately long, thick, well-furnished, fluffy, or plumed. Hair must be at least 5 cm long. The color is even along the entire tail.

COAT
Semilong to long, soft, silky hair without woolly undercoat. Ruff and britches well-furnished in winter. Pure white coat. Reddish-brown (auburn) or cream symmetrical markings at the base of the ears separated by a white blaze. Another colored patch running from the croup to the tip of the tail. The arrangement of these markings is called a "van" pattern. Main recognized colors: red and white, cream and white.

NOTES
Allowable outcross breeds: none.

FAULTS
More than three colored patches on the body. No blaze on the face. Markings unevenly distributed. Tail color starting too far up the back. Disqualify: bicolor and solid patterns. Absence of coloring on the ears and tail.

CHARACTERISTICS
This particularly hardy, sturdy, very lively cat loves to swim. Although the breed was once reputed to be aggressive, selective breeding has made Turkish Vans friendly, especially toward other cats. Independent, playful, and with a strong character, they are very affectionate and often possessive toward their owner. They are excellent companions and have a moderately loud voice.
Turkish Vans can adapt to apartment life, although a large yard with water is better. They grow slowly and take three to five years to reach their full beauty. They require only weekly brushing, except during considerable pre-summer shedding.

(▼) F.I.Fe   (■) L.O.O.F.   (★) C.F.A.   (♦) T.I.C.A.

York Chocolate

Country of origin: United States

A brown-coated city dweller

This new breed created in the United States is named after New York City and its brown coloring. The first York Chocolate kittens were born to housecat parents in the 1980s on Janet Chiefari's farm in New York state. The father was a longhaired black cat, and the mother, also longhaired, was black and white. The old-type Siamese ancestrors of both parents contributed the chocolate gene.

York Chocolate

GENERAL
Old-type Siamese appearance. Male weighs 7 to 8 kg. Semilonghaired.

HEAD
Nearly round. Rounded skull. Slightly domed forehead. Moderately long muzzle. Nose without break. Chin in line with tip of nose (■).

EARS
Fairly large, well-spaced. Slightly rounded tips.

EYES
Fairly large, well-spaced, slightly oval, lemon-shaped. Color: gold to green (■).

NECK
Long, thin.

BODY
Long, midway between Oriental and foreign types. Should not be heavy. Fine-boned with slender muscles (■).

LEGS AND PAWS
Long and fine-boned with firm muscles. Small, rounded paws. Long hairs between the toes.

TAIL
Long, thin, straight, tapering to a slender tip. Well-furnished.

COAT
Semilong, fine, soft, silky hair. Very fluffy tail. May have a ruff. Color: solid chocolate, solid lilac, and these same colors in a bicolor version (■). Kittens are much lighter than adults. Tabby markings and tipping are acceptable up to 18 months.

NOTES
Allowable outcross breeds: none.

FAULTS
Head too Oriental in type. Weak chin. Oriental-type eyes. Heavy body. Disqualify: white spots or lockets (■).

CHARACTERISTICS
These lively, energetic cats are good hunters. Playful and affectionate, they are good companions.

(▼)F.I.Fe   (■) L.O.O.F.   (★) C.F.A.   (◆) T.I.C.A.

Pixie Bob

Country of Origin: United States

In 1985, Carol Ann Brewer, a breeder in Washington state, had a female cat named Pixie who was polydactyl (with more toes than normal). After mating, possibly with a small bobcat, Pixie produced a litter in which some kittens resembled the father (spotted coat, broad ears, etc.). They were called Pixie Bobs. The new breed was recognized by T.I.C.A., which published a standard in 1998. The same year, France also approved the breed.

Pixie Bob

GENERAL
Medium to large in size, slender.
Weight: 4 to 10 kg.
Wild appearance.

HEAD
Broad with prominent
forehead. Long, broad
muzzle. Very strong
chin.

EARS
Broad at the base, roun-
ded at the tips, well-
spaced. Lynx tips desi-
rable.

EYES
Slightly oval, moderate-
ly deep-set. Color cor-
responding to that of
the coat.

BODY
Long, strong. Prominent
shoulders and hips.

LEGS AND PAWS
Long. Muscular. Strong
boned. Large paws with
fleshy toes.
Polydactylism accepted
(6-7 toes on the fore-
paws; 5-6 on the hind
paws).

TAIL
Short, thick, flexible.

COAT
Short or long hair. Silky,
wooly, resilient, water-
proof. Spotted tabby
(dark spots on a light
background). Well-mar-
ked ticking, gray under-
coat (◆).

(▼)F.I.Fe   (■) L.O.O.F.   (★) C.F.A.   (◆) T.I.C.A.

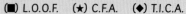

Part 2

CATS, HUMANS, AND HISTORY

HISTORY
SYMBOLS
ART AND
COMMUNICATION

Cats Throughout History

The collection of images cats have generated throughout the millennia is like a staggering vista between two opposite worlds. From one era to the next, from one country to another, cats have been themselves and their opposites, gods or devils, lucky charms or the source of all evil. No other animal has unleashed such passion, such hatred or such adoration. Masters of the universe in ancient times, despised and tortured during the medieval era, cats clearly have an extraordinary personality in order to make a comeback as dignified and fascinating animals in the eyes of our contemporaries. What has been the perception of cats since they first approached humans? How are their behaviors and attitudes interpreted? How is this "supporting actor" used?

The Perception of Cats Throughout History

Depending on the era, cats have inspired various extreme feelings. In ancient Egypt, cats were assimilated to the moon and the sun, and were elevated to the rank of the gods. Their fortune was quite the opposite in Europe during the Middle Ages.

Cats as Gods

Revered and refined, cats saw their hour of glory under the skies of the Orient.

During the transition from the Middle to the New Empire from 1785 to 1557 BC, Egyptians worshipped Bastet, the cat-goddess with the body of a woman and the head of a cat. A symbol of love and procreation, Bastet was worshipped in Bubastis, which became the capital during the reign of the Libyan kings, and in Saqqara, where the Bubasteion temple

was erected. Raising sacred cats, to whom supplications were made during annual festivals, was a common practice. They were given bread soaked in milk and fish from the Nile to eat. They were then displayed in baskets so that the people could pay homage to them. When these sacred cats died, an embalmer wrapped them in a shroud and treated their bodies with cedar oil.

The practice of mummifying cats started with the XXIIth Dynasty (950 BC). Later the practice became more rooted in custom. Mummies were more numerous in the XXXth Dynasty, during which the Greek culture spread throughout the land of the Pharaohs, and in the IVth century BC, during the Persian occupation of Egypt. The discovery of sixteen necropolises of cats in the sanctuary of Bastet, the cat-goddess, in Saqqara and in Bubastis, the largest of which are located in Beni-Hassan, illustrates this custom.

When these mummy cats were sent by boat to Europe, they were first preserved in the

Cat on a Papyrus (plant). Taken from the tomb of Beni-Hassan, Egypt. École des Hautes Études, Paris. Photograph, J.-L. Charmet collection.

Natural History Museum in London. But there were so many of them that the decision was made to use them as fertilizer. Recent X-ray research on these ancient treasures has led to great revelations. These cats were in fact quite young, mostly between 2 and 4 months or 9 and 17 months. One detail sheds new light on Egyptian customs. The evidence of strangulation around the necks of the kittens indicates that they did not necessarily die of natural causes before being plunged into natron and then embalmed.

Nevertheless, the Egyptian religion devoted to cats left its mark. Its sphere of influence reached as far abroad as Gaul, where the discovery of amulets, statuettes and sistrums - in particular in the city of Toulouse, where these objects probably date back to the first century BC, - goes hand in hand with the identification of cat remains in Great Britain, Budbury, Gussage All Saints and Danebury. These places testify to the fact that cats were pervasive and well established.

For many years, the Egyptian veneration for cats supplied fodder for Greek authors. Herodotus described the mandatory period of mourning that families underwent at the death of the animal. According to tradition, the family members shaved off their eyebrows as a sign of grief. Diodore of Sicily wrote about the Egyptian passion for cats. According to one story that occurred during a crucial time when the Egyptians feared a war with Rome, King Ptolemy Aultete, father of Cleopatra, was unable to save a Roman who had accidentally killed a cat from being lynched. The laws governing the murder of sacred animals were so strict that even the king could not disobey them.

Cats were sacred. They could influence the decisions of their worshippers. According to Polybe, an historian, cats held a strategic position during one military event in the VIth century BC. The event in question was the siege of Peluse led by Cambyse II, King of Persia. The enemy seized cats and placed them

265

The goddess Bastet with two kittens.
Bronze statue, late period,
Mariémont Museum (Belgium).
F. Gourdon collection, Paris.

at the front lines of the fighting. This trick caused a hasty surrender by the Egyptians, who refused to have their sacred animals be the target of choice during battles.

Cats were also revered in the Orient. According to legend, Mohammed chose to sacrifice his garment and cut off his sleeve rather than wake his cat, Muezza, who was sleeping in his arms. In the XIIIth century, Sultan El-Daher-Beybars bequeathed an entire park called "The Cat Orchards", or Gheytel-Qouttah, to stray cats.

Cats were held in very high esteem in the Far East. Buddhist monks raised sacred cats. In Japan, the Kyoto palace opened its doors to a white cat that had given birth to five kittens. The temple dedicated to the cat named Maneki-Neko, which shows the cat seated with one paw raised in greeting, proves to what extent cats were worshipped in the Land of the Rising Sun.

The Sun Cat

Likened to the Sun, cats had the power to bring about dawn each new day.

The goddess Bastet had a solar-like appearance that was rooted in her ancestry. She was the daughter of Ra, the Sun God, just like her sister Sekhmet, and was called "The Eye of Ra." Cats, which were likened to goddess, were therefore confused with the sun. However, this resemblance was based more on behavior than appearances.

Indeed, it was thanks to the snake-hunting activities of the cat that the sun brightened the universe. When the cat-goddess confronted Apopis, the dragon-snake that was permanently plunged into dark and chaotic atmospheres, she freed the sun from its dark grave. In the vignettes of *Livre des morts* (*Book of the Dead*), we clearly see the cat poised to cut off Apopis' head if the formidable serpent dares to approach. We can deduce that the world awakes to find light everyday thanks to the vigilance and bravery of the cat.

Considered to be the guardian of the night by the Egyptians, the cat was thought to be a hero, keeping watch in the dead of night. He played a crucial role in the nightly crossing of the solar boat as it sunk into Amenta, the kingdom of the dead. The same scene was replayed every night. Ra, the Sun, crossed the twelve regions of Egypt as the twelve hours of daylight trickled away. At six o'clock, he is overcome by sleep as he crosses the threshold into the underworld. Accompanied by the dead he is assigned to lead into the afterworld, he is merely a cadaver forced to make these nightly crossings. In the eighth hour, however, a crucial event occurs: Apopis appears suddenly and blocks the way of the advancing solar boat. The proud, rash cat then rises up and announces, "I am Atoum, the Holy Cat of Heliopolis." Then he turns to the dead and says, "O you, vindicated dead, who fought against the spirit of evil when you were alive, I will keep the evil spirits away from you in Amenta because I am Atoum of the Heavens, Atoum of the beginning and the end of the world." The strong cat with masterful powers, decapitates Apopis and clears the way for the solar boat to resume its journey. The cat's intervention allows the sun to be born again in the twelfth hour.

The snake, which is accused of suffocating the Day, is omnipresent in Egyptian culture. Serpents are found on objects dating back to the XIIth dynasty (1901 - 1785 BC), in the form of ivory "worship staffs". These staffs depict cats raising a knife against a serpent, symbolizing Ra's battle against darkness. The *Book of the Dead* recounts this episode and speaks of the Great Cat, who lives in the Persian tree in the city of Heliopolis, along with Ra, and who battles the dragon-snake, Apopis, for the emergence of dawn.

This very common identification of cats with the Sun is also seen in the steles of the New Empire.

The Moon Cat

Cats were likened to the Moon, which influenced their gestation.

Bastet, the salutary deity, friend to men and children, protector of pregnant women, pitted against her twin sister, Sekhmet, who represented destructive heat, was considered to be the moon goddess. She embodied the heat

Girl holding a cat whose tail is being bitten by a rooster. Source: Bordeaux. Late 1st century or early 2nd century AD. Museum of Roman Civilization, Rome. G. Dagli Orti collection, Paris.

A Precious Guide

In the Greek, Roman and Gallo-Roman world, the belief was that cats accompanied their masters after death. The funeral stele of Salamine (420 BC) is one illustration of this belief.

The stele of Laetus shows an identical scene, but places more emphasis on the guide role played by the cat at all stages of life. This architectural work, which dates back to the late 1st century, the early 2nd century AD, and which was extracted from a Roman city wall in Bordeaux in 1831, depicts a small girl holding a kitten in her hands. The mission of the kitten is to protect the child from the hazards of life put in her path. The fundamental role cats play with children has been well represented in the world of art throughout past centuries. Showing children surrounded by their toys and their pets was an established custom among both the Romans and the Gauls.

that impregnated. In *Iris and Osiris*, Plutarch further develops this association between the cat-goddess and the moon. At the time, it was thought that female cats could be in gestation seven times during their life and could give birth to a total of 28 kittens. This calculation is equal to the number of days in the lunar month.

The Greeks likened their goddess, Artemis, the personification of the Moon, with Bastet, the cat-goddess. This likeness is easy to make because according to Greek mythology, when Artemis was being chased by the monstrous python, she supposedly transformed herself into a cat and took refuge in Egypt.

The comparison between cats and the moon was based on a physical detail. The Greeks were intrigued by feline eyes, which dilate and retract according to the intensity of light. At the time, they could not provide a scientific explanation for this phenomenon. They thought that the pupil enlarged and shrunk according to the phases of the moon.

The association between cats and the moon has been a source of inspiration for architecture throughout history. The portal of the Saint-Michel de Lescure church, which is located near Albi and which is a veritable Roman Benedictine masterpiece (1150), has frescos depicting a parade of 24 cat heads. It illustrates a cosmic calendar made up of alternating suns and moons above animal and plant designs. Twenty-three feline heads in arcs of circles stand out with a twenty-fourth, more massive head placed on the keystone. This represents the twenty-four hours in a day and brings together the alternation of day and night.

Wooden cat statue, late period.
Limoges Museum, on loan from the Louvre
Museum (France). F. Gourdon collection, Paris.

The Devil Cat

Considered to be Satan's helpers, cats were detested, burned and subjected to the worst forms of abuse during medieval times.

In the Middle Ages, especially between 1180 and 1233, cats became victims of accusations of the worst sort with their strange and misunderstood behavior. They were associated with imaginary crimes that the pagans attributed to the Christians and the Christians attributed to the Gnostics and the Jews. They were involved in diabolical rituals organized by heretical sects. Cathars thought the devil took the form of a cat. In 1230, William of Auvergne, Bishop of Paris, described Lucifer as a toad or a cat in his writings.

The Cursed Black Cat

Their color raised concern and caused them to have a fatal destiny.

People hated and despised black cats. This aversion to black cats goes back a long way. It dates back to Psammetic II, one of the Pharaohs of the XXVIth dynasty (594 – 588 BC), who took a hammer to the statues of the Ethiopian usurpers and called down a curse on black Ethiopians. This idea endured into the Middle Ages, when Ethiopians were compared to demons.

Fear of the year one thousand unleashed the animosity of the clergy on cats. Later, Gregory IX, Pope from 1227 – 1241, wrote in a bull that the devil was like a black cat whose followers would kiss his genitals before engaging in an orgy. In 1307, the Bishop of Coventry was accused of worshipping a black cat, as were the Templars during their trials at that time.
The medical profession pronounced an anathema on black cats. One illustrious Milanese doctor, Jerome Cardan, warned his patients about cruel, audacious black cats, saying that because they were cantankerous and moody, they could cause melancholia in people. The age of cat massacres was about to begin.

The return of the crusades and the Black Death epidemics helped to perpetuate the notion of the devil donning the body of a cat. This negative image was still alive and well in the XVth century. In Alsace, the devil was said to travel with his henchmen pulled by a team of four black cats. In the XVIIth century, during the Tagharim, a barbarian ceremony in Scotland, which is still called "Devil's supper", cats were impaled alive on a spit and then roasted for two days. They were continually replaced during these two days so that the piercing mewing, which were thought to cause the devil to appear, would punctuate this fatal ceremony.

The Witch's Accomplice

Mixed up with witchcraft, cats aroused hatred and vengeance.

Flexible, nocturnal and silent, cats were able to slip stealthily into houses. They were suspected of doing evil and practicing witchcraft. They suffocated children in their cradles and when the parents pummeled this wicked animal, the bruises and wounds did not appear on the body of the cat, but on the body of an old woman who, by her own confession, had transformed herself into a tomcat or a she-cat.
Cats became a major ingredient in the recipes concocted by witches and were used in all kinds of potions.
The hide of a black cat would be filled with barley, wheat and oats. Once stuffed with these grains, it was placed in a fountain

A witch preparing a potion. Next to her we see a broom and a black cat. Folk style postcard by Böske Kardos, Hungary, early XXth century. Private collection. Photo by J.-L. Charmet, Paris.

269

Louis XIV is credited with banning the fires of St. Jean in Paris, at the Place de Grève, where cats were burned in the presence of the king. When the fires were not out in the open, they were in the cathedrals. In 1638, a man by the name of William Smyth caused quite a stir in England when he had a cat roasted in the most holy place of the Ely cathedral. During the reign of Charles VII (1660 – 1685), the effigy of the Pope was burned during solemn processions, not in the form of a simple portrait, but in the form of a thick figurine stuffed with live cats. This guaranteed a dramatic effect and the crowd could not contain its excitement. Finally, during country fairs, the entertainment program would list cat shooting. Suspended in a basket, the captive animal would gesticulate and whine as arrows pierced its body.

for three days. The hide was then dried and ground, resulting in a powder with formidable effects. When thrown from the top of a mountain on a windy day, these seeds scattered across an entire region, ravaged the ground and rendered it sterile.

The despised, reviled cats were tortured and then burned during traditional festivals. Some cities in the north of France and Lorraine such as Arras, Metz and Ypres in Flanders, earned the reputation of having cat phobias. During the summer solstice, cats were thrown into the flames from the top of high towers before a jubilant crowd. Only black cats with white spots were spared in the St. Jean holocaust because they bore the mark of an angel or the hand of God. The tradition in Metz up until 1733 was to sacrifice and burn 13 cats. In Ypres, these cruel rituals continued until 1817.

An Evil Animal

All their evil powers were concentrated in their head and their tail.

Starting in the Middle Ages, literature was filled with examples attributing a slew of flaws to cats. Proverbs, which were widely illustrated in Flemish painting, are evidence of this. Wily, crafty and deceitful – this is the image of cats portrayed in books, paintings and other works of art. The cat is depicted as a hypocrite in the character of Tibert in *Roman de Renart* (*Book of Renart*) (XIIIth century), and riddled with flaws when portrayed as Grippeminaud in *Pantragruel* by Rabelais. Cats also represented the negative image of justice. After all, the linings of judges' robes were sewn out of cat fur. The evil power of cats was confined to their heads and tails. Conventional wisdom in the XVth century warned young girls not to step on the tail of a cat or she would have no chance of finding a husband during that year. A literary tail by Madame d'Aulnoy dating to 1697 recounts the misfortunes of a princess changed into a cat by a wicked fairy. In order for the young girl to be rescued, her prince charming had to cut off the head and tail of a cat and throw them in the fire in order to elim-

inate once and for all the parts of the body that resembled evil.

One of the traditions of Poitou is quite eloquent in this respect. According to this legend, when God wanted to create cats, the devil told him, "Make the cat if you want, but his head shall belong to me." The cursed head of felines had the distinctive feature of holding the brain, the seat of strange virtues. Although cat meat was considered to be a delicacy, especially in Spain and Italy, its brain was of no value; it acted like a poison that make people go mad. As for the tail, it was intriguing because it was in constant motion, even while the cat's asleep. The tail was suspected of being inhabited by a strange force. It was therefore deemed necessary to kill the worm, the venom, the serpent or the hair of the devil that was causing this disturbing movement.

Cats and the Imagination

Idealized and transformed, cats became something else in the imaginations of people – sometimes thought of as wise, sometimes as a mother and sometimes as a wife.

She-cats and Their Bodies

With her ability to give birth or to adopt suggestive attitudes, the female cat was a woman's double.

Mother Cats

Cats became legendary because of their exemplary behavior in their roles as mothers.

Despite the difficulties in exporting cats out of Egypt, the Greeks began to pray to Bastet, the Egyptian goddess with a cat's head in the IVth century BC. The goddess of music, dance and joie de vivre, Bastet was at first the protector and nursemaid of royal children. Then she became the goddess of maternity. She protected pregnant women and newborns.

Although she carried out her mission in the Great Castle of Ra, she became very popular by extending her protection as a nurturing mother to all the children of Egypt.

Many earthenware talismans and amulets depicted a cat with a woman's head and swollen breasts surrounded by kittens. She was associated with the features of the god Bes, the attendant during birthing and nursing. Both of them played a ritual role during birth. Bastet ensured that gestation proceeded smoothly, encouraged labor, nursed the babies and cared for them. Some statuettes depict the she-cat lying down feeding her young and watching them play, while others show her standing, holding three of her attributes: a sistrum used to chase away evil spirits from the beds of young mothers; the willow basket used by obstetrician priestesses; and an aegis, a medallion with an effigy of a lion or a cat to reinforce the power of protection.

The fecundity of she-cats and their exemplary maternal behavior were undoubtedly decisive factors in giving Bastet this protector image.

The cat as a Woman

She-Cats resembled women because of their behavior and their charm.

The link between the goddess Bastet and cats, which produced the mother cat cliché, led to the superimposing of women and cats, honing the similarities between the two. The image took full shape in the Middle Ages at a time when misogyny was the rule, tipping the balance in favor of the negative side of this comparison. In fabliaux and other satirical works, the affinities between women and cats had strong sexual connotations. According to *Le Dit de Chaste-Musart* (The Tale of Chaste Musart), women could be compared to three predators: the she-cat prowling around, the vixen lying in wait, or the she-wolf carrying off her prey.

In the XIth century, the poem of Troubadour Prince William X depicts the cat as an instrument of torture used by two women on a male victim. The story tells of the poet's encounter on a road in Auvergne. Two women with loose morals mistake the Troubadour for a pilgrim. William finds this charming and pretends to be mute so as not to give himself away. Ermesent and Agnes believe they have found the perfect man to quench their desires without risking their reputation, but they nevertheless remain cautious. In order to test the muteness of the poet, they run a cat up and down the back of the poor man, who is scratched to the point of bleeding. In spite of his wounds, William passes the test and his act of heroism does not leave him disappointed.

The theme of the she-cat turning herself into a woman is prevalent from ancient times to the Middle Ages and is found in several forms of literature. In *The Cat and Venus* Aesop tells the story of a cat who falls in love with a young man. In order to fulfill her love, she entreats the goddess to change her into a woman. But she turns back into a cat when she forgets her new form and chases after a mouse. This tale inspired La Fontaine in *The Cat That Turned into a Woman*, in which the feline nature of the woman and the femininity of the cat merge and are intertwined together.

Feline Intelligence

Their intelligence and extrasensory abilities put cats on a higher level.

Cats and Religion

Despised by the clergy, cats nevertheless inspired those who built cathedrals.

Around the year 700, cats appeared in pictures in the Lindisfarne Gospels in Ireland. *The Book of Kells*, which is composed of works of art by artists in a monastery around 800, is filled with illustrations of cats. An Irish poem written by a monk around the end of the VIIIth or the beginning of the IXth century, and later put to music in 1953 by Samuel Barber, describes the charms of the cloister when the presence of a cat brightens up the lives of the monks.

CATS IN HELL

Cats are not forgotten when the fury of demons is evoked. Indeed in 1863 in the *Dictionnaire infernal* (Dictionary of Demonology) by Collin de Plancy, the three heads of the demon Bael are made up of three devilish animals: the toad, the spider and, of course, the cat.

*"Le Jardin des délices terrestres,"
close-up of the left panel:
the creation of man and woman
by God the Father. Jérôme Bosch
(1450 – 1516), Madrid, Prado
Museum, G. Dagli Orti collection,
Paris.*

Bonne de Luxembourg, around 1345). The *Livre d'heures* (Book of Hours) written by Jeanne d'Evreux around 1325 shows a cat playing with a woman's skein while she is busy spinning. In *Heures à l'usage de Paris* (Hours Intended for Paris), completed in the XVIth century, which contains prayers to be recited during the day and pictures of animals, the cat is shown with his paws bound, held captive by two rats taking him away in a boat. We also see in this series of drawings a giant triton seize the cat by the nape of his neck and threaten him with his whip.

Cats as Soothsayers

Be they witches or magi, their gestural messages were heard.

Cats could predict the future and foreshadow pleasant or untimely visits based on the position of their body. The direction in which a cat extended his paw while cleaning himself indicated the direction from which the visitor would come. The body part he was licking and cleaning indicated whether it would be a man or a woman. Cats were also able to predict a long illness. When the cat abandoned the home of a sick person or left the bedside of his protégé, it meant that he had guessed the exact moment of death. Finally, cats were also veritable weather indicators. If a cat lifted his paw above his ear while cleaning himself, it was a sign of rain.

Use of Cats in History

Thought to be lucky charms, cats lived in harmony with the world. They chased away rodents and became pets.

The Magic Cat

He healed, enriched and fertilized the earth.

Cats as a Cure

He both caused disease and cured pain.

According to the Swiss doctor Conrad Gesner, author of *Historia animalium* (1551), cats could

Two centuries later we see the Celtic cross of Muireadach, which dates to the Xth century in Monasterboice, with two cats lying on its base, holding a fledgling and a kitten in their paws. An English bestiary dating back to the XIIth century, which portrays Christ baptizing creation, situates the cat between the rabbit and the squirrel, paying close attention to his environment. Left out of Biblical texts, this animal became the source of new interpretation. In France in the XIIth and XIIIth centuries, psalter Jean Pucelle depicts a tomcat and an old man warming themselves by the fireplace (*Livre de prières* [Book of Prayers], written by

cause serious respiratory problems. If some of their fur was accidentally swallowed, it could lead to suffocation. Their noxious breath could cause the death of those who were bold enough to sleep in their presence. Doctors (Ambrose, Pare, Matthiole) advised people not to breathe in air contaminated by dogs and cats. If a cat simply looked at the patients, it was enough to throw them into a sheer panic. To treat all these problems, the doctors resorted to specific preparations. The remedies were made out of cat meat, liver or excrement. They were recommended for hemorrhoids, varicose veins, lumbago, gout, fever, kidney stones and certain eye disorders.

Cats and Money

He had the power to make his master rich.

Legends link cats, the animal of the poor, to sudden, unexpected fortune. We see this in the famous fairy tale *Puss in Boots*, where Charles Perrault depicts the poverty of the miller who gives his son a cat by way of an inheritance. The legend of the Venice Fountain recounted in Albert de Statd's *Annals*, written at the end of the XIIth century, is another example. Chased by hordes of Attila's men, the people of Aquilee take refuge on the island that later became Venice. Just before leaving for this island, a rich man asks a poor man to become his partner. The poor man has hardly any money to furnish capital. His only fortune is his two cats. But once he hands them over to his partner, these two animals start to act like lucky charms by waging war against the rats swarming the Venetian soil. They are later sold at a high price and the city of Venice is born, rid of its plague.

The story of the Englishman Richard Whitington, set at the end of the XIVth century, also illustrates the power of the cat to make fortunes. The adventurer leaves for India with only a cat for baggage. The cat is loaded on a ship and then brought back to shore when the ship sinks. He is let loose in a rat-infested land and he undertakes a never-ending hunt. The lord of the land offers a reward

to the cat by appointing him generalissimo of the armies and to the owner of the cat, whom he promotes to advisor. Nicknamed "Milord Cat" or "Lord Pussy," Richard Whitington went on to become the Lord Mayor of London where he built the palace that now houses the London Stock Exchange.

In peasant traditions, cats were frequently associated with money. One knew that in order to become rich, one simply had to place a purse containing money near a cat just before going to bed and to whisper in the ear of the cat, "Do your duty!". The next morning, the purse would be filled with louis d'or. All that remained was to reward the cat with a thick stew. The only drawback was that the cat used to make the fortune served nine masters on a rotating basis. When he took the soul of the ninth, he headed for hell. The cat sets himself up as a victim in this story because once his owner makes his fortune, he wastes no time in getting rid of the cat.

Cats and the Earth

They were associated with telluric forces.

The presence of cats was beneficial for crops. They added vitality to the roots, the grass and the sprouts. In Béarn, a cat buried alive in the field would kill the weeds. This was due to the power of communication of the cat. His life force reached the seedbed, gave strength to the seeds and helped them prevail over undesirable plants. According to another belief, if a cat was nailed to the base of a diseased tree,

Cats protecting silkworms. The cat-spirits were supposed to keep away the rats that were so fond of silkworms. The flowers are good omens; they protect the silkworms from epidemics.

Popular Chinese imagery, early XXth century. Reproduced in the book by Father H. Doré on superstitions in China. B.N. (National Library) - Paris J.-L. Charmet collection.

CATS AS CHARMS

Cats were lucky charms in matters of the heart. In the Middle Ages, a woman who wanted to keep her husband faithful had to keep one ritual alive: she had to trap the cat under a basin for two days, make him breathe urine-soaked bread, coat his paws with ointment, etc.

According to Germanic folklore, if a young girl was followed by a cat to the doorstep of the church, she would be lucky in love.

Another belief was that if a virgin leaving a ball was lucky enough to cross the path of a calico cat, she would soon find the man of her life.

Cats were less favorable to men, however. If a man loved cats, he would not find a wife.

the tree would be healed. Finally, if the body of a cat was buried or built into a wall, it would guarantee solidity and strength for the entire edifice. Cats sacrificed during ceremonies were compared to plant spirits. Their death ensured a fertile and prosperous year for the whole community. Cats and grass were sometimes closely linked. In Franche-Comté, the expression "kill the cat" at the end of the harvest meant cutting down the last sheathes.

However, cats could also bring curses with their power over nature. They symbolized the cold, winter and even vermin and evil influences that could endanger the autumn or spring sowing season.

Useful Cats

They rid the people of the rodents that destroyed the harvest and began to be appreciated as pets.

Cats as Hunters

They came to replace weasels and civets.

When a man invited a cat to live in his home, it was in exchange for a service. He expected this talented predator to eliminate all the rodents infesting the house, from cellar to attic. The same contract earned cats their keep on boats, and, in fact, bought them long voyages from one continent to another, which established feline geography and expanded the range of breeds.

In the Xth century, Welsh laws established under the reign of Howel Dda, set the value of cats based on their age and their hunting abilities. In Venedotie (in the North), cats were worth one penny from birth until they opened their eyes, 2 pence until they caught their first mouse and 4 pence once they become adults. In any case, cats had to "see, hear and kill mice."

In the Middle Ages, cats replaced civets and weasels. Striped cats, which are still called Syrian cats in Italy, were the most highly valued in terms of being good hunters. Soderini

of Florentine (1526 – 1597) extolled their talents in a country where striped cats had first taken up residence.

Cats watched over the grain reserves in houses and in monasteries. Households were reluctant to feed cats in order to make them more efficient. Starting in 1730 though, cats were driven to the attic by brown Norway rats. In the XXth century, they no longer prevailed over rats.

Cats as Pets

His role as a seducer took precedence over his work as a ratter.

It is still not known where cats were first domesticated. Was it in Persia or Egypt? Doubt still remains due to the fact that bones were discovered in two different places – at an archeological site in Jericho dating back to 6700 BC, and a site in the Indus Valley in Harappa, which dates back to 2,000 BC. Despite the presence of remnants found at the levels of dwellings, it is not clear whether cats were actually domesticated per se.

More likely, this phenomenon began in 4000 BC. People along the Nile in Egypt began to adopt a more sedentary lifestyle and agricultural practices. This brought wild cats closer to their dwellings because these animals were attracted to the prey that sought refuge in their fields and attics.

Little by little, the wild cats began to tolerate other animals and then attempted to get closer to humans. They gradually overcame their fear and were transformed physically, abandoning the camouflage skin that was no longer needed so far from the bush. They took up residence in houses and used their sharp fangs and furtive swipes of the paw to rid the houses of the rodents, vipers and cobras that slithered around on the ground.

Thus the cat entered the age of domestication. The El Licht hieroglyphs describe how cats were integrated into Egyptian houses.

This is when cats began to win over people in high positions.

Birds drinking from a dish at the house of Ciceron. Roman mosaic art from Pompei.
Naples Archeological Museum, G. Dagli Orti collection, Paris.

ORIGIN OF THE WORD CAT

Linguist are not unanimous on the origin of the word cat. Ancient Egyptians used an onomatopoeia to label cats – *meow* or *myeou*. This corresponded to the phonetic transcription of the hieroglyph for cat. Copts used the term *chau*. It should be noted that the word *tom* [cat] is an anagram from Atoum, the sun god likened to a cat. The Greeks called cats *ailuros*, from the words aiol and ouros, which are translated as "wagging tail." In Latin, felis was first used to designate wild cats, then weasels and finally cats in the writings of Ciceron (1st century BC). The word *cattus* replaced felis when domesticated cats from the Orient were introduced into Rome. The word was used for the first time in a scientific context in the agronomy treaty of Palladius entitled *De re rustica*, which dates back to the IVth century. The word catus does appear in the Bible in the Book of Baruch, but is used in reference to a bird of the night. According to Isidore of Seville, *catus* comes from captare – to take, or from cattare – to have a piercing look. In the VIIth century, the term used for cats was *musio*, *murilegus* or *muriceps* (one who captures mice).

The word catus translated into several languages:

- Roman languages: *gato* in Portuguese and Spanish, *gatto* in Italian;
- Celtic languages: *cat* in English;
- Slavic languages: *kochka* in Russian;
- Germanic languages: *Katze* in German;

In France, the word *chat* was certified in 1175, while the word *chatte* appeared in the XIIIth century. The word *chaton* dates to 1261 and the word *chatière* dates to 1275.

The Cardinal playing with his cats of whom he was particularly fond. In "Richelieu" by Maurice Leloir, early XXth century. Selva Photographs, Paris.

During the XIth dynasty (2134 – 1991 BC) in Egypt, cats became the favorite pets of the Theban king, Mentouhotep II. Other personalities of the time also cherished cats: Queen Tiyi, wife of Amenophis III (1400 – 1362) and Prince Thoutmosis, older brother of King Amenophis IV (1363 – 1346). In private tombs, cats were depicted lying under the chair of their master, indicating their role as pets. Cats could also be seen parading across papyrus - talented hunters lying in wait for waterfowl.

Much later, when they were able to cross the borders of this sacred world, cats began to tour the world, taken aboard boats as they set off to explore or colonize. They reached India around 500 BC and then other countries in the Orient, but did not reach Japan until 999. They arrived in Europe belatedly. The Romans brought them into both the south of Russia and the north of Europe 100 years after the birth of Christ. At the same time, cats were landing in Norway with the mercenaries returning from Byzantium. Four hundred years later, they reached Latvia.

It took many years until they penetrated into the New World. They were brought by French Jesuits to Quebec in the 1500's. They accompanied the pilgrims on the Mayflower and headed to America in 1620. They were so well loved on the great continent that the Society of Library Cats was founded there in their honor.

After suffering through a period of hell that lasted throughout the entire Middle Ages, cats began to arouse deep feelings. As Daniel Defoe, author of *Robinson Crusoe*, pointed out, very few English families in London did not own a cat in 1630. In 1700, cats were given increasingly more important places in the homes of Turks, who were enamoured with them. Throughout all of Europe under Louis XIV and XV, many socialites enjoyed the company of cats: Marie Leszczynska, wife of Louis XV; the Duchess of Maine, wife of one of the sons of Louis XIV; the Duchess of Montespan; Princess Palatine, wife of the Duke of Orleans and the Marquise of Deffand.

Intellectuals got away from Descartes, whose idea of the animal-machine seemed outdated and inappropriate. Cats were restored to favor thanks to François-Augustin Paradis de Moncrif, who dedicated an entire book to cats (1727). After authors such as Chateaubriand, Victor Hugo, Théophile Gautier, Honoré de Balzac, Alexandre Dumas and Charles Baudelaire came Champfleury, a realist author, who expressed his "felineophile" feelings in the book *Les Chats* (Cats), published in 1869. Steinlen, a drawer, created a new feline silhouette in his album entitled, *Des chats, images sans paroles* (Cats, Pictures without Words) (1897). Émile Zola, François Coppée, Pierre Loti, Stéphane Mallarmé, Paul Léautraud, Jean Giraudoux and Colette were all cat lovers.

Friends of politicians from Richelieu to Churchill to Poincaré, Clemenceau and de Gaulle, cats had their fans. The ideal confidant, they in turn won over American presidents. Abraham Lincoln (1809 – 1865) adopted three scrawny, hungry cats. White House galas were never held without Slippers, President Roosevelt's cat (1858 – 1919). John F. Kennedy (1917 – 1963) used to cuddle his cat, Tom Kitten. Among our contemporaries, Socks, Bill Clinton's cat has been written up in the press.

In Great Britain, Sir Winston Churchill (1874 – 1965) bequeathed part of his fortune to his cat, Jock.

Soft and reassuring, cats allowed the admirers who loved their soft fur to pet them. They entertained toddlers. They won over comfortable places in hearts and homes. Although a roof over their heads was guaranteed, they nevertheless maintained their independence, making them undoubtedly the only animal that could get away with being so demanding for a friendship sometimes aloof…

Cats as Symbols Throughout the Ages

Although doubt remains as to the date when cats first appeared in Egypt, it is thought that around 4000 BC Egyptians domesticated cats and turned them into hunters, fishers and more importantly, ratters, since rats had become a national plague on the harvests. This role allowed the cat to gain respect and admiration and to finally become a guardian god who governed the family.

Egypt. Cat sarcophagus in finished and painted wood. 332-330 BC. Louvre Museum.
G. Dagli Orti collection, Paris.

Cats rose to the ranks of Totem (Myeo). They entered the pantheon of the Egyptian gods, first portrayed as the god Ra (the Sun), who killed Apopis the snake, god of the Night, every morning. They also represented Nafdet, the destructive goddess of snakes. During the XXIIth dynasty in Bubastis, the cat even took over for the lioness as guardian of the sacred Temple in the form of the goddess Bastet. Also called Bast or Pacht, this goddess with the head of a cat was the goddess of love and a symbol of femininity. Priests of this goddess were constantly on the alert for the slightest signs from the sacred "catery," which they considered to be omens. When the cats died, they were embalmed. In the XIXth century, hundreds of thousands of mummies were discovered. Unfortunately, however, they aroused little interest and most were sold off as fertilizer. A person who accidentally killed a cat could be subject to the death penalty. Contrary to popular belief, cats were killed frequently, but only by priests and the official caregivers of the cats. This was undoubtedly not only a means of selection and curbing overpopulation but especially of offering an ex-voto to the goddess.

Osiris (the god of harvests reminiscent of the sun) was also symbolized by a cat. Cats were therefore the symbol of both the moon and the sun. Herodotus and Plutach offered several explanations: the fact that the variations in the pupil of the cat were assimilated to how high the sun was in the sky; the fact that she-cats loved the moon; their nocturnal activities; their eyes that glowed in the dark and the changes in pupil diameter, which was also similar to the phases of the moon. The symbol of the moon was the one that endured throughout the years.

Cats had become such important members of the family that when they died, all members of the family shaved their eyebrows as a sign of mourning. If a fire broke out, it was more important to try to save a cat than a human. If a person was unable to save the cat, he had to spread cat ashes on himself and parade through the streets mauling himself.

The Persian king, Cambyse II, won the battle of Peluse because his soldiers brandished shields with cats strapped to them and the Egyptians, not wanting to hurt the animals, surrendered. The greatest festivities, the Bubastides, occurred during the second month of the flooding season. Men and women went down the Nile, dancing, laughing, singing and making music. The Temple was open to everyone during this time and the goddess was brought out in procession. The celebration was for the goddess of fertility and the protector of the harvests.

China and India discovered cats shortly after Egypt did. They were perceived as helpful animals because of their hunting abilities. Their beauty gained them acceptance as pets, essentially for women. In China, the rustic god, Li-Shou, had cat-like features and in India, the fertility goddess, Sasti, was the equivalent of Bastet.

The cats that were so jealously guarded by the Egyptians were stolen by the Greeks in Luxor and Thebes during cultural and commercial exchanges and consequently introduced into Europe. Legend has it that the tension between Rome and Egypt stemmed from cats. When Caesar occupied the banks of the Nile in 47 BC, a Roman who had killed a cat was stoned by the people of Alexandria, who rose up against this occupying force. Hostilities ensued and eventually led to the death of Mark Anthony and Cleopatra. From then on, cats were outlawed in Roman-held Egypt. Whether legend or reality, this story illustrates the power cats represented at that time. In Greece, the equivalent of Bastet was the goddess Artemis, who created the cat.

As Pline the Ancient attests in his book *Histoires naturelles* (Natural Stories), the Roman world had come to appreciate cats not only for their hunting abilities, but also for their beauty (numerous frescos and mosaics testify to this) and for their independent nature – freedom incarnate.

Roman colonies therefore spread the worship of Bastet throughout Europe (and even transposed it to the worship of Diane), which is undoubtedly one of the underlying reasons for the superstition linked to this animal in Europe.

Cats were introduced in Japan around the VIth century. According to custom, every temple owned two cats in order to keep mice

away from the manuscripts. Legend has it that emperor Hidi.jo, a great lover of cats, ordered that cats should be pampered. They were pampered to such an extent that when cats were needed to protect the silkworms against mice, rather than disturb them, pictures of cats were instead painted on doors or else bronze, porcelain or wooden statuettes were set up to trick the mice. Of course, this was not very effective and cats came to personify helpless,

Dreaming cat. Asian engraving. Selva collection, Paris.

Le Fort des Chats assiegé par Mer, et par Terre, par les Rats et les
Souris, ou il y est Mort du temps jadis plus de dix huit cens mil Rats,
et Souris, dont les Chats on remporteé vne grande Victoire Sur eux, leur
ayant fait lever le Siege, et les ayant contraints de ne plus paroître.

XVIIth century caricature. B.N.G.
J.-L. Charmet collection, Paris.

evil, selfish devils. In the Middle Ages, the
Japanese distinguished good luck cats by their
"tortoise shell" fur (white, black and tawny)
and malevolent cats by their forked tail and
their ability to change themselves into witches.
However, cats again saw their hour of glory
when it was forbidden to confine adult

cats. The Japanese adoration for cats was not
cloaked in religion however. Disciples of yoga
took a liking to the sleeping position of the cat
(lying in a curled up position), which was the
ideal position to regulate vital body fluids. A
symbol of purity, cats became the intercessor
between perfect and unique Buddha and his
faithful followers. And yet, when it was time
for Buddha to ascend to Nirvana, he is said
to have been sleeping and consequently
arrived late, which was considered to be most
irreverent.

The Arabs of the VIIth century saw a pure
spirit in cats, unlike the unclean spirit they saw
in dogs. They worshiped the Golden Cat
before Islam, and Mohammed also looked
favorably on cats. Indeed, according to legend,
when Mohammed's cat, Muezza, was sleeping
in the prophet's sleeve, Mohammed chose to
cut his clothes rather than disturb his companion. The cat was grateful. His master then
affectionately stroked the back of the cat with
his hand three times, thereby granting the cat
seven lives and the ability to always land on
his feet when he fell.

As for the introduction of the cat into Europe,
there are two theories.
The first theory refers to the Roman legion-
naires under Julius Caesar who reportedly
brought cats into Great Britain via a Roman
tribe called the "Friends of Cats" established in
the Netherlands.

The second theory is that when the Egyptian
general, Gosthelos, fled to Portugal, he of
course took his cats with him. His descendants later became the monarchs of Scotland,
the point from which cats began to conquer
the United Kingdom. In the meantime,
Egyptian priests landing with their cats were
well liked by the Franks and the Celts.

In Gaul, there was very little interest in cats in
the IVth and Vth centuries. They were more
well liked in Northern Europe than in
Southern Europe. Cats were liked in
Germania because they had eliminated the

rats and in Scandinavia, cats accompanied the goddess of beauty and love, Freja, also known as Freyja in other Nordic countries.

Hordes of barbarians from Asia bringing with them the plague and the brown rat, caused cats to spread throughout all Europe. They were sold for a small fortune and benefited from protective laws so that they could fight the rodents. For example, any person who killed a cat that guarded an attic had to pay a fine in the form of meat, wool, milk or wheat that was equivalent to the length of the body of the victim when held by the end of the tail with its head level to the ground. However, this favorable period for the cat ceased with the arrival of Christianity in the XIth, XIIth and XIIIth centuries, except during the Crusades, when the black rats returned. Cats, considered to be arrogant, slowly faded into obscurity. The Church attributed strange and evil powers to the cat in order to destroy the myths and various forms of pagan worship associated with this animal. It had no choice but to object to this feline symbol of femininity, sensuality and sexuality.

Hundreds of thousands of cats were chased, crucified, skinned alive or thrown into the fire because they were the companions of witches, who would come to the Sabbath disguised as black cats. They shared their fate in this respect. Justice was on the side of the clergy in the fight against debauchery in the name of elevating the Spirit. Judges did not hesitate to directly implicate cats in witch trials. The Inquisition unleashed all kinds of violence against this animal such as the dreadful throw-

ing of cats into the fires of St. Jean or the fairs in Flanders, which were actually cat hunts. Belgium threw its cats off the tops of cathedral towers. Germany forced cat owners to cut off the ears of the cat. Not to be outdone, France had a custom of walling up live cats in the foundation of the house in order to protect the house against evil spirits. Cats were exterminated to such an extent that in Europe they were later itemized as an actual asset on inventories, and in wills and estates.

Thus in the Middle Ages cats were considered to be symbols of evil and Satan.

Once again, it was an invasion of rats, this time the gray rat (also called sewer rat) in 1799, that helped clear the good name of cats. A decree in Colbert ordered all ships of the Royal Navy to carry two cats aboard in order to ward off rodents.

During the Age of the Enlightenment everything linked to witchcraft was demystified.

Around 1885, the Pasteurian era also contributed to the feline return to grace. The knowledge that diseases could be transmitted by infinitely small beings known as microbes lead to a phobia of animals, which were potential carriers. Cats, however, were a symbol of cleanliness because they spent hours on end cleaning themselves and therefore became the most approachable animal. Thus began another period of glory: sculptors, painters, storytellers, fable writers, philosophers, poets and writers all lent distinction to the cat, who was often their companion in solitude.

Cats were at times symbols of good and at times symbols of evil. Art illustrates the various periods cats have endured and testify to the myriad ways man has viewed them.

Cats in Art and the Media

The cat has been represented frequently in art and the media over the centuries according to its status as either demon or god, hunter or companion animal, or simple illustration of beauty and grace. Nevertheless, as Christabel Aberconway's collection confirms, few painters throughout history have been "cat lovers."

Egypt. Cat hunting in a papyrus thicket. Relief from the Old Kingdom. Vatican Museum. F. Gourdon collection, Paris.

Cats in Painting and Sculpture

Prehistoric times

From this period, we have a bone sculpted into the profile of a cat (from the Pyrénées-Atlantiques Department in southwestern France) and a cave painting discovered in Gabillou (in the Dordogne Department in southwestern France) apparently representing the head of a cat.

Egypt

Egypt has yielded the first abundant iconography.

Apart from sacred images, the cat appears on so-called "ostraca," or small pieces of pottery that Egyptians used like notebooks to record their thoughts, notes, and drawings.

This media was used to create caricatures of cats, who were often drawn in human attitudes leading flocks of geese or serving mice. Some consider these pieces of pottery to be the origin of animal fables.

The Egyptians saw nature as mystical. Cats were often represented on amulets, objects which were both mystical and aesthetic.

The theme of "the cat under the chair" long remained the archetype for bas-relief (with sexual connotations when the chair belonged to a woman).

A papyrus dating from 3200 B.C. from the *Book of the Dead* describes a cat killing Apopis, the dragon-snake of darkness and enemy to the sun god (Ra). Generally, the cat is represented holding Apopis with one foreleg and brandishing in the other the knife with which he will cut off his victim's head. This scene symbolizes the sun obliterating the night and allowing the solar cycle to begin anew.

During the New Kingdom (1560-1080 B.C.), painters used cats as a theme in royal tombs. The British Museum has one example: the tomb of Nebamum, where a cat is used like a pointer dog in bird hunting. Another example, found in the Valley of the Kings on the tomb of the scribe Nakht, shows a cat crouching under a table eating fish.

In the late second millennium B.C., in the city of Bubastis, the main deity was Bastet, the goddess of fertility and protector of families and crops. After being depicted as a lion woman, she became a cat woman or simply a cat (like other leonine goddesses who were intermittently depicted as cats: Pakhet, Nout, etc.). Once a symbol of the sun, the cat became a symbol of the moon and therefore governed femininity.

The Greco-Roman period

Among the few representations of cats in the Greco-Roman world are a famous mosaic from Pompeii showing a cat seizing a duck and a bas-relief from the 5th century B.C. showing a cat confronting a dog.

In terms of sculpture, the Greek funerary stele exhibited at the Athens Museum of Archaeology shows two young Greeks amused by a dog's antipathy toward a cat.

A stele from the Gallo-Roman era found in Alise-Sainte-Reine in France's Côte d'Or Department shows a young man holding a cat. The Bordeaux Museum has a tomb bearing the sculpture of a young girl, her cat, and a rooster. Dating from the medieval era, the Saint-Pierre Cathedral has a choir stall featuring a cat catching a mouse.

Athenian with a cat on a leash. Greek bas-relief, around 510 B.C. Athens. National Museum of Archaeology.
G. Dagli Orti collection, Paris.

The Medieval period

Cats were rarely represented during the Middle Ages, due to their bad reputation. Some exceptions include Tibert, a cat in *Le Roman de Renart*, featured in the Strasbourg Cathedral; the sculpture of the rat-hunting cat of Saint-Germain-l'Auxerrois in Paris; and the painting of a domestic cat at its masters' feet in Le *Mois de février* from *Les Très Riches Heures* du *Duc de Berry* by Pol de Limbourg.

Still, numerous (often later) pictorial representations bear witness to the link between cats and sorcery established by the Church. Examples include Hans Thoma's lithography *La sorcière* [*The Witch*] (1870), Hermann

Vogel's wood engraving by the same name (1890), and Queverdo's *Le départ pour le sabbat* [*Going to the Witches' Sabbath*].

Before the 15th century, the cat was represented rarely and only anecdotally in paintings: *The Sacrifice of Abraham* by Benozzo Gozzoli (1468-1484), *Esau Selling his Birthright to Jacob* by Michel Corneille, and Luca Giordano.

Jan de Beer (1475-1518) included a cat in his *Annunciation of the Virgin*, but cats were virtually absent from sculpture.

Sixteenth century

In the early 16th century, as the cat's image improved, it was included in several paintings as a subject. In *Adam and Eve* (1504), Albrecht Dürer depicts a cat as peaceful and gentle, as opposed to a snake. In this painting, the cat is unaware of the presence of the dog and the mouse, as human sin has not yet upset the harmony that reigns over Earth. This representation of a cat dozing at the couple's feet has virtually become a classic, especially for Flemish artists such as Franz Pourbus the Elder (1570) and Pietr Jansz Saenredam (1797).

In these three paintings, the cat is represented as one animal among others as a reminder that Adam was given the duty of naming them all. Leonardo da Vinci lovingly represented cats in many pieces in various realistic attitudes.

Seventeenth century

In their paintings, Philippe de Champaigne (1602-1674, *Les pèlerins d'Emmaüs* [*The Pilgrims of Emmaus*]) and Charles Le Brun (*Le sommeil de l'enfant Jésus* [*The Sleeping Infant Jesus*], 1655) introduced cats into the foreground.

The Annunciation was a recurring theme involving cats. Often indifferent to this major event, the cat appears to be drawn by the forces of evil. Le Tintoret must have shared this ambivalence toward cats, for the cat in his *Annunciation* bears a malevolent expression.

Jérôme Bosch also linked the cat to the evils of hell in his *Jardin des délices terrestres* [*Garden of*

Earthly Delights], but very anecdotally and naturally, since he depicted the devil in this form. This malevolent role appears frequently in representations of the Holy Family, including that by Baroccio (1563) and *Portrait de famille* [*Family Portrait*] by Georg Pencz (1541), which shows a cat stalking a goldfinch. This bird was known for its particular fondness for thistles, an allusion to Christ's crown of thorns. The cat eyeing the bird, a symbol of

Christ the redeemer, embodies the evil that threatens the salvation of humanity.

Representations of the Holy Family by many other painters also include cats, but without a goldfinch: Leonardo da Vinci, Giulio Romano, Vermeyen, Murillo, Rembrandt, Frans Floris de Vriendt. Cats also appear in Christ's life during times of celebration: The

Wedding at Cana by Giuseppe Mazzuoli, *Feast in the House* of Levi by Paolo Veronese, or, more traditionally, in Veronese's *The Last Supper*, featuring a cat sleeping at Judas' feet, once again depicted as an accomplice of evil. The dog-cat opposition, a symbolic allusion to the battle between good and evil, appears once again in several paintings, including *The Last Supper* (1481), painted in the Sistine Chapel by Cosimo Roselli.

The cat's presence in scenes following the Resurrection symbolizes Christ returned from the dead and now eternal. According to Valériano, the cat embodies the moon and therefore signifies the beginning and end of all things.
The life of the Virgin Mary is another pretext for numerous appearances by felines in pieces including *La visitation* [*The Visitation*] by Theodor van Loon.

Religious painters rarely depicted cats as companions, with the exception of the cat in St. Jerome's cell.

In the theme of the Vanities, the cat symbolizes the sense of sight. To this allegory were added the metaphors of feminine beauty and earthly love (*Allégorie de la vue* [*Allegory of Sight*], 1616, by Jan Saenredam; *La vue* [*Sight*], 1666, by Barent Fabritius; *Portrait de jeune femme tenant un chat* [*Portrait of a Young Woman Holding a Cat*], 1525, by Bacchiacca; and *Vanité* [*Vanity*], attributed to Pietr Wtewael).

Illustrating the passage of time, the theme of "clawing" symbolizes the fleeting nature of earthly pleasures (*Enfants jouant avec un chat* [*Children Playing with a Cat*] by Jan Miense Molenaer, *Le coup de patte du chat* [*Clawing Cat*] by Prud'hon, *Charité* [*Charity*] by Cornelis van Haarlem). Meanwhile, an imaginary world based on the medieval bestiary gave rise to parody animal concerts. There was a true craze for this genre, especially among Flemish painters: *Le concert de chats* [*The Concert of Cats*] by David Teniers the Younger and an etching in which Jan Brueghel uses cats in place of notes on sheet music.

During the Baroque era, Rembrandt included cats in only one painting, *Le ménage du menuisier* [*The Woodworker's Household*].

Having become a household animal, even among the middle class, the cat began appearing in pastoral compositions by Jacques Callot, Abraham Bosse, and David Teniers the Younger (*Le concert des chats* [*The Concert of Cats*]). The painter Jordaens included cats in his drinking scenes.

Gerard Terborch also included cats in his *La famille du rémouleur* [*The Grinder's Family*], as did Velasquez in his *Fileuses* [*Spinners*] (around 1657). Some consider these cats as symbols of freedom.

An etching by Pierre-Paul Prud'hon shown in the 1798 Exposition features a huge cat sitting at Liberty's feet as she tramples her chains.

Chien gardant du gibier
[*Dog Guarding Prey*] *by François Desportes (1661-1743).*
International Museum of Hunting, Gien, château (France).
G. Dagli Orti collection, Paris.

Eighteenth century

During the Age of Enlightenment, Watteau painted cats full of grace and goodness.

Chardin painted a lovely cat in *La blanchisseuse* [*The Laundress*] but was more cruel in his other paintings, depicting the cat as pilfering and sneaky.

Eighteenth-century artists rediscovered cats as a hunters that coexisted with game (François Desportes, Jean-Baptiste Oudry, and Gilles Colson). Louis Le Nain painted a contented cat curled up peacefully at the corner of the hearth.

Swiss painter Gottfried Mind (1768-1814), nicknamed the "Raphael of Cats," produced numerous paintings featuring cats, which he idolized. He even sculpted them from chestnuts. But cats returned to the flat background in paintings by François Boucher, Jean-Honoré Fragonard, and Maurice Quentin de la Tour.

With rare exceptions, cats were treated in a conventional manner in European art. Cats were traditionally depicted as greedy and pilfering, curled up in a chair or in the arms of their mistress.

Nineteenth century

However, feline representations abound in nineteenth-century pictorial art, including *Julie Manet* by Pierre Auguste Renoir, *La mort du cochon* [*Death of the Pig*] by Louis Léopold Boilly, *Miss May Belfort* by Toulouse-Lautrec, and *L'atelier du peintre* [*The Artist's Studio*] by Gustave Courbet.

Apart from the famous *Olympia* with her black cat, Édouard Manet composed a superb piece featuring a white cat and a black cat sitting on a roof in the moonlight: *Chats de Champfleury* [*Cats of Champfleury*]. Géricault painted a white cat full of goodness and melancholy.

The two kittens at the center of Gaugin's painting entitled *Where Do We Come From? What Are We? Where Are We Going?* illustrate innocence.

Cats are also present in paintings by Maurice Denis, including *Le goûter* [*The Snack*] (1919) and *Hommage à Cézanne* [*Hommage to Cézanne*].

Some nineteenth-century, so-called "bourgeois" painters were almost entirely devoted to cats. One hundred eighty-two of these specialized painters have been recorded, including Philippe Rousseau (*L'importun* [*The Intruder*], 1850) and Louis-Eugène Lambert (*Famille de chats* [*Family of Cats*], 1887) in France and Charles Van den Eycken in Belgium.

Twentieth century

This abundance of cats in pictorial art continued into the twentieth century with works like *Le corsage à carreaux* [*The Checkered Blouse*], *Le*

Julie Manet by Auguste Renoir (1841-1919). Musée d'Orsay, Paris. Giroudon collection, Paris.

chat blanc [The White Cat], and La petite fille au chat [Little Girl With a Cat] by Pierre Bonnard. These pieces suggest new facets and unique attitudes for feline subjects.

The many cats in the world of Balthus (Mitsou, Quarante images [Forty Images], Le chat de la Méditerranée [The Cat of the Mediterranean]) contributed to the erotic atmosphere the artist cherished.

Another amazing painting is that by Douanier Rousseau, who drew a Portrait of Pierre Loti (or of Edmond Achille Frank?) and his cat, adding a more naïve aspect to his work.

An ardent admirer of cats, Théophile Alexandre Steinlein (1859-1923) made portraits of thousands of cats of all breeds in all settings. He also helped decorate the "Black Cat" cabaret.

Japanese artist Foujita (1886-1968) produced many self portraits featuring a cat on his shoulder (Self Portrait, 1928, Centre Pompidou). His far eastern calligraphy is admirably well-suited to his lithographs.

Fernand Léger, a modernist painter, surrounded his mistress with cats and books in La femme au chat [The Woman With a Cat] (1921). Francis Picabia, Marc Chagall (Paris par la fenêtre [Paris Through the Window]), Salvador Dali, and Pablo Picasso (Chat dévorant un oiseau [Cat Devouring a Bird]) all painted cats. But not until the twentieth century did cats enter the world of painting under their own name: Rapinou by Suzanne Valadon, Lulu by Vollard, Sita by Cecilia Beaux, etc.

A huge cat lover, Léonor Fini represented cats as "individuals in their own right," beautiful, magical, natural, innocent, very sensual, and rebellious in a world where the borders between animal and human were blurred. According to Fini, her attraction to these animals was not mysterious; she was simply moving "toward a perfect being, more beautiful than all others." Many of these paintings show sphinxes, women with the body of a cat.

Fini created masks, costumes, theater and dance sets (Les demoiselles de la nuit [The Young Women of the Night], a 1948 ballet by Roland Petit) inspired by her fetish animal. She spoke about her love of cats to her friend Stanislao Lepri (Coup de foudre [Love at first sight], 1972, De père inconnu [From an Unknown Father], 1975).

Contemporary fantasy art often features black panthers or cats as symbols of femininity. Pieces include Katzen Portrait by German painter Carl Rohring (1980), in which the head of a cat is surrounded by feathers and dried flowers forming a fanciful head of hair like a woman's.

Cats in Literature

Ancient times

Among the writers and poets of ancient times who mention cats are Homer, Plutarch, Aesop, Virgil, and Ovid.

Aesop tells us that a female cat in love with a handsome young man asks for help from Venus, who agrees to turn her into a woman métamorphosée en femme [The Woman Who Was Turned into a Cat]). But the cat remains a cat and, despite her transformation, can only chase a mouse across the room. In his Metamorphoses, Ovid describes the transformation of Diana, Apollo's sister, into a cat.

The Middle Ages

In the twelfth century, the cat is found in farces and fables including the Roman de Renart featuring Tibert, a cat who embodies deceit, cruelty, and slyness, just like Renart. Stories of witchcraft also abound in cats.

The Renaissance

In the sixteenth century, opinions on cats were still divided. Ronsard and Rabelais shared a repulsion for these animals, while Montaigne (Essays) and Du Bellay defended them passionately. Du Bellay even composed a two hundred-verse epitaph in memory of his cat, Belaud.

The Classical Era

In the seventeenth century, writers denounced women's hypersensitivity with regard to cats (Scarron).

Fable writers echoed public condemnation of the cat and helped fuel their negative image. La Fontaine still considered the cat a selfish, smarmy, mischievous animal.

He used a cat for his caricature of the canon.

Le chat botté et son jeune maître [Puss in Boots and His Young Master]. Illustration for Charles Perrault's story Puss in Boots. Épinal print, around 1840. Private collection. J.-L. Charmet collection, Paris.

His cat appeared sixteen times, but the outcome was never in the cat's favor. La Fontaine's cat is the "Attila of rodents," a sly, cruel, deceitful hunter (*The Cat, the Weasel, and the Little Rabbit*) who selfishly snubs his friends (*The Cat and the Two Sparrows*). The names of La Fontaine's cats reveal his scorn: Raminagrobis, Raton, Rodilard, Grippe-Fromage, and Grippeminaud. Rabelais' "stuffed" cats resemble Raminagrobis. Rabelais characterizes the cat as a hypocrite and uses cats to satirize men of the law and their leader, Grippeminault.

In Charles Perrault's *Stories or Tales From Olden Times* (1697), the feline character Puss in Boots, clever but loyal to his master, is once again a bearer of good luck. As with all fairytales, the author is inspired by folk tradition. This work illustrates how a poor and abandoned younger son gets revenge with the help of his cat. In this very symbolic work, the lunar forces embodied by the cat's magic oppose the solar forces represented by royalty.

In *The White Cat* by Contesse d'Aulnoy, from her *Contes nouveaux ou les fées à la mode* [*New Tales or New-fangled Fairies*] (1698), the cat is again portrayed as a wonderful, protective guide (tutelary genius) who brings luck to the person he serves. Here again, we encounter a multitude of symbols, and the old balance is restored: three solar kingdoms versus three lunar kingdoms. M.-L. von Franz sees in these two tales the need for the hero to recover his shadow (his cat), that is, to reintegrate his anima into his conscious personality. Based on a Freudian interpretation, Bruno Bettelheim explains that man must learn to trust and accept his unconscious.

Eighteenth century

The first work truly dedicated to the glory of the cat, *Les chats* [*Cats*] by François Augustin Paradis de Moncrif, appeared in 1727. This author depicts cats as independent and merry, forming sorts of republics and approaching humans out of pure kindness, rather than servitude like dogs. Emotionally and physically, these cats exude grace. But this extravagant work was mocked by Voltaire.

In *Natural History*, Buffon (1749-1804) defends the dog's sincerity, as opposed to the cat's deceitfulness. Chateaubriand (1768-1848), an admirer of the cat's independence, rose up against Buffon. He admitted a desire to improve the cat's image and described cats lovingly (including Micetto in *Memoirs from Beyond the Tomb*).

Nineteenth century

In *Les peines de coeur d'une chatte anglaise* [*The Heartbreak of an English Cat*], Balzac uses the cat as a mouthpiece to denounce the hypocrisy of British Puritanism. He admitted that this work brought him into the domain of comparative psychology. Just like La Fontaine, he was thinking of *La chatte métamorphosée en femme* [*The Woman Who Was Turned into a Cat*]. Nineteenth-century writers celebrated the cat's ambiguity, mystery, and individualism, as well as its relationship to the supernatural. For the same reasons that cats were largely exterminated in the seventeenth century, they were loved in the nineteenth century. Baudelaire's "mysterious cat, seraphic cat, and strange cat" perfectly illustrates this notion in two poems from *Flowers of Evil*: "The Cat" and "Cats." The cat's flexible body and silky fur play an important sexual role.

Romantic writers were impassioned by the mystery and magic associated with felines.

Verlaine extolled the cat's virtues in "*La femme et la chatte*" ["*The Woman and the Cat*"].

Indeed, mystery and fantasy appear in literature about cats in the nineteenth century and later in the twentieth century.

The extraordinary Cheshire Cat in *Alice in Wonderland* (Lewis Carroll, 1865) is a perfect illustration of the absurd and the nonsense linked to this enigmatic animal.

The poet Edward Lear, a master of nonsense, depicted cats as both companions and literary subjects ("*The Owl and the Pussycat*"). Absurdity is the opposite of common sense and, in this regard, the cat again proves its independence through its rebellious, mysterious spirit.

While for Émile Zola the black cat symbolizes wrongdoing as a witness to a murder (*Thérèse Raquin*), for Edgar Allan Poe the black cat evokes a certain uneasiness linked to evil. The animal seems to unleash dark forces, with guilty sexuality and lechery.

In *The Cat That Walked By Himself*, Rudyard Kipling describes an animal clever enough to retain its freedom. He complies with folk tradition by creating a bestiary to illustrate human nature, as opposed to later twentieth-century authors like Louis Pergaut and Maurice Genevoix, who observe the cat objectively in its natural environment.

Twentieth century

Twentieth-century writers continue to celebrate the cat while moving beyond romanticism and seeking to better understand and discover the cat.

Pierre Loti attempts to penetrate the "strange window" of the cat's eyes to reach the "unknown" inside its little brain. The cat often appears to be dictatorial in contemporary literature. Cats do not stray; they exercise their freedom. The author thus feels he is chosen anew each day.

Robert Sabatier feels as though he lives in his cat's home. Graf Bouby (Jean Blot) calls his owners his "slaves." In *L'homme pressé* [*The Man in a Hurry*], Paul Morand admits, "I had a hundred cats, or rather, a hundred cats had me." People who believe that cats love them are opposed by those who are convinced that cats love only the advantages that humans give them—essentially domestic comforts. This

does not bother Cocteau, who sees the cat as the visible soul of the home, or Baudelaire, who sees cats as "familiar spirits" in the house that give life to objects.

Michel Tournier coined the term "suradaptation" to illustrate the cat's ability to disappear, blend in, and reappear in the house. According to Renée Massip, "some houses need a cat," like Maurice Genevoix's Rou, a

Back cover of The Thousand and One Nights by Lucien Lafargue, 1912. Selva Photographies collection, Paris.

superb cat torn between the delights of freedom and the pleasures of domestic life, and Rémo Forlani's Finette.

Other authors believe that cats like both their owner and their home and are prepared to follow their owner even into uncomfortable situations (for example, Christopher Simon and Anne Frank). Colette describes the world of animals realistically. Yet, she lapses into anthropomorphism with regard to cats named One and Only, Dernière, Kapok, Mini-Mini, etc. Colette illustrates the cat's lack of modesty in *La maison de Claudine* [*Claudine's House*]:
While cats were reputed to bring luck in love in the fifteenth century, they are now a symbol of pleasure, sensuality, and sexuality (*Chat beauté* by Paul Guth, *Graf Bouby* by Jean Blot, *Blues for a Black Cat* by Boris Vian, and *A Cat's Life* by Yves Navarre).

Authors link women and cats closely, sometimes making them one and the same ("*La femme et la chatte*" ["*The Woman and the Cat*"] by Paul Verlaine, *Cat on a Hot Tin Roof* by Tennessee Williams, *La femme du boulanger* [*The Baker's Wife*] by Maurice Pagnol). While cats sometimes turn into women, they also become rivals of women (*The Cat* by Simenon and *La chatte* [*The Female Cat*] by Colette).
In *Particularly Cats*, Doris Lessing describes a woman who must get rid of a female Siamese cat in order to keep her husband.
While the Egyptians already called the cat a "sorrow swallower," Paul Léautaud describes the cat as a refuge and a true friend in his

Profile of Colette with cat. Drawing by Jean Texcier, 1926. Private collection. J.-L. Charmet collection, Paris.

Journal littéraire [*Literary Journal*] peppered with thoughts and anecdotes about cats.

Today, cats inspire and play a role in the author's meditations (*A Cat's Life* by Yves Navarre and *Graf Bouby* by Jean Blot). Boris Simon believes that cats can make man better: The cruel leader of the pack in his *Passage de l'homme-chat* [*Passage of the Man-cat*] discovers a love for cats and recognizes their loving nature and vulnerability. As a result, he becomes able to communicate respectfully with others.
The cat can act as the writer's mirror. In Louis-Ferdinand Céline's German trilogy (*North, Castle to Castle, Rigodon*), there is an obvious parallel between the personality and behavior of the author and that of the cat Bébert.
The cat's death is thus experienced as a double trauma, often accompanied by feelings of guilt (*Le chat des Briarres* [*The Cat of Les Briarres*] by Renée Massip, *The Age of Reason* by Jean-Paul Sartre).
Jules Laforgue and François Maynard composed funeral prayers for their cats (in the manner of Du Bellay's epitaph).
Jean Cocteau illustrated the cat's enigmatic nature in *Beauty and the Beast* (with the Beast in the film appearing as a frightening and loving monster-cat).

However, in contemporary literature, cats (black, of course) are still often linked to witches and the devil. In *The Curse*, a story from *The Mutilated*, Tennessee Williams portrays a cat and a man linked by a ruthless fate. Still, the cat can have a positive effect: In his story *La patte du chat* [*The Cat's Paw*], Marcel Aymé revisits the ancient belief in the power of cats to bring rain by swiping their paw behind their ear.
René Barjavel is one of many writers who believe in metempsychosis. For him, cats are reincarnations of human beings.

Over the ages, some constant themes emerge in the way writers see cats: cats and writing, cats and pleasure or sexuality, cats and women, cats and the absurd, the sacred or diabolical cat, and always the eternal mystery of the cat.

Cats in Movies

There are cat trainers in the movie industry: the Briton John Holmes and the American Frank Inn, who selected cats in several different categories: humpbacked cats who appeared to be arching their backs, scary-looking cats with bristly hair, yawning cats, cats who licked their chops, etc. According to him, "The best feline actors are big eaters," because they work not for petting, but only for cat food.

Among the cat actors in 1920 was Pepper the Cat, a character in the movie *Down on the Farm* who was very attached to Mak Sennet. Pepper was affectionate and got along wonderfully with Frederich the Mouse and Teddy the Great Dane.

In 1952, a cat named Rhubarb played the main character in a movie by the same name. He was an aggressive, vicious, perfidious cat. Arthur Lubin used this skittish cat, the sole heir of an old, misanthropic billionaire, to caricature American society with its gangsters and conciliatory police, its flashy advertising and its fetishism.

Rhubarb, a true star in his time, was paid a very high salary. He also received two Patsy Awards (equivalent of the Oscar for animals).

Many cats, some more interesting than others, have appeared in films of varying quality. On screen, they represent the traditional themes associated with cats:
• The supernatural: *The Cat From Outer Space* by Norman Tokar, *Un jour, un chat* by Jasny Jones, the cat in Ridley Scott's *Alien*, *La féline* by Jacques Tourneur, *Cat People* by Paul Schrader, *Black Cat* by Edgard George Ulmer, based on the story by Edgar Allan Poe.
• Sensuality, sexuality, women: *La féline* by Jacques Tourneur, *Cat People* by Paul Schrader, *La femme du boulanger* by Pagnol with the cat Pomponnette.
Still, despite this handful of films, it seems that cats have not yet found their true place in the movies.

Cats in the Comics

Comics and cartoons are always swapping characters. Some cats born in the comics have

Felix the Cat.
Selva collection, Paris.

become cartoon characters (including those of Walt Disney), while others born in animated features have moved into comic strips (*Felix the Cat*).

From 1911 to 1944, George Herriman, an author of comic strips published in the *New York Journal*, immortalized the cat and its craziness. It has been said that President Wilson read this comic strip directed at the members of his Cabinet. Herriman's lisping cat (of unclear gender) with the evocative name of Krazy Kat is in love with a mouse named Ignatz. This ill-tempered mouse is indifferent to Krazy Kat's advances and spends its time hurling bricks at everyone as policeman Offissa Pupp, hopelessly in love with Krazy Kat, looks on.

Poetry and the logic of the absurd already reigned in this imaginary world that probably inspired Otto Messmer and Pat Sullivan to create the adventurous *Felix the Cat*, featured first in movies and later in comic strips (1923).

Walt Disney's cats are generally strays chased by the dog Pluto. Exceptions include Nip, who spends his time trying to irritate Mickey, and especially Big Pete, a black cat gangster whose shady schemes are foiled by Mickey.

Hanna Barbera's cat Tom defends the house from attack by two little disdainful mice who have made their home in the wall. As can be imagined, they spend their time looking for food and bothering Tom, leading to mad dashes in which anything goes. This story was so successful that *Our Gang*, the magazine that published it, was retitled *Tom & Jerry* in 1942. These adventures were also successful in the movies, as were the antics of Sylvester and Tweety.

Most postwar comic strips featured humans with dogs as pets (Milou, Idéfix, Rantanplan). When cats did appear, it was either to highlight a dog (Hercule and Pif) or to wreak havoc. The cat in *Gaston Lagaffe* is a robber, complainer, and troublemaker.

Azrael, the feline companion of the wizard Gargamel (in *The Smurfs* by Peyo), is a vile cat who is as deceitful and cruel as his master and as demonic as cats were reputed to be in the Middle Ages.

Fritz first appeared in Robert Crumb's notebooks in 1959, but the first strips were not published until 1965. According to his creator, Fritz is a young, sophisticated, very hip feline student living in a huge, modern residence hall with millions of other animals. This cat behaves like an unscrupulous, cynical, ambitious, cocky young man. His adventures always have a happy ending.

A European counter-culture born in the 1970s and equivalent to the American underground (with Fat Freddy) featured Matiolli's *Squeak the Mouse*, a sort of very modern *Tom & Jerry*. In 1978, Jim Davis created the irresistible *Garfield*, a fat orange tiger cat, for the *Herald Tribune*. This short-tempered, lying, lazy, bossy cat makes life difficult for his owner, Jon. Yet, the two cannot live without each other and understand one another. Americans probably see these characters as a couple sharing a home. Garfield's motto is "cats are invincible."

In comics, as in other forms of artistic expression, the same themes and symbols are associated with cats:
- cats as domestic animals (Felix, Garfield, etc.);
- cats as animals who are erotic and in love (Fritz by Matiolli or Edika);
- cats as cruel, hypocritical animals (*Raspoutine* and *Premières enquêtes* by Sokal);
- cats as discrete and clever animals (*Chevalier and Gheebrant*, *Chaminou* by Macherot, Stanislas, *Supermatou*, *Le chat*, alias Jacques Bertrand by Greg);
- cats as cursed animals (*Fat Freddy*, *Maido et Maildur*);
- cats as symbols of the supernatural (the cats in Mandrake, Gogol's telepathic cat in *La foire aux immortels* by Bilal, *The Many Lives of Felix*, *Poussy et Krazy*, *Ottag* by Rebuffi, *Les huit jours du diable* by Convard).

Cats in Caricatures

Russian artists ridiculed their sovereign, Czar Paul I, and caricatured him as a huge, horrible cat.

Louis Wain drew over one thousand cats a year and gave them human expressions. Siné produced comic strips and even plates, basing his caricatures on cats. The same is true of Barberousse and Dubout.

Felix's pranks was even used as one of the official tuning test patterns for the TV network NBC from 1928 – 1930. Lindbergh also chose Felix as his mascot for his aeronautical undertaking.

According to Marcel Brion, French science-fiction author, "Felix is not just a cat, he is THE cat." The famous feline lives in a world of fantasy, where everything is possible, from filling the coal cellar with music notes from a

Mice burying a cat. A recurring theme in Russian mythology: the weak always prevail over the strong. Caricature of the burial of Czar Peter the Great. Russian popular imagery, 1850. Institute of Slavic Studies, Paris. J.-L. Charmet collection, Paris.

Cats in Cartoons

In 1911, G. Harriman created Krazy Kat, whose characteristics were described earlier. Krazy Kat was one of the most poetic characters in cartoons.

Created in 1920 by Otto Messmer, Felix, one of the first stars of talking cartoons, was a huge success. A picture portraying a couple of

saxophone, to offering the birds chirping overhead to two little old men he runs into who are sad because their canary died. He is constantly amazed. His whole world revolves around two signs springing from his head: the exclamation mark and the question mark.

A cheerful character, he takes pleasure in scoffing at life and is proud of his ability to get by on his own. He is as bold as he is mischievous and as lucky as he is ingenious.

During World War II, Fritz Freleny and Chuck Jones created the characters Sylvester and Tweety Bird for Warner Brothers, a studio looking more for gags than for a picture of reality. The protagonist in the story is Sylvester, a big pussycat who is constantly scheming to catch the little bird, often through acts of kindness.

The couple is similar to the Metro Goldwyn Mayer characters, Tom and Jerry, created by Fred Quinky, William Hanna and Joseph Barbera. The audacious mouse always wins following a frantic chase by the clumsy Tom. However, the big cat evolved over the years into a quiet father, scolded by the frisky Jerry - an anthropomorphism of the characters.

Fritz the Cat was born out of a cartoon. Ralf Bakshi first presented this hero, created by Crumb, in 1971. Fritz is a cat full of flaws, though he could have easily been any other animal.

In the world of Walt Disney, cats are often treacherous when they play supporting roles. The two Siamese cats in *Lady and the Tramp* are terrible liars and the cat in *Cinderella* is none other than Lucifer himself.

In *Pinocchio*, Gepetto lavishes care on an adorable, happy pussycat, while Pinocchio is betrayed by a deceitful and hypocritical cat, who is the accomplice of the fox.

Cats play good guys when they have a leading role such as in *That Darn Cat* and the *Aristocats*, which gives an extraordinary image of a cat world (or a human world?) where the aristocrat cats (Duchess, etc.) are portrayed as being just as benevolent as the proletarians (Romeo, etc.).

Walt Disney also devoted other films to cats such as *The Cat from Outer Space*.

Cats in Heraldry

Heraldic bestiaries draw upon cats in particular as a symbol of freedom. The banner of the migrant people from the North (Alains, Sueves and the Vandales) had the silhouette of a cat with a bright silver burst against a black background.

Furthermore, the old Roman Legion went to battle wearing a symbol that had half of a red cat against a violet backdrop, in order to stimulate the desire to defeat.

Cats and Aristocratic Coats of Arms

The good name of cats was truly cleared when they began to appear on coats of arms, which helped contribute to the ennoblement of cats. German author Bertrand de Walkliet testifies to this in his book (1530). The builder of his *Tour du Chat* (Cat Tower) erected a tower with a cat on top.

In the XVIth century, some of the oldest noble families bestowed upon felines the honor of becoming a family symbol. Cats thus appeared on hundreds of coats of arms in Burgundy, Germany, Holland and Italy.

We note, for example, the silver head against a sky-blue backdrop on the Dekaten coat of arms, and the two cat heads facing each other on the Platen coat of arms.

In heraldic tradition, the entire cat is said to be "frightened" if he is lurking, "passing by" if his tail is fluffed out and "bristled" if his arched back is higher that his head and his fur standing on end.

In order to serve as a reminder that cats are night loving hunters, they were often painted with mice against a black background.

On some coats of arms, cats are portrayed as extraordinary animals. On the Chaffaux coat of arms, a cat armed with a scythe is standing in front of a house. The Heighs chose a female cat with the face of a woman wearing a bonnet. The Dobekatz coat of arms shows a cat wearing a necklace and soaring off a high rock. They also were used to represent the motto: "Everything through love, nothing through force" for the Dukes of Burgundy as well as the Kersaint saying, "Bad cat, bad rat."

Cats as Clan Symbols

Cats were also used by families whose name contained syllables such as "cat" or "chat" and their derivatives. The Scottish clan Chattan displayed a mountain cat on their coat of arms. The Catesby clan had a spotted cat on theirs. There was even one coat of arms that showed a cat holding a mouse in its mouth. It apparently belonged to Dick Whitington (or Lord Cat), who became rich and powerful thanks to his fearless cat Fritzy, who according to legend, saved Whitington's entire crew.

However, despite the use of cat imagery in heraldic art, felines did not figure prominently on coats of arms because of their twofold image.

Although they, in fact, embodied freedom and adaptability, their lack of forthrightness and their fearlessness had negative connotations. They are not found in symbols of the French Revolution. With the advent of the Republic, they appeared on one symbol in particular that extolled the virtues of liberty. It showed a cat crouching down at the feet of a goddess resembling Libertas, a deity of Olympia.

The first representation of Liberty showed her next to a cornucopia with a cat and a bird tumbling out with string around the paws.

After the fall of royalty in France and the end of heraldic art, cats started to figure prominently on merchants' signs, often illustrating odd legends.

Cats and Bourgeoisie Signs

The domestic nature of cats with its hint of independence, as well as their superb silhouettes and their proverbial mischievousness all sparked the imagination of shopkeepers. Consequently, there was a flourish of signs for shops and inns along the lines of "The Big Cat," "The Black Cat" or "The Laughing Cat" (The Smoking Cat, The Dancing Cat, etc.).

In 1935 on Boulevard Saint-Germain in Paris, a sign with a large cat wearing glasses marked the spot of one of the first well-established opticians in Paris.

And who could forget the sign designed by A. Willette for the most famous cabaret of Montmartre - "the Black Cat," a truly free-spirit kind of place.

Cats on Stamps

Many countries such as Luxembourg, Poland, the Netherlands, Yemen and Romania, among others, have used cats to symbolize or represent a tale, legend or a character linked to that country. In 1957, the Republic of Cuba issued a stamp in honor of the fiftieth anniversary of the Jeanette Ryder Foundation. The stamp depicted her as an animal protector, with two dogs beside her and a cat on her lap.

Spain commemorated the exploits of Lindbergh by including the silhouette of a cat in the lower right-hand corner.

Cats in Advertising

Given that cats have such strong powers of suggestion in terms of symbols, it is not surprising that they were used in advertising.

Symbol of Comfort and Warmth

In 1885 one of the first famous cats in product advertising was the big black and white pussycat stretched out on an armchair for Old Tom Gin (a name often given to English cats at the time). Since cats spend a great deal of their time sleeping, they need comfort and warmth. Thus they began to appear one by one on car cushions (Fiat), sofas (Cinna), next to boilers (Technal, Techibel) and fireplaces (Supra).

Symbols of Family

Cats are also the guardians of the family and they first appeared in

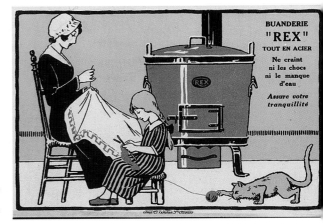

"Rex" laundry room in steel. Advertisement for a washing machine with a mother sewing and her daughter knitting. Silva collection, Paris.

this role way back in the time of the Egyptians. One tobacco company chose the cat for two reasons. The first reason was its name: Catlin Tobacco Company. The second reason was that it had chosen to illustrate the advertisement with a cat defending a tobacco box that was sheltering her young. A cat guarding the house can be also pitted against a rat burglar, in order to show how efficient an alarm system is (Brink's).

Symbol of Cleanliness

Cats are always busy cleaning themselves. Cleanliness has long been associated with cats. In 1943, the Axton-Fischer Company used a white Angora cat cleaning itself to show that the filters on its cigarettes cleaned the impurities out of the smoke inhaled. The detergent and soap maker, Le Chat, used the symbol of the cat to promote the image of its products. Omo detergent, Fée household cleaning products and Manshion Polish also used this image.

Symbol of Softness and Femininity

Because cats have such soft fur, they have been used to promote wool (Chat botté) and women's legs (wearing Dim hose or shaven with a Philips razor). The purring cat adds the idea of pleasure to the image of softness (Dim). Of course, these advertisements mainly target women. The symbol of femininity brought out by cats has also made its appearance in advertising. Women have been transformed into cats such as with the idle woman for Cinna sofas. Conversely, cats have been changed into women for Boucheron jewelry.

Symbol of Silence

Elegance and beauty are conveyed by felines in order to promote household equipment (Kano kitchens or Selles bathrooms) in addition to their ability to move silently. Cats do not like a lot of racket. Thus they were also seen in advertisements next to dishwashers (Miele) or vacuum cleaners (Moulinex).

Symbol of Visual Acuity

Another symbol – that of vision - is best illustrated by a black cat with yellow eyes. This cat became the symbol of Marshall automobile headlights and lent his look to that of the Canon auto focus camera. According to Laurence Raphael (*le Chat dans la publicité* [Cats in Advertising], Lyon, 1986), the most widely used symbols in advertising are silence, softness, beauty, luxury and femininity.

In 47% of advertisements, advertisers are trying to sell household supply products, since cats are perceived to be protectors of the home.

Women are the main target (in 40% of cases they are the sole target as opposed to 15% for men), because cats appeal to emotions and feelings. In 43% of cases, cats are evocative enough to be used alone. In 32% of cases, they are accompanied by a woman, as opposed to only 6% of cases when they are accompanied by men. It should be noted that the breed of the cat can also be suggestive. In fact the percentage of purebreds used increases from 33% to 81% when the products being introduced are luxury products.

Symbol of Evil

In advertising, the evil role of the cat is only highlighted when the advertisement needs to be dramatic. Cats, therefore, are perceived as having a good name in our day and age, because advertisers would not choose an evil animal.

Cats, Music, and Dance

Ancient Music

In ancient Egypt, Bastet was the most popular cat-goddess, but there was another deity with the head of a cat – the god of music.

Classical Music

However, this animal only inspired a few compositions throughout history. The most famous are: *Fugatta del gatto* by Domenico Scarlatti, *Duetto buffo du due Gatti* by Rossini (melodious exchange of expressive meows), *les Berceuses du chat* by Maurice Ravel, *le Faucon et la Petite Chatte* by Stravinski and the meows of the white cat and the puss in boots in Tchaikovsky's *Sleeping Beauty*.

Contemporary Music

More recently, we see *Cats*, the musical by Andrew Lloyd Weber (1981), which drew its inspiration from *An Old Possum's Book of Practical Cats*, a collection of humorist poems such as *the Old Gumbie Cat* or *Rum Tum Tugger*, written by poet T.S. Eliot for children. In this story the cat is constantly seen sitting down (doorstep, armchair or in front of the fireplace).

Once night falls, however, the cat prowls around the house and amuses herself by tangling up the curtain cords for example.
It is difficult to convey in French the full humor of the characters and the plays on words with the cat names, but Frenchman Jacques Charpentreau successfully created a modern performance adapted to the French civilization.

This musical comedy, which is brilliantly staged by a troop of singers-dancers-actors, musicians, choreographers and producers, illustrates certain characteristics of cats: extremely sensual and exuberant at the same time, but also cold and mysterious.

Apart from this show, a text that was not published by Eliot because it was deemed too sad, was a smashing success. The show in question is Memory with Elaine Paige. It was Barbara Streisand, however, who made it famous throughout the whole world with the song of the little she-cat, Grizabella, who was banished from society because of her pitiful appearance, and especially because she dared to show her despair.

Two Cats Signing. Cover of "Songs Without Words." s.d. XXth century. Selva collection, Paris.

Cats in Photography

There are three main categories of cat photographs: those showing the animal in its usual habitat, those that are more like documentaries and those that are fantastical photography.

Photograph by Yann Arthus Bertrand

Photographs of Daily Life

There are numerous portraits of cats in modern iconography.

In addition to photographs, there are also many advertisements, posters, calendars, etc. that depict cats. Often an attempt is made to bring out the tenderness or innocence of this animal by showing kittens or by emphasizing the beauty of familiar poses, pouncing cats or cats' eyes.

One example is the black and white Christian Louis poster (1968), in which a white cat lying on a sheet is looking at the camera with its right eye since its left eye is hidden by glasses. There is also the color photograph by Bruno Maso entitled *le Chat magnifique* (The Magnificent Cat), with a low-angle shot of a white cat coming toward the camera against a jet-black background. The newborn kitten photograph by the great amateur cat photographer, Mieko d'Eugène Smith, symbolizes all the fragile promises of new life.

Documentary Photography

Witnesses of their times, photographers have portrayed the image or function of cats in present-day society. André Kertesz spent several days observing a woman feeding stray cats in the street and shot *Une scène de rue à Paris* (Scene from a Paris Street) in 1929. New York photographer Harry Warnecke reconstructed an observed street scene (1925) for a superb photograph of a policeman stopping heavy traffic in order to allow a mother cat holding her kitten in her mouth to cross the street under the stunned gaze of a crowd of curious onlookers.

The 1952 photograph of a pregnant woman lying next to a cat by Lowie Elliot Erwitt portrays serenity, life and birth.

Fantastical Photography

Among the most famous fantastical photographs is that of Philippe Halsman (1906 –1979) entitled *Dali Atomicus*. Dali is shown suspended in space along with his chair and easel. The photograph had to be re-shot 26 times with patient cats who found themselves projected to the right at the same time as a waterfall. And then in 1980 we see the very personal vision of Sandy Skoglung in the photograph of radioactive cats walking around in a gray room where a grandfather watches his wife hunt for something in the refrigerator.

Photographers have made entire books about cats.

Les Chats (Cats) by Yann Arthus Bertrand is a magnificent album where this talented photographer once again demonstrates his great sensitivity and sometimes-caustic sense of humor. No other album brings to light so clearly the intimacy and love between a cat and his master.

Hans Silvester also produced a beautiful piece of work in his album *Les Chats du bonheur* (The Mediterranean Cat), in which he captures feline gestures against a backdrop of Greek villages.

Part 3

CATS AND THEIR OWNERS

THE SOCIAL ROLE
OF CATS

BEHAVIOR

REARING

DAILY LIFE

Social Function of Cats

A little like "indoor crickets" – a name given to cats because their purring is sometimes as loud as than crickets and cicada put together – cats have come to be recognized as pets in their own right. Moreover, cats are taking over as "man's best friend" in many European countries, France, England, Germany and the United States.

More autonomous and requiring less space, cats have many traits that attract people in this day and age. People who are rushed and stressed find tenderness and understanding in the touch of a cat, with just a hint of the mischievousness and unpredictability that gives cats their special charm.

A Family Affair

Contrary to the typical clichés that portray cats as the companions of choice of writers, night owls and single women, most cat owners are families with two children, a house and a yard. In France, the rate of cat ownership is

A cat and its family.

66% among people who live in houses (62% with a yard) and only 25% among apartment dwellers. Sixty-six percent of cats live in cities with a population of fewer than 100,000 people. In this country, there are 8.4 million cats and 1 out of every 4 households has at least one cat. Cats are essentially taken in out of a love for animals. In rare cases, cats are acquired in order to chase mice, but much more often, they are acquired as company for the children. More than 85% of farmers own a cat, followed by merchants, craftsmen and business owners. Only 36% of executives, professional people and unemployed persons share this happiness. Whereas dog owners tend to limit themselves to the canine species, cat owners often own several different species, mixing birds or dogs with cats in their singular love for animals. Although cats have all too often been the poor cousins of veterinary medicine, more attention is being paid to their health in this end of the century, although they still do not receive a lot of medical treatment. In Europe as in the

United States, veterinarians are now specializing in feline medicine and opening up feline clinics. Entire scientific journals are now devoted to this species.

Cats are becoming more strongly attached to people, something thought to be impossible a few centuries ago. Consequently, they are taking on a status similar to dogs: man's faithful friend and first among pets.

In that respect, however, the question remains as to whether cats will ever be truly domesticated. Domestication, in fact, involves controlling reproduction. Herein lies one more paradox with cats. It remains difficult to control the reproduction of thoroughbred cats, who never give birth when the breeders want them to, and yet free-roaming alley and neighborhood cats give birth to litters without a second thought!

Thus the domestication of cats is a work in progress in which we as owners all have the privilege of participating every day.

Cats and Children

Due to preconceived notions and biases, babies and consequently adults, are deprived of the joy of living with a cat. When cats try to jump into the baby's cradle to sleep, the erroneous assumption is made that they have bad intentions and are trying to suffocate the baby.

Two reasons explain why cats are attracted to babies. First, with the baby spitting up curdled milk, the cat cannot help but be attracted to this newfound source of delicacy. This is one reason why cats seek out the cradle, either to lick it or to sleep there. Second, like cats, babies sleep a lot and always in a particularly warm and cozy cradle. In other words, all these temptations bundled into one single being will only serve to attract the cat.

It is wise to keep the cat out of the baby's room during the first few months of life. Care should be taken though to ensure that the cat does not associate the presence of a baby with the absence of attention for him.

During the early development stages, however, both the cat and the baby should be allowed to

A child and her cat

freely interact with each other as they wish. Some mornings, for example, you may see the cat waiting in front of the bedroom door for the baby to wake up. Then he might hop up on the table and offer his flank for a few caresses while the baby eats his breakfast. These types of interaction, which are clearly initiated by the cat, may begin as early as five months.

When motor function development begins so do the chasing/running games and the cat may sometimes experience a few difficult moments when the child discovers that his tail moves!

Between the ages of 18 and 24 months young children exhibit the classic aggressive behaviors seen in normal development. During this period, the cat owner must be vigilant and always be nearby when the cat and child interact. Otherwise an unfortunate scratch is always possible. The child must also be taught at this stage to respect the cat, although the cat has his own ways of commanding respect!

For instance, Florence, who at six months was completely fascinated with the dog that would come lick her feet and lie down next to her, clearly began to exhibit inviting behavior and to call out to the cat at the age of eight months. She expressed her pleasure upon seeing the cat with high-pitched shrills and by holding our her hands and smiling in the cat's direction. However, since she did not live with

A teenager and her cat.

the cat and only saw it every two weeks, she was not able to "tame" and to handle the cat in the way she wanted until she was two years old.

More so than any other animal, cats can help children make contact with their environment through kinesthetic stimulation and help them to safely explore the immediate environment. Seeing a cat strolling by illicits an immediate and spontaneous response from the child, who cries out to show his joy and excitement, sometimes even forgetting the toothache that kept him awake. These shrieks sometimes cause the cat to run away. This is because both the temperament of the cat and how early or late socialization occurs (which ideally should occur before the age of five weeks), will largely determine the quality and the very nature of the interaction between the child and the cat.

The diversity of feline temperaments also explains why children will not necessarily have the most interactions with the family cat. It may be the grandmother's cat, the older sister's cat or the neighbor's cat that captivates the child and responds to his invitation to interact.

No matter what their age is, children learn to adapt their behavior to the desires of the cat. In short, they learn patience. The cat is a partner who helps them enter the adult world with the help of games.

Quite simply, the cat teaches life skills: patience, respect for others and the ability to control one's gestures and vocal and body expressions.

When Cats Go to School

Some teachers have decided to hire an unusual teaching assistant – a cat. It may be their own cat that lives at the school or a cat they found whose temperament is especially well adapted to their lifestyle.

For example, Sylvie Thevenon tells of her first semester as a young teacher in a Paris neighborhood where discipline was something that was difficult to teach her students.

"The animal arrived unexpectedly a month and a half after school started when one of the children brought in an abandoned cat who had recently been wandering around the newly built school."

From that moment on, the dynamics of the class changed completely. Clearly, nothing could be done that day unless the kitten was included.

All the children began asking questions, wondering if they could keep the cat. They also gave their opinions about the best way to care for it and hold it and, with a very pronounced sense of justice or injustice, about where it should sleep. They thoroughly discussed the "cuddling" time everyone would be allotted.

For once, all the children in the class were expressing themselves and the normal rules of speaking were totally different. They made no references to either the leaders or the teacher! In this respect, the presence of the animal completely changed the behavior of the children. It gave rise to new modes of speaking and listening and gave each student a place, value and a role to play. It brought the class together as a coherent group that was complementary and united by the project. The animal became a true agent of cohesion and it stimulated and motivated that class.

The presence of the animal had numerous consequences throughout the year. Among the most striking was that the children who had trouble concentrating on a task for a long time and who had difficulty situating themselves in time and space discovered that they were able to have projects and stick to them. They improved their concentration skills and became more active and determined. They were also better able to honor their commitments and to accept taking on responsibility. It was almost as if the children "forgot themselves" in the presence of the animal.

The children discussed how to show respect for the animal and how not to bother it. They shared their experiences with their class and also with children in other grades. Stories circulated around the school and works were displayed (little books, poems, drawings, etc.).

For all these reasons, and above all because of the hilarious daily routine that resulted, the presence of the animal became indispensable since it had given the children the opportunity to let others see their true selves without fear of rejection.

The Therapeutic Role of Cats in Hospital Environments

Cats know where hospitals are and many colonies of cats live around hospitals and clinics where the medical staff and often the patients feed and pet them.

Rather than forbidding this practice in the name of hygiene and cleanliness, many doctors and psychiatrists have used their patients' interest in cats to help speed up their recovery or even provide help when traditional medicine fails.

Child psychiatrist Boris Levinson, whose dog Jingles happened by chance to participate in a consultation one day, described the first experiments using animals to facilitate therapy. Normally Levinson did not allow his dog to be in his office. That day, however, he was meeting with parents who were bringing in their autistic son for a last-ditch consultation before most likely having to commit him. Levinson had agreed to see them outside of his usual office hours and his dog stayed in the office. The child said nothing throughout the entire consultation until the very end when the doctor was discussing a second appointment with the parents. The child who had been silent for so long asked if the dog would be there the next time.

From then on, Boris Levinson deliberately used his dog. When he first published his results, he exposed himself to ridicule by his colleagues, who could not resist asking him if he paid his dog.

However, the trend to use pets as therapeutic aids soon began in the United States and eventually took hold in Europe. Dogs were the first animals to be used, but cats are now used regularly for elderly persons and in psychiatric environments.

Obviously, medical personnel who rely on animal-facilitated therapy must use animals with which they have a good rapport. If medical personnel are not familiar with cats or are afraid of them, it is better to choose another species or to refrain from using animals at all. At the Paul-Giraud hospital in Villejuif, France, cats have become invaluable medical assistants under the attentive and affectionate supervision of the medical staff.

"I prefer cats to dogs. We adopt dogs, but cats adopt us. You might say they trust us. They understand us," stated a 58-year old patient who had been receiving care in a specialized unit for over 22 years. Thanks to the presence of cats living around the hospital and to the attentive care of a devoted staff, he was able to get back on track and return to reality. The medical staff plays a very important role because although cats help the patients open themselves up to the world and develop positive behaviors, at the other extreme, it is also possible for patients to become too involved in a relationship that is too exclusive. Cats can be wonderful catalysts for relationships and emotions, but the medical staff must guide

Stray cat.

these relationships in order to provide healing, or at least improvement for the patient.

Without getting into the psychiatric aspects, numerous studies have shown that simply petting a cat, talking to it or reading in its presence, without any other special interaction, is enough to lower blood pressure.

Other studies have demonstrated that cardiac patients (those who have suffered from a heart attack or other coronary problems) may live longer in the presence of cats.

Cats can help humanize hospital environments and establish relationships between patients and hospital staff.

All too often, hospital staff members fear that the presence of cats will increase their already heavy workload. However, once cats are brought in, they systematically realize that their presence facilitates their relationships with patients, lessens patient aggressiveness and makes everything easier.

Shared Cats, Garden Nomads

In cities everywhere, wherever cats live in colonies, a network of solidarity, sharing and dialogue is established, which ethnologists are now beginning to study seriously. Women who are sometimes referred to as "cat grannies" help feed these nomadic cats and contribute to maintaining the charm in these places even though they sometimes drive public officials, who want to keep cemeteries clean and well-groomed and free from roaming cats, to

despair. After all, what would the Capitol, the Forum of Rome or the Père-Lachaise cemetery be without cats? They would undoubtedly be places without a soul.

This situation is well accounted for in the new pet protection law published at the beginning of 1999, which henceforth establishes true protection laws for these free-roaming cats. Sterilized, identified, and sometimes vaccinated whenever possible, these cats can now stroll along with confidence under our delighted gaze. Just like with those who feed the pigeons, there are people who take great delight in caring for cats they cannot take into their homes. The cats repay them well as they are generous with their affection.

Cats and the Elderly

Cats make excellent pets for elderly persons for all the reasons stated above, but also because they are so autonomous. Nevertheless, it is important to choose a good-natured cat that is not to lively and that is well socialized if children will be visiting regularly.

Longhaired cats should be avoided because they require daily brushing and sometimes-daily eye care. But there again, it all depends on the nature of the elderly person or couple.

Of course there is still the painful problem that sometimes prevents an elderly person from enjoying the company of a cat. And that is the question of, "But what about after I am gone, Dr?"

This desire to ensure that the cat continues to live a comfortable life even after the person

---

BUSINESS CATS – THE PROFESSION OF THE FUTURE

Trends from the United States have more chance of taking root here if they fulfill genuine expectations. For a long time now, many merchants and even post offices have let their cats wander around in their shop or office.

Today, media and advertising agencies do not think twice about allowing their employees to bring their dogs to work. Since cats do not especially like being transported, when businesses have a cat, the cat generally lives there and becomes the office mascot. Cats are used to veterinary offices, but they can also work for big companies, where they clearly change the atmosphere and create an environment of cohesion around them.

dies is entirely understandable. The concern is especially valid in cases where the elderly person lives alone or is a widow. A friendly "adoption" arrangement is the best solution to keep from depriving an elderly person of this daily dose of happiness. After all, how many cleaning women, household assistants, friends or relatives would contribute to giving the elderly person a sense of security by promising to look after the cat if it has the sad surprise of seeing its master gone on before him…

Often, elderly persons will not be able to enjoy the company of one or more cats with their mind at ease unless they have this guarantee. However, the children or grandchildren of these persons should not feel guilty if they cannot take on such a commitment. There are enough cat lovers out there to testify to human solidarity and their ability to share.

Bear in mind, nevertheless, that for both young and old alike, the death of a cat is a particularly sensitive time. It may even lead to depression or illness in cases of people who are fragile or sick (people suffering from multiple sclerosis, for example). Those in the entourage of the grieving person should be sure to provide plenty of support for him or her. The grieving process is especially difficult for elderly persons who have already lost a spouse and for whom the cat was the only living testimony to their life together. The same holds true for adolescents whose parents are divorced and who just lost the cat that sometimes was the only memory of their parents' marriage and their childhood. Pay close attention to loved ones in these situations and support them in difficult times. "The pain of a cat, is pain all the same."

Cat Rearing and Behavior

In spite of their reputation for being independent and autonomous, cats can be trained at a young age and they exhibit a clear aptitude for learning. Take as but one example the case of a kitten that was reared with young puppies and that learned by imitation to lift its leg to urinate! Nevertheless, kittens can only be taught natural behavior sequences, which can be either positively or negatively reinforced and thereby shape their behavior. The extremely rare artists who work with cats in circus environments have to rely on pure art. They take note of their cat's interesting behaviors, reinforce these behaviors and then display them on scene in order to enhance their value. Motivation is almost more important with cats than with dogs. Furthermore, motivation in this case means the same as motivation with humans. In other words, the cat has to want to do something in order to do it. Pavlov's beloved method of using food as bait for motivation, which was so effective with dogs, is not so effective with cats. A cat's attachment to his master and his love of games are sources of motivation that are a thousand times more effective. The fact that neurophysiologists even refer to the notion of motivation shows the degree of intelligence they attribute to cats.

Rearing a Kitten

Advanced knowledge about feline behavior now indicates that psychomotor development begins with gestation, thus before birth, just as with humans. The behavior of the mother will influence the behavior of her future kittens and their abilities to learn.

A team of British researchers also proved that sociability towards humans may be genetically determined and may be a character trait that kittens inherit from their fathers. For now, this is the only influence the father is known to have on his offspring, since he does not care for the kittens after they are born.

The bulk of learning occurs nevertheless during the period from birth to six months.

Training and learning are also possible as adults, depending on the temperament of the cat and the teaching skills of the owner.

With kittens, behavior takes shape around three main hubs within the litter:
- learning, which plays an important role;
- the role of the mother, which is more and more seen as being important at the very beginning of development;
- socialization, which will determine to a large extent how a kitten behaves as an adult.

In fact, we even talk about intra-specific socialization, which means establishing all the communication behaviors specific to the feline species. These behaviors are established very early on, especially as compared to dogs, and they are essential to the proper develop-

Kittens in a Group

ment of the kitten and his emotional stability. They begin to be established around the second week after birth and continue until the seventh week, sometimes a little longer.

During this period, it is important to provide kittens with what ethnologists call "an enriched environment." In other words, they need specific sources of stimuli that will arouse their senses and spark their intelligence.

Contact and games with other kittens are essential to development before the age of eight weeks. Inter-specific socialization, the process of learning social behaviors directed toward other friendly species (humans, dogs, rabbits, etc.), also occurs during this period and ends around the third month. The nature and strength of the bond that develops between the cat and his owner will depend on the quality of this inter-specific socialization. It is possible to influence the sociability of a cat by having various people handle the kitten during the first few weeks of life. This will make for a good-natured cat. The cat will learn to adapt to everyone, but overall, will not be extremely attached to one person in particular. Conversely, the kitten can be handled by only one or two people maximum,

which will consequently make for a cat with only one master, who will be extremely attached to his future owner.

Cats must also be taught about other species they will later have to live with at a young age, as it will be infinitely more difficult to familiarize them later on. This is especially true for toddlers who, in the eyes of the cat, are an entirely separate breed from the human race! It is sometimes difficult for cats to accept young children, who are unpredictable, able to emit very shrill sounds, and to take advantage of the moment when adults are not paying attention to pull on the whiskers, tail or ears of a passing cat. It is important to familiarize cats with young children, especially in cases of grandparents who only have the children over from time to time.

Grooming, feeding (after weaning) and defecating and urinating behaviors are certainly all inborn to some degree, but the mother also teaches them to kittens soon after birth. Around the 15th day, kittens are capable of licking their front sides. Starting at three weeks, kittens can answer the call of nature in a litter box on their own. As of the fourth

Example of a Maine Coon in an enriched environment.

week, kittens are able to eat the same food as their mother, imitating her behavior and acquiring her food preferences in so doing. Kittens also learn to drink fresh water at this age. As the taste of water is different from the taste of milk, it is important to train them quickly.

In order to prevent the cat from becoming a finicky eater, it is important to give young kittens foods with different textures and tastes (dry food, croquettes and pâtés with different flavors).

At Home with the Owner

When a young kitten is adopted, its training is limited. The kitten is normally already house broken and generally, the owner needs simply show the kitten the litter box once and the kitten will remember where it is and come back to it systematically.

The kitten also learns, for no apparent reason, where the refrigerator and everything else that gives him access food is located!

It is more difficult to train a cat not to bother the table and your dishes and food. In fact, it is normal behavior for cats to jump up on the table or the kitchen work space. If you wish to eliminate this behavior, a sharp "no" will suffice. You may accompany that with a sharp sound (snapping your fingers or clapping your hands).

If, however, the cat is normally allowed to jump up on the table and to walk on the table, it is extremely difficult to keep it off a table set for guests. All you can do in this case is shut the dining room door!

Giving the cat unrestricted access to all rooms in the house is generally the simplest way to operate. Nevertheless, it is easy to restrict access to the baby's room, although the rules must be established at the right time, in other words, one month before the baby is born.

Social Behavior

As paradoxical as it may seem, cats are social animals. Even though they sometimes prefer to avoid contact (especially with some of their congeners), cats do show a true talent for communication with humans in optimal living conditions.

Nature has given cats particularly subtle and varied means of communication, which enable them to detect the presence and emotional state of other cats or animals. They can therefore make an informed decision about whether to approach the other animal or not.

When an encounter with a congener is unavoidable and not desired, all means of communication are deployed in a dissuasive strategy where bluffing is the name of the game.

Since cats are basically visual animals, they are especially sensitive to contrasts in light (they can distinguish differences of 10–12%) and to movement. They are able to detect a mouse moving at the ridiculous rate of 144 m/hr.

"ENRICHED ENVIRONMENT"

Buried in this conventional term is simply the idea of raising kittens in a diverse environment with respect to physical space, senses and relationships. All studies have shown the benefits for kittens who are exposed, even if only for a few minutes a day, to diverse objects (little balls, brown paper bags, cardboard boxes, etc.) and to pieces of wood on which they can climb. There should be objects big enough for them to hide in (cardboard boxes are a veritable gold mine!) as well as various sounds (television, children playing and crying, music, etc.). Kittens raised in these conditions showed preliminary signs of play well before the age of five weeks (the normal age for these activities). Their development was clearly accelerated and greatly improved.

The objective of having an enriched environment is to promote harmonious behavioral development in kittens and to enable them to adapt in any circumstance. Kittens raised in this manner have well-developed exploratory behaviors.

Color is not a decisive factor for cats. They can only detect blue and green with certainty. Contrary to common thought, cats are not able to see in complete darkness. However, they require six times less light than humans do to distinguish an object with the same degree of clarity. This means that they distinguish beings and depth better than humans do at night.

Moreover, their whiskers provide an excellent additional source of information because they provide keen detection of objects thanks to gradients in heat and turbulence, which direct their nose and taste buds to the most favorable angle.

The final olfactory advantage cats have is their vomer-nasal passage, which links the buccal cavity and the nasal cavity. At the top of this passage is the Jacobson's organ, which is lined with olfactive cells that are directly linked by nerve pathways to olfactory bulb. Because of this anatomical particularity, cats are considered to be macrosmic (animals that can detect a single odorant molecule whereas humans require several hundred). Cats therefore have a keen sense of smell and thus, emotions.

Cats are generally thought to have a musical ear. They can detect differences of one tenth in high frequency tones and difference of one fourth in average frequency tones. It is also clear that in familiar settings, cats respond to their name and can distinguish their name from other names in the family. Most likely they are also responding to the voice tone and intonation of their owner because if it happens to be the veterinarian saying their name at his office, cats generally remain stone faced, once again proving their attachment to their owner. Although cats can subtly analyze the behavior of others, they also allow their emotions to show, either directly or by leaving traces of their path. This deferred, or distance communication essentially involves leaving deposits of odors and visual marks.

Odor deposits, which include urine and feces deposits and sudoriferous gland secretions, are

WHAT IS THE TEMPERAMENT OF THE CAT?

This question was incongruous just several decades ago but now, thanks to studies on colonies of free-roaming cats, we know that cats have different temperaments:
- the suspicious cat: always on the alert, on the defensive, does not explore a lot of unknown territory, does not interact with unknown congeners, runs from human strangers;
- the sociable cat: always likes contact (mutual licking, social games), seeks out and initiates contact;
- the intermediary cat: neither sociable, nor suspicious, responds to solicitations even from strangers but does not initiate contact, not an active communicator but has an even-keel temperament.

A child playing with her cat.

THE BREEDER – A SECOND MOM

As the inescapable middleman between the kitten and his future owner, the breeder and his/her family play a big role in determining the behavior of a kitten. The breeder is the "human reference" for the kitten.

This is one reason why whenever cats are destined for families with young children, it is important between the second and seventh week for the kitten to have contact either with the young children he will be living with (even if only once a week) or with other children close to the breeder. This may seem tedious or complicated, but it is nonetheless the best way to end up with a kitten that is perfectly adapted to his future life. The same holds true for cats that will have to live with dogs in their adult life. It is important that the breeder himself have dogs or that he be able to put his litters in contact with good-natured dogs.

Systematic handling can deepen the future bond between kitten and human. The kitten is handled everyday during the socialization period (picked up, pet and talked to for 5 – 40 minutes per day). If the breeder does the handling himself, the kitten will bond more easily with an owner who is single. If the kitten will go to live with a family, two or three different people, preferably of each sex, should do the handling. These people should also have as good a relationship with kittens and the mother cat as the breeder. If the mother cat is fearful, it is preferable to do the handling when she is not present.

Cats use five main postures
to communicate:
1. Friendly
2. Confrontational
3. Defensive
4. Aggressive
5. Threatening

awakening, and scratches anything that happens to get in the way of his paws. Others believe that when a cat scratches an object, it leaves secretions from the small glands located between the plantar pads. These glands are activated by fear, especially when the cat is at the veterinarian's office, and cat therefore leave their mark as well as visual traces in the form of slashes in softer material (leather sofas are often left in a sorry state!).

The latter theory explains why commercial scratching posts do not work well. They do not convey a story. It is of course through direct communication that cats show their true talent as comedians and bluffers and sometimes their sense of tragedy.

When cats encounter other cats, they use postures and vocal sounds and they transmit subtle messages to the other cat through movement of their whiskers and ears.

There are five main postures, depending on the emotions of the cat and the messages he wishes to communicate.

The arched "cat back" is the best known posture and the term is even used in everyday language. In this posture, the cat makes itself appear as frightening as possible. Its fur stands on end to make it look larger, his tail is puffed out like a bottlebrush and its pupils are extremely dilated.

Conversely, during a friendly encounter its fur lies flat and its tail is bent in characteristic fashion.

When a cat is in a threatening position: crouched down, growling, and with its claws extended, it is important not to interpret this posture as being a posture of submission as with dogs. In this position, the cat is ready to do anything to get out of the bad situation in which he finds himself and it will bite if the other party persists.

Fights between cats are always spectacular to hear. In fact, there is often a lot of noise for nothing, which is just fine. Except for fights between male cats during mating season, when biting is serious, cat fights are more often than not merely long periods of waiting and preparing for battle backed up by growling. When the attack is launched, it is brief and lively,

often referred to as "marking." It should be noted, however, that the very notion of marking presupposes that the odor deposit instills fear and causes the one who just smelled it to flee. This is the case with most Felidae, but with cats on the contrary, the odor deposit, especially if it is a urine deposit, incites the passerby to cover over this deposit with another deposit and to continue on his way without fear. Consequently, the term odor deposits is more accurate as it does not make assumptions about the function of this behavior.

Recently, some of these substances were isolated and synthesized in the form of a spray. The sprays were reported to have a calming effect, but at any rate they cannot solve everything. In cases of behavioral problems, it is always important to seek the advice of your veterinarian.

Cats also leave their mark by scratching trees, furniture and sometimes the edge of the sofa. Several theories have been proposed. Some see this scratching as simply an original form of stretching. The cat stretches, especially upon

larger than normal hair and is embedded in a sanguineous sinus, which creates hydraulic suspension. Their sensitivity to the slightest movement of air is therefore amplified.

Arranged in groups of four or five in four rows around the nose, the whiskers change position according to the activities and emotions of the cat. During waking activities (chasing, lying in wait or friendly encounters), the whiskers are positioned in a arch of a circle. They are quickly pulled down during an attack. There are also vibrissa above the carp under the anterior side of the forelegs, just above the eyes and a few tufts on the jowls.

Well Adapted Communication Strategies

At least three different personalities live inside the head of the cat:
- the hunter: very discrete, wants to see without being seen, moves silently;
- the show-off: struts around during mating season, removes intruders from its path by arching its back and makes more noise than the others in order to protect its secret garden. A devilish bluffer, it does nonetheless step aside sometimes, since the rule among cats is to give the right of way to the first one to arrive;
- the charmer: has taken up residence with humans for good, its needs are provided for (food), it is sheltered from the worries of living with others, it has all the time in the world to develop specific behaviors that would normally not be expressed except in these particular living conditions. Purring, kneading behavior, social licking behavior (licking the eyebrows

punctuated by impressive vocal sounds, and then it is over as soon as it began.

These behaviors are frequently seen in games between two adult cats living together. Only experience will tell if it is really just a game or whether you need to take one of your cats to the veterinarian to be treated for aggression. When cats chase something or lick themselves, their ear pinna may be flipped back in order to obtain information, but they are always perfectly straight.

Finally, it is not unusual to see that the ears are not symmetrical in their movements. This is because cats do not have "eyes in back of their heads" and they skillfully use the stereophonic gifts nature has given them and also because they are generally apt to change moods and the movement of their ears indicates the slightest variation.

Whiskers are a form of vibrissa, the hair that is distinctly characteristic of mammals (except humans). The whisker base is five to six times

Neutral cat

Angry cat

Aggressive cat

Happy cat

EARS AND WHISKERS – VALUABLE INDICATORS

Ear movements are sometimes the only indication of a cat's emotions. Equipped with a well-controlled musculature, the ears position themselves according to the whims of the cat's moods, which can vary from one minute to the next. Straight up, pointing slightly forward, moving or working independently (it is not unusual to see that only one ear turns toward the source of a noise), they indicate a cat that feels confident, as he takes in information about the surrounding environment. When the pinna are facing forward or when the ears are pointing toward the source of a sound, they indicate that the cat is on the alert. In situations when cats are on the defensive, the ears lie flat laterally and are perfectly symmetrical, giving their forehead the characteristic smooth, bulged out appearance, and betraying intense anxiety. When the pinna are pulled back, it is already too late – aggression has already started (see pictures as shown opposite).

of his owner when he comes home at night) and vocal sounds so rich and expressive that they are taken at their word, are all signs of domestication and its consequences.

Cats organize their lives around different areas. They have areas for resting, eating, eliminating waste, and playing. There is also a temporary area for reproduction. If the cat is free roaming, there is a hunting area, which can be quite a large area (several hectares).

Respecting this organization can avoid a lot of problems. Not respecting these areas on the other hand, can be the source of many behavioral problems.

In an apartment, it is important for the elimination area to be as far as possible from the eating area. The resting area will vary depending on the amount of sunshine and the mood of the cat. The proximity of the owner or one of his family members also plays a role. Cats always look for sources of heat (radiators, comforters) and it is not unusual to see a cat sleeping next to the fireplace or on a piping hot radiator. Since cats are less sensitive to heat than humans, they take enjoy it as much as possible.

The play area is the biggest area in their field of investigation because it is during their crazy chases (where they alone know what they are actually chasing) that they cover the most ground. Cats are particularly fond of high up places (such as the table or the top of the wardrobe) and the climbing they require. Cats are filled with joy when they can be at the same level as their owner's, face allowing them to have their own style "cat-to-cat" interaction by rubbing against their owner's cheek or forehead just like they would with another cat.

Eating Behaviors

Gourmet by nature, cats owe many of their habits to their Egyptian ancestors and domestication.

Felis lybica and Felis ornata are the two most likely ancestors of the cat. Originally from the desert, they both had few opportunities to drink and had to be satisfied with the meager prey they often hunted, which was essentially mice.

Cats have maintained this sobriety in terms of water (even though in actual fact they drink more than we think) and have stayed in the habit of eating many small meals in a twenty-four hour period. Thus, cats eat ad libitum and may eat as many as 15 – 16 meals, consuming an average of eight grams per meal. The time spent eating is always very short – 15 minutes total per day. But the frequency with which they come to their feeding dish, which is generally when the owner is nearby, leads one to believe that all they do is eat!

POISONS

Among the most frequent causes of poisoning are:

- Organophosphorous and carbamate insecticides: salivating, vomiting, diarrhea and convulsions;
- Organochlorine insecticides: hyperactivity, vomiting and convulsions;
- Antifreeze (ethylene glycol): vomiting, cardiac problems, convulsions, coma and death;
- Anticoagulants (dicoumarol, antivitamin K): lethal internal hemorrhaging;
- Paracetamol (toxic starting at 50 – 60 mg/kg): loss of appetite, vomiting and jaundice;
- Aspirin (toxic starting at 25 mg/kg): vomiting, depression, coma and death;
- "Toxic" plants which, when ingested, can cause:
    - Digestive problems: ficus, mistletoe, holly, rhododendron, azalea, etc.;
    - Kidney problems: philodendron, ficus;
    - Cardiovascular problems: cylclamen, mistletoe;
    - Nervous system problems: mistletoe, Japanese mimosa, and philodendron.

Some cats prefer to eat at night, others spread their meals out over regular intervals and still others prefer to eat during the official meal-times of the family.

As the ultimate nibblers, cats come back to their dish often to savor a small mouthful. Note that their digestive system is perfectly adapted to this eating pattern and that cats generally do not tolerate being fed once a day very well, unlike dogs.

The ideal system, both in terms of cats' pleasure and their health, seems to be to distribute dry food ad libitum along with fresh water, and to give them pâté or croquettes twice a day.

Cats are only moderate water drinkers. They drink nine to ten times a day, drinking about 12.6 ml each time. They are highly sensitive to odors and they hate plastic dishes that retain bad odors. They prefer glass or heavy porcelain dishes by far.

Some unconventional cats like to drink direct-ly from the tap, sometimes using their paw. Others are particularly fond of bath water, but the main source of water should always come from the owner!

As an "informed consumer," cats assumedly control their food intake according to their needs. Statistics show in fact that only 6 – 12% of the feline population is obese as opposed to 20 – 30% among canines. Nevertheless, it is necessary to be reasonable and to limit the overall amount of food a cat consumes in a day, even if the food is distributed in self-service style.

As for the variety of food to give the cat's palate, your cat will let you know! Reputed to be difficult by some of the advertising agen-cies, some cats do prove to be loyal to a certain brand, texture or even a certain flavor throughout their entire life.

It is clear nonetheless that unlike a dog, a cat would rather starve to death than eat some-thing he does not like. Therefore, you are not giving into the cat's every whim by buying dif-ferent flavors and varieties. That being said, a kitten's palate can be trained. This is done by first giving the mother and then later the kit-tens food that is varied in texture (pâtés, canned food and dry food) and in flavor when the litter is weaned from the mother. This practice will make for easy-going cats.

Waste Elimination Behavior

House training is one of the behaviors closely associated with cats. It is a behavior that is acquired very early on, from the 22nd to the 39th day. Prior to this time, cats respond to stimula-tion by their mother, who licks the anal-geni-tal area after each feeding in order to stimulate urination and defecation.

True neurological control over this behavior is not fully operational until three to four weeks. At 30 days, kittens begin to approach the lit-ter box or loose dirt for the first time. The behavioral sequence is triggered soon after and the kittens scratch the litter, eliminate and then cover their feces. Among especially meticulous cats, the latter part of the sequence can sometimes reach the walls of the litter box itself, making the noise they clearly wanted to hear!

Contrary to what happens with dogs, there is no noticeable difference between male and female elimination behavior. Both eliminate by crouching down. If your cat emits a strong spray of urine horizontally, he is not relieving himself, but rather depositing his odor.

Any elimination in an inappropriate place (sink, shower stall, bedroom, etc.) should be checked out for possible behavioral problems.

Grooming Behaviors

Along with sleep, grooming is probably one of the cat's biggest activities, to such an extent that Pasteur is credited with saying, "cats are clean animals because they spend all day grooming themselves."

In addition to the cleaning function in the strict sense of the word, grooming has an important calming effect. When cats lick themselves or when they are licked by another (as with kittens licked by their mother), endorphin production is triggered, the same

This frequent behavior is not a cause for alarm. In nature, wild carnivores do not eat only meat. Their diet is also partly made up of vege-tables in order to maintain a balanced diet and provide them with a source of energy. A cat that eats grass, therefore, is simply replicating an ancestral behavior, even if its diet is otherwise perfectly balanced. Undoubtedly, cats are also sensitive to some of the tastes and odors of grass. Nonetheless, even though grass is said to be a purgative, it is important to have your cat de-wormed regularly in order to eliminate intestinal parasites.

British Blue cats (mother cat and kitten) during grooming.

hormones that are produced to counteract the sensation of pain. An anxious cat, for example, will lick itself more frequently than another cat, even at the risk of mutilating itself and pulling out hair.

Because it can be done to others, the licking behavior has a social function that is clearly illustrated in the mother-kitten relationship. Functional as of the 15th day of life, grooming is done with the particularly rough tongue and also with the paws. The front paw is moistened with the tongue and then serves as a sort of washcloth to reach the ears. The back paws are used to reach the ears and the back, sometimes with a little too much zeal. We can see the classic autopodal reflex – the paws begin to move when the side of a parasite-infected ear, typically mange, is scratched. However, we may also see another, non-pathological reflex when we stroke the cat's lower back – the cat's tongue makes licking movements in time with the stroking!

Reproductive Behaviors

Cats reach puberty at an early age – around six months and sometimes even earlier if they are exposed to a lot of sun. Thus kittens born in the spring are less precocious than kittens born at the beginning of summer. The latter kittens will have their first heat at the beginning of January or February, depending on the weather

Mother cat nursing her kittens

conditions. If cats are not purebreds and if you do not want them to reproduce, it is preferable to have them spayed as soon as possible based on the advice of your veterinarian. Moreover, since some infectious diseases can be transmitted through biting, which occurs frequently when tomcats fight, it is pointless to expose your cat to additional risks if you do not want to carry on his line. In addition, studies on female cats have clearly shown that early sterilization can help prevent breast tumors later on. Some owners believe it is useful for their female cat to have one litter before being spayed, even if it means killing the kittens. This is utterly cruel for the mother cat and there is no scientific basis for it. Of course the maternity experience is extremely gratifying for both the mother and her owner when the pregnancy is desired. But it is not based on any biological or behavioral imperative.

Cats are mature between the ages of 6 and 12 months. Hormonal secretions give the male cat facial aspects that are different from a prepubescent cat or a neutered cat. His cheeks develop to the point where they can truly be called jowls and he generally becomes lanky at the same time when female cats are in heat, from spring to the beginning of autumn because both chasing the she-cats and fighting with other males are exhausting. Frequently, these fights result in abscesses, which require a visit to the veterinarian for an appropriate treatment (prescription of antibiotics and in some cases, surgery in order to lance the abscess and allow the puss to drain).

Female cats can first start gestation as of the age of five months. However, as a precaution, it is recommended to wait until she is eight or nine months old. The period of heat, which lasts four to eight days, is followed by a period of rest for eight to ten days. If the cat does not become pregnant, this cycle will continue to repeat itself from spring through autumn.

One biological peculiarity is that ovulation in the female cat is triggered by mating, which means that mating must occur several times in a row in order to have successful fertilization. This practice can lead to kittens from the same litter with different fathers.

A female cat does not allow a male to approach her unless she is receptive. When she is receptive, she first meows languorously and plays the "untouchable tease" by rubbing her nose and lips on the ground and rolling on the ground. She makes a characteristic vocal sound, sometimes repeatedly, with a distressing and uneasy cry.

Mating is always an impressive sight to behold for the novice, but opportunities to witness it are relatively rare, since the frolicking preferably occurs at night.

Generally, the female has calmly watched the fights that the males start over her pretty eyes. After the fights, she does not necessarily choose the most courageous male, as has been shown in recent studies.

In response to her cry, the male makes a characteristic meow in a low, diphthong voice after having copiously sprayed the encounter spot with his urine. The female then adopts a suitable position, lying flat on the ground with her croup lifted. Her tail moves to one side opening up the anal-genital zone. Coitus occurs fleetingly, and the female reacts violently. The male penis is equipped with little spines that help stimulate the vagina but can also be painful. The female may turn toward the male violently and sometimes bites him. A female can be covered more than seven times. The ensuing ovulation does not automatically suppress the heat behavior.

Nothing in life prepares the female cat for the upheaval associated with gestation and yet, in 99% of cases, she adopts a maternal behavior with her young that is always admirable. Gestation lasts from 58 – 71 days. Before giving birth, the cat looks for a warm, cozy place such as the bottom of a wardrobe, a straw basket or a shoebox. She should be left in peace for the big moment. The mother cuts the umbilical cord herself and eats the placenta surrounding each kitten. Since the placenta is so rich, she will not be hungry again for one or two days after giving birth. As soon as they are born, each kitten heads for a breast and will always return to the same one for three to four weeks.

Just because the mother is nursing does not mean that she cannot be in heat again, some-times as soon as 15 days after giving birth. Therefore if you only want to have one litter, plan to have your veterinarian perform surgery as soon as possible. This will not bother the kittens in any way once they reach the age of three weeks.

Since ancient times, cats have had the reputation of being fertile and prolific. Some cats continue to be fertile well past the age of 13 or 14 years. Tri-colored cats have the reputation of being able to give birth to three litters per year. The average is generally around two, with four to six kittens per litter.

Locomotive Behavior

Tightrope walkers without equal, cats are like artists working without a net, whether they are climbing down out of a tree as fast as a high-speed train, or climbing on your knees.

Their natural ease stems from several gifts: joint and muscle flexibility, an unequaled sense of balance and excellent vision that enables them to locate obstacles.

As swift as a horse, cats can adopt a gait in two or four stages and walk at four different paces: walking, ambling, trotting and galloping.

Climbing is child's play for them even on seemingly smooth surfaces. His claws are powerful allies even though cats that have been de-clawed seem to manage quite well.

Cats always know how to get back down the same way they came up, unless they become frightened at the top and the shouts of the owner, who is even more scared, prevents them from using their skills to get back down. Pay attention to the risks involved in attempting to get a cat down from a tree or another delicate situation. Scratching can occur and the cat will hold on tightly to his rescuer, sometimes with a death grip.

Finally, the popular notion that cats always land on their feet is a myth. Granted with anything above the seventh floor, the cat will fall at a constant speed and his injuries will not be any more serious. But unfortunately, they often suffer fractures or pneumothorax at this altitude that can seriously endanger their life.

The falling cat test

two heights, some parachutist cats manage to escape unharmed while others end their lives prematurely. Be careful with balconies, especially in cities, where pigeons and other birds can tempt the cat to stick its nose out a little farther than it should.

In contrast to humans, it was thought that animals had only their instincts to go by until the XVIIIth century. At the opposite extreme, the notion of cat intelligence was exaggerated and confused with what was simple learning (complex though it may be) and true intelligence (according to J.-P. Chaurand in *Le Comportement du chat et ses troubles* [Cat Behavior and Problems], ed. du Point Vétérinaire, 1995).

A True Actor

Like a situation comedy with all kinds of humor, cats are never without ideas. They put on a pitiful face if mealtime is missed, loiter about their empty dish, look their owner straight in the eye and meow. Their voice is husky, coming from deep down. It is the cry of a beggar. Then they turn into a tramp, checking out trashcans with their nostrils wide open. It would be surprising if they did not find an old bone, a few scraps of ham or the leftover meat of the youngest child who does not like

A cat purring with pleasure in the arms of its owner.

At anything under one and a half meters, a cat does not have time to turn around and ends up falling on one body part or another and damaging it. With anything in between these

---

PURRING: THE MYSTERY OF HOW IT IS TRIGGERED PERSISTS

Purring is a murmur specific to Felidae that a cat emits when its mouth is closed, causing a sound and a laryngeal vibration. It expresses an intense emotional state, which could be pleasure or pain. Some cats that are in the terminal phase of cancer or that suffered from a traffic accident purr intensely, expressing their pain and anxiety. For a long time, it was believed that purring came from a specific organ. Actually purring is an aerodynamic phenomena made possible by coordinated movements of the glottis and larynx and the adjacent muscles. Nevertheless, purring is still a voluntary behavior that humans cannot activate intentionally. Petting generally stimulates purring, but not always.

Since kittens purr more frequently than adults, it is now believed that purring is a means for the cat to express dependence on its mother, and more generally, on the person caring for it (owner, veterinarian or veterinarian's aid). With domestic cats, purring can become a means of communication with humans. Up to you to figure out what the cat is trying to tell you!

beef steak. At any rate the cat always has a solution – the closet! With one swipe of the paw, it knocks down the whole pile of little tarts and dry food. One would have to be deaf not to react to this cataclysm.

Another place where the cat reveals its humor: the litter box. Has the litter not been changed?

It walks around its toilet, sniffs it, steps one foot in and immediately takes it out of this foul heap of odors that is a magnet for a diseases of all sorts like a devil on springs. However, there are also scenes where the cat has no humor. If it misses a landing while doing its acrobatic feats, it is ashamed and hides in a corner out of sight and licks itself for a long time, focusing his energy on this substitute grooming, which is an attitude specific to cats when they are ill at ease…

ANIMAL INTELLIGENCE TESTS

- The lowest level on the scale consists of assessing an animal's ability to establish a relationship between two events or between one event and the response that it is supposed to give.
This in itself is learning at varying degrees of complexity.
- The highest level consists of subjecting the cat to a series of problems (finding food, for example), that are all different, but that have one point in common that it can latch onto if it discovers it. The experiment therefore measures how long it takes for the cat to improve its performance and to stop making errors in situations that are different each time. There are many variations on this test and in particular, one called the "inversion" test.
Food is hidden under one of two objects first, then under the other. This test can also be done with three objects, which makes it particularly difficult. The alternation between the two objects is always the same during the various problems to which the cat is successively exposed. If it shows an improvement in his performance during the last series of tests, it is clear that it has grasped the common element in all these problems.
Another series of tests consists of asking the animal to find means of obtaining food. In the case of a chimpanzee, for example, boxes are stacked up so that it may climb on top of them and reach a bunch of bananas.
Motivation is sometimes a problem when it comes to experiments with cats. When they are in their natural environment, we observe very elaborate behaviors. For example, Nounours, the European cat, had been designated by its four housemates to jump from the table onto the refrigerator and with a swipe of the paw, knock the package of dry food on the ground for the enjoyment of the other cats who were then able to calmly eat it. Nounours was also in charge of opening the door, a task at which it excelled.
Despite the inherent limits to their validity, all these tests and trials help establish a system to rank the degree of animal intelligence. Ranked at the top are primates and Rhesus monkeys, with cats falling somewhere in the upper average.

Cats and Daily Life

Even though Moncrif wrote in 1727 that "by virtue of their meticulous cleanliness, cats could teach us a lesson or two," and although according to Pasteur "cats are the only clean animals" in creation, cats do nonetheless require some care on a daily basis.

Daily Life

As a factor that determines quality of life, a cat's familiar environment should always be looked after. Of course that does not mean you need to wait until you move into Versailles in order to enjoy living with a cat. But, as in many other areas, cats always prefer quality to quantity.

Indoor cat

In an Apartment

Granted, 25m² seems to be a minimal space for an apartment cat. However, even reduced to this limited space, a cat owner can still provide the cat what it needs to savor its favorite joys – high altitude surveillance and daily stretching – by adding a few shelves, maybe a wardrobe that is not too high and a nice scratching post (sometimes an old tree trunk will do the trick better than a patented scratching post).

The cleanliness of the litter box is crucial to prevent behavioral problems associated with house-training, especially in small spaces where odors can spread easily.

Some owners are able to successfully train their cat to answer the call of nature on the balcony (if they have one). However, this practice requires that the cat control its desire to jump up on the edge of the balcony with all the risks involved. Depending on the specific abilities of each cat, the owner can give the cat more or less freedom, but most often he should supervise the cat.

Even the most acrobatic of cats is not entirely protected from a fall caused when he thought he could catch a bird flying or an even more nasty fall when it gets carried away chasing an infrared light… Just like with babies during bath time, caution and supervision are strongly recommended when cats are on the balcony.

In a House

If the house has several floors, it is wise to place a litter box on every level, even if the cat lives alone without any other cats. This will facilitate the life of your cat and prevent annoying accidents.

If there are several cats, it is preferable to set up as many litter boxes as cats (up to a reasonable limit of four boxes). Frequently, all the cats use the same litter box even if some boxes are reserved for urine and others are only for defecation.

Of course, the ideal (for the person cleaning the house, that is) would be for cats to have the brilliant idea to answer the call of nature outside, but this behavior is not always given, as evidenced by the pleasure some cats take in coming back inside to urinate or defecate in their litter box. Summer is obviously the best time to try to inculcate these good manners, especially since in the winter cats are too lazy to go out!

Generally speaking, cats deal well with the daily absence of their owner because their sleep patterns are often timed with our working hours.

Moreover, even though cats are often very attached to their masters, they seem to have more emotional autonomy than their friends the dogs, and the anxiety separation disorders classically seen in dogs is rarely seen in cats. This may be explained by the fact that it is also true that cat owners have fewer departure rituals than dog owners do.

Whether cats live in an apartment or in a house, they need to be protected from a certain number of household accidents.

Green plants are among the temptations that should be extracted from Mr. Cat's teeth, especially if the plant appears to be toxic in nature (see attached list).

You could, on the other hand, arrange harmless plants in such a way that the cat will be attracted to them and will spare your other plants.

This strategy can also be applied to the garden, where sometimes the cat's talents as a gardener are not fully appreciated, especially when it plows up the freshly-sown seedbed or decides to attend to the call of nature in the impatiens freshly planted that morning.

A lot could be gained by planting a small corner of Labiatae (thyme, mint and catnip – but be sure to ask for the real stuff because some seed vendors have the annoying habit of selling wild oats in place of catnip and calling it "catmint."), along with couch grass to which cats are not adverse. It appears that when cats have benign digestive problems, they willingly eat couch grass.

Living with "Neighbor" Cats

If you are fortunate enough to live in an individual house, there will invariably be problems with cohabitation. Generally, cats resolve these problems rather well, although often noisily. But the fury and noise worthy of Shakespeare that pussycats can unleash at night should not cause their owner to tremble. This is a bluffing strategy that cats push to the limits.

The bites, scratches and abscesses that may result are more frequent with full-grown males than with other cats. Neutering or spaying is always advisable because this operation protects the cat from numerous infectious diseases, some of which can be lethal. This operation can be performed starting at the age of six months (or even a little earlier, depending on the development and maturity of the cat and the season. Female cats that are five months old in January will be much more pre-

Mixed breed in a tree trunk

323

Angora Turk in a garden.

BRUSHING

For short or medium-haired breeds, you can use a curry-comb, which will really separate the fur. For longhaired breeds, now is the time to do a brushing with a soft brush.

Brushing helps restore the fullness and fluffiness of the fur.

Bathing will change the appearance of the coat and it will take two days for the fur to regain its natural consistency.

Cats then provide the "finishing touches" themselves, with the grooming tool nature gave them – their tongue. It is sometimes necessary to limit their enthusiasm, especially with longhaired breeds. Indeed, licking too heavily in one area of the coat can cause the fur to become tangled and stuck together. In this case, the best solution is to put a collar on the cat (which can be quite elegant) until it is time to show the cat during a contest.

cocious than cats that turn five months old in November). The procedure also helps prevent overpopulation and needless problems with the neighbors.

Gardeners, Take Pity on Slugs and Mice

Many products commonly used by gardeners are toxic for cats. Unfortunately, even gardeners who love cats often find themselves in a bind when they underestimate a cat's abilities to go exploring in narrow, hard to reach places. As a precaution (this also applies to children), it is better to ban rat and slug killers from the garden for good.

Hygiene

House-Training

Some cats are so meticulous with their litter box that the owner is forced to change the litter after every use.

American Shorthair in its litter box

Without exaggerating, the litter box should be checked every day and maintained according to the type of litter used. Bentonite or sepiolite-based litters have the distinctive feature of clumping around urine to form small balls that can be periodically removed at least every three days. Feces remain intact and are removed in the same manner with a small shovel. The advantage of this type of litter is that it limits odors that not only bother owners (and their guests), but also the user(s) of the litter box. Odors that are too strong will repel the cat and sometimes lead him to answer the call of nature in a less appropriate, albeit more inviting, place (shower stall, bathtubs, flower pots, etc.).

Traditional, non-clumping litter needs to be changed every day.

For longhaired cats, it is recommended to trim the hair around the anus so as to avoid the nasty surprise of finding feces stuck there.

Coat Maintenance

Even for shorthaired cats, weekly or even daily brushing is a good way to check the cat to see if all is well and that there are no little wounds, parasites, etc. In this way, cats generally get a little tender loving care of a slightly different kind. With longhaired cats, brushing is imperative. Kittens must be taught young to tolerate the session, which should never end with scratching. If the cat is not patient enough, several short brushing sessions could be done. Purebred cats that will be shown on a regular basis, must be trained at a young age to tolerate being handled and bathed. Go easy during the first bath and be attentive to any signs of anxiety so as not to create any aversions in the future champion. Unfortunately, aversions can be instilled very quickly.

For cats with outdoor access, it is necessary to be vigilant especially in spring, when cats shed their hair and when the rainy season hits with full force. Longhaired cats, even if they spend a long time grooming themselves, are not sheltered from having their hair become matted and compacted into sometimes voluminous masses. These mats then become an inviting

Grooming of a Burmese Sacred Cat

spot for parasites, which cause serious dermatological problems. Be sure to get to the groomer and the veterinarian in time (a general anesthesia may sometimes be necessary).

It is normal to find whiskers from time to time on pillows, the sofa or other places where the cat is used to sleeping. There is no cause for concern. Cat whiskers are a particular type of hair but are shed more slowly than hair.

Eyes and Ears

The eyes should only be cleaned if they are watery and even then, it is always preferable to seek the advice of a veterinarian before applying a cleaning product. In fact, epiphora (watering) does not normally occur in cats. If watering does occur, it may be an indication of a problem with the tear glands or eyelids, or an infectious or viral disease. Persian cats, whose faces are very flat, require frequent eye care. Use products recommended by your veterinarian.

The ears should not be cleaned unless you notice the presence of yellowish or brownish deposits. If your cat is scratching its ear furiously or tilting its head, you should take it to the veterinarian as soon as possible and refrain from using any product that could conceal a foreign object. Never use cotton swabs (which would only push the foreign object further into the eardrum) and ask your veterinarian what products to use.

Teeth

At four months old, cats begin to get their adult teeth, especially the fangs, which have a different morphology from baby teeth.

It is almost illusory to try to brush cats' teeth. However, you should regularly check the color of the teeth and look for possible tartar buildup. Regular crunching promotes chewing and prevents tartar buildup, or at least limits buildup if it has already started. Therefore, do not

Ear care on a Maine Coon kitten

Show cats are required to have their claws trimmed or they will be disqualified. The best way to trim the claws seems to be to sit down and to hold the cat in between your thighs on its back. Reassure the cat by petting his stomach between every few cuts.
Using guillotine clippers, trim the tip of the claw, staying well above the pink triangle, which is fleshy part of the claw matrix. Cutting any lower will cause heavy bleeding and a pain that the cat will remember during the next session.
If your cat is used to this operation, it will integrate it as part of the ritual process with you and trimming its nails before a show will not be a problem.
You can also take advantage of this opportunity to trim the hair growing between your Persian's digits.

Trimming the claws of an Abyssinian

deprive your cat of the pleasure of eating dry food. Accustom it to eating dry food and to drinking fresh water at a young age. If the tap water is hard water, mineral water is recommended. Your veterinarian will check the state of the teeth during annual check-ups and if necessary, suggest de-scaling, which is a mild treatment requiring a brief anesthesia.

Claws

The act of scratching objects is part of normal behavior for cats. However, this behavior does not always fit well with sedentary apartment life. Indeed, although scratching trees is not a problem for the owner of a cat that has free access to the yard, scratching the leather sofa or expensive furniture can seriously compromise community life.

When cats have to live in apartments, it is important to forbid them from scratching objects you do not want them to scratch, starting at a young age. A simple "no" along with a sharp noise (clapping your hands) will suffice to correct this behavior. If a young kitten exhibits this behavior often, especially upon waking, you should give it one or more objects that can be used as a scratching post. Cats do not always accept commercial scratching posts. Often a piece of wood (birch, pine, and even olivewood) will do the trick better. Scratching posts should be changed regularly since cats eventually grow weary of them.

"De-clawing" a cat involves a mutilating surgical operation since it consists of amputating the last phalanx of the cat's front paws, definitively removing the claw and its root (the claw is equivalent to human fingernails, which cannot be removed without their base). This operation should not be performed without first discussing all the aspects with your veterinarian.
Various studies have shown that this ablation does not compromise the cat's hunting and jumping abilities. In Quebec, this operation is widely practiced and cats there do not seem to have any particular problems with motor functions. However, bear in mind that depending

on the nature of the cat, scratching, along with vocal sounds and characteristic growling, is a means of advertising or issuing a warning about impending aggression (biting). Cats with agile paws, who can no longer use scratching to defend themselves after being operated on, have been known to start biting without going through any other process.
Claws should be trimmed approximately every three to four weeks, for cats that do not get exercise. It is better to have two people, one to hold the cat down without force and one to look closely at the claw before trimming it. Special clippers are sold at veterinarian offices. It is important not to cut the living tissue part of the claw or it will start to bleed. In order to spare you cat, it is perhaps wise to accustom it gradually to these manicure sessions and to ask your veterinarian to show you how to proceed.

The Milestones of Life

The Birth of a Child

For a cat that belongs to a couple, the birth of a baby is a major event that will necessarily change the relationship. Indeed, despite all the good intentions of the owner, the cat will never again have the same relationship with the couple.

Before the birth, it is important to start accustoming the cat to no longer having access to the nursery, especially if the cat was in the habit of roaming in the apartment or house freely without restriction.

During your stay at the maternity ward, think about giving the baby's first blankets to the father. He can take them home and leave them out in the open in a small basket. The odors will give your cat(s) some indications of the new arrival and facilitate introductions.
When you come home from the hospital, think about taking the time to make introductions. Both the baby and the cat will be sensitive to what you say and understand more than you might think.

Later on, be sure to continue paying attention to the cat and try not to only shower him with affection when your baby is sleeping (or he will associate the absence of the baby with an abundance of attention). Rather, you should pet him and talk to him in front of your baby, which will also help the baby become a cat lover later on.

The temptation for cats to adopt babies sometimes pushes them to risky behavior, such as wanting to sleep in the cradle. Indeed, the cradle is a warm, pleasant place, sometimes with the delicious aroma of curdled milk (your cat does not necessarily have the same opinion of regurgitation as you do!). Be careful therefore to channel your cat's impulses by possibly giving him doll cradle of his own.

As the baby grows and depending on the nature of the cat, you will generally be surprised to see how tolerant the cat is vis-à-vis your child (a tolerance that is generally limited only to the child or children of the family). The cat is a wonderful source of life lessons for the child. Around the age of 15 months for example, the child will start to discover that the cat has a funny tail. A simple growl from the cat is enough to make the child understand that respect for individuals is important. However, during this age when the child is discovering everything fearlessly, you need to be vigilant and always ensure mutual respect.

Moving

Moving is a big event for cats, who are sometimes said to be more attached to places than people. Some cats prove this by returning to their old house, sometimes making very long journeys. There was one old cat, for instance, that in all likelihood made the roundtrip between Lyon and Barcelonette, in the South of France, disappointed to find its old house abandoned.

During the move, it is wise to lock the cat in one room with food, a litter box and a few toys. If possible, wait until the very last to bring the cat and put him in a room that is relatively arranged.

A move between two different apartments generally does not pose a problem. The cat will quickly take possession of its new territory. If the cat is moving from a house to an apartment, plan to arrange the apartment so that it can jump and climb in order to help it become accustomed to being deprived of freedom and access to the outside.

If the cat moves from an apartment to a house, it is wise not to let it outside for three to seven days and thereafter to monitor it when it goes outside, either by watching or going outside with it. From then on, let it go outside more and more frequently, but keep a box of cat food nearby to bring it back!

Vacations

Cats really do not like to travel in cars or any other means of transport. For this reason, it is always better to find a friend who can stop by your house to feed the cat and change the litter, especially for short trips.

If you rent a vacation house, even for a month, your cat will not get used to it unless you take it there regularly, something you can start accustoming it to at an early age. Sometimes a cat's ability to adapt is staggering, such as the case of the cat that got used to travelling with his owner on a motorcycle at an early age.

Some cats that are used to living in an apartment during the year, may be depressed when they return from the vacation in the country in September. If your cat seems to be lacking energy or appetite, or if it starts to urinate inappropriately, do not hesitate to take it to the veterinarian.

A cat in its transportation basket.

TRIPS

Cats may be irritated by travelling in cars, buses or subways, even for short trips (such as going to the veterinarian). Heat, dim light and silence may reassure your cat. Put him in a willow basket cage or even a simple, thick cardboard box for trips (do not worry, he will not suffocate). Line the box with a paper towels and put a cloth under him.
If the cat is emotional, it may have an accident within the first five to ten minutes. If this happens, remove the paper towels so that it may finish the trip dry.
One trick is to place the willow basket in a slightly filled litter box. Urine will then flow through the basket into the litter box, leaving the cat dry. This trick also protects the seats and floor covering in your car. If the trip is long, give the cat food (preferably dry food) and fresh water periodically when you make meal stops. Do not leave food in its cage or box however.
A tranquilizer may be useful for air travel. Consult your veterinarian.

A Sick Cat

Before hospitalizing a cat, even under the best of conditions, the best interests of the cat and the owner's possibilities should always be discussed with the veterinarian. The amount of stress on the cat and the strength of the bond between the cat and its owner are aspects veterinarians specialized in feline medicine will consider as factors that may influence the morale of the animal and its ability to recuperate.

It may be wiser to simply take the cat to the clinic to receive treatment (day hospitalization) unless the owner can come by the clinic once or twice a day to visit his cat and give him food, which the cat often accepts more readily when given with such a loving heart.

Part 4

KNOWING THE CAT

ANATOMY
PHYSIOLOGY
NUTRITION
GENETICS
PREVENTION
DISEASES

Anatomy and Physiology

The cat's physiology is very similar to that of other animal species. Like all mammals, the cat is homeothermal, able to maintain its internal organs at a constant temperature (between 38 and 38.5°C). Its skin is covered with hair. After mating, the fertilized eggs are sheltered in the female's uterus and nourished by extensive exchanges through the placenta. At birth, kittens are nursed by their mother.

Cats are often described using well-established images that distinguish them from other species: they are depicted as silent but noisy during mating, mysterious, independent, territorial, adept at hunting, nocturnal and able to see in the dark, agile, meticulous about grooming, sleeping often, curled up and purring at the corner of the hearth, etc. These attributes are based on the behavioral characteristics of felines, as well as their remarkable physiological adaptations as fearsome predators. All these special features are simply adaptations for survival in a wide range of environments, where felines effectively track and hunt prey and spend the rest of their time recovering and rebuilding their energy reserves.

The cat is a mammal, built according to the guidelines of this large group of animal species. Yet it is a specialized mammal, perfectly adapted to its predatory status. This adaptation primarily involves the functions enabling it to interact with its surroundings: the musculoskeletal system and the nervous system. To a lesser extent, even the autonomic functions (circulation, respiration, digestion, and elimination) are involved.

The Musculoskeletal System

Anatomy

The musculoskeletal system includes the skeleton, joints, muscles, and tendons that allow the bones to move in relation to each other.

Skeleton and Bones
Bone tissue (connective tissue consisting essentially of calcium) serves as a support, accounting for nearly the entire skeleton. It also plays a protective role, especially with regard to the central nervous system and the thoracic organs. It is involved in regulating phosphorus and calcium metabolism. It protects the bone marrow, where blood cells are produced.

The cat's skeleton consists of 279 to 282 bones. Generally, these bones are long, small, and thin but highly resistant.

Trunk
• Spine: 50 to 54 vertebrae divided into five segments or regions, including seven cervical vertebrae, thirteen dorsal or thoracic vertebrae, seven lumbar vertebrae, three sacral vertebrae, and twenty to twenty-four caudal or coccygeal vertebrae (tail).
• Thorax: sternum consisting of eight sternebrae; thirteen pairs of ribs, nine of which are sternal.

Limbs
Forequarters
41 bones, including:
• the thoracic girdle: simple clavicle and scapula;
• one upper arm bone: the humerus;
• two forearm bones: the flat, arched radius and the longer ulna;

• thirty-six bones in the hand: five fingers (four complete external fingers and one internal, incomplete thumb). The carpus consists of seven bones, and the metacarpus includes five bones. There are fourteen phalanges (three in each external finger and two in the thumb).

The claws are the cornified part of the digital extremity. Each is curved and flattened laterally. The claws are very sharp and retract automatically into a cutaneous sheath when the cat is resting or walking.

The paw pads are generally located underneath and behind the fingers and toes. It is by way of the paw pads that the limbs touch the ground. There are five digital pads on the forefoot, one on each finger. The large, triangular palm pad or metacarpal pad in the center of the hand is shaped like a club or heart on a playing card. A small, rounded, not very pronounced carpal pad is located at the top of the hand.

FINGER STRUCTURE OF THE CAT
DORSAL, PALMAR, VERTICAL CROSS-SECTION,
DISTAL EXTREMITY *(from P.C. Blin)*

A: *Middle phalanx*
B: *Distal phalanx*
C: *Claw*
D: *Cutaneous fold of the claw*
E: *Digital pad*
F: *Joint cavity*

1 – *Joint surfaces of the phalanges*
2 – *Ligament of the 2nd and 3rd phalanges*
3 – *Extensor tendon of the finger*
4 – *Flexor tendon of the finger*
5 – *Relaxed elastic ligament*
7 – *Fatty portion of the digital pads*
8 – *Cutaneous covering*

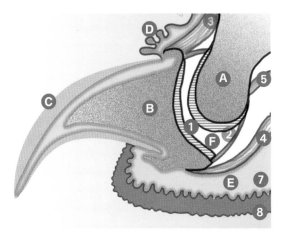

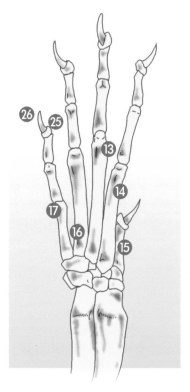

DORSAL VIEW OF THE HAND

13- *3rd metacarpal*   14- *2nd metacarpal*
15- *1st metacarpal*   16- *4th metacarpal*
17- *5th metacarpal*   25- *Ungicilar crest*
26- *Apex of phalanx*

SKELETON OF THE CAT

1- *Mandible*
2- *Frontal bone*
3- *Cranium*
4- *Cervical vertebrae*
5- *Thoracic vertebrae*
6- *Rib*
7- *Lumbar vertebrae*
8- *Ilium*
9- *Sacrum*
10- *Caudal vertebrae*
11- *Ischium*
12- *Femur*
13- *Patella*
14- *Fibula*
15- *Tibia*
16- *Tarsus*
17- *Metatarsus*
18- *Phalanges*
19- *Metacarpus*
20- *Carpus*
21- *Radius*
22- *Ulna*
23- *Sternum*
24- *Humerus*
25- *Scapula*

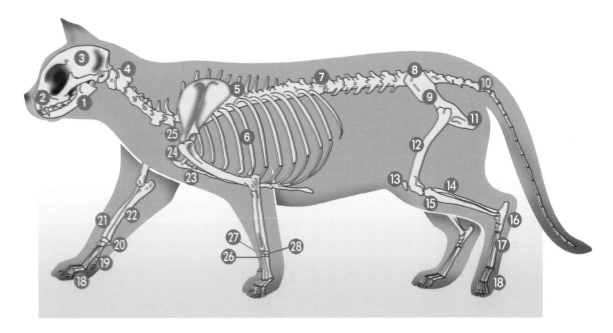

Hindquarters

39 bones, including:

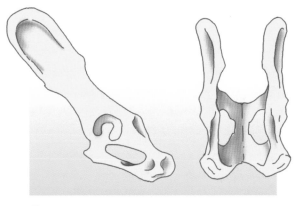

COXAL BONE OF THE CAT

– one in the pelvic girdle: the nearly straight coxal bone, which extends horizontally;
– one in the hip: the long, cylindrical femur;
– three in the leg: a long, thick, flat patella; a long tibia; and a styloid fibula;
– four complete toes and one internal toe (variable with relation to the foot);
– seven bones arranged in two rows in the tarsus;
– four curved bones in the metatarsus.
The cat has an angled hock, a fairly long shin, and a compact digital region with highly arched, very closely spaced fingers and toes.
There are five fleshy pads on the plantar surface: one large, trilobed digital pad surrounded by four others.

Head

The frontal bone is extremely short. The cranium is voluminous and globular, with large temporal fossae and orbits. The jaws are powerful and short.

Joints

The joints are remarkably flexible and mobile. The limbs can rotate fully without dislocation. The skeleton is very flexible, and the tail can assume almost any position.

Muscles

"The active organs of movement, the muscles are contractile, or able to shorten temporarily under the influence of a stimulus. They can thus mobilize the anatomical elements of the bones, to which they are attached. They are also elastic and highly toned. They give the living being its shape and characteristic postures" (Barone).

There are three major types of muscle cells, based on their structure and physiology:
- the striated skeletal muscle cells (muscles capable of voluntary contraction);
- the striated cardiac muscle cells (which contract rhythmically in the absence of a nerve stimulus);
- the smooth muscle cells of the organs, which are regulated by the autonomic nervous system (sympathetic and parasympathetic).

The fleshy part of the muscles is dark red and has a strong, characteristic odor. The tendons are generally pearly white, thin, and fragile but resistant.

The head is characterized by highly developed, complex, overlapping cutaneous muscles and powerful masticatory muscles.

The cervical region includes a thick mass of muscles arranged in four layers.

The abdominal muscles are highly developed and give the abdominal wall its fleshy texture and thickness.

The croup and hip muscles are large.
The special features of the limb muscles are based on the number of digits in the hands and feet. The limbs contain rotator muscles (for pronation and supination, enabling a 180° rotation of the palm or plantar surface of the hand or foot).

The hindquarters, more powerful than the forequarters, are always ready to spring the animal into motion. In the cat, running is a series of long, low bounds. Cats are sprinters, not distance runners. Their muscles and claws enable them to scale and climb with ease. They can

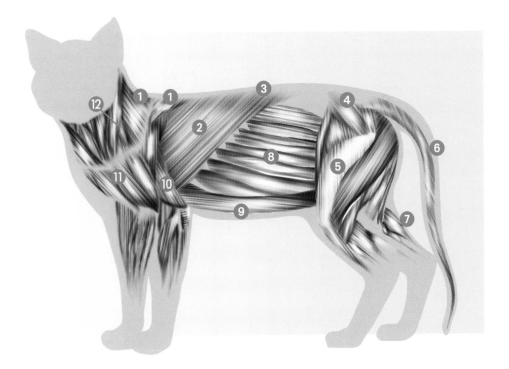

MUSCLES OF THE CAT

1 – *Trapezius muscle*
2 – *Latissimus dorsi muscle*
3 – *Thoracolumbar fascia muscle*
4 – *Gluteus medius muscle*
5 – *Tensor fascia lata muscle*
6 – *Sacrocaudalis muscle*
7 – *Gastrocnemius muscle*
8 – *External abdominal oblique muscle*
9 – *Rectus abdominus muscle*
10 – *Triceps brachii muscle*
11 – *Cleidobrachialis muscle*
12 – *Cleidocephalicus muscle*

jump very high and are able to land on their feet when the fall is high enough.

The Physiology of the Musculoskeletal System

The musculoskeletal system has a dual role: It ensures the cohesion and solidity of the body as a whole, and it enables the animal to move about in order to fulfill its needs by acting on its environment.

The Bones and Joints

Bones
The skeleton is a frame around which the other tissues are arranged. Consisting mainly of hydroxyapatite crystals and based on calcium and phosphate (99% of the body's calcium is stored in the bones), bone is not a fixed structure. It is a living tissue that is constantly renewing its external surface, or periosteum, and producing blood cells in its innermost part, the bone marrow.

The structure of the joints depends on the bones they connect. Long bones have synovial joints. Synovial fluid is a shock-absorbing, lubricating liquid that enables the perfect mobility of the individual parts, including the joint cartilage covering the ends of the bones (or epiphyses), the synovial membrane, the articular capsule, and the ligaments.

Cartilage
Thanks to its flexibility, cartilage significantly reduces friction during joint movement and distributes and balances the stresses sustained by the joint, thereby preventing injury to the underlying bone. Cartilage can withstand a strain proportional to the force applied along its surface, thanks to a network of complex proteins that either retain or release a large amount of water according to the stress sustained. Water accounts for 70% of cartilage by weight, and the fibrillar network over 25%.
Articular Capsule and Synovial Membrane
The articular capsule consists of collagen and elastic tissue. It ensures joint cohesion through its solid attachment to the bone tissue.It is not very vascularized but is well-innervated.

Synovial fluid is formed through filtration from the many capillaries in the synovial membrane.

Muscles and Movement

Like all felines (in the Felidae family), the cat is a carnivore. Its diet is more exclusively carnivorous than that of the dog. To hunt prey, it can mobilize its 279 bones and 30 teeth powerfully, rapidly, and precisely. It has very powerful muscles supported by a skeleton that is well adapted to jumping, climbing, and combat.

The cat can quickly develop considerable force with relation to its weight. However, it cannot maintain this effort very long; like all felines, the cat lacks endurance. In a single bound, it can reach impressive heights with relation to its size. Using its claws, as needed, it can climb up a vertical tree trunk. But coming down is sometimes an insurmountable task: A frightened cat that has clambered to the top of a tree may be completely unable to get back down.

The locomotor muscles are called striated muscles because of the way their cells look under a microscope. They consist of clusters of cells rich in myofibrils, or tiny filaments that slide against each other to cause the cell to shorten and the muscle to contract. The contractile force is then transmitted to the bones by the tendons, which form fibrous ropes attached to the bone surface. Each muscle contraction is caused by a stimulus from the nervous system. One nerve cell, or neuron, regulates several dozen muscle cells. This set of nerve and muscle cells is called a motor unit.

The energy necessary for muscle contraction comes from a chemical fuel called ATP (adenosine triphosphate). The normal use of this compound requires oxygen. When there is not enough oxygen in the blood to meet this requirement, ATP is used differently, and byproducts like lactic acid accumulate in the muscle and blood, leading to fatigue and the inability to sustain effort. The muscle is an engine with a suboptimal yield. Only 25% of the energy used is transformed into movement, with the rest being dissipated as heat.

The coordination of the contraction of the various muscle groups is important for successful combat. In cats, this orchestration by the brain and cerebellum is very effective, enabling highly precise motions even at great speeds, as well as rapid changes in the direction of movement.

Cats have five digits on each forefoot and four on each hind foot. Supple and extensible, they allow the cat to move in complete silence, with the paw pads acting as shock absorbers and the claws retracted. The retractability of the claws can be a nuisance when the cat is running over flat ground (a dog's claws, for example, serve as spikes) but eliminates all noise. Encased in a sheath that protects them from constant wear, the cat's claws remain curved and very long. They are fearsome weapons. Still, owners of excessively sedentary cats must provide a scratching area for their cat to wear down and trim its nails.

The Nervous System

Anatomy

Central Nervous System (CNS)

The encephalon includes:
- The brain, weighing 20 to 28 g. It is compact, globular in the back, and has a truncated anterior stem. It measures 35 mm long, 37 mm wide, and 26 mm high. Its circumvolutions, or folds, are not very pronounced. The brain contains 80% water (9 to 11% protein and 6% fat). The hypothalamus, located in the median, central part of the brain, regulates the endocrine system;

- The cerebellum (involved in postural activity) and the brain stem (which regulates autonomic activity) in the hind section of the brain. Its surface is divided into wide lamellae. The cerebellum weighs 3 to 5 g;

- The whitish, cylindrical spinal cord inside the spine weighs 7 to 9 g. Emerging from each side of the spinal cord are the roots of the

EXTERNAL ANATOMY OF THE CEREBRAL HEMISPHERES

Dorsal view of the encephalon
7 – *Suprasylvian fissure*
8 – *Marginal fissure*
9 – *Crucial fissure*

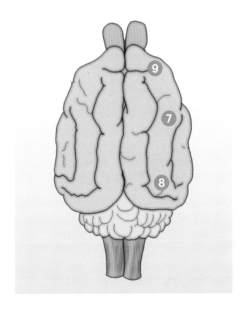

EXTERNAL ANATOMY OF THE CEREBRAL HEMISPHERES

Left-hand lateral view

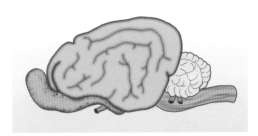

spinal nerves. Running inside are the sensory motor and associative paths.

Peripheral Nervous System

The peripheral nervous system is the set of all nerve fibers grouped as follows:

- cranial nerves (twelve pairs: olfactory, optic, acoustic, vagus nerve, etc.);
- spinal nerves connected to the spinal cord (thirty-six to thirty-eight pairs, including eight cervical, thirteen dorsal, seven lumbar, three sacral, and five to seven coccygeal nerves).

Autonomic Nervous System

The autonomic nervous system regulates the body's autonomic activities (organ function and the coordination of various organ functions).

It includes, in particular:
- The sympathetic nervous system, with its nerves and ganglia. Sympathetic nerves run from plexus to plexus to the organs. The thoracic ganglia become aortic or pulmonary cardiac filaments. The sacral ganglia branch into hypogastric nerves running to the pelvic organs;
- The parasympathetic nervous system. This system is the opposite of that above. It is formed of a cranial section and a pelvic section.

The Eye

The nearly spherical eyeball sits inside the orbit. Its volume is 4.5 to 5 cm³, its weight is 10 to 11 g, and its horizontal diameter is 19 to 22 mm. The wall of the ocular cavity consists of three layers, or tunicae:

- the external tunica (sclera and cornea);
- the middle tunica (uvea: choroid, ciliary body, and iris);
- the internal tunica (retina with papilla and optic nerve).

The eyeball contains the aqueous humor that fills the anterior cavity and the vitreous humor (2.8 cm³), separated by the lens, a transparent, refractive, biconvex organ (8 mm thick, 0.5 cm³, 1.4 g) that plays an essential role in focusing.

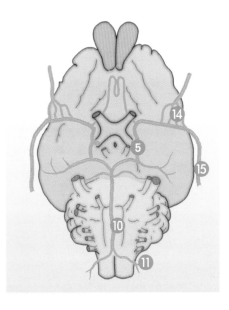

EXTERNAL ANATOMY OF THE CEREBRAL HEMISPHERES AND BLOOD SUPPLY

Ventral view
 5 – *Internal carotid artery*
10 – *Basilar artery*
11 – *Vertebral artery*
14 – *Epidural rete mirabile*
15 – *Maxillary artery*

337

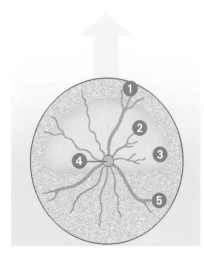

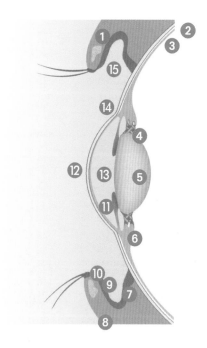

The cornea is the transparent, anterior part of the external tunica. The uvea, a vascular, innervated tunica, includes the anterior lamina of the iris, the ciliary body, and the choroid. The iris, located in front of the lens, separates the posterior chamber of the eye from its anterior chamber.

The iris, an aperture that is greenish-blue, yellow, etc. and marked by many concentric or radiating striations, allows light to pass only through the pupil.

The size of the pupil regulates light penetration. In bright daylight, it closes to form a very narrow, vertical slit. In semi-darkness, it opens into a circle.

The thin, densely pigmented choroid located between the retina and sclera consists of a network of vessels. It supplies blood to the retina and the anterior segment of the eye. The upper half of the back of the eye is formed by the tapetum lucidum, consisting of cells that reflect and break down light, ensuring good night vision. The optic nerve connects the retina to the brain.

The Physiology of Sensory Functions

The sensory functions allow the animal to perceive and assimilate variations in all forms of energy. Exteroception enables an animal to detect external information: light energy (vision), sound energy (hearing), etc. It thus involves the five senses: sight, hearing, smell, taste, and touch (tactile and thermal sensations). To these must be added proprioception, or the perception of the position of one's own body in space, based on the membranous labyrinth of the inner ear and numerous receptors in the muscles, tendons, and joints. The sensory functions also include interoception, or the often unconscious perception of a great deal of information that comes from the organism itself: composition of the gastroduodenal contents, arterial pressure, chemical composition of the blood, etc.

Smell and Taste

These two senses are considered indivisible in carnivores. Taste, which is not highly developed, complements the sense of smell.

Olfactory Acuity

A cat's sense of smell is not as effective as a dog's. In the cat's predatory activity, this sense takes third place behind sight and hearing. Still, the cat's sense of smell is by no means underdeveloped. It plays an important role in the animal's social relationships and is involved in eating. Any disturbance to the sense of smell will cause the cat to refuse food.

The cat is a so-called macrosmatic species, in which the olfactory region of the brain occupies a large portion with relation to the entire developed brain. This ratio is approximately 6, versus 0.3 in humans, for example. The cat's odor detection threshold is very low, although variable based on the odorous substance and on learning. When the concentration of the odorous substance increases, so does sensation, but much more slowly. Smell is therefore a subtle, qualitative sensation. But odor is not as well quantified. The sensation occurs approximately one-half second after the perceived volatile substance comes into contact with the mucosa. After a certain period (one to two hours) of intense stimulation, the receptors become desensitized. This olfactory fatigue occurs with all odors. Adaptation occurs when an odor that is constantly present is no longer perceived (due to a gradual increase in the detection threshold).

Odor Perception

By nature, odor molecules are volatile substances at normal temperatures. They reach the olfactory organ, located above and behind the nasal fossae, during inhalation. Another point of access is the so-called retronasal passage, through which air reaches the olfactory organ during exhalation. When the oral cavity contains food, this process contributes to the sense of taste.

The interaction between odor molecules and the receptors in the mucosa triggers an electric phenomenon, creating a sort of computer card called an olfactory image. This card is carried by the olfactory nerve, then read thoroughly and interpreted by the brain. The image is so rich in possibilities that it could code countless different odors. The cat's ability to discriminate odors is considerable. It can recognize even the most complex chemical mixtures.

Taste

The sense of taste is developed in cats, which have over four hundred taste buds. It is commonly accepted that cats can detect the four basic taste sensations: sour, bitter, sweet, and salty. Sour and bitter sensations are very well perceived, much better than in dogs, making cats very wary with regard to possible toxins.

Salty flavors are also detected by the entire tongue surface. Sweet flavors are recognized only at high concentrations. These thresholds fit well with the carnivorous diet of cats, which may also have specific receptors for certain compounds in meat that they require (such as taurine).

Hearing

Auditory Acuity
With its highly developed sense of hearing, the cat can detect a wide range of sounds at very low intensities. The cat's range of per-

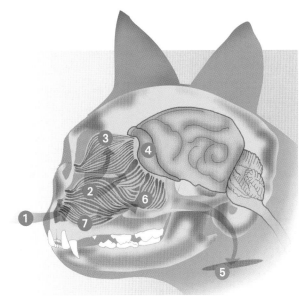

NASAL CAVITY OF THE CAT

1 – *Air entering through the nostrils*
2 – *Meatus nasi medius*
3 – *Dorsal turbinate bone*
4 – *Olfactory bulb*
5 – *Nasopharynx*
6 – *Ventral meatus*
7 – *Ventral turbinate bone*

ceived vibrations is approximately three times greater than that of humans. Cats can hear lower sounds and especially much higher ones: In the ultrasound range, at frequencies above 20,000 hertz, cats seem able to perceive sounds up to 60,000 Hz! Very low intensity (approximately 5 dB) suffices, with the perceived sensation increasing largely as a function of intensity. Cats are thus able to distinguish slight variations in pitch, regardless of intensity. The concepts of auditory fatigue, adaptation, and persistence are much less pronounced in feline hearing. Cats can locate the source of sound by moving their ear flaps in different directions, each moving independently of the other.

Auditory Perception
The pinnae capture sound waves and transmit them to the outer auditory canal. Sound is thus initially reinforced through resonance (as when one speaks into a tube). The eardrum vibrates and transmits these vibrations to the osselets (hammer, anvil, and stirrup), which serve as a transformer, since the resistance to

EAR OF THE CAT

1 – *Pinna*
2 – *Chain of osselets*
3 – *Semi-circular canals*
4 – *Cochlea*
5 – *Eardrum*
6 – *Tympanic bulb*
7 – *External auditory canal*

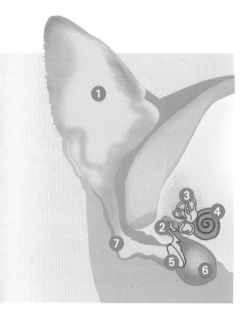

sound propagation is not the same in air (outer ear) and water (inner ear). The solid osselets transmit sound waves between the two media without information being lost through reflection.

The information is coded electrically in the cochlea, a sort of spiral passageway lined with vibratory cells connected to nerve cells. These cells are bathed in the fluid, or endolymph, contained in the cochlea. They form the organ of Corti, which is connected to the vestibulocochlear nerve.

Vision

Our fascination with cats is largely based on their facial expression, with their vertical pupils and eyesight that does not seem to diminish at night. Indeed, the cat's eyes are well-adapted to nocturnal predation. Like humans, cats have fully frontal eyes directed forward. This makes the cat one of the mammals with the best binocular vision (approximately 120°), allowing it to better perceive outlines and distances. On each side, this binocular vision is complemented by monocu-

lar vision of approximately 80°. The cat's lens (the eye's "autofocusing" device) is highly mobile and enables rapid focusing on prey.

The Eye and its Parts
The structure of the eye is the same in all mammals. Light penetrates the cornea, then the anterior chamber, which is filled with a liquid called the aqueous humor. After passing through the pupil, light is then diverted by the lens, which works like a regular convex lens. Light then passes through the posterior chamber to the retina.

The eye is equipped with groups of muscles that enable it to move in all directions. It is protected by the eyelids. Cats have a third eyelid that is highly mobile and can sweep over the entire surface of the cornea, cleaning it and covering it with a protective liquid film.

Color
Color perception requires that the retina contain photoreceptors called cones. But the sensitivity to many shades of color is based on families of cones that are sensitive to different wavelengths of light. Primarily nocturnal, or

VISUAL FIELD OF THE CAT

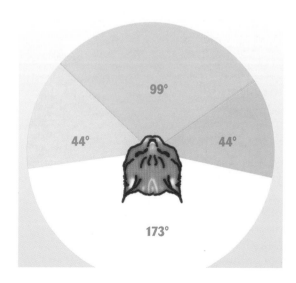

monochromatic, species such as rats have one type of cone. These animals distinguish objects based only on their light intensity. Cats are dichromatic, meaning they have two sorts of cones. We may thus assume that they can perceive two colors and the shades that result from mixing these two colors, from red to green. Humans are trichromatic, meaning we have three families of cones whose associated stimulation allows us to detect shades of color in the entire visible spectrum.

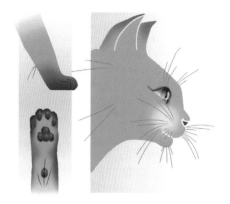

Nocturnal Vision

The cat's nocturnal vision, however, is much keener than ours. Other cells, the rods, are involved in this function. Cats have 200 million rods, versus only 120 in humans. In addition, the tapetum in the lower part of the back of the cat's eye serves as a mirror, reflecting light that is "unused" by the retina and enabling this light to be saved and returned to the retina. The cat's tapetum is easy to see when your car headlights shine into a cat's eyes.

Form and Motion

The perception of form, motion, and probably outlines is linked to a certain specialization of the retinal cells: some cells respond only to the perception of lines arranged in a specific direction. In short, some cells detect vertical elements, others detect horizontal elements, and still other cells detect each angulation (in increments of 10 to 30 degrees). The displacement of these lines during motion enables more effective perception. In other words, the more an object or animal moves, the better the cat perceives it.

Touch

Skin is a highly effective tool, able to detect very slight differences in pressure and temperature. Tactile receptors are not distributed evenly over all parts of the body. The most innervated regions are the face and extremities (paws and paw pads) and the anal and genital regions. The cat has vibrissae (whiskers) on its muzzle that are a sort of large, extensively innervated hair with a highly developed tactile role.

In the event of overstimulation, the perceived sensation turns into pain. In fact, physiologists have demonstrated the existence of receptors that become active only when the stimulation is great enough to injure the skin. This means that pain may, in some ways, be considered as a separate sense. Tactile and thermal sensitivity serve to alert and protect the animal when a stimulus becomes dangerous, and specific sensitivity prevents an already altered region from being re-exposed.

Proprioception and Balance

Cats are well-known for their remarkable sense of balance that enables them to walk along very narrow walls or fences and easily right themselves during a fall so as to land on all fours. This ability is based on the subtle, unconscious, and virtually constant detection of the head's position in space and of muscle and tendon tension. Each movement is detected three-dimensionally by highly sensitive receptors in the inner ear. In the same manner, muscle receptors, or spindles, and tendon receptors constantly compare the tension in each muscle group. All this information is thoroughly analyzed by various structures in the brain (particularly the frontal region) and cerebellum, leading reflexively to the immediate correction of movement to maintain balance during motion.

This system is disconnected very rarely, only during phases of deep sleep.

Organ Sensitivity

Although information from the autonomic functions rarely reaches the conscious level, these functions are under close surveillance by a whole battery of specialized receptors that oversee their activities: for example, blood composition, pressure, concentration, and volume, as well as the contents of the large intestine, are constantly regulated.

There are so many of these specialized receptors that the neurons carrying information back to the brain form the majority in mixed nerves (that is, both sensory and motor nerves). For example, in the vagus nerve, the main nerve regulating the heart, bronchi, stomach, intestine, and bladder, only 10% of the nerve cells are involved in regulation. The remaining 90% are sensory cells from these same organs.

The Integumentary System

Anatomy and Physiology

The integumentary system includes the skin and its phanerae (hairs, cornified appendages).

Skin

The cat's skin is loose, elastic, and highly resistant. Depending on the region, it varies from 0.4 to 2 mm in thickness. A cat weighing 2 kg has a body surface of 0.15 m2, and a cat weighing 6 kg has a surface of 0.3m2.

The skin's main role is to act as a barrier between the external and internal environment by limiting permeability thanks to hair and the cornified layer of the epidermis. This barrier works in both directions. It is essential in limiting the loss of substances, particularly water, and in preventing the excessive penetration of foreign elements.

The outermost layer of the skin consists of the epidermis and epidermal appendages (hair follicles, sebaceous and sweat glands, claws, paw pads).

The epidermis is a supple, watertight, resistant external envelope. Its cornified layer is an adaptation to life on land. The epidermis is not vascularized. It consists of several layers of cells and is covered by a surface film of desquamated cells, proteins, and especially lipids (waxes and sterols). It has one layer of cells packed very closely together. All of this thus forms an impermeable barrier.

Special cells called melanocytes produce melanins, or pigments that protect the skin from sunlight, and store it in vesicles, the melanosomes, which are then transmitted to the neighboring keratinocytes.

All these cells truly work as a team to perform the functions of the skin and protect it from damage.

CROSS-SECTION OF THE SKIN

1 – Epidermis
2 – Dermis
3 – Hypodermis
4 – Capillaries
5 – Nerves
6 – Hair follicle
7 – Sweat gland
8 – Sebaceous gland
9 – Subcutaneous fat
10 – Arrector pili muscle
11 – Secondary hairs
12 – Primary hair

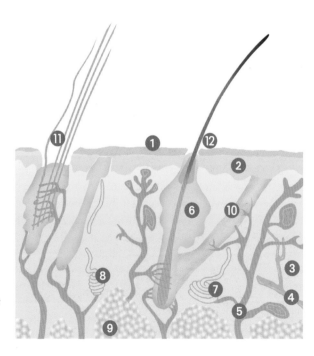

Given the skin's exposure to the external environment, it is not surprising that it also contains cells with a defensive role, a bit like the white blood cells. It also contains many cells that modulate the sensory function of the dermis.

The dermis, the main part of the skin, ensures passive protection against external trauma. It is a connective component that supports the epidermis and provides it with nutrients and hormones, thanks to its vascularization. With its many receptors, the dermis is also the center of the skin's sensory function.

The hypodermis is a looser connective tissue characterized by richly vascularized adipose cells. Fat serves as an insulator and a form of energy storage.

Hair

The hair has a special role in protecting the skin against cuts, scrapes, temperature extremes, and chemical substances. The hair follicle is an invagination in the epidermis that generates hair from a matrix, or bulb. In carnivores, there are three kinds of follicles:

• one main primary follicle containing the main or guard hair, which is approximately 4 cm long in most shorthaired cats,
• two lateral primary follicles that generate the awn hairs (secondary or tectorial hairs),
• these three follicles are surrounded by some fifteen secondary follicles that produce the down hair.

There are several categories of hair (grouped differently, depending on the author):

• The outer coat or guard hairs (primary hairs): long, thick, straight, pigmented, spatulate at the distal end. Protective element of the coat, abundant in the upper parts of the body.
• The awn hairs (also for protection): bent at the end and pointed at the tip, giving them a clublike appearance.
• The intermediate or heterotype hairs: These

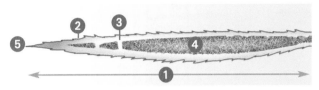

DISTAL PORTION OF THE HAIR

1 – Distal ("spatulate") portion
2 – Cuticle
3 – Cortex
4 – Medulla
5 – Tip

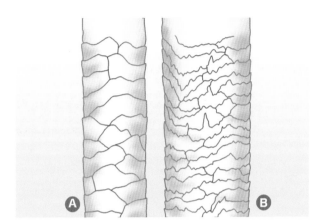

TYPES OF SCALES

A – Pavimentous
B – Denticulate

hairs are wavy and slender at the base, also ending in a club. They play a protective role.

Undercoat, down hair, underfur: thin, wavy, very dense hairs involved in thermal insulation.

The tactile hairs and vibrissae are special types of hair found primarily on the muzzle. They are connected to nerve cells and play a sensory role.

Hair growth is constant and cyclical. Each cycle consists of three main phases (anagen, catagen, and telogen). During anagen, or the growth phase, approximately 0.3 mm of hair is generated per day (guard hairs). Catagen is a transitional phase preceding the telogen "rest" phase. Telogen is the longest phase, especially in winter. Grouped entry into the anagen phase is observed at certain times of the year.

This is seasonal shedding, which is regulated essentially by the light-dark cycle. Grooming occupies much of a cat's time and is facilitated by its very agile, scraping tongue with cornified papillae. During grooming, cats ingest a large quantity of hair, especially during periods of shedding. This can lead to the formation of hairballs in the intestine and cause digestive disorders.

Cutaneous Glands

The sebaceous glands are linked to the hair follicle. They secrete an essentially fatty substance and are involved in the formation of the cutaneous film. There are two types of sweat glands: apocrine glands, which open into the hair follicle, and eccrine glands, which open directly onto the skin. In carnivores, the eccrine glands are limited to the foot pads. They seem to play an important role in increasing traction. Apocrine glands are distributed over the entire body surface and produce an alkaline liquid that is rich in proteins. But their flow is minimal and varies only slightly based on body temperature.

In some areas, including the face, the glands produce special substances, or pheromones, that are very important in the cat's marking of its familiar surroundings and in its social relations. Cats that appear to be relieving an itch by rubbing their cheeks against a vertical object are actually marking their presence.

The Circulatory System

Anatomy

The circulatory system is a closed circuit of hollow tubes through which blood and lymph flow.

This system includes:

- A **heart**, or central motor organ. Through its rhythmic contractions, the heart ensures the movement of blood in pulmonary circulation (right auricle-left ventricle) and systemic circulation (left ventricle-right auricle). After being oxygenated in the lungs, the blood from the veins is pumped into the aorta, the longest and most voluminous artery, from which it supplies the entire organism.

The globular, rounded heart is located in the thoracic cage between the 4th and 7th ribs. It is greatly slanted from front to back, lying almost flat against the sternum. The heart weighs 15 to 20 g in the cat (0.4 to 0.8% its body weight).

- A **vascular system** including:
- arteries that carry blood from the ventricles

HEART

1 – Right ventricle
2 – Right auricle
4 – Cranial vena cava
5 – Brachiocephalic artery
6 – Left subclavian artery
7 – Aorta
9 – Pulmonary vein
10 – Caudal vena cava
11 – Left atrium
12 – Left ventricle
15 – Left pulmonary artery

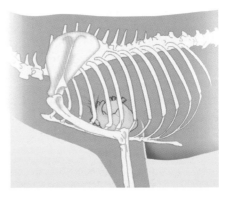

PROJECTION OF THE HEART IN THE THORACIC CAGE

Left lateral side
From the 4th to 7th rib behind the forequarters

344

of the heart to all parts of the body. The arteries branch into arterioles;

• capillaries, very thin vessels connecting the smallest branches of the arterioles to the first branches of the veins. The capillaries enable the exchange of gases, nutrients (nutritional elements used by the cells), metabolites, and heat;

• veins, which carry blood from the capillaries to the right auricle of the heart. The caudal vena cava carries blood away from the hindquarters, pelvis, and abdomen; the portal vein carries blood from the abdominal digestive organs and spleen to the liver.

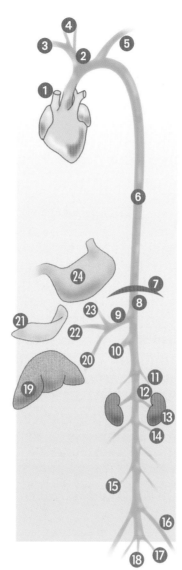

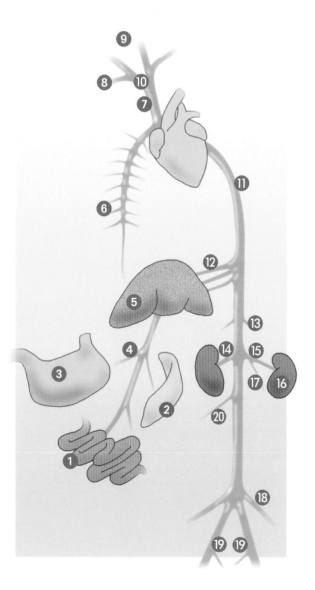

General Circulation

Blood circulates thanks to the contraction of the ventricles and the presence of valves (tricuspid valve, mitral valve). The right side of the heart (right auricle) receives blood from the peripheral veins and sends this blood to the lungs after contraction of the right ventricle.

In the lungs, blood releases carbon dioxide (CO_2) and recovers oxygen (O_2). The left side of the heart (left auricle) receives oxygenated blood from the lungs and pumps it to the rest of the organism after contraction of the left ventricle, thanks to the aorta.

• A **lymphatic system.** This set of ganglia, or lymph nodes, is located along the pathway of lymph vessels in the lymphocenters. Lymph (a clear fluid, the most abundant extracellular liquid) circulates through this system.

The lymphatic system defends the organism from attack by foreign bodies and also includes the central lymph organs (thymus and bone marrow). The thymus is a transitional organ that regresses in adults. The spleen and tonsils are peripheral lymph organs.

The Physiology of Circulation

The higher animals are composed of billions of cells. Most of these cells are isolated from the external environment and thus unable to draw from it the nutrients and oxygen they need. To solve this problem, the circulatory system serves as an internal conveyor belt enabling the renewal of the interstitial fluid bathing the cells. It is the vital system par excellence: any interruption of the circulatory system leads to nerve disorders within seconds and irreversible damage in minutes.

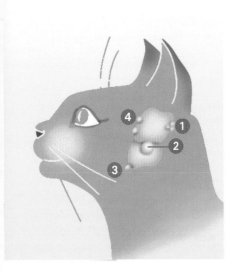

LYMPH NODES OF THE HEAD

1 – *Lateral retropharyngeal lymph nodes*
2 – *Medial retropharyngeal lymph node*
3 – *Mandibular lymph node*
4 – *Parotid lymph node (variable)*

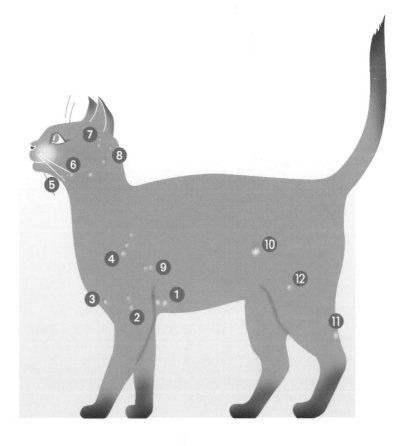

CLINICALLY EXPLORABLE LYMPH NODES

1 – *Accessory axillary lymph nodes*
2 – *Axillary lymph nodes*
3 – *Ventral superficial cervical lymph node*
4 – *Dorsal superficial cervical lymph nodes*
5 – *Medial retropharyngeal lymph node*
6 – *Mandibular lymph nodes*
7 – *Parotid lymph node*
8 – *Lateral retropharyngeal lymph node*
9 – *Cranial mediastinal lymph nodes*
10 – *Cranial mesenteric lymph nodes*
11 – *Superficial popliteal lymph node*
12 – *Superficial inguinal lymph node*

Blood

Blood is a viscous, heterogeneous liquid consisting of a liquid portion, or plasma, and a globular portion including the red blood cells (red blood corpuscles), white blood cells, and platelets. It serves as a carrier and protector. It enables the transport of:

- respiratory gases: oxygen and carbon dioxide,
- cellular fuel energy,
- waste produced by the cells,
- substances that regulate cell activity, such as hormones,
- heat between the sites of production and elimination.

Blood also plays a major role in protecting the organism. The properties of hemostasis and coagulation stop bleeding in the event of a break in a blood vessel wall. Certain cells, the macrophages, act as a cleaning service to remove any internal debris or external invader. Finally, the immune system can detect any foreign body that has been "memorized" and effectively eliminate it.

Red Blood Cells

Shaped like disks, the red blood cells contain hemoglobin, a protein that contains iron and carries oxygen. Their walls are highly elastic, enabling them to squeeze through the narrowest capillaries. Their average life span is approximately two months. After hemoglobin is destroyed by specialized cells, it is turned into bilirubin, a pigment that is itself transformed and eliminated through the bile and urine, to which it gives a yellowish or greenish tint.

White Blood Cells

The white blood cells, or leukocytes, act both as a cleaning service and an army to fight off invaders. They actually consist of various specialized types of cells that cooperate actively and constantly exchange information, thanks to chemical messengers called cytokines. The white blood cells can detect any foreign body or waste and destroy, swallow, and digest it. They have a great ability to learn, the immune function, which enables them to effectively recognize any previously encountered element (antigen) and attack it with specific antibodies. This memorization ability is put to use in vaccination.

Platelets

The platelets are tiny cells that become active as soon as an abnormal component is present in the blood or when they come into contact with connective tissue at the site of a small vascular tear. The platelets adhere to this area and rapidly agglomerate into a sort of plug. At the same time, the vessel contracts locally, and bleeding quickly stops. This is known as hemostasis.

Blood and Circulation

Total blood volume: 65 to 70 ml/kg weight.
Red blood corpuscles (red blood cells): 5.5 to 10 million per microliter.
Leukocytes (white blood cells): 8,000 to 25,000 per microliter.
Platelets: 300,000 to 500,000 per microliter.
Hemoglobin: 80 to 140 g/l.
Hematocrit (percentage of red blood cell volume compared to total blood volume): 24 to 45.
Glucose: 0.7 to 1.1 g/l.
Sodium: 145 to 155 mEq/l.
Potassium: 4 to 4.5 mEq/l.
Calcium: 62 to 100 mg/l.
Protein: 54 to 78 g/l.
Total lipids: 1.5 to 6 g/l.
Cardiac output (resting): 150 to 280 ml/min.
Heart rate (resting): 120 – 140.

Blood Circulation

Blood always follows the same route through the circulatory system. Blood oxygenated in the lungs flows to the heart through the pulmonary veins. It is then pumped to all the cells in the organism by the left part of the heart by the aorta and then the various arteries supplying blood to the organs. Thanks to the veins, which converge into the two venae cavae, the blood returns to the heart (right side), where it is pumped to the lungs by the pulmonary arteries.

The Heart

The cat's heart is approximately the size of a walnut. Thanks to special cells that automatically trigger each beat, the heart beats an average of 120 to 150 cycles per minute at rest. Contraction occurs during the systolic phase, and filling occurs during relaxation, or the diastolic phase. The heart's output is approximately one-half liter of blood per minute. During effort, heart rate and output increase, providing the muscles with more blood, and therefore more oxygen and energy, per unit of time. These variations are associated with the implementation of the autonomic nervous system. During rest, the parasympathetic nervous system slows the heart. During effort, or in the event of fear or stimulation, the orthosympathetic nervous system stimulates the heart.

The Vessels

Blood leaves the heart under high pressure via the arteries. Arterial pressure (or tension) can be measured with a Doppler effect tensiometer and varies from 130 mm of mercury (mmHg) at systole to 90 mmHg at diastole. Expressed in cm of mercury, as by doctors, this gives a value of 13/9. A cat's pressure is therefore not much different from a human's. The artery walls are semi-elastic, providing flow resistance that leads to a drop in pressure toward the capillaries. The highly elastic veins offer little resistance to strain; the pressure in the veins is thus very low.

The very thin capillaries are the circulatory system's reason for being: They are the site of the exchanges that enable renewal of the interstitial fluid. When blood enters the capillaries, it loses some water when it supplies oxygen, energy substrates, and hormones to the cells. When blood leaves the capillaries, water returns from the cells carrying carbon dioxide, waste, and any substances secreted by the cells. The amount of water that leaves the blood through capillaries is slightly greater than the amount that returns. The excess then passes through a second return circuit, the lymph vessels, whose contents, or lymph, returns to the blood in the thorax. The other roles of lymph include carrying elements such as cells and very large molecules which are produced in some tissues and cannot cross the capillary walls.

The blood flow to an organ may be highly variable. In some organs, the arteries can actively contract (vasoconstriction) or relax (vasodilation), operating like a sort of faucet to regulate blood flow through the organ. This process is controlled by the brain and spinal cord through the orthosympathetic nervous system, which resolves conflicts and sets priorities when several organs require increased blood flow at once, or in the event of a threat to general circulation. Many hormones can also act locally to modify vessel activity. For example, this occurs during digestion, when hormones produced by the intestine regulate the blood supply to this organ and the flow of absorbed elements.

After bleeding, or when the oxygen requirement increases suddenly, certain organs, particularly the spleen, can quickly put into circulation many brand new red blood cells. The spleen also captures old red blood vessels and destroys them.

The Respiratory System

Anatomy

The respiratory system includes:
- the nostrils;
- the nasal cavity, which is always very short;
- the larynx, a hollow organ that regulates air flow between the pharynx and trachea;
- the trachea, a single, flexible, wide tube (8 cm long) which is a continuation of the larynx;
- the bronchi, passages branching off from the trachea into the lungs to ensure air circulation;
- the two lungs, a right lung and a left lung. Spongy and elastic, they share the thoracic cavity with the heart. Each is surrounded by the pleura. The lungs account for 1% of the body weight.

The right lung, which is longer, consists of four lobes: the caudal, middle, cranial, and accessory lobes.

The left lung consists of three lobes: the caudal, middle, and cranial lobes.

The Physiology of Ventilation

The term "respiration" can be interpreted in two different ways. Strictly speaking, it means the gaseous exchanges between a cell and its surrounding environment, or the consumption of oxygen and elimination of carbon dioxide. In a broader, more general sense, respiration is the back-and-forth movement of air through the respiratory system. In this latter sense, "respiration" is synonymous with "ventilation," the preferred term. Ventilation is closely linked to the circulatory function, which it complements. One of the parameters used to describe the combined efficiency of the two systems is the ventilation/perfusion ratio, whether applied to the entire respiratory network or to a more limited portion.

The cycles of ventilation (inhalation, then exhalation), which are the source of respiratory volume, enable the renewal of air in the alveoli (alveolar air), which has a different composition from atmospheric air. This composition is maintained constant during rest and under conditions of thermal neutrality.

In cats, the ventilatory function plays three different roles:

• It plays the leading role in regulating the quantity of oxygen carried by arterial blood, expressed by its partial pressure (PaO2, or 95 to 100 mmHg);
• It is involved in regulating the acid-base balance in arterial blood, by regulating the partial pressure of carbon dioxide (PaCO2, or 35 to 40 mmHg);
• Finally, since cats cannot sweat, the ventilatory function is actively involved in combating heat by eliminating it through water vapor.

The Airways
Air penetrates the respiratory passages through the nostrils. As needed, and especially when it is hot, the cat can also breathe through its mouth. After the air passes through the nasal fossae and pharynx, it reaches the trachea and bronchi before being distributed into the pulmonary alveoli. The airways are not only simple passages for air movement. As air moves through the airways, it is also heated and takes on water vapor until it is saturated (approximately 6% water vapor at 38°C). This process is used maximally in combating heat: The animal breathes quickly to eliminate a large amount of heat. This mode of ventilation is called thermal polypnea (panting).

As air travels through the airways, it is also filtered by numerous cilia on the cells of the mucosa and by the secretion of mucus that forms a sort of conveyor belt to carry away dust and dirt particles to the pharynx, where they are swallowed. Finally, the nasal fossae are the center of olfaction, and the vocal cords cause air to vibrate in the larynx, enabling the cat to meow.

In cats, as in humans, the trachea and bronchi are equipped with muscles that contract to limit the diameter of these passageways and significantly increase the resistance to air flow. This bronchoconstriction remains moderate in healthy animals. It is a process justified only by its ability to be inhibited during effort, in order to increase air flow through the respiratory system. In some respiratory disorders, such

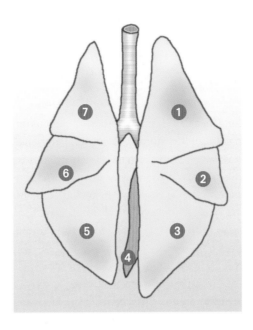

LUNGS OF THE CAT

1 – *Right cranial lobe*
2 – *Middle lobe*
3 – *Right caudal lobe*
4 – *Accessory lobe*
5 – *Left caudal lobe*
6 – *Left cranial lobe (caudal portion)*
7 – *Left cranial lobe (cranial portion)*

as bronchial asthma, bronchospasms can greatly limit breathing and have serious consequences, leading even to death from asphyxia.

The Movement of Air

Lung mechanics is the study of the motor forces enabling air movement through the use of muscles in the respiratory system. During inhalation, the diaphragm, or muscle separating the thorax from the abdomen, contracts and increases the volume of the thoracic cage toward the back. It is aided by the external intercostal muscles.

This increase in thoracic volume creates a depression in the space between the lungs and thoracic wall (pleural cavity), enabling air penetration. Under normal conditions, during rest and at thermal neutrality, exhalation then follows passively: The elasticity of the lungs and thorax returns them to their resting position, forcing air out. Still, some muscles, particularly in the abdominal wall, can contract as needed to speed exhalation.

The cat's resting respiratory rate varies from 20 to 40 cycles per minute. The amount of air mobilized during each cycle, or tidal volume, is approximately 30 ml. The product of the respiratory rate and the tidal volume gives the respiratory volume, which varies from 0.5 to 1 liter per minute during rest. During effort, this volume increases, thanks to an increase in the tidal volume and especially the respiratory rate.

Hematosis

Hematosis means all gaseous exchanges between the alveolar air and the blood. It is produced by purely passive phenomena involving the partial pressure gradients of gases between the air and the blood. Because oxygen is more concentrated in the alveoli than in the blood arriving in the lungs, it passes from the air to the blood. Carbon dioxide follows the opposite route. The animal's only means of acting on these exchanges is to vary these partial pressures by modifying respiratory volume. Any increase in respiratory volume (hyperventilation) speeds the renewal of alveolar air and increases gaseous exchanges. Receptors located in the carotid arteries and aorta constantly analyze the composition of arterial blood and adapt ventilation to any change, in order to always maintain the same partial pressure values for oxygen and carbon dioxide.

The Digestive System

Anatomy

The digestive system consists of the group of organs used in digestion.

Digestive Tract

The short, wide oral cavity (always pink) has a broad opening or mouth bordered by two lips: the upper lip with thick whiskers (vibrissae) and the lower lip with a free, slightly scalloped edge.

The palate is covered by a small number of serrated, bumpy crests. The tongue lacks a median furrow and is short and wide. Large, conical, cornified papillae cover the tongue, making it a real rasp that is quite useful in grooming.

The teeth are characterized by highly developed canines, reduced incisors, and more functionally adapted molars: the front molars (premolars) are designed for cutting, and the molars are designed for grinding.

There are two consecutive sets of teeth:

- the milk teeth, baby teeth, or deciduous teeth:
2 (I3/3 C1/1 P3/2) = 26
- the adult or permanent teeth:
2 (I3/3 C1/1 P3/2 M1/1) = 30
(I = incisors, C = canines, P = premolars M = molars).

In other words:
- the upper jaw contains six incisors, two canines, and eight molars (six premolars and two molars);
- the lower jaw contains six incisors, two canines, and six molars (four premolars and two molars).

The incisors are very small, compact, and closely spaced.
The canines are pointed and evenly conical.
The carnassial is the last premolar in the upper jaw (P3) and the only molar in the lower jaw (M1).

The pharynx connects the oral cavity to the esophagus and is also linked to the nasal cavities. The esophagus is long, wide, and highly dilatable. The stomach has a volume of 300 to 350 ml.

The cat's intestine is typically short. The small intestine is 1 to 1.7 m long, and the very short large intestine is 20 to 40 cm long.

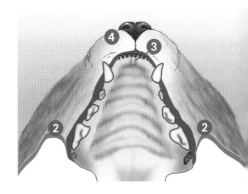

PALATE OF THE CAT

2 – Commissura of the lips
3 – Incisive papillae
4 – Upper lip

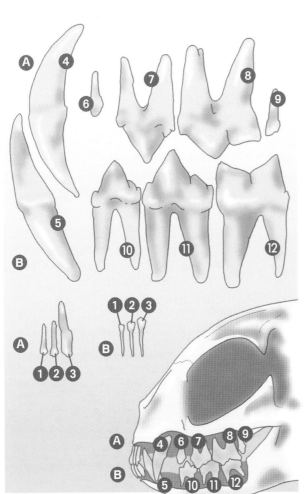

TEETH OF THE ADULT CAT

A – Upper incisor teeth
B – Lower incisor teeth

1 – Central incisor
2 – Divider incisor
3 – Corner incisor
4 – Upper canine
5 – Lower canine
6 and 7 – Upper precarnassials
8 – Upper carnassial
9 – Postcarnassial
10 and 11 – Lower precarnassials
12 – Lower carnassial

(Barone, 1976)

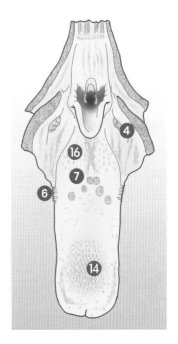

TONGUE OF THE CAT

4 – Palatine tonsil
6 – Foliate papillae
7 – Circumvallate papillae
14 – Conical papillae
16 – Filiform papillae

Visceral surface

1 – Lateral right lobe
2 – Medial right lobe
3 – Lateral left lobe
5 – Medial left lobe
6 – Caudate process of caudate lobe
7 – Papillary process of caudate lobe
8 – Gall bladder

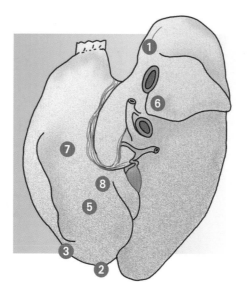

CROSS-SECTION
OF THE ABDOMEN OF THE CAT

1 — Right kidney
2 — Liver
3 — Pancreas
4 — Ascending colon
5 — Descending duodenum
6 — Greater omentum
7 — Jejunum
8 — Ascending duodenum
9 — Spleen
10 — Descending colon
11 — Left kidney

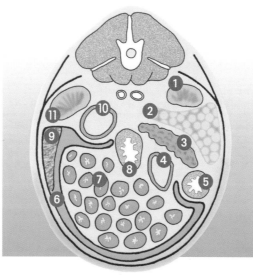

PLAN OF THE ABDOMEN IN THE CAT
Left lateral view

1 – Left kidney
2 – Descending colon
3 – Jejunal mass enclosed in the greater omentum
4 – Bladder
5 – Spleen
6 – Stomach
7 – Liver

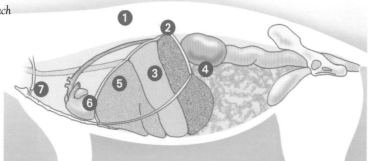

The average total capacity of the intestine is approximately 250 ml. The large intestine begins with a curved cecum.

The colon ends in a short rectum and an anus with two anal glands (anal sacs) that produce a strong-smelling secretion particular to each animal. This secretion is used in marking territory and in recognition between cats.

Ancillary Organs

The voluminous liver (80 to 150 g) is divided into seven lobes. The excretory duct consists of the hepatic and cystic ducts, which lead from the gall bladder and converge in the bile duct, which opens into the duodenum together with the pancreatic duct.

The **pancreas** is an organ attached to the duodenum (first portion of the small intestine). It is a combination of two distinct glandular tissues:

- the exocrine gland, which produces the pancreatic juice emptied into the intestine;
- the endocrine gland, which releases two hormones (insulin and glucagon) into the blood. This gland weighs 8 to 10 g, and its pancreatic duct opens near the bile duct in the intestine.

The cat's narrow, long **spleen** is constricted in the middle and sits on the left between the abdominal wall and the stomach. This wine-colored organ weighs 5 g. It keeps red blood cells in reserve and destroys old ones.

The Physiology of Digestion

All living beings must draw from the external environment the elements they need to meet their energy requirements, in order to develop and maintain their structure. Food ingested intermittently is a complex, heterogeneous substance that is often insoluble in water and impossible to assimilate directly. Digestion is therefore the extensive transformation of this food into nutrients that the body can absorb.

Functions of the Digestive Tract

This transformation involves the primary mechanical reduction in size of ingested pieces of food into smaller and smaller particles. The second process is the enzymatic attack of the various components in food. The combination of these mechanical and chemical phenomena leads to the release in the intestinal lumen of simple forms that can then be absorbed.

This dual mechanical and enzymatic process involves the convergence of several basic functions of the digestive tract:

• A motor function: Food is transformed mechanically. It is ground up and mixed with secretions, then passes through the different segments of the digestive tract in a manner adapted to the transformations that occur in the tract;

• A secretory function involving glands that are highly specialized (salivary glands, pancreas) or diffuse (glands in the gastric mucosa and small intestine);

• An absorption function centered in the small intestine that ensures the passage of basic elements to the internal environment.
The digestive tract also has complementary functions:

• An excretory function: The digestive tract is involved in the elimination of endogenous wastes, certain medications, etc.;

• An immune function, as for any tissue acting as a barrier between the external and internal environment;

• A regulatory function: The digestive tract plays an active role in internal regulation.
The entire tract is lined with a greatly folded mucous membrane which significantly increases the contact surface between the contents and the walls of the tract. In fact, a small intestine measuring a total of 1.7 m long has a surface area of 100 m²!

Role of the Different Parts

Schematically, the digestive tract is divided into three segments:
• An oral segment involved in the early stages of ingestion, storage, grinding, and maceration. This segment includes the oral cavity, pharynx, esophagus, and stomach;

• A middle segment (small intestine), to which the stomach contents are transferred only after a sufficient reduction in particle size, and where most of the digestion and absorption takes place;

• A terminal segment (large intestine), where the fermentation, dehydration, and final formation of stools occurs before defecation.

The Oral Segment

The cat's compact, globular cranium enables it to develop optimal masticatory force. The cat's mandible, like that of all carnivores, exerts only vertical movement serving mainly to grind and slice prey with the incisors and canines. Actual mastication (use of the molars) is minimal. Saliva initiates the absorption of the alimentary bolus and lubricates the esophagus.

The stomach is a pouch connected to the esophagus and duodenum by two sphincter openings, the cardia and the pylorus. It works as a reservoir by adapting to the quantity of food ingested, up to a maximum volume of 400 ml. This volume is over 65% of the total digestive volume. Food is then transformed into a fluid mass, or chyme, by powerful motor activity and especially by a highly acidic secretion that dissolves and breaks up food particles. An enzyme called pepsin begins to break up the proteins it is able to access.

The Middle Segment

The small intestine (1 to 1.7 m long) is the most important segment in the processes of digestion and absorption, especially its initial parts (duodenum and jejunum). It is in these parts of the small intestine that enzymatic activity is the greatest, because the chyme consists of particles small enough (less than 2 mm in diameter) to provide a large contact surface, and the pH, neutralized by the alkaline secretions of the liver and pancreas, is optimal for enzymatic activity. The main enzymes involved are trypsin and chymotrypsin for protein, lipase and phospholipase for lipids, and amylase for starch. The cat's enzymatic equipment is well-adapted to its natural diet. Proteins and lipids are well-digested by cats, while carbohydrates are not as well digested. The pancreas is the main source of the necessary enzymes. Bile is involved in the emulsification of fats in the duodenum, a process necessary before fats can be attacked by lipase. The mucosa has transit systems adapted to most of the basic elements produced by enzyme hydrolysis.

The motor activity of the small intestine is characterized by the alternation of different contractile modes. Localized, undistributed contractions called segmental contractions mix the substrates and put them into contact with enzymes or the mucosa. Coordinated contractions spread over several dozen centimeters, or peristaltic contractions, move the contents further along the tract.

The Terminal Segment

The cecum is not highly developed in carnivores. The colon, measuring 20 to 40 cm long, able to extract a large amount of water from its lumen, and equipped with an adapted motor function, dehydrates and molds the stools. Segmental contractions predominate in the colon. A few enzymatic activities still occur in the terminal segment, but they mainly involve the microflora it contains. The numerous bacteria that colonize this part of the digestive tract are not harmful to the animal. Quite the opposite—their presence limits the propagation of other bacteria, or pathogens, that could lead to digestive disorders.

Stools are stored in the large intestine until defecation. After the animal seeks an appropriate spot and assumes a characteristic posture, defecation follows by an involuntary, coordinated contraction of the rectum combined with the relaxation of the anal sphincter.

The Liver

The liver is an organ with numerous functions. By producing bile, it contributes to digestion by ensuring, in particular, the emulsification of lipids thanks to surfactants called bile salts. Bile gets its color from pigments produced by the metabolism of hemoglobin contained in the red blood cells.

The liver also works as an antitoxin, transforming many of the external substances that might penetrate the organism, including medications, and allowing them to be eliminated. In the cat, this function is not as efficient as in other species. For this reason, the elimination of many medications is much slower in cats than in dogs or humans. Sometimes, the cat's body transforms medications into certain byproducts, or metabolites, that are not found in the other species. For example, paracetamol, an ingredient in many pain relievers, is metabolized into toxic components in cats. A single 500-mg tablet can result in death.

Finally, the liver has many metabolic roles. It can store, transform, and release the elements produced during digestion. It actively captures the carbohydrates in food, storing glucose as glycogen and releasing it as needed. Similarly, it transforms lipids from the small intestine and puts them into circulation in an appropriate form. This mobilization can, however, easily become deregulated in cats, whose liver suffers under the prolonged storage of fats. This condition is known as hepatic lipidosis. Last, the liver also plays a key role in processing proteins and vitamins.

The Reproductive System

Anatomy

The reproductive system is involved in procreation and contributes to maintaining the species.

The Male Genitalia

Formed by the set of organs involved in producing sperm and depositing it into the genital passages of the female, the male genitalia include:

• Two gonads, the testicles, which have two different functions: an exocrine function in producing gametes (spermatogenesis, or sperm production), and an endocrine function in producing hormones (secretion of testosterone, the male hormone that is the basis for the secondary sexual characteristics, spermatogenesis, and male sexual activity);

• The sperm passages, or excretory ducts, of the gonads (vas deferens and urethra), which nourish the sperm (spermatozoa + semen), store it (thanks particularly to the secretions of auxiliary glands including the epididymis and prostate), and send it to the portion involved in mating;

• A portion involved in mating, the penis. During mating or coitus, the penis deposits sperm into the genital passages of the female (insemination).

The testicles are globular and located below the anus (2 g).

The yellowish, bilobed prostate surrounds the urethra. Cats do not have seminal vesicles.
The penis is short, curved backward, and ends in a conical glans covered with tiny erectile barbs with a cornified tip that become rigid during ejaculation and disappear after castration.

The Female Genitalia

The female genitalia include:
• Two gonads, the abdominal ovaries. They are involved in the development (oogenesis) and release of ova (ovulation), as well as the

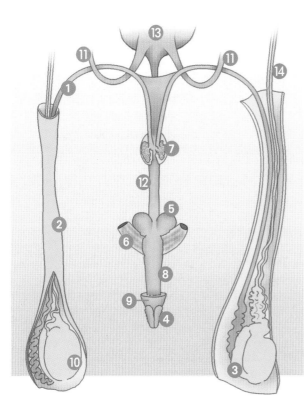

GENITALIA OF THE MALE CAT

1 – Vas deferens
2 – Spermatic cord
3 – Epididymis
4 – Glans penis
5 – Bulbourethral gland
6 – Ischiocavernosus muscle
7 – Prostate
8 – Penis
9 – Prepuce
10 – Testicle
11 – Ureter
12 – Urethra
13 – Bladder
14 – Testicular vessels

(from J. E. Crouch, 1969)

FREE PORTION OF THE PENIS

1 – External opening of the urethra
2 – Glans penis
3 – Os penis
4 – Inside of prepuce

GENITALIA OF THE FEMALE CAT

1 – Ovary
2 – Fallopian tube
3 – Uterine horn (open on the right)
4 – Uterine cervix
5 – Vagina
6 – Opening of the urethra
7 – Vulva
8 – Urethra
9 – Ureter
10 – Bladder
11 – Adipose tissue

(P. Eckstein and S. Zuckerman, 1960)

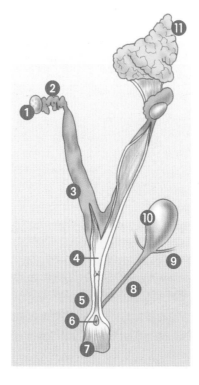

PRE-MATING POSITIONS OF THE FEMALE CAT

1 – Lordosis
2 – Presentation of the genital organs

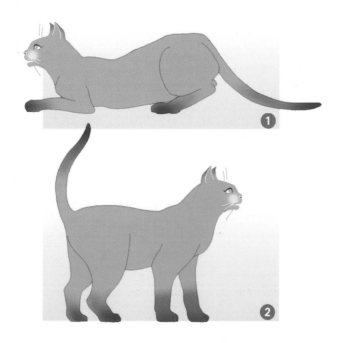

secretion of sexual hormones (estradiol, progesterone);
• Genital passages, or oviducts, that capture the ovules and are the site of fertilization; the uterus, which receives the eggs and ensures their implantation and gestation;

• A portion involved in mating, including the vagina and vulva, a passage that receives the penis during mating and provides a channel for newborns during parturition, or birth.

The ovaries are located quite far forward, near the kidneys.
The oviducts are short, narrow, and not very sinuous.
The uterus includes two long, nearly straight horns.
The vagina is long and wide.
There are four pairs of mammary glands, or teats: one pectoral pair, two abdominal pairs, and one inguinal pair.

The Physiology of Reproduction

Male Sexual Activity

Puberty: 7 to 12 months
Male sexual behavior includes several phases:
• Seeking a partner: Signals issued by the female indicate her degree of receptivity and attract the male. The female will accept the male's advances only during estrus, or heat.

• Behavioral synchronization: In male cats, the preparatory phase of mating is fairly long. Body posture and mimicry are definitely important signs and symbols during the courtship behavior, play, and fighting that precede the acceptance of the male by the female.

• The sexual act: The male mounts the female, firmly grasps the scruff of her neck in his teeth, and lies down on top of her. The female then crouches flat against the ground and stretches her hindquarters out and up. Next, the male moves his loins to bring the penis against the vulva of the female until it penetrates the vagina, triggering a "mating cry." Remember that the glans penis of the male cat is covered by many tiny, conical papillae that become rigid during mating and "form tiny spikes that must temper the female's sensual pleasure and even cause her pain, as evidenced by her cries" (Leyh, 1871).

"Is it love that makes the male cat's partner cry out?" (M. Bashô, 1664-1694).

Coitus lasts five to ten seconds.
Sperm consists of two parts:
- cellular elements, or spermatozoa, produced by the testicles;
- a liquid or seminal environment produced by the secretions of the glands along the genital tract.
Volume of a single ejaculation: 0.01 to 0.4 ml.
pH: 7 to 8.
Number of sperm per ejaculation: approximately 60 million.
Length of sperm: 55 microns.
Artificial insemination consists of collecting sperm by various methods, then diluting and storing it before inserting it into the female's genital passage using special instruments. Preferably, sperm should be harvested using an artificial vagina, but males must be accustomed to this manipulation.
Cats can ejaculate two to three times per week, without the quality of the semen being diminished.
Diluted semen is inserted within forty-eight hours of ovulation.
Generally, two inseminations are conducted twenty-four hours apart.

Female Sexual Activity

Puberty: 4 to 12 months
Shorthaired breeds mature earlier (Abyssinian, Birman, Siamese: 4 to 6 months). Persians reach sexual maturity at 1 year old. In most cases, the first heat occurs in spring around the age of 7 months. The reproductive stage of life ends late (at 15 years old or more).

Sexual cycle: Throughout the entire reproductive stage, the female genital organs undergo structural modifications that always occur in the same order at periodic intervals, at a well-defined rate for each species. These cycles are interrupted only by gestation. Cats have a seasonal cycle that occurs only at a certain time of year (mating season is mainly January to October). But a certain number of female cats (Siamese-type shorthaired cats living indoors) have virtually no period of sexual quiescence (anestrus). Anestrus can be stopped by increasing the length of light exposure. The female cat's sexual cycle lasts an average of fifteen to twenty-eight days. It can be divided into four periods that correspond to the different phases of ovarian activity:
• Proestrus, or the period of follicular maturation (the ovarian follicle contains the future ovule). This phase lasts one to four days.
• Estrus (heat), or the period during which the female cat seeks to mate, which triggers ovulation. In most cases, the cat is a so-called "induced ovulation" species, meaning that if mating does not occur, neither does ovulation. The number of ovules released (two to eleven) depends on the number and especially the frequency of mating (three times every three to four hours). Ovulation occurs twenty-four to thirty hours after mating. During estrus, the female cat displays true courtship behavior (calling, rubbing against objects, pacing up and down on the hind legs, lordosis). Estrus lasts four to ten days.
• Metestrus, a phase which does not occur if the cat has mated, in which case it is replaced by the beginning of gestation. If mating has not occurred, or if mating has occurred with a sterile male, a phase of false pregnancy (without maternal behavior or the onset of lactation) lasting thirty to forty days may be observed.
• Diestrus or anestrus, or the period of sexual quiescence. This phase is of variable duration, depending on the breed and environmental conditions (lighting, isolation from males, etc.).

Fertilization: The initiation of new life through the union of two gametes in the upper part of the oviduct. Female cats display two particular phenomena:

• Superfecundation, or the fertilization of different ovules from a single ovulation by sperm from different fathers. In the litter, the kittens thus come from several different fathers.

• Superfetation: 10% of pregnant cats will go into heat and accept mating (from the 21st to the 24th day of gestation). This leads to the development of fetuses of different gestational ages in the same litter. Live, stillborn, and premature kittens are produced at birth.

Progestation, or the stage during which the eggs freely migrate, are distributed in the uterus, and undergo segmentation. The eggs enter the uterus four to six days after ovulation.

Implantation, or the **attaching of eggs** to the uterus, that is, the active penetration of eggs into the uterine mucosa prepared for this purpose. Physiologically, thanks to the placenta, this is the beginning of a special relationship between the mother and fetus. Implantation occurs thirteen to fourteen days after ovulation. Gestation, or the stage during which the female carries the young. This stage lasts sixty-three to sixty-eight days.

Pregnancy diagnosis: Since hormonal tests are invalid in female cats, the diagnosis is established based on data from clinical, X-ray, and, most recently, ultrasound examinations:

• Clinical examination: Bilateral enlargement of the abdomen apparent around the 30th day. Generally, the fetuses can be detected through abdominal palpation starting around the third week. The fetuses can be recognized by their "beadlike" arrangement and uneven, more or less hard and bumpy, quality;

• X-ray examination: Gestation can be detected with X-rays starting on the 21st day. The skeletons of the kittens appear around the 36th day and become very clear starting on the 40th day.

• Ultrasound examination: The diagnosis can be made starting on the 20th day. Fetal movements appear on the 28th day.

After the sixth week, the various parts of the fetus become perceptible.

The hygiene and care of the pregnant cat should include a diet higher in calories than the maintenance diet. The female cat should be dewormed prior to gestation to prevent the fetuses from being contaminated through the placenta. A spacious queening box with a blanket should be prepared to shelter the mother and her young and placed in a quiet, warm place.

Parturition (birth): All mechanical and physiological phenomena leading to the expulsion of the fetuses and afterbirth through the female genital passages at the end of gestation. Early signs include a temporary decrease in rectal temperature. Milk secretion begins several days before birth. Just prior to giving birth, the female becomes nervous, often retreating to the prepared nest. Parturition lasts approximately six hours, with ten to sixty minutes between expulsions. The average number of kittens per litter is three to five. The birth weight of kittens is 100 to 125 g. A female can have five litters in two years. A female giving birth for the first time is known as a primipara. The mother severs the umbilical cord and licks each kitten vigorously. She remains in one place for twenty-four to forty-eight hours. The kittens first begin nursing one to two hours after birth.

Nursing

During the first forty-eight hours, the queen does not leave her young. They nurse very frequently—approximately once every twenty minutes. The kittens drink an estimated 2 to 3 ml of milk each time. Their weight increases very rapidly (it should double in seven days).

After each nursing, the female licks her kittens, focusing on their anogenital region. Having a meal and being stimulated by their mother's tongue causes the kittens to eliminate urine and stools, which the mother eats. The kittens move around very little at first, and their eyes are closed. They open their eyes between the 10th and 14th day. Around three weeks old, the kittens begin to explore, and they learn very quickly to relieve themselves outside the nest. If the kittens encounter solid food, they will try to eat it. Gradually, the consumption of solid food increases the time between nursings. Weaning is generally complete between one and one-half and two months after birth. Lactation then declines rapidly, since the maintenance and secretion of milk depends on the stimulation of the teats during nursing.

Controlling Reproduction

Permanent sterilization:
• Ovariectomy (excision of the ovaries) before puberty (6 to 7 months in age) or during sexual quiescence;
• Ligation and section of the oviducts;
• Orchidectomy (excision of the testicles) between 6 and 10 months in age.

Temporary sterilization:
• Preventing heats by administering synthetic progesterone (medroxyprogesterone acetate or megestrol acetate). The repeated use of these products has some risks (pyometra, diabetes, obesity, mammary disorders);
• Interrupting estrus with progesterone;
• Interrupting gestation through induced abortion, which should be conducted before the thirteenth day following mating (before implantation), using synthetic estrogens or prostaglandin (PGF2 α) before the 40th day.

Inducing estrus:
• Cohabitation with females regularly in estrus;
• Providing lighting for over twelve hours per day;
• Hormone therapy:
- PMSG (for eight days), ovulation six to seven days after the beginning of treatment.
- FSH (for five days): ovulation four to six days after the beginning of treatment.
- HCG (one to three injections): ovulation twenty-four hours thereafter.
- GnRG (two injections): estrus on the second or third day.
- Antiprolactin (one injection): estrus twenty-four hours thereafter.

The Urinary System

Anatomy

The urinary system is involved in the formation and excretion of urine (that is, the nongaseous purification of the blood, as opposed to the gaseous purification that occurs in the lungs). It includes a glandular portion consisting of two kidneys, and excretory passages, or urinary tracts.

Kidneys

The kidneys are voluminous glands located on the left and right side of the lumbar region. They rest against the dorsal wall of the abdominal cavity. They are smooth, globular, and weigh an average of 10 to 20 g each (together, they account for 1/20 of the body weight). They are yellowish in color and covered by a network of three or four interlobular veins converging into the hilus.

Urinary Tracts

• The ureters: In each kidney, urine is collected by the renal pelvis. From there, it is carried by the ureter to the bladder. The ureters are narrow in diameter and have thin walls;
• The bladder, a single, medial, distensible, relatively small and rounded reservoir with a thick muscular wall covered by the peritoneum. When the bladder contracts, urine is flushed into the urethra during urination;

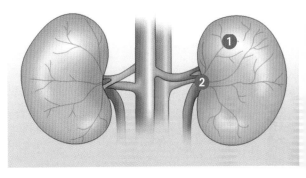

KIDNEYS OF THE CAT
Ventral view

1 – Interlobular veins
2 – Hilus of the kidney

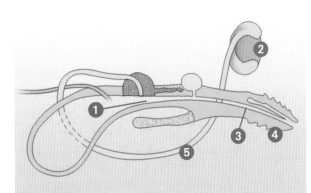

ARRANGEMENT OF THE PELVIC AND PENILE URETHRA

1 – Pelvic urethra
2 – Testicle
3 – Spongy portion of the urethra
4 – Free portion of the penis
5 – Ductus deferens

359

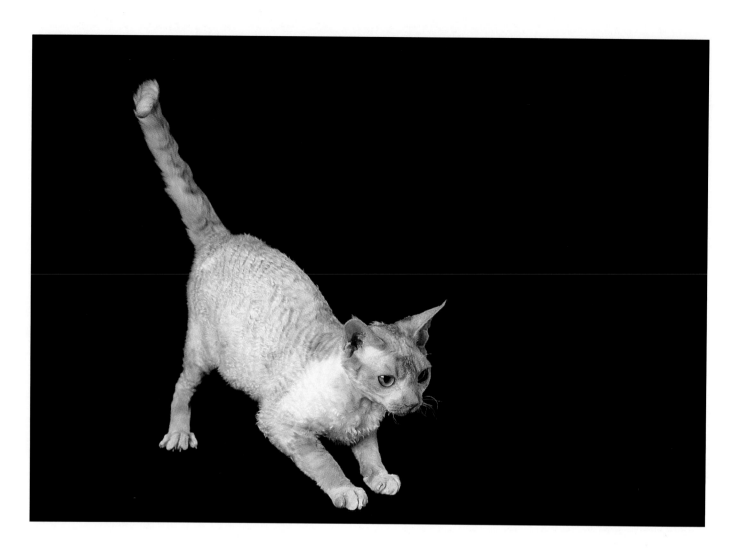

• The urethra, a long duct common to urine and sperm in males, short and independent in females.

Physiology

Elimination

Besides the liver, the other organ with a major role in elimination is the kidney. With a rich blood supply—the kidneys constantly receive approximately one-fourth the heart output—they filter the blood and eliminate the waste it contains, including the pigments derived from hemoglobin, urea, creatinine, the products of hormonal breakdown, and substances of external origin (xenobiotic substances). Since this filtration also leads to the loss of certain precious elements (glucose, sodium, calcium, amino acids, etc., and even water) the kidneys selectively sort and recover the desired elements after the formation of glomerular filtrate.

Urine Formation

The basic unit in which urine is formed is a highly folded tube called the nephron. The kidneys consist of nearly one million nephrons. Each nephron is supplied by a small capillary that undergoes passive filtration: Blood pressure causes water and all the elements that can pass through the pores of the filter to leave the capillaries. This region is called the glomerular chamber. In a cat weighing 3 kg, it forms 6 to 12 ml of glomerular filtrate per minute, or approximately 8 to 16 liters per day, although its blood volume is a mere 200 ml. This shows the significance of the reabsorption functions based in the nephron. Thanks to a series of specialized carriers, the walls of the various parts of the nephron constantly transfer precious elements from the urine to the blood. These transfers also lead to the passage of water and concentrate the urine. The cat is a big water saver: in the event of dehydration, it can produce highly concentrated urine (over five times more concentrated than blood). Under normal conditions, the total quantity of urine produced per day is 10 to 15 ml per kg of body weight.

Urine

Quantity: 10 to 15 ml/kg of weight/day.
pH: 5 to 7.
Density: 1,018 to 1,040.
Urea: 800 to 4,000 mg/kg of weight/day.
Creatine: 12 to 20 mg/kg of weight/day.

Urination

Urine is carried from the kidneys to the bladder by the ureters. The cat's bladder has such a large capacity that a cat can easily go over twelve hours without urinating. During urination, urine is expelled from the body through the urethra, a passageway that is different in males and females. In males, it opens at the tip of the penis, which faces backward during rest. As before defecation, prior to urination the cat seeks an appropriate spot and assumes a characteristic posture. Then a reflex is triggered, and the bladder is completely emptied. Under some conditions, cats can release small quantities of urine in various places. This activity, called urine marking, is linked to the cat's social behavior and governs the relationships between individual cats. Castrated animals usually do not display this behavior.

The Main Stages of a Cat's Life

A cat's life expectancy is approximately ten years, although it is not uncommon for cats to reach 15 and even 20 years old. From a kitten weighing 100 g at birth to an adult weighing 2 to 7 kg (depending on the breed), a cat spends its life playing, grooming, and sleeping, all of which is punctuated by meals.
Although a cherished companion, the cat retains its predatory instinct, evident even in its play.

Kitten grooming itself.

At Birth

After a gestation period of sixty-three to sixty-eight days, the female cat gives birth to a litter of one to ten kittens weighing 70 to 150 g each. The average birth weight is 100 g and varies according to a number of factors, including:

• Sex: Females are slightly lighter than males;
• Breed: Newborns of large breeds like the Norwegian Forest Cat are heavier than those of other breeds;

• Litter size: In litters of over five kittens, newborns are lighter.

• The mother's diet during gestation: If the mother's diet is unbalanced or insufficient, the fetuses can suffer from malnutrition, and she may produce lighter, weaker kittens that may even have birth defects.

From Birth to Adulthood

The mother cat licks each newborn kitten to remove the membrane that envelopes it. This licking behavior continues well beyond birth, as mothers lick their kittens to stimulate and awaken them. The first thing a kitten does after birth is to seek its mother's teats.

THE MOTHER'S MILK

In the first few days following birth, the mother cat lies on her side to make her teats accessible to her young. The kittens' first attempts at suckling produce not milk but colostrum, a substance different from milk in appearance and composition. In particular, colostrum contains numerous antibodies that the kitten absorbs in massive quantities during the first sixteen hours of life. These antibodies protect the kitten from germs in its environment for a few days to a few weeks. A few days later, the mother begins producing milk for her nursing kittens. Like colostrum, feline mother's milk is high in antibodies. For this reason, when kittens do not receive colostrum, they should be given feline mother's milk within sixteen hours of birth so that they can absorb the antibodies. Still, colostrum is always preferable, since, in addition to antibodies, it contains other elements lacking in milk.

At birth, kittens cannot regulate their body temperature and are thus very fragile and highly dependent on their mother to keep the nest warm. The rectal temperature of very young kittens is approximately 37°C, rising gradually to 38 to 38.5°C by the age of seven weeks. Thus, it is best to heat the queening box to 33°C the first week after birth and 30°C in the following weeks, decreasing the temperature to 28°C around the fourth or fifth week after birth and 26°C thereafter.

The Kitten's Development

A kitten acquires many abilities between birth and adulthood. The major changes occur before weaning, while the kittens are still nursing.

The Five Senses

At birth, the kitten already has a sense of smell keen enough to find its mother from a distance of 50 cm. Similarly, it is able to distinguish the three basic flavors: sweet, salty, and bitter (it dislikes salty and bitter). However, kittens are born blind and deaf. They acquire the senses of sight and hearing almost simultaneously.
Hearing develops when the kittens are around five days old, but they cannot orient themselves to sound until they are about fourteen days old. They do not have the hearing ability of an adult until the age of one month, at which time they learn to recognize their mother's voice.
Kittens first open their eyes seven to fifteen days after birth and acquire depth perception three or four days later. The simultaneous acquisition of sight and hearing requires a few days of adaptation.
Although far from nimble, kittens have a sense of balance from a very early age.
They have difficulty coordinating their movements before they are two weeks old. They begin walking on four legs at around seventeen days old and are agile enough to scratch an ear with a hind leg around three weeks old.

Dental Development

It is fairly easy to determine a cat's age based on the date when baby and adult teeth first appear, since one needs only to open its mouth (see table at right).

Main Areas of the Body

Not all the main areas of the body develop at the same rate. Kittens are born with a relatively large head; then the limbs grow longer, making the kitten look quite tall and gangly. Finally, the rest of the body catches up, eventually attaining typical adult proportions.

ERUPTION OF TEETH IN KITTENS

Deciduous Teeth (weeks)
Permanent Teeth

Incisors		
1st	2 to 3	3½ to 4 months
2nd	2 to 4	3½ to 4 months
3rd	3 to 4	4 to 4½ months

Canines		
	3 to 4	5 months

Premolars		
2nd		4½ to 5 months
3rd		5 to 6 months
4th		5 to 6 months

Molars		
1st		4 to 5 months

Kitten Growth

A kitten's growth can be gauged by measuring its weight gain, an easy parameter to record. All kittens in the litter must be weighed every day at the same time. By recording this measurement, we can see the change in weight for each kitten and also compare kittens to each other.

A kitten should gain weight every day. There are a few guidelines for determining whether a kitten is developing properly. If the kitten does not gain weight for two consecutive days or if it loses weight, we must determine the cause: insufficient feeding by the mother, illness, etc. Normal growth in kittens from birth to adulthood occurs in three phases:

• **The neonatal period**, or approximately the first four days after birth, during which the rate of growth is highly variable, particularly with relation to birthing conditions. Kittens that had a difficult birth may stay at the same weight, but weight loss is rare.

• **During the strict nursing** period of the first four weeks, growth is regular and linear, and it is even possible to predict weight as a function of age. Thus, the weight at seven to ten days is equal to twice the birth weight, and the weight at four weeks is equal to four times the birth weight.

Growth during the strict nursing period is directly dependent on the quality of lactation and the mother's care of her kittens.

• **The pre-weaning period** is a time of dietary transition occurring when kittens are four to seven weeks old. At approximately four to five weeks old, the kittens' growth rate declines; this corresponds to a decrease in lactation associated with temporary undereating. Around the seventh week, another growth spurt occurs, indicating the end of weaning: The kitten is now consuming enough solid food for its growth to continue. Even during

---

DIGESTIVE CAPACITIES

At birth, the kitten has a digestive tract adapted to digesting mother's milk. Feline mother's milk is rich in protein, fat, and lactose, or milk sugar. Thanks to an enzyme called lactase, the kitten is able to digest this lactose. Gradually, the kitten's digestive capacities change. Thus, many adult cats, having lost this enzyme, are unable to digest lactose and therefore milk. Undigested lactose travels through the small intestine to the large intestine, where bacteria cause it to ferment. This fermentation leads to acidic diarrhea.

As the ability to digest the lactose in milk decreases, the kitten gradually acquires other enzymes, including amylase, the enzyme enabling the digestion of starches.

The significant contribution of protein to the caloric value of feline milk is an early precursor in kittens to the strictly carnivorous diet of adult cats. Because cats cannot store protein, they require a great deal of protein in their diet.

Female cats nurse their kittens until they are six to seven weeks old, but kittens acquire the ability to chew and digest solid food around four to five weeks old. At this age, kittens tend naturally to begin nursing less often.

CHANGE IN FELINE DIGESTIVE CAPACITIES AS A FUNCTION OF AGE.

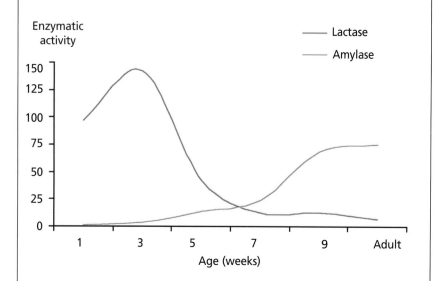

Example of lactase, the enzyme enabling the digestion of lactose (milk sugar) and amylase, the enzyme enabling the digestion of starch (Kienzle, 1987 and 1993).

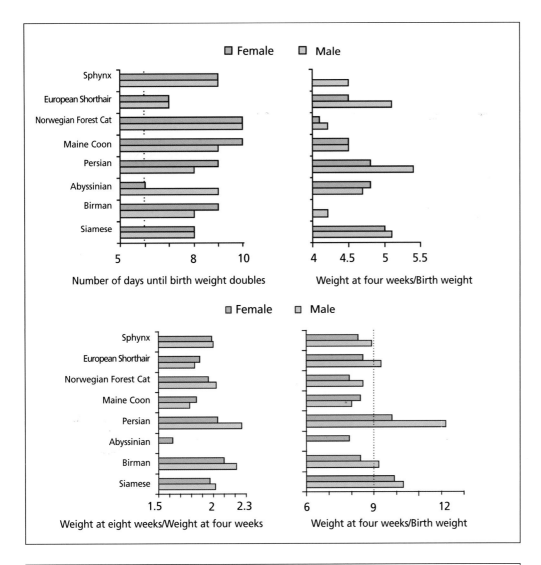

STANDARDS FOR GROWTH DURING THE STRICT NURSING PERIOD IN VARIOUS FELINE BREEDS, FOR BOTH SEXES
(Dubos, 1997).

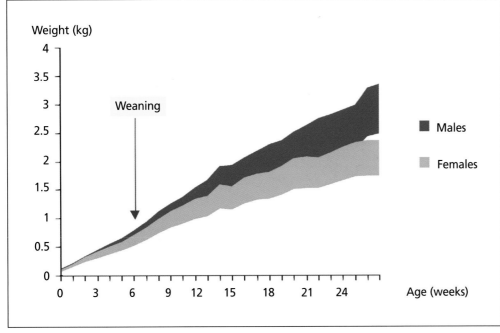

EXAMPLE OF GROWTH CURVE FOR KITTENS *(Siamese and Oriental)* *(Dubos, 1997).*

this transition period, the kitten continues to gain weight. The weight at eight weeks is generally equal to twice the weight at four weeks, or eight times the birth weight.

• **The post-weaning period** starting after eight weeks signals the beginning of the kitten's autonomy and corresponds to the expression of genetic potentialities. Individual variation is fully expressed at this time. The kitten eats by itself when it wants and grows to its full adult size. Once the cat reaches full size around ten to twelve months, it should maintain a constant weight.

Factors Influencing Kitten Growth

Among the factors influencing kitten growth are intrinsic factors determined by genetics (breed, sex, gene pool of the parents, hormonal mechanisms) and extrinsic factors involving the environment in a broad sense. These extrinsic factors are based essentially on the mother's and then the kitten's diet and are tempered by health and social conditions (breeding, living space, and maternal behavior).

Intrinsic factors include:

• Breed: As for most living species, the heavier the breed, the faster the growth.

• Sex: Sexual dimorphism is highly indistinct at birth and increases with age. Males become significantly heavier than females between six and twelve weeks old. Males thus have a higher growth potential than females, but this potential is delayed, with growth in males lasting a few weeks longer than in females.

• Family factors: Kittens receive half their genetic material from their mother and half from their father, with all this material being reworked to a certain extent. Family traits within a single breed may result in individuals that tend toward obesity or have a particular body size or type. These factors are especially important in selective breeding.

• The mother's weight: This parameter is not independent of breed and family factors. The heavier the mother (large in size and healthy), the faster the growth. This is explained partly by the quality of the mother's milk.

GROWTH AS A FUNCTION OF THE MOTHER'S WEIGHT. FACTORS INFLUENCING VARIATIONS IN WEIGHT

(Loveridge, 1987).

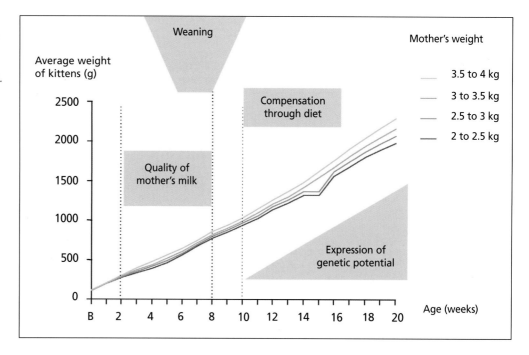

• Individual genetic factors: The combination of the maternal and paternal genotypes produces a unique individual and leads to individual variation within a single litter. Thus, to better estimate a kitten's growth, it is best to use the average of the parents' measurements.

• Hormonal factors: Following birth, certain hormones synthesized in the kitten's body guide its growth. Unlike humans, kittens rarely suffer from endogenous hormonal disorders that affect growth. Juvenile diabetes is marked by metabolic disorders, rather than growth disorders. Hypothyroidism is very rare, and dwarfism is unusual. Finally, the rare defects that result in the abnormal secretion of sex hormones seem to have little effect on growth in kittens. In addition, early spaying or neutering alters neither weight nor stature development, that is, growth to full adult size. However, the use of hormone therapy in kittens can greatly upset the natural endocrine balance and thus modify growth. This type of treatment should be used with great caution and for medical reasons only.

Many environmental factors determine successful growth.

• Hygiene of the cattery and surrounding stress
Nursing is a stressful period for the mother and a sensitive time for kittens. Strict hygiene must therefore be observed starting before birth and must involve both the equipment made available to the queen and the location of the queening box or nest. Inadequate hygiene will make the mother and her litter more susceptible to problems. In addition, when the mother is constantly disturbed, nursing suffers.

Just like for all young, a kitten's growth occurs during sleep. In the first few days of life, a young kitten sleeps almost constantly and nurses when awakened by its mother's licking. As it grows, the kitten will spend more time playing and exploring its environment, and less time sleeping. Still, the quality of its sleep is very important. In addition, certain hormones secreted under stress can have a serious effect on hormonal balance and growth. Thus, a stressful environment can harm a kitten's well-being, as well as that of its mother, and can compromise growth that began under optimal conditions. The nest environment and the litter must be protected from disturbances in the home, excessive changes in temperature, unusual visits, etc.

• Litter size
Kittens in large litters normally weigh less than those in small litters. This weight disparity may even increase in the first weeks of life, since a large litter must share the same amount of mother's milk as a small litter. Kittens from large litters (six or more) are lighter until they are about two months old. It is only after weaning, when kittens receive a solid diet, that this disparity tends to lessen.

• Nutritional factors
The mother's diet during gestation influences the birth weight and viability of her kittens. From birth to weaning, a kitten's diet is composed only of mother's milk. The quality and quantity of this milk are therefore determining factors in kitten growth and health. Both the mother's and the kittens' diet must be considered.

Nursing queens have greatly increased dietary requirements. During gestation, the queen accumulates dietary reserves. At the start of nursing, her reserves are used for producing milk. Since the mother's body is focused primarily on milk production, if she is underfed she will begin by losing weight. Next, her milk production will decline.`

A queen allowed free access to food during gestation and lactation will recover her initial (pre-gestation) weight at weaning (six to seven weeks after the kittens are born). If the queen receives only 50% of her dietary requirements from five weeks before giving birth until the end of lactation, she will lose up to 33% her initial weight. The primary conse-

AVERAGE COMPOSITION (%) OF CAT MILK, COW'S MILK, AND HUMAN MOTHER'S MILK.

Cat milk

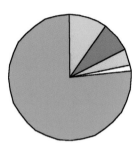

Cow's milk

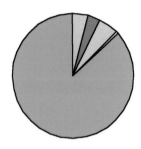

Human mother's milk

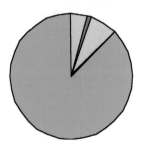

☐ Fat
◼ Protein
☐ Lactose
☐ Minerals
◼ Water

RATIONAL DIET FOR THE NURSING QUEEN

Milk production requires a great deal of energy. For a kitten to gain one gram, it is estimated that it must ingest at least 2.7 g of milk. This means that during lactation, the queen must produce the equivalent of one and one-half to twice her own weight in milk. The dietary requirements of a nursing queen increase during lactation and are based on the number of kittens in the litter, although not proportionally.

A specially adapted, complete, and balanced food must therefore be offered freely to the mother. She must also have access to clean water at all times. A diet for lactating females must be richer than a maintenance diet. It must be higher in energy (calories), and therefore enriched in fat, but also in protein, taurine, and minerals, particularly calcium and phosphorus. Even with a specially adapted food, the queen cannot possibly consume the amount of food necessary to cover all these requirements, since they are so great. She will thus draw on the reserves her body built up during gestation. This phenomenon is normal and inevitable but need not be excessive. As a point of reference, let us note that a female cat gains approximately 40% her initial weight during gestation, still weighs 20% more after giving birth than before mating, and recovers her normal weight at the end of lactation. The queen's dietary consumption increases steadily throughout lactation until weaning is complete. Indeed, even though the kittens may nurse less and less frequently, the mother must rebuild her reserves and compensate for the losses incurred in the first phase of lactation.

In sum, the body prepares for lactation during gestation, and lactation continues based on the dietary contribution after birth.

VARIATION IN THE QUEEN'S FREE CONSUMPTION OF FOOD THROUGHOUT THE REPRODUCTIVE CYCLE.

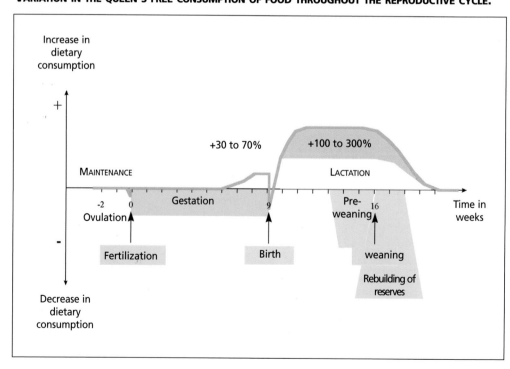

quence of this malnutrition is the queen's lack of attention toward her kittens—she becomes irritable when they try to nurse.

This change in the mother's behavior, combined with the kittens' malnutrition due to an insufficient milk supply, compromises the future of the litter.

The malnutrition of kittens during nursing has several possible causes: a malnourished mother, as we have just seen, but also highly insufficient lactation (very large litter, mother producing little milk) or insufficient nursing (mother not allowing sufficient nursing, too many kittens, stressful environment, not enough peace, etc.).

In all these cases, the kittens decline rapidly. Dehydration, hypoglycemia, and a decrease in body temperature are observed, and death follows. Several phenomena explain this very rapid decline:

• Because its liver is not yet mature, the kitten depends on glucose produced during the digestion of lactose from an external source (milk). In the case of underfeeding, hypoglycemia is inevitable and can lead to coma.

• A kitten's kidneys are immature at birth. The newborn is therefore not yet able to regulate the flow of water and minerals. Consequently, it must drink often, in small quantities. Any factor that limits nursing exposes kittens to rapid dehydration.

• Young kittens, especially newborns, are unable to regulate body temperature and fight temperatures that are too low because they do not have the necessary fat reserves. The steady, sufficient ingestion of milk and the mother's care during nursing (licking) and in the nest (mother's body heat) are essential to preventing hypothermia. The kittens' rectal temperature should thus be monitored, particularly if their weight remains the same from one day to the next.

Substitute Mother's Milk

When to Use
If the kittens are orphaned, if the litter is too large, or if the mother's milk cannot be consumed (due to a mammary condition), it may be necessary to administer a cat milk replacer. Feline mother's milk produces a certain amount of growth in kittens. Therefore, if the kittens do not gain weight over two consecutive days and no disease is detected, the mother's milk may be insufficient, with the kittens not receiving enough for growth. In this case, bottle feeding a milk replacer as a supplement to the mother's milk is a good solution for preparing all kittens in the litter for weaning.

How to Choose
Cat milk replacer, or substitute mother's milk, may be chosen based on various criteria:

• Composition of the milk. It is best to administer a type of milk that is as similar as possible to the mother's milk. Cat milk is fairly concentrated, similar to dog milk in composition, and much richer than cow's milk, particularly in fat, protein, and minerals.

Even though the composition of commercial substitute mother's milk is not always clearly indicated, a few guidelines can aid in making a selection. Kittens are adapted to digesting milk, that is, to digesting protein, fat, and lactose, all of animal origin. However, they are not yet well supplied with enzymes for digesting starch. Therefore, it is best to choose a milk with as little starch as possible, and, more generally, with as few ingredients of plant origin as possible (except oil, which provides essential fatty acids). The milk should contain all the necessary minerals (calcium, phosphorus, magnesium, sodium, chlorine, potassium), trace elements (iron, copper, zinc, iodine, selenium, fluorine, manganese), and vitamins (A, D3, E, K, C, B-group vitamins), as well as a certain number of essential amino acids (such as tryptophan and arginine), without forgetting the essential fatty acids (linoleic, linolenic, and arachidonic acids). Finally, kittens, like adult cats, require taurine in the diet.

• Dilution of the milk. The dilution recommended by the manufacturer must be considered in conjunction with the indicated composition. Substitute mother's milk is generally sold as a powder that must be mixed with water. Depending on the product, it is recommended that one part powder be diluted in two or three parts water.

Cow's milk, skim (ml)	600
Low-fat fromage blanc (g)	190
Lean ground beef (5% fat) (g)	90
Soybean oil (g)	30
Egg yolk (g)	20
Mineral and vitamin supplement (g)	10

• Ease of administering, cleaning, etc. Usually, manufacturers supply bottles with nipples more or less adapted for kittens.

• The results obtained. This is by far the most important criteria. Kittens must grow (gain weight) steadily without diarrhea, etc.

Hygiene and Feeding Schedule

The method used for bottle feeding is at least as important as the quality of the milk administered. The feeding schedule must be regular over 24 hours, both day and night, with feeding occurring more frequently the younger the kitten: from seven bottles every 24 hours in the first week to two in the sixth week, with solid food being offered by the time the kitten is thirty days old. Strict hygiene must be observed during feedings, as kittens are fragile and must be protected from infection:

• The person who prepares the milk and administers the bottles must be sure to wash his or her hands prior to these activities;

• Before the bottles are filled with milk, they must be thoroughly cleaned (with a bottle brush) and rinsed in very hot water. They must also be sterilized regularly;

• The milk must be prepared just prior to feeding;

• Unless the manufacturer indicates otherwise, the milk must be prepared using water that has been boiled and cooled to a temperature of 37 to 38°C before feeding;

• At each bottle feeding, the kitten must be allowed to suckle freely;

• When the kittens are young, the caregiver should stimulate their perineum with a warm, damp cloth during suckling to imitate the mother's licking behavior and thereby stimulate urination and defecation.

Weaning

Weaning is the change from a milk diet to a solid diet. Weaning is a physiological necessity, for both the kitten and the mother. The kitten's nutritional requirements increase steadily, while lactation begins to decline around five or six weeks after birth. A milk diet thus becomes insufficient to fulfill the litter's dietary requirements. At the same time, the kitten develops, its digestive capacities increase, and its body becomes ready for a solid diet.

By four to five weeks old, the kitten may start to show interest in its mother's food, at first licking the food around its mother's mouth. So as to be accessible to kittens, the food dish must be wide and have fairly low edges. In addition, in the case of dry food, the pieces must be small enough for kittens to pick up. With a specially adapted diet, it is best if the food given to the mother during lactation is the same as the food the kittens will be given after weaning. This helps prevent adding the stress of dietary change to that of weaning.

The time of weaning is based on a number of criteria, some of which are contradictory: For the mother, especially in the case of large litters, weaning fairly early prevents too many of her dietary reserves from being depleted. For kittens, weaning is highly stressful (change in type of diet, separation from the mother's nest) and need not be early, to the extent that a sufficient quantity of milk is available.

In practice, weaning can begin when the kittens' growth rate decreases. The kittens' consumption of solid food must be monitored and should increase steadily starting when they are four weeks old. Kittens can be weaned when they consume approximately 20 g of dry matter per day, or approximately 25 g of dry food or 70 g of canned food, generally when they are around six to seven weeks old.

For kittens raised on a bottle with a milk replacer, the number of daily feedings should be reduced in the week preceding the chosen weaning period (for example, going from four to three bottles per day) and, after each feeding, the kittens should be offered a bowl of solid food moistened with the substitute mother's milk. During the week chosen for weaning (when the kittens are around five weeks old), the kittens should be offered the solid food before bottle feeding. One or two bottles per day may still be necessary, depending on the kitten. The kitten's weight is the golden rule—it must increase steadily. The kittens must be weighed in the morning, prior to the first meal. Gradually, the amount of food made available between meals should be increased, first as a soupy mixture, then as solid food soaked with less and less milk, then with the milk gradually being replaced by water. By the end of the week, the solid food should be moistened with water alone.

Even though weaning should occur gradually, the weaning period must not be too long. The kittens should be prepared for weaning starting at four to five weeks old, and weaning should be complete by the time they are seven weeks old. This will allow the mother to recover from this period of great stress on her body.

Very early weaning (at four to five weeks old) is necessary under some circumstances (orphaned kittens, feline infectious peritonitis, etc.). If early weaning is done properly and the kittens are fed carefully, the stronger kittens will be affected very little. However, morbidity (the number of sick kittens) may increase in the weaker kittens, especially in the case of underfeeding.

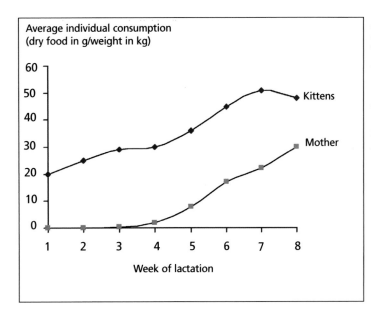

Average individual consumption (dry food in g/weight in kg)

Week of lactation

AVERAGE DIETARY CONSUMPTION OF THE MOTHER CAT AND HER KITTENS

(*average of three kittens per litter*) (*dry food in g/weight in kg, with dry food at 4.5 kcal/g*)

(*from Legrand-Defretin and Munday, 1995*).

Weaning is a necessary evil in the lifecycle. It is a required step toward independence but also a highly stressful period for kittens. Weaning must therefore be carried out with utmost care.

Adulthood

Cats spend approximately one-third their time sleeping and one-third playing, with the last third divided between eating and grooming.

When a cat has free access to the outdoors, it will willingly hunt small prey (mice, young birds, small birds) that it may or may not eat, when it is fed elsewhere. Even if it does not have access to the outdoors, a domestic cat will still exhibit this predatory behavior. Indeed, all cats are drawn to moving objects and can spend hours kicking a ball around.

A cat that eats only mice must consume eight to ten mice per day to fulfill its dietary requirements. Hunting mice is not easy, and just spotting one is not enough to catch it. Hunting is very time-consuming, and failure is frequent. Still, cats do have terrific assets for hunting and catching prey. They have keen senses of hearing, sight, and smell, mobile whiskers, sharp claws, great nimbleness, and one particularly special skill—the ability to move without making a sound.

Normal weaning							
Weeks	1	2	3	4	5	6	7
Number of bottles/day	7	6	5	5	4	2	
Solid food					+	++	+++
Early weaning							
Days	1-7	8-14	15-21	22-28	29-31	32-35	36-42	43-49
Number of bottles/day	7	6	5	3	3			
Solid food					+	++	+++	+++

For example, six bottles per 24-hour day means one bottle every 24/6 = four hours, including at night.

SAMPLE FEEDING SCHEDULES FOR MILK REPLACER.

(adapted from Campanac, 1985).

The Claws and Teeth

A cat's claws have several special features: They grow constantly throughout the cat's life, are slightly curved, and are sharp and retractile, being attached vertically.

A cat's ability to extend its claws has several consequences. First, with its claws retracted, the cat can move silently, thanks to its delicate paw pads. Next, cats can retract their claws to protect them, as they are valuable hunting and fighting weapons. Finally, when the claws are extended, they serve both as fearsome sharp, slicing weapons and as a precious tool for climbing trees.

Thanks to the shape of its claws, a cat can easily sink them into its prey or enemies, like a set of tiny knives. Clawing, even in play, always leaves at least a nice scratch on the skin.

It is entirely possible for owners to clip their cat's claws, but several precautions must be taken. First, owners must use a specially adapted nail clipper that is in good condition. Next, the cat must be held firmly, so that the paw does not slip when the nail is clipped. Finally, once the owner is well-equipped and well-positioned, he or she must take the end of the cat's foot, lightly squeeze the tip of the toe between two fingers, and cut in the direction of the claw (unlike when clipping human nails) to avoid crushing it. When a claw is extended in this manner, two areas become apparent: a pinkish area near the toe and a lighter area near the tip. The light area is what must be cut, as the pinkish area is the nail root and contains blood vessels. The cat is equipped with four claws on each hind foot and five on each forefoot. The fifth of these front claws is called the dew claw (it is located on the toe corresponding to our thumb). This claw must be monitored, since if it is not clipped, it could curl around into the skin and injure the paw. Many cats willingly use tree trunks or, when unavailable, a vertical plank as a scratching post. Scratching serves to file the nails, not so much to wear them down as to renew them, as scratching removes the old outer layer of the claw to expose the underlying sharper claw. Some cats will actually clip their nails on their own—you may see them chewing on a nail as if to bite it off.

After its claws, a cat's teeth are its second line of natural defense, especially its fangs. A cat's teeth are better adapted to seizing, shredding, and tearing prey than to chewing food, which is often swallowed whole.

Water

Some cats may be good swimmers, but they are fairly rare. Cats' general aversion to water is evident in their behavior while drinking. Cats probably originated in the desert and drink very little. Their urine is highly concentrated. Cats that consume prey also drink water, but not as much, since 60% of the prey's body is water, whether it is a mouse or a bird. Similarly, cats that eat wet food from a can tend to drink very little or not at all, while those that eat dry food drink in addition to eating. Cats will consume water in small quantities, drinking from ten to twenty times per day. It is therefore essential that cats have access to clean water at all times. The belief that dry food promotes disease, kidney-related disease in particular, is absolutely false. Still, it is essential to make sure that the cat drinks enough water for proper kidney functioning.

Spaying and Neutering

Approximately 50% of domestic cats, both male and female, are altered. Altering poses no particular problems, except with regard to diet, since the change in status causes an increase in appetite and a decrease in caloric requirements, both in males and females. Consequently, altered cats should either be given less food or a food lower in calories to prevent them from becoming overweight. Owners can even accustom their cat to receiving less food one to two weeks before the scheduled operation. Thus accustomed, the cat will adapt even more easily to its new status.

Life Expectancy

Although some cats reach the record age of 30 years old, a cat's average life expectancy is ten years for altered cats. In whole cats, life expectancy decreases to six years for females and five years for males. This difference can be explained by the tendency of whole cats to stray and therefore be more exposed to risks including both traffic and contagious disease, infections, parasites, etc. Indeed, whenever cats have access to the outdoors, they tend to come into contact with other cats either to reproduce or to fight for territory or mates. These close encounters promote the spread of disease and ultimately shorten the cat's life. Still, the number of elderly cats continues to rise, indicating a better adapted diet, vaccinations that are more common and more effective, and improved medical care.

Old Age

The number of elderly cats in the feline population continues to grow. Of the 8.2 million cats in France, slightly more than 30% are over 8 years old, and 900,000 (11% of France's total feline population) are over 11 years old. Just like in humans, old age is a separate stage in a cat's life. Aging is a natural, unavoidable phenomenon in cats as in other species. It appears in a number of ways: decreased energy, a tendency toward lethargy, difficulty walking, lack of appetite, and a greater frequency of various illnesses including cardiac problems (ventricular hypertrophy), particularly due to the decreased elasticity of the arterial walls, respiratory difficulties due to the decline in pulmonary functioning, susceptibility to infection due to a weakened immune system, frequent kidney disease, tumors, and endocrine problems such as hyperthyroidism, diabetes, etc.

The majority of overweight cats are between 6 and 10 years old, with older cats tending instead to be thin. Obesity is a risk factor in a large number of diseases, such as diabetes, skin problems, etc., but thinness should not be favored for this reason. Indeed, a cat that does not consume enough calories will lose weight, but if the cat does not consume enough protein, it will lose muscle, and its immune system will become weaker.

A cat's appetite may decrease with age, both because of frequent mouth problems (gingivitis, ulcers, tumors) and because of a decline in digestive capacities. The quality and quantity of the diet should therefore be monitored for cats over 10 years old. Elderly cats tend also to drink less and can quickly become dehydrated, so the amount of water in their diet and their water consumption must be monitored as well. In addition, many illnesses occur more often in elderly cats than in young cats. For example, kidney failure is more common in older cats, in part because of the slow onset of this illness. Elderly cats should be monitored by a veterinarian so that any illness can be treated as soon as possible. One veterinary examination per year is recommended throughout a cat's life, for example at the time of vaccination. One examination every six months is strongly advised for cats over 12 years old.

From birth to old age, the cat is primarily a carnivore and a hunter, independent and proud. From a very early age, cats are drawn to moving objects. As adults, they love petting just as much as roaming in the great outdoors. Whatever the breed, and at all stages of life, cats are fascinating animals to observe and live with.

Elderly cat walking through a meadow.

373

Food
and Nutrition

Proteins, fats, carbohydrates, vitamins and minerals, trace elements...
Each nutrient in a diet plays a unique role. Excess amounts, as well as deficiencies, of any one of these elements can have a negative impact on a cat's health. Therefore, it is necessary to gain a full understanding of the types and amounts of food required by the domestic cat, bearing in mind that a cat's dietary needs vary dramatically from those of humans and dogs. Contrary to commonly held views, cats do not have a biological need for variety in their diet. In fact, cats have a poor sense of taste and primarily choose their foods instead using their highly developed sense of smell. So while foods proclaiming tasty lamb and delectable chicken flavors appeal to owners, their formula may not meet a cat's nutritional needs. Some owners who feed homemade foods unwittingly give their cats an unbalanced diet, which can lead to serious health problems. Dieticians study the specific needs of cats at various life stages, such as lactation, pregnancy, growth, maintenance, old age, or sterilization. They then create a diet that meets specific nutritional, caloric, digestibility, performance, and prevention requirements, rather than simply selecting appealing ingredients, such as chicken, lamb, fish, or liver. Some diseases can be treated and even cured by feeding a special diet. But even the most healthful food is useless if the cat refuses to eat. Therefore, a food's appeal is vital. Modern commercial cat foods, particularly premium brands, offer appetizing foods that meet the nutritional needs of individual cats.

Feline Nutrition

"The cat's dependence on man for its nutritional needs has followed the progression of the feline population. The new sedentary and dietary behaviors have resulted in the appearance of new diseases, prompting increased research in the field of feline nutrition."

Prof. James G. Morris, Ph.D.,
University of California, Davis,
at the Société Française de Félinotechnie-
Royal Canin Symposium, Paris, March 1998.

374

Driven by veterinary and scientific research, we are now moving beyond the traditional concept of nutrition (building and maintaining the organism and providing energy) to include its preventive dimension, linking health and nutrition.

Nutrition serves three functions:

1 - **Construction and maintenance**: This is the role of proteins, minerals, trace elements, and vitamins.
2 - **Supply of energy:** This is the role of fats and carbohydrates.
3 - Prevention: Based on our newly acquired knowledge, we now know that certain nutrients play a role in minimizing the risk of urinary tract, digestive, and skeletal disorders and stave off the problems that develop with age.

Since humans domesticated the cat, we have the responsibility to provide a healthful diet that meets the true nutritional needs of our small companion, not simply foods that appeal to our own sensibilities. That is the first step in showing respect for animals.

Nutritional Needs of Cats

All nutrients—we have discovered fifty to date—have a specific function. A deficiency in any given nutrient will have a serious impact on a cat's health over time.
What, exactly, is a nutrient?

It is a type of chemical that can be used as is to feed living cells and that can be absorbed without prior digestion (glucose, amino acids, etc.). A nutrient most often arrives in the digestive tract in the form of complex molecules that are separated during the digestive process and then absorbed as simpler elements.

NECESSARY NUTRIENTS FOR CATS

Proteins	Fats	Carbohydrates		Minerals		Vitamins
		Starch	Fiber	Macro Elements	Trace Elements	

Where are they found?

Proteins	Fats	Starch	Fiber	Macro Elements	Trace Elements	Vitamins
Beef, poultry, fish, liver, eggs, brewers yeast, etc.	**Animal:** Poultry fat, fish oil **Vegetable:** Soya oil, etc.	Grains (corn, rice), alimentary pastes	Corn bran, beet pulp, green vegetables wheat bran	Bone meal, mineral salts, etc.	Liver, vitamin and mineral complexes	Liver, brewers yeast, vitamin and mineral complexes

What is their function?

Proteins	Fats	Starch	Fiber	Macro Elements	Trace Elements	Vitamins
Source of essential fatty acids for: Growth, reproduction, muscle development, healthy, glossy coat, etc.	**The best energy source:** Vital for a healthy coat and an immune system	**Energy source**	**Essential for:** Movement through the digestive tract, firm stools, and a healthy digestive tract	**Essential for:** Strong bones and teeth, muscle function, and nervous system function	**Essential for:** Renewal of blood cells, liver function, organ function, healthy coat	**Essential for:** Sight, reproduction, healthy bones, cell function and integrity

A cat must always have access to fresh water.

Cat eating a mouse.

Water

Water is the foundation for all life, animal and plant alike. Though a cat can survive for several weeks without eating, he will die within two days without water. Water makes up two-thirds of a cat's body. The amount of water that an individual cat requires varies considerably, depending on the type of food (dry or moist) consumed.

Proteins

Build bones, muscle tissue, and the nervous system

Proteins are made up of chains of amino acid linked end to end. Some amino acids cannot be synthesized by the body. These are called essential amino acids and must be included in the diet. Deficiencies can result in serious medical conditions. Protein content of food is, of course, important, but even more so is the quality, or biological value, of those proteins. High-quality proteins include fish, eggs, and red meat. Tendons and connective tissues provide proteins of low quality.

An essential amino acid meriting closer attention is arginine. A cat lacking sufficient quantities of arginine in its diet is unable to convert ammonia to urea, resulting in dangerously high, and potentially deadly, levels of ammonia in the blood. Another essential amino acid

for cats is taurine. Without adequate amounts of taurine, the retina of the eye atrophies, eventually resulting in total blindness if no steps are taken to correct the diet. Other problems arising from taurine deficiency include dilated cardiomyopathy and reproduction disorders.

Lipids - Fats

Lipids, commonly referred to as fats, provide energy and also add palatability to food. Lipids are made up of fatty acids and glycerol forming chains of varying lengths. Some are saturated, others are unsaturated. Fatty acids provide energy, contribute to the composition of cell membranes, and are neurotransmitter precursors.

These latter two functions rely on essential fatty acids, so named because cats cannot synthesize them, and therefore must obtain them from their diet. Cats differ from dogs in that, in addition to taurine, they require dietary linoleic acid and arachidonic acid (available only from animal sources), because they lack the necessary enzymes to metabolize these fatty acids. If a cat's diet contains only essential fatty acids of plant origin, the cat will have deficiency.

Carbohydrates

Better known as sugars, carbohydrates are provided primarily by plants. We distinguish between those carbohydrates that provide

ILEAL DIGESTIBILITY OF PRIMARY PROTEIN SOURCES USED IN DOMESTIC CARNIVORE DIETS	
Source	Ileal digestibility (%)
Sodium caseinate	99
Powdered eggs	100
Dehydrated poultry meat	94-96
Dehydrated beef	93-95
Fish meal	92
Poultry meal	90
Soy	90
Corn gluten	86
Cracklings	93-95

Ileal digestibility: Measured at the end of the small intestine (the ileum). This determines real digestibility, that is, the actual nutritional value for the animal excluding the nutrients consumed by the bacterial flora of the large intestine.

energy and those that do not, such as fiber, which aids passage of food through the digestive tract.

Energy-providing carbohydrates include starches and soluble sugars, such as lactose. Cooked starches are more digestible, but cats digest considerably less starch than dogs. Kittens readily digest lactose while nursing, because their body still produces the enzyme lactase. However, most adult cats are lactose-intolerant, and therefore, should not be given milk (see section on the Main Stages of a Cat's Life).

Carbohydrates that do not provide energy are referred to as dietary fiber. Quantities must be carefully controlled. Too much fiber and absorption of some nutrients is diminished; too little and movement of fecal waste through the large intestine slows, resulting in flatulence. Fiber content may be adjusted under certain circumstances. Fiber can be increased in an attempt to reduce an obese cat's weight, since higher amounts of fiber decrease the caloric content of food and absorption of other nutrients.

Two Types of Fiber

•**Non-soluble**: Fiber contained in corn, leeks, wheat bran, and beet pulp that cannot be broken down by the bacteria of the large intestine. This type of fiber is particularly important for regularity.

• **Soluble**: 25% of beet pulp fiber and 100% of pectin can be broken down in the digestive tract. This fiber is what keeps the intestinal flora in balance and helps maintain a healthy colon.

These two types of fiber must be included in food in the proper quantities and proportion. Diets lacking sufficient fiber often result in loose stools or diarrhea. Excessive amounts of fiber produce too much fecal matter.

Law requires that crude fiber content be listed on commercial foods. However, the figure on the package can be misleading since it only pertains to non-soluble fiber content.

Minerals

Though only small quantities are present in the body, minerals play many physiological roles.

Since they are interrelated, their absorption is interdependent. Therefore, cat foods should contain an optimal balance of minerals. Minerals are divided into macronutrients and trace elements. Macronutrients are so named because the dietary requirements are measured in grams, whereas trace elements are measured in milligrams. Macronutrients include calcium, phosphorus, sodium, chlorine, potassium, and magnesium.

Vitamins

Vitamins are essential to life. They are classified as fat-soluble (A, D, E, and K) or water-soluble (C and B).

With regard to Vitamin A, cats' needs differ from those of dogs. Cats are incapable of converting beta carotene from vegetables to retinol (Vitamin A). Unlike humans, cats do not synthesize Vitamin D from sunlight.

TWO GROUPS OF ESSENTIAL FATTY ACIDS

Omega-6 fatty acids are found in vegetable oils and poultry fat. They help maintain a healthy, glossy coat.

Omega-3 fatty acids are primarily found in fish oils. They play a role in many body systems, including the nervous and immune systems, cell membrane integrity, and act as anti-inflammatories.

These acids are extremely fragile and prone to turn rancid. Therefore, the fatty acids in foods must be preserved. Modern preservation techniques used in the manufacture of commercial pet foods are highly effective.

Minerals: Functions and Sources

MACRONUTRIENTS

	FUNCTION	SOURCES	DEFICIENCY	EXCESS
Calcium (Ca)	Bone construction, transmission of nerve impulses	Bone meal, calcium carbonate, calcium phosphate, dairy products	Anorexia, tooth loss, osteomalacia (mature cats) rickets (young cats)	Over mineralization, stunted growth, secondary deficiency of trace elements
Phosphorus (P)	Bone construction, cell membrane structure, energy metabolism	Bone meal, phosphates, meat, and fish	Anorexia, infertility, osteomalacia (mature cats) rickets (young cats)	Kidney disorders, osteofibrosis, stunted growth
Sodium (Na) and Chlorine (Cl)	Maintain fluid and electrolyte balance	Cooking salt, bacon, cheese	Polyuria, weight loss, stunted growth, dry skin	Oxalate urinary tract stones, intense thirst, diarrhea, convulsions, high blood pressure
Potassium (K)	Regulation of fluid balance, energy metabolism	Potassium salt, vegetables, meats	Anorexia, muscular weakness, high blood pressure, heart disorders	Kidney and heart disorders
Magnesium (Mg)	Bone construction, nervous system, energy metabolism	Bone meal, magnesia, magnesium salts	Nervous disorders, growth retardation, convulsions, irritability	Increased risk of struvite urinary tract stones, diarrhea

TRACE ELEMENTS

MINERAL	FUNCTION	DEFINIENCY	EXCESS
Iron (Fe)	Transportation of oxygen (hemoglobin, myoglobin)	Anemia, generalized weakness, susceptibility to infection	Digestive disorders (vomiting, diarrhea)
Copper (Cu)	Synthesis of hemoglobin, melanin, and collagen	Anemia, bone disorders	Hemolysis, jaundice, liver damage (?)
Zinc (Zn)	Renewal of the epidermis, protein synthesis, reproduction	Growth retardation, bone disorders, skin disorders, increased susceptibility to infection, infertility	Vomiting, appetite loss, pancreatic fibrosis, secondary iron and copper deficiency
Iodine (I)	Thyroid hormones (thyroxin)	Growth retardation, skin disorders, sterility, goiters, hair loss	Goiters, appetite loss
Manganese (Mn)	Catalyst for various metabolic functions	Bone development and reproduction disorders	Dull coat
Selenium (Se)	Works in conjunction with Vitamin E, cellular anti-oxidant, ensures membrane integrity	Cardiomyopathy	Appetite loss, growth retardation (?), hepatitis, kidney disease.

NOTE: Symptoms not observed in cats are indicated with a question mark (?).

Vitamins: functions and sources

VITAMIN	FUNCTION	SOURCES
Vitamin A *(retinol)*	Vision, growth, immunity	Cod liver oil, liver, eggs
Vitamin D *(calciferol)*	Metabolism of calcium and phosphorus, absorption of calcium	Sun (UV), cod liver oil, eggs.
Vitamin E *(tocopherol)*	Antioxidant, maintain muscle cell structure	Milk, grain germ, eggs.
Vitamin K	Blood clotting	Fish, liver, grains
Vitamin B1 *(thiamin)*	Metabolic processes for utilization of carbohydrates for energy, maintain neurological functions	Grains, bran, yeast.
Vitamin B2 *(riboflavin)*	Metabolism of amino acids and fats	Grains, milk, yeast.
Vitamin B6 *(pyridoxine)*	Metabolism of proteins, fats, carbohydrates, and iron	Grains, milk, fish, yeast.
Niacin *(nicotinamide)*	Integrity of skin tissues	Grains, yeast, fish, eggs.
Vitamin B9 *(folic acid)*	Metabolism of proteins, synthesis of hemoglobin	Yeast, liver
Vitamin B12 *(cobalamin)*	Metabolism of proteins, synthesis of hemoglobin	Iron, fish, dairy products
Vitamin B5 *(pantothenic acid)*	Integrity of skin tissues	Liver, fish, dairy products, rice
Biotin	Integrity of skin tissues, metabolism of carbohydrates, fats, and proteins	Yeast, natural ingredients
Choline	Metabolism of fats, maintain liver health	Natural ingredients

Therefore, these two vitamins, derived from animal sources (liver is a particularly rich source), must be provided in the cat's diet, demonstrating once again that the cat is indeed a carnivore. However, cats do not require Vitamin C.

Basic Nutritional Requirements

Health Maintenance in Adult Cats

Assuming that fresh water is freely available, an ideal maintenance diet can be defined based on our understanding of a cat's dietary needs. The diet should be appetizing and maintain ideal body weight.

Proteins: While cats require the dietary taurine provided by proteins, they also must consume more protein by body weight than dogs. Protein requirements are expressed in relation to caloric content. Cats require 80 grams of protein per 1,000 kcal.

Lipids: In addition to providing energy, fats make foods more appetizing. However, the greater the fat content, the more food a cat will eat, possibly leading to obesity.

Experts generally agree that 10% crude fat on a dry matter basis is sufficient for an adult cat on a maintenance diet.

Of course, fats must be of high quality and provide sufficient quantities of essential fatty acids (linoleic and arachidonic acids).
Deficiencies in these two fatty acids can result in growth retardation, infertility, hair loss, fatty liver disease, and clotting disorders.
A healthy diet will include balanced quantities of animal and vegetable fats.

Carbohydrates: Though cats do not require starch in their diet, it is a good source of energy. Since carbohydrates are not as appetizing to cats, overeating is less likely, and therefore the risk of obesity is reduced.

ADULT CAT AT IDEAL WEIGHT: EXAMPLE OF A COMPLETE, NUTRITIONAL DRY FOOD

KEY VALUES	
Protein (%)	32
% animal protein	86
Fats (%)	13
Metabolic energy (kcal/kg)	3,850
Magnesium (%)	0.08
Taurine (%)	0.15
Urinary pH	6 - 6.5
Digestibility (%)	85

INGREDIENTS
chicken or turkey meat and by-products, corn meal, rice, cracklings (dehydrated beef proteins), corn, poultry fat, poultry liver, Scandinavian fish meal, brewers yeast, beet pulp, corn fiber, soy oil, egg powder, DL methionine, mineral salts.

RECOMMENDED DAILY ALLOWANCE		
WEIGHT (IN KG)	GRAMS PER DAY	
	MINIMUM	MAXIMUM
2 - 3	30	50
3 - 5	50	75
5 - 7	65	100

ADULT CAT WITH OBESITY TENDENCIES: EXAMPLE OF A COMPLETE, NUTRITIONAL DRY FOOD

KEY VALUES

Protein (%)	37
% animal protein	92
Fats (%)	10
Metabolic energy (kcal/kg)	3,500
Magnesium (%)	0.08
Taurine (%)	0.15
Urinary pH	6 - 6.5
Dietary fiber (%)	11

INGREDIENTS

Chicken or turkey meat and by-products, corn meal, corn, rice, cracklings (dehydrated beef proteins), poultry fat, poultry liver, Scandinavian fish meal, brewers yeast, beet pulp, corn fiber, soy oil, egg powder, DL methionine, mineral salts.

RECOMMENDED DAILY ALLOWANCE

WEIGHT (IN KG)	GRAMS PER DAY	
	MINIMUM	MAXIMUM
2 - 3	30	50
3 - 5	50	75
5 - 7	65	100

SENSITIVE OR FINICKY ADULT CAT: EXAMPLE OF A COMPLETE, NUTRITIONAL DRY FOOD

KEY VALUES

Protein (%)	33
% animal protein	92
Fats (%)	22
Metabolic energy (kcal/kg)	4,550
Magnesium (%)	0.08
Taurine (%)	0.15
Urinary pH	6 - 6.5
Dietary fiber (%)	88

INGREDIENTS

Chicken or turkey meat and by-products, corn meal, corn, rice, cracklings (dehydrated beef proteins), poultry fat, poultry liver, Scandinavian fish meal, brewers yeast, beet pulp, corn fiber, soy oil, egg powder, DL methionine, mineral salts.

RECOMMENDED DAILY ALLOWANCE

WEIGHT (IN KG)	GRAMS PER DAY	
	MINIMUM	MAXIMUM
2 - 3	30	50
3 - 5	50	75
5 - 7	65	100

A moderate, balanced amount of soluble and non-soluble fibers is a healthy addition to a cat's diet.

Minerals and trace elements: Recommended daily allowances of trace elements are provided in the table below. A range, as well as an optimal amount, for each element is listed.
A calcium and phosphorus (necessary for bone growth) ratio of 1:1 to 2:1 is recommended. Cats can tolerate high levels of table salt (NaCl) if they have free access to fresh water. If protein content is high, potassium must be increased. Signs of potassium deficiency include growth disorders, lethargy, and muscular weakness.

Cats must consume at least the minimum amount of magnesium. Signs of deficiency include growth retardation, lethargy, convulsions, and muscular weakness. However, an excess can be just as dangerous. If urinary pH is not sufficiently acidic (pH > 6.5), magnesium increases the risk of struvite calculi (stones), also called magnesium ammonium phosphate calculi.

RECOMMENDED DAILY ALLOWANCE OF MACRONUTRIENTS *(in g/kg of dry matter in a diet of 4,000 kcal/kg dry matter)*

	Range		Optimal	
	Minimum	Maximum	Minimum	Maximum
Calcium	0.8	2.0	0.9	1.6
Phosphorus	0.6	1.6	0.8	1.2
Sodium chloride	0.25	4.0	1.0	2.0
Potassium	0.4	1.5	0.5	1.0
Magnesium	0.05	0.2	0.1	0.16

Recommended daily allowances for trace elements are provided in the following table.

RECOMMENDED DAILY ALLOWANCE OF TRACE ELEMENTS *(according to Kronfeld, 1991)(in mg/kg of dry matter in a diet of 4,000 kcal/kg dry matter)*

	Range		Optimal	
	Minimum	Maximum	Minimum	Maximum
Iron	80	400	90	400
Copper	5	250	12	40
Zinc	50	1,000	80	180
Iodine	0.35	7	0.55	3.8
Manganese	0.1	500	20	90
Selenium	0.1	5	0.25	0.5

Vitamins: Deficiencies and excesses vitamin A are equally harmful. Signs of deficiency include reproductive disorders, retarded growth, vision disorders, skin diseases (hyperkeratosis), and diminished immunity. Excessive consumption of vitamin A, as might be seen with cats fed an exclusively liver diet, produces lethargy accompanied by deforming cervical spondylosis, in the advanced stages of which the vertebrae of the neck fuse.

Cats do not synthesize vitamin D, so it must, therefore, be provided in the diet. Excessive consumption can produce ectopic calcifications in the kidney, liver, and other tissue.

The role of vitamin E is better understood now than it was in the past. It is an antioxidant that acts against free radicals (against cell aging) and boosts immunity. Deficiency is evidenced by fatty deposits that are yellow-orange in color.

Recommended daily allowances are provided in the following table.

RECOMMENDED DAILY ALLOWANCE OF VITAMINS

(by kg of dry matter in a diet of 4,000 kcal/kg of dry matter)

	Range		Optimal	
	Minimum	Maximum	Minimum	Maximum
A (IU)	6,000	6,000	8,000	25,000
D3 (IU)	500	5,000	600	1,500
E (IU)	30	600	50	150
K (mg)	0.1	100	2	10
B1 (mg)	5	150	10	20
B2 (mg)	4	80	6	30
Pantothenic acid (mg)	5	150	10	25
Niacin (mg)	40	1,200	70	200
B6 (mg)	4	120	8	20
Folic acid (mg)	0.8	24	1.5	3.1
B12 (mg)	0.02	0.6	0.05	0.1
Biotin (mg)	0.07	2.1	0.1	0.3
Choline (mg)	2,000	7,200	2,100	3,000

The Pregnant and Lactating Cat

Gestation in cats lasts sixty-six days on average. Average litter size is three to five kittens weighing approximately 100 grams each.

The queen puts on weight during pregnancy. Up to 40 days, she accumulates the reserves that she will need during the late gestation period and lactation.

Weight gain during the last 26 days is essentially equivalent to the in utero growth of the kittens. Food intake naturally increases during pregnancy. From onset of gestation, a queen should be fed a diet high in fats, such as foods formulated for kittens and lactating/gestating cats. This will increase the survival rate of the kittens at birth. Particular attention should be given to taurine content: a minimum of 0.1% in dry food and 0.25% in canned food.

Food must not be acidic, or the skeleton of the fetus will not develop properly. The daily quantities fed should be increased by 10% each week during the first eight weeks of pregnancy. However, feeding should not be increased to the extent that the queen becomes overweight, or she could have difficulties at delivery.

The period during which the queen is lactating is also crucial. A mother cat will produce 1 1/2 to 2 times her weight in milk (particularly high in proteins and fats in cats). As a result, lactation demands much greater energy expenditure than gestation.

A lactating cat requires as much as twice or three times the daily calories of a cat on a maintenance diet. No matter how much or how rich the food provided, a lactating cat will not consume enough to meet all her energy needs.

The excess 20% body weight (essentially stored in fat reserves) at delivery, as compared to weight at mating, is typically utilized for extra energy during lactation.

Once the kittens are born, high-calorie food should be constantly available so the queen can feed freely. During this period, kitten food is ideal.
This diet should be fed until the kittens are weaned, at which time, the queens diet is gradually returned to a maintenance diet.

WEIGHT AND FOOD CONSUMPTION OF A CAT DURING REPRODUCTION

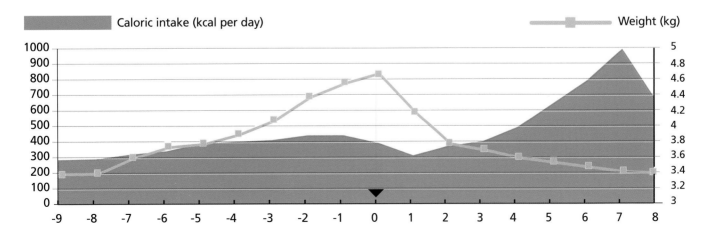

GROWTH OF KITTENS UNTIL WEANING

According to Festing, Humi, Rosenstein

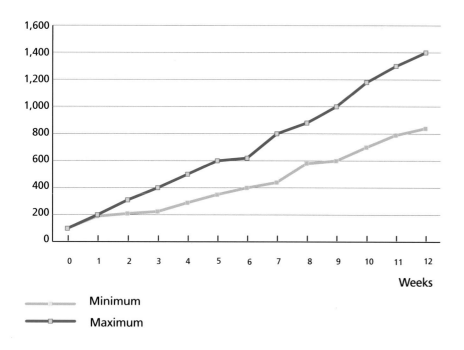

Weeks

--- Minimum

--- Maximum

Growing Kittens

Kittens are nursed for five to seven weeks. Initially, kittens drink colostrum, the liquid produced by the nursing cat before her milk comes in. Colostrum is rich in antibodies, which provide young kittens with vital early protection against infectious diseases. Kittens grow extremely rapidly, gaining approximately ten to fifteen grams per day. They double their birth weight within ten days, and by the age of seven to eight weeks, weigh five to seven times more than when born.

It is helpful to weigh kittens daily, and at the same time every day. If a kitten does not gain or loses weight, or cries often, a milk supplement should be provided. Cow's milk is not a good milk substitute for kittens, because it contains too much lactose and not enough calories (see Main Stages of a Cat's Life).

Commercial milk replacement preparations adapted specifically to the needs of nursing kittens are available. Hand-feeding a kitten is, needless to say, a repetitive, time-consuming task.

A bottle may be used to feed kittens (the kitten should be held upright) or a flexible rubber tube may be introduced into the stomach. (Note: This procedure should be performed only by a qualified veterinarian or experienced breeders.
Bottles and nipples must be sterile, since kittens at this stage of development are very vulnerable to diarrhea-causing bacteria.

CALCULATING AVERAGE INTAKE FOR KITTENS UNTIL WEANED

According to Bains, Cornell University, Monson.

	Average weight of kitten (kg)	Caloric requirements (kcal/kg)	Caloric requirements (kcal)	Quantity of milk per day* (ml)	Quantity of milk per feeding X number of feedings
Week 1	100 to 200 g	400 to 380	40 to 75	35 to 70	(6 to 12 ml) x 6 to 7 feedings
Week 2	200 to 250 g	380 to 350	75 to 90	70 to 80	12 ml x 6 feedings to 16 ml x 5 feedings
Week 3	250 to 350 g	350 to 300	90 to 110	80 to 100	16 ml x 5 feedings to 25 ml x 4 feedings
Week 4	350 to 470 g	300 to 250	110 to 120	100 to 110	(25 to 27 ml) x 4 feedings

* For a caloric value of the milk approx. 110 kcal/100 ml

COMPARISON OF CAT'S MILK TO COW'S MILK

According to Zottmann

Analyses	Dry matter (% raw)	Protein (% dry matter)	Fats (% dry matter)	Lactose (% dry matter)
Cat's milk	20 - 25	35 - 42	26 - 42	13 - 17
Cow's milk	12 - 13	24 - 38	28 - 30	35 - 39

Weaning

Kittens should be weaned very gradually. Beginning at the age of three weeks, solid kitten food can be made available, though the kittens will eat only a little solid food at this time. Kittens progressively increase their intake of solid food and decrease nursing. When first introducing solid food, a milk substitute may be mixed with the food to make it more appealing.

Once the kittens reach five weeks of age, the queen will begin weaning them on her own. If kitten food has been provided at an early age, the kittens will switch more readily to their new food source. However, kittens who nurse exclusively will have greater difficulty, consume fewer calories, and as a result, their growth will slow during this period.

Kittens should be gradually separated from the queen, making sure that the kittens always have access to solid food. After a period of time, kittens should be completely separated from the queen during the day, spending only the night with her. Once they are completely weaned, kittens may be moved to a new environment around the age of seven or eight weeks. A 24-hour fast with limited water availability will help stop lactation.

Dietary needs of kittens

The only requirement for feeding kittens is that they make the transition from liquid to solid food. The diet fed to the queen at this time is ideal for kittens, since this high-calorie food contains large amounts of quality proteins and is rich in vitamins and calcium.

A kitten's digestive system changes during the first few weeks. Digesting lactose, the primary sugar in milk, becomes increasingly difficult, but kittens slowly develop the ability to digest starches from grain sources.

However, this progression takes time. To avoid the risk of diarrhea associated with weaning, feeding a food containing less than 30% starch to dry matter is recommended. Diarrhea, which dramatically slows growth and causes dehydration, can have dire consequences in very young animals.

Since dry food is convenient, it should be fed to kittens from a very young age, though it is a good idea to moisten it with kitten formula early on, then with beef broth or water as they grow. Competition between littermates will encourage all of the kittens to eat the dry food, provided the feeding dish is large enough for all to feed at the same time. Three to five meals per

CONSUMPTION OF SOLID FOOD BY KITTENS
According to Legrand-Defrein

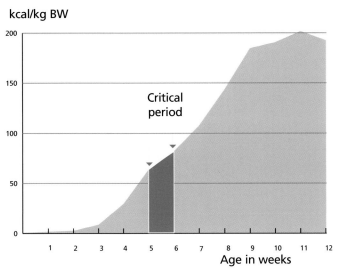

EVOLUTION IN A KITTEN'S ABILITY TO DIGEST CARBOHYDRATES AS COMPARED TO ADULT CATS
According to Kienzle.

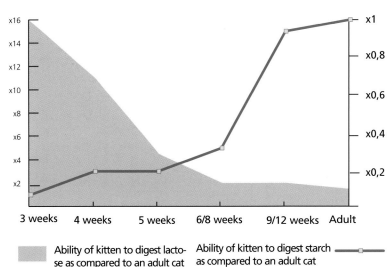

383

KEY VALUES

Protein (%)	28
% animal protein	84
Fats (%)	23
Metabolic energy (kcal/kg)	4,400
Magnesium (%)	0.08
Taurine (%)	0.15
Phospohrus (%)	0.6
Digestibility (%)	86

INGREDIENTS:

Poultry fat, chicken or turkey meat and by-products, rice, corn starch, corn meal, corn, poultry liver, Scandinavian fish meal, brewers yeast, beet pulp, corn fiber, soy oil, egg powder, DL methionine, borage oil, and mineral salts (including chelated iron, copper, zinc, and manganese).

RECOMMENDED DAILY ALLOWANCE

Weight in kg	Thin Grams/day MIN	MAX	Ideal Grams/day MIN	MAX	Overweight Grams/day MIN	MAX
2 - 3	30	50	25	45	-	-
3 - 5	50	75	40	65	30	55
5 - 7	65	100	55	90	45	75

day is appropriate. The amount of liquid added to the kibble should be decreased gradually until none is added by the time the kittens are fully weaned. Kittens should always have access to clean, fresh water.

Above all, the diet fed to a just-weaned kitten must be rich in calories. At eight weeks of age, a kitten consumes three times more calories per kilogram of body weight than an adult cat (200 to 250 kcal/kg). The daily ration will vary between 30 to 50 g of kitten food, depending on the weight and breed of cat. Energy requirements remain extremely high until the age of twelve weeks, then gradually decrease as the animal enters a slower growth period. However, kitten food may be fed until the age of one year, the age at which growth normally stops and the kitten is considered an adult.

The Geriatric Cat

Improved medical treatment and specialized diets have worked together to prolong the life expectancy of cats. Average life expectancy is fourteen years, but it is not unusual to encounter cats that have reached the age of twenty or older. The oldest cat on record reached thirty years of age.

The nutritional needs of geriatric cats differ from those of younger animals. Geriatric cats are more prone to health problems, including chronic renal failure, oral health problems, tumors, bone and muscle degeneration, cardiovascular disease, and diabetes mellitus. Most of these diseases can be alleviated, prevented, or entirely cured through diet.

Special nutrients: Aging is a complex process during which production of free radicals increases. An animal is protected from these free radicals by antioxidants. As a cat ages, his defense system weakens. An older cat may benefit from a diet enriched with vitamins C and E. Vitamin C may help protect against dental and oral health problems, while vitamin E, which limits production of free radicals, attenuates the effects of aging. These two vitamins also boost the immune system. The daily allowance of these two vitamins for cats aged ten years or older is five to six times higher than for normal maintenance.

Other adjustments must also be made to the older cat's diet. Since appetite and absorption decline with age, a high-calorie, appetizing food is recommended. Softer kibble is also helpful since the older cat may have difficulty chewing.

The scientific community was divided for many years regarding the possible need to reduce protein content in an older cat's diet. Research demonstrates that doing so does not retard aging of the kidneys in any way and can only contribute to muscle loss and weakening of the animal's immune system. However, a decrease in phosphorus is recommended. In addition, after a certain age, foods that increase urine acidity should be avoided, since they favor the development of oxalate calculi, which occur with greater frequency in older cats.

DISTRIBUTION OF CATS NOT MANTAINING IDEAL WEIGHT

% of feline population

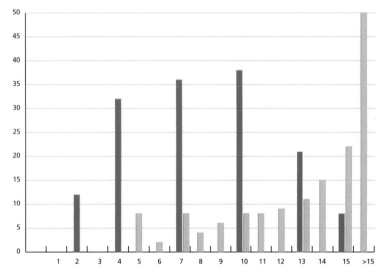

Age (years)

■ Overweight cats
■ Underweight cats

Spaying, Neutering, and Obesity

Owners often opt to have their pets spayed or neutered not only to prevent pregnancy, but to avoid undesirable sexual behaviors such as vocalizing in females and pungent marking in males. Spayed or neutered cats are calmer, less likely to roam, and live on average two times longer than cats that have not been spayed or neutered. There are, however, two side effects of this procedure. Caloric requirements decline, while at the same time, free feeding increases by 25% in males and 18% in females, resulting in an average weight gain of 26% in cats allowed to feed freely following spaying or neutering.

This weight gain, which eventually leads to long-term obesity, is directly linked to the fat content of food. The higher the fat content, the more appetizing the food, and the more fattening. The cat consumes more food, and therefore more calories, while energy requirements have decreased. This excess energy is stored as fat.

Obesity has several adverse health effects. Obese cats are four times more likely to develop diabetes mellitus, three times more likely to suffer from lameness, and two times more likely to have non-allergic skin disorders.

In addition to these common maladies, and as a result of increased life expectancy in spayed and neutered cats, sterilization has more long-term effects, such as increased frequency of urinary calculi (stones) (see Nutrition and Health). Therefore, a cat's diet should be modified following neutering or spaying. Fat content should be no more than 10%, and quantity should be controlled in order to avoid overeating.

In the weeks leading up to the surgery, the new diet can be introduced gradually to prepare the cat and avoid added stress. This adjustment in diet is necessary to reduce the risk of obesity.

By having your cat spayed or neutered, you help control the pet population and make a contribution to society as a whole. A female cat can produce as many as 220 offspring in only 24 months. In addition, since spayed and neutered cats lack sexual desire, they are less likely to stray, and therefore, less likely to be injured or killed by automobiles or to exposed to contagious diseases from contact with other cats.

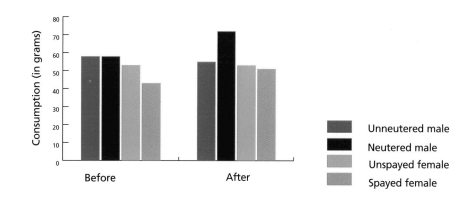

AVERAGE AMOUNTS CONSUMED (IN GRAMS) PRIOR TO AND THREE MONTHS FOLLOWING SPAYING OR NEUTERING AS COMPARED TO NON-SPAYING OR NEUTERING

Legend:
- Unneutered male
- Neutered male
- Unspayed female
- Spayed female

SPAYING AND NEUTERING: WHEN? HOW?

Veterinarians spay and neuter cats almost daily. However, not all use the same procedure. Tube tying and vasectomy are of little use since they do not eliminate the undesirable behaviors caused by the male hormones. Not all specialists are in agreement regarding the appropriate age for sterilization. Generally, cats are sterilized between six to twelve months of age, before sexual behaviors have been established. Spaying a female at a relatively young age (six to eight months) reduces the chance of an undesired pregnancy. In Europe, veterinarians prefer to perform an ovariectomy (removal of the ovaries), while in the United States, an ovariohysterectomy (removal of the ovaries and uterus) is the procedure of choice. This latter procedure is more invasive, but eliminates the risk of future uterine infections. However, uterine infections are extremely rare in females that have undergone an ovariectomy. In the United States, debate in veterinary circles is currently focusing on sterilization of extremely young cats between twelve and fourteen weeks of age. This approach does not seem to have any behavioral or medical side effects, nor does it affect growth, though males castrated at a very young age are likely to reach a slightly larger size than unneutered males. Whether sterilized at three months or twelve, kitten food must be fed until the end of the growth phase, increasing the likelihood of obesity. Opinions will undoubtedly change over time, but the practices currently in place in Europe are satisfactory.

	YOUNG ADULT	MATURE CAT	GERIATRIC CAT
Age	Sterilization to 5 years of age	6 - 9 years of age	Ten years of age and
older			
Kcal/kg/Fat (%)	3,500 kcal/10%	3,500 kcal/10%	4,000 kcal/16%
Urinary pH	6.2 (range 6.0-6.4]	6.6 (range 6.4-6.8)	7.0 (range 6.8-7.2)
Potassium citrate	-	+	+
Phosphorus	1.00	0.8	0.6
Vitamin E	-	+	+
Borage oil	-	+	+

The appropriate diet for a sterilized cat varies with age. From castration to the age of five years, a diet containing 10% fat and targeting a urinary pH of 6.2 with phosphorus content of 1% is suggested. From six to nine years of age, a slightly higher pH of 6.6 and extra vitamin E is advisable. Cats over the age of ten have a tendency to lose weight. Therefore, fat-content should be increased to 16%, while targeting a neutral pH in order to protect against formation of oxalate calculi, which are more common in older animals. Phosphorus should be reduced to 0.6% to maintain renal function and vitamin E intake increased.

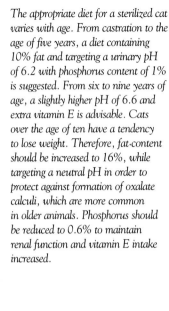

Obesity decreases life expectancy. Adult cats up to the age of ten years are the most prone to obesity.

Nutrition and Health

The previous section covered the dietary needs of healthy cats. This section will focus on the role of diet in preventing and treating various health disorders.

All feeding practices that put a cat at risk must be eliminated. Young , healthy cats that consume excessive amounts of fat run the risk of becoming obese.

A diet of only liver (that your cat will consume with glee) invariably leads to bone and joint disorders as a direct result of the vitamin A overdose (liver is very high in vitamin A). Extreme cases can result in fusion of the vertebrae of the spinal column.

An obese cat whose food intake is suddenly reduced runs the risk of hepatic lipidosis. Frequent changes in food cause digestive problems, including vomiting and diarrhea.

Hepatic Lipidosis

Feline hepatic lipidosis (also referred to as fatty liver) is a disease in which fats accumulate within the liver cells, interfering with the proper functioning of this organ. Hepatic lipidosis is the leading disease of the liver in the United States, the country with the highest proportion of obese cats. Obesity occurs most often in cats between the ages of 4 and 12. Sterilized cats are more likely to become obese, as are females.

The onset of hepatic lipidosis occurs when an obese cat stops eating. This form of anorexia, which some equate with the psychologically-based anorexia found in humans, can be triggered by stress, including disease, changes in routine or surroundings, arrival of a new animal or person, or a sudden change in diet.

If a cat does not like the food offered, he will not eat; unlike dogs, cats will literally starve themselves to death. If there are several pets in the home, the owner may not notice that one cat is not eating, particularly since the cat typically remains energetic. Sometimes, an owner will note (with pleasure) a slight weight loss. However, weight loss corresponds not only to loss of fatty tissue, but also of muscle mass, since body proteins are not being replaced with sufficient intake of protein.

After the cat has not eaten for several days or weeks, the liver suddenly stops functioning and signs of hepatic lipidosis appear, including jaundice, hepatic encephalopathy (blank stare, excessive salivation), followed by coma lasting several days, then death. A definitive diagnosis is based on a liver biopsy, since these symptoms are not specific to hepatic lipidosis, but merely indicate cessation of normal liver function.

Cats suffering from hepatic lipidosis need to be treated under the care of a qualified veterinarian. Treatment focuses on force-feeding the animal a special liquid diet using a syringe or feeding tube until the animal regains his appetite. Typically the cat begins feeding on his own within two or three weeks. Reintroducing the cat to food (whether liquid or solid) must be done gradually with small meals. Outcome is favorable if the disease is detected early and appropriate treatment is provided.

This disease can be avoided by closely monitoring an obese cat that is being placed on a reduction diet. When the new diet is introduced, the owner should make sure that the cat is eating. A new diet should be introduced in stages, gradually replacing the old food with greater quantities of the new over a period of two weeks.

Food Allergies

A food allergy is an inappropriate response of the body to a foreign substance, which is normally absorbed by a healthy cat. Some foods are not recognized by the immune system and trigger a rejection mechanism. Most food allergies are caused by proteins. Intense itching, particularly on the head, ears, neck, and forelegs is the primary symptom. Digestive disorders, including vomiting, diarrhea, and abdominal pain may also be associated with food allergies.

In fact, food allergies are quite rare; they are responsible for only one percent of all skin disorders. Food allergies should not be confused with food intolerance, which does not trigger an immune response (lactose intolerance, histamines present in poor quality foods, excessive fermentation in the large intestine, etc.).

Diagnosing a food allergy is extremely difficult, since it is necessary to identify the specific food responsible for the symptoms. In order to do this, the cat is often fed a diet composed of ingredients other than those typically used in cat foods. Lamb meat is commonly used for this type of diet. If the symptoms disappear (this can take several weeks, or even months), the old food is reintroduced to see if symptoms reappear. If they reappear in less than one week, a food allergy is confirmed.

A food allergy is treated by feeding hypoallergenic food.

Diet and Urinary Calculi

Let us immediately dispense with an old wives tale: No, kibble does not cause urinary stones. However, it is true that cats are more susceptible to the formation of calculi than other species, though occurrence is only 1%. Understanding of this affliction has improved in recent years. We now know that there are several types of urinary calculi in cats. The nutritional approach for treatment varies depending on the composition of the calculus. Not all urinary problems indicate the presence of calculi. A kidney disease or inflammation of the bladder (of bacterial origin or caused by a tumor) are equally common causes.

Symptoms of urinary calculi accompany the onset of what was previously known as feline urologic syndrome (FUS). The current term, feline lower urinary tract disease, is more accu-

Cats should be maintained at their ideal weight. Though the likelihood of a cat becoming obese increases around the age of seven, cats over ten years of age tend to lose weight. Fat content can be increased for the older cat without any harmful effect and protein content maintained at an adequate level.

DIMENSIONS INDICATIVE OF A CAT'S PHYSICAL CONDITION
According to Scarlett.

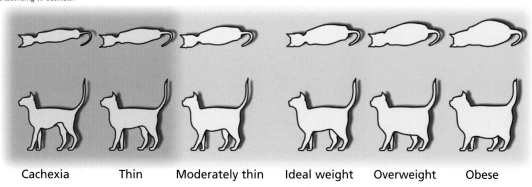

| Cachexia | Thin | Moderately thin | Ideal weight | Overweight | Obese |

rate (FLUTD). Common symptoms include: Frequent trips to the litter box, straining, painful urination, and bloody urine. If a stone travels to the lower urinary tract, the urethra may be blocked. In this case, the cat is unable to urinate, and if left untreated, will die within 24 to 48 hours.

Urolithiasis: Magnesium ammonium phosphate stones (struvite) were much more common prior to the 1990s, before most manufacturers revised the composition of their foods. These types of stones are most common in young male and female cats between one and six years of age. Male cats, due to the structure of their anatomy, have greater difficulty expelling stones. Sterilized, sedentary, obese, or inactive cats generally urinate less frequently. When urine remains in the urinary tract for extended periods of time, a cat is predisposed to formation of stones.

Urine pH is by far the most important factor in the formation of struvite. A slightly acid pH (below 6.5) inhibits formation of stones. Conversely, alkaline urine favors mineral precipitation, particularly if there is a high concentration of magnesium. Dietary recommendations are simple: Food must create an acidic urine and contain a limited quantity of magnesium (less than 400mg/1,000 kg). Protein determines the amount of acidification. Proteins of animal origin generally increase acidity, whereas those of plant origin do not. Acidifying agents, such as methionine, ammonium chloride, or phosphoric acid (the most effective) may also be added. However, excessive acidity is also harmful. Chronic acidosis in an adult cat can lead to potassium loss.
In the early and late stages of life, acidification of urine is not recommended: In kittens, growth may slow and bone demineralization result. In cats over ten years of age, a different type of calculus is observed and, therefore, a more alkaline urine is appropriate.

Oxalate uroliths were very rare in the past, but their incidence is on the rise as a result of the dietary preventive measures mentioned above.

This type of stone is most common in older cats. Males (neutered or whole) are more susceptible to this type of stone, as are certain breeds, including the Burmese, Himalayan, and the Persian. This type of calculus develops in alkaline urine containing high quantities of oxalate and calcium. Diet has an effect on the formation of this type of calculus. A diet rich in sodium, vitamin D, and lactose, but low in fiber and phosphorus improves intestinal absorption of calcium. The ideal diet should not acidify urine, be rich in magnesium, and have a low concentration of calcium.

Reconciling the unreconcilable: The frustrating fact of the matter is that the nutritional recommendations for preventing the formation of struvite and oxalate calculi are directly opposing. Therefore, a middle ground must be found. Acidifying agents should not be administered if food promotes acidity. The focus should be on attaining moderate acidity_a pH of approximately 6.5, lower if there are struvite calculi to be dissolved. Note: Calculi must be analyzed before determining the appropriate dietary treatment. Finally, acidifying foods should be avoided for very young or geriatric cats.

The Influence of Feeding Methods: In addition to food composition, the manner in which the food is consumed also plays a significant role. Urine concentration promotes formation of calculi of any type. Diluting the urine increases trips to the litter box and reduces the likelihood of stones. Cats should always have access to fresh water (replaced at least daily). Food quality also plays a role. If it is highly digestible and energy-rich, water loss resulting from defecation will be kept to a minimum.

Moreover, researchers have established that the secretion of stomach acids during digestion makes urine more alkaline. The greater the amounts of food consumed, the greater this effect.

Therefore, feeding several small meals is recommended. Free feeding of dry foods (within daily quantity guidelines) encourages the cat to drink more often and therefore promotes more stable urine acidity. Finally, during hot weather, a cat should have access to a cool area, because urine pH rises sharply in extreme weather conditions.

Taste

Though domestic carnivores have a better sense of smell than humans, the same is not true of taste.

Taste is simply a sensation that is perceived by stimulation of receptors (sensory cells) located primarily on the tongue, but also throughout the mouth and pharynx. The sense of taste allows animals to evaluate the appetency of a food, and to reject a toxic product, which is generally characterized by a bitter taste. The sense of taste stimulates salivary, pancreatic, and gastric secretions and instills a general sense of well being.

These receptors, called taste buds, are located on the upper surface of the tongue, as well as on the palate, epiglottis, and pharynx. On the tongue, taste buds are grouped in papillae. There are four types of papillae: Filiform, fungiform, calciform, and foliate. Filiform papilla, located on the upper surface of the tongue, do not play a role in taste. Instead, they sense the texture of food.

The number of taste buds varies considerably from one species to the next. Dogs have many more than cats, but far fewer than humans. This "handicap" is offset by a highly developed sense of smell.

At the base of the taste buds are nerve fibers connected to three nerves the glossopharyngeal, facial, and vagus nerves. The information gathered by these nerves is transmitted to the thalamus, the area of the brain responsible for taste.

Flavors

Researches believe that domestic carnivores are able to distinguish between sweet, sour, salty, and bitter, though not much solid proof

exists to support this assertion. Nevertheless, it is worth studying taste preferences. Studies analyze a cat's behavior when offered two different types of food, thus determining which taste the cat prefers.

- Sweet: Unlike other mammals, cats do not have a great attraction to sweet tastes. They do not distinguish between plain water and sugar water. However, if the sugar water is diluted with a salty solution, the cat prefers it.

Actually, it appears that cats have nerves specific to water that mask sweet tastes.

- Sour: Receptors for sour solutions are distributed across the surface of tongue. If a food is too sour, it is rejected.

- Salty: Cats have a higher perception level for salty flavors than other species. They are able to eat very salty foods.

- Bitter: Bitter flavors are perceived by the taste buds located on the posterior portion of the tongue. Cats are very sensitive to bitter flavors, which typically indicate toxic substances.

Perception of taste varies from one animal to the next. Some authors have proposed different classifications. They claim that cats possess a nucleotide-based system. Since nucleotides are present in meat, this would account for cats' preference for meat products.

Modification of Taste

Several factors can modify taste perceptions. Sense of taste fades with age, and some illnesses affect taste perceptions (though studies have not been carried out on humans). Some medications, such as tetracycline, also alter sense of taste. Regarding the food itself, studies have found that cats are more eager to eat canned food that has been warmed slightly. Researchers believe that heating the food decreases any salty or bitter taste in the food.

Premium foods administer precise amounts of acidifying agents appropriate to the age of the animal, thus reducing the likelihood of formation of oxalate calculi and struvite.

OPTIMAL URINE pH

Growing kitten
Weaning to five years of age:
pH 6.2; range 6.0-6.4

Adult cat
Five to nine years of age:
pH 6.6; range 6.4-6.8

Geriatric cat
Ten years of age and older:
pH 7; range 6.8-7.2

Cats are finicky eaters. They prefer shallow (dog bowls are too deep) glass, porcelain, or ceramic dishes rather than plastic or stainless steel. Cats enjoy food that has been briefly heated in the microwave.

POOR SENSE OF TASTE

Number of taste buds by species

Chicken	24
Duck	200
Cat	**473**
Dog	1,706
Humans	9,000
Pig	15,000
Goat	15,000
Rabbit	17,000
Calf	25,000

Food Preferences of Cats

Preferences are developed from experience. When a kitten begins to eat solid food during weaning, he invariably prefers the food that his mother eats. If a new food is offered to a cat in a stressful situation, the cat will reject this food in the future because it is associated with an unpleasant experience, a phenomena called neophobia. Neophobia should be distinguished from aversion, which corresponds to refusal to eat a food that has made the cat sick.

Other factors also play a role. Cats prefer products of animal, rather than plant, origin. Some cats prefer fish over beef. Though cats are not particular about fat content, the presence of fats gives foods a texture that cats enjoy. Cats are particular about texture, as well as the size of each bite; they dislike overly small pieces.

Eating Behavior of Cats

Normal behavior

Cats are by nature nibblers. If left to their own devices, a cat will eat between ten and sixteen small meals per day. An interesting observation is the fact that total darkness inhibits eating. Meals last only two to three minutes. A cat drinks ten times per day on average.

Cats generally prefer commercial foods over homemade foods.

Studies have revealed the following general preferences (though behavior varies considerably from one individual to the next). Cats

A HIGHLY DEVELOPED SMELL

Breed/Kind	Olfactory Mucus	Dedicated Brain Zone
Dog (1)	20 to 170 cm²	10 to 50 times bigger than for humans
Cat	25 cm²	6 times bigger than for humans
Human	4 cm²	

(1) Whether of small or large bread

favor foods containing amino acids associated with animal proteins. Cats love liver. Not all will choose fish over red meat; this preference varies considerably.

There is also a correlation between food preference and the length of the fatty acid chains. For example, cats refuse to eat fatty acid chains of moderate length contained in some vegetable oils, such as coconut and palm oils. Regarding texture, cats seem to prefer extremes, either very wet or very dry food. In terms of canned food, cats typically choose foods with chunks over mousse preparations. Though cats are strict carnivores, they are, on occasion, attracted to some vegetables, including catnip, valerian, sage, mint, and olive, though they simply wish to chew, not consume, these products.

Food preferences seem to be strongly influenced by experiences encountered at a very young age. Kittens imitate their mother's eating behaviors, and in most cases, will forever favor the food that they ate when first introduced to solid food.

Drinking is also a taught behavior. A mother cat will teach her kittens to lap from a saucer. From that time on, fresh water must always be available.

The Pathology of Eating Behaviors

Anorexia: Refusal to eat is observed in a wide range of disorders. Treating the underlying illness does not always restore appetite. A cat that has been removed from her normal environment and placed in a kennel or hospitalized may refuse to eat. In serious cases, administering a drug such as diazepam often restores appetite.

Ingestion of non-food objects: This behavioral disorder is called pica. One of its variations concerns primarily Siamese and Burmese cats who chew on cloth, particularly wool, using their molars. If wool is not available, they will turn to other materials, including cotton or synthetics. An extreme example is that of a cat whose owners moved all cloth out of the cat's reach. The cat destroyed a mattress in order to chew on the stuffing. Though the behavior is generally rather sporadic, these animals are capable of causing considerable damage in only a few minutes. Little is known about the cause of this behavior. However, it is more common in young cats and decreases in frequency if the cat has free access to plants or dry food. It does not seem to be linked to a deficiency, but it regresses when the diet is rich in fiber.

If this behavior continues despite all dietary efforts to the contrary, the following solution may work. Wet a used piece of clothing with perfume or hot sauce, and leave it within reach of the cat. He will soon associate his undesirable behavior with a disagreeable taste experience.

Cats also exhibit dangerous behaviors, including chewing electrical cords, twine, or string. The last two can cause deadly intestinal obstructions. Again, "aversion" techniques may put a stop to such behaviors. A less bothersome behavior is abnormal sucking, such as sucking on the owner's skin or the teats of a dog or another cat. This disorder differs dramatically from that of "wool suckers." It merely reproduces infant behavior. The cat does not chew, but acts like a kitten, massaging with its front paws in typical kitten fashion.

Food aversions: A cat may develop an aversion to certain types of foods for various reasons. The classic case is hiding a pill in a piece of food. The cat will generally develop an aversion for the type of food that was consumed at that moment. She will also tend to refuse food eaten at a time when she was having digestive problems such as vomiting or diarrhea. This behavior is also observed in humans, who avoid foods that they believe have made them sick in the past. This is an adaptive behavior. In the wild, cats will refuse to eat damaged prey, since it is more likely to contain endotoxins.

Predatory behaviors: This is not, strictly speaking, an eating behavior disorder in cats. Even if fed a proper diet at home, cats invariably develop this behavior, preying on hapless birds and rodents. This behavior is highly desirable in the country where cats are sometimes kept for strictly utilitarian purposes. However, the friends of animals living in urban areas would prefer that their sprightly companion not proudly present them with captured birds, mice, and squirrels. We now have ways to promote or inhibit this predatory behavior.

To promote hunting behavior, a queen with strong hunting skills is selected, since she is the one who will teach the art of hunting to her offspring, who should remain with their mother as long as possible. It is useless to starve a cat in the hopes that she will develop predatory behaviors, since these behaviors are not dependent on hunger. There are various approaches for inhibiting these types of behaviors. These include selecting non-hunters or poor hunters as parents and separating the kittens from the mother as early as possible.

Commercial Food or Homemade?

Cat lovers are sometimes inclined to prepare a "little something" for their beloved pet. It is possible to provide a healthy diet containing all the nutrients (proteins, fats, carbohydrates, vitamins, and minerals) contained in twelve mice per day, not to mention the various birds and plants consumed, but the cat's natural diet would have to be replicated in the kitchen. Commercial foods are now the simplest solution and guarantee a healthy, balanced diet. But it took a long time to reach this point. Decades of intense research and innovation in manufacturing techniques were required to produce today's premium foods.

Foods Prepared at Home

Using fresh ingredients to feed a cat is possible, but a few basic rules must be followed.

Birds will be less vulnerable if a cat wears a collar fitted with a small bell. If cats take an interest in pet birds or rodents, aversion methods may be tried. The simplest is to place mousetraps upside down around the cage of the object of the cat's attention. If the cat comes prowling around, the mechanism will be triggered and frighten the cat.
Some experts suggest the following: Spray a body deodorant at the cat at an angle (not toward the eyes) two or three times per day. This will slightly irritate the nasal membranes. Next, spray this same deodorant around the cages housing your cat's coveted prey. The cat will develop an aversion for these spots. Be careful however not use the deodorant that you use on yourself, or your cat could develop an aversion to you!

- The food must have a high animal product content and be enriched with vitamins and minerals;
- The diet must be balanced, and contain sufficient amounts of proteins, energy, etc.;
- Ingredients must be weighed from time to time to verify that the correct amounts are being incorporated;
- The owner must make sure the cat is eating the entire meal and not sorting out only his preferred choice morsels;
- In addition to the meat, rice or pasta, green vegetables, and vegetable oil, a vitamin and mineral supplement containing calcium and phosphorus in a 2:1 ration must be incorporated. Cats require about fifty different nutrients. A vitamin and mineral supplement formulated specifically for cats (available from most veterinarians) is the only way to be sure that all necessary minerals, trace elements, and vitamins are included in the diet.

Ingredients for Foods Prepared at Home

Meats vary considerably in quality. Meat with a high collagen content (tendons, connective tissues) does not provide high-quality dietary protein. Intermediate quality beef, such as stew or cheek meat, is a good choice. These meats can be served raw or lightly cooked, but not boiled. Pork, on the other hand, must be cooked thoroughly to protect against parasitic diseases. Poultry, which may be cooked by any method, contains particularly high quality fats. None of these meats provide all of the vitamin and mineral (especially calcium) needs of cats.

Regarding raw preparations labeled "for animal consumption," provided they do not contain tendons and connective tissues, they may be of acceptable quality, but normally contain a high percentage of fat. They should be used only on occasion.

Quantities of offal should be limited. Special care must be taken with regard to liver since it contains large amounts of vitamin A. It must make up no more than 10% of a cat's diet. Lung has been fed to cats for centuries. It is a source of moderate quality protein and can be fed from time to time to sedentary cats lacking energy.

Fish is also an excellent source of high-quality protein. It must be cleaned and cooked, since the viscera may contain the vitamin B1 blocker thiaminase, which can lead to nervous disorders. The disadvantage of fish is that it contains a lot of bones, which may get caught anywhere in the digestive tract. A distinction is made between fatty fish (more than 8% fat), such as mackerel, sardines, salmon, or herring, and low-fat fish (less than 5% fat), such as cod, pollock, skate, or bream, and moderate fat fish, such as flounder, dab, and all flat fish.

Eggs (provided the whites are cooked) and dairy products are sources of high-quality proteins. However, not all cats are alike when it comes to lactose, the sugar in milk. Though kittens have sufficient lactase, the enzyme necessary for the digestion of milk, adult cats are sometimes lactose intolerant. However, yogurt, which does not contain lactose, is easily digested and can even help maintain

SERVING FOR A 4 KG ADULT CAT ON A MAINTENANCE DIET

QUANTITY PER DAY	INGREDIENTS
80 g	Meat - Beef containing 5% fat, lean fish
40 g	Green vegetables - Green beans, leeks, carrots, zucchini
80 g	Cooked white rice of cooked noodles
1 teaspoon	Soy, canola, or grape seed oil
As directed	Vitamin and mineral supplement (Ca/P = 2:1)

Suggested quantities are for a moderately active cat and should be adjusted to suit the unique needs of each individual cat.

healthy intestinal flora. Unfermented cheeses are also typically well tolerated.

Grains provide most of their energy in the form of starch. Starch must be well cooked, or it will be difficult to digest. Puffed grains for animal consumption are good energy sources. Rice must be well cooked and sticky.

Vegetables provide fiber, or bulk, which dilutes energy and speeds passage through the intestinal tract. Unfortunately, cats do not like vegetables, so they must be surreptitiously added to the diet. Well cooked, puréed potatoes are acceptable. Dry vegetables such as chickpeas and beans are not recommended because they cause gas.

The addition of soy, grape seed, or canola oil incorporates high-quality essential fatty acids (Omega 6 and 3). Peanut and olive oils are also acceptable. Rounding out the perfect meal, a vitamin supplement will fill in the gap if there happens to be a deficiency in the homemade diet, particularly calcium or fat-soluble vitamin deficiencies.

Commercial Foods

There are three types of commercial food: Wet, moist, and dry.

Canned foods
These foods, which contain 70 to 82% water, are sterilized in vacuum-packed cans. Primary ingredients are meat and meat by-products. These products are available in a number of different textures, including mousse, pâté, and chunks of various sizes. Cats seem to have distinct opinions as to which presentation they prefer. Canned foods also contain grains and vegetables that are cooked to perfection during the sterilization process. They provide all necessary vitamins and minerals.

Semi-moist foods
These foods, which contain 30 to 60% water, have a limited market. They are stabilized by adding preservatives such as glycerin, propy-

lene glycol, or ascorbic acid. This type of food is presented in the form of sausages or ground meat.

Dry food (kibble)
These foods contain 7 to 10% water and 90 to 93% nutritional dry matter. They are undoubtedly the wave of the future.

In the United States, where commercial foods originated, the pet food market is mature and sophisticated: 70% of all dogs and 60% of all cats are fed commercial foods. Meals prepared at home by the owner are increasingly rare. Of all commercial foods, dry represents 80% of sales for dogs and 65% of sales for cats.

In Europe, this market has existed for less than twenty years, but its growth curve indicates that European consumers are following the same trend. Currently, 41% of all dogs and 54.5% of all cats are fed commercial preparations.

Dry foods account for 54% of all dog food sales and 22% of all cat food sales in Europe.

Consumption has increased 4% by volume and 8% by value for dry dog food; 8% by volume and 16% by value for dry cat foods. Wet canned food sales have fallen 3% per year by volume and have stagnated by value.

In the dry food line, premium brand commercial cat foods are growing at a rate of more than 20% per year. Several factors can explain this new interest in dry, particularly premium brand, foods.

• **Performance to cost ratio:** There is a perfect balance between performance and cost. The nutritional makeup of the food is adapted to the specific needs of each animal, and it contains more than 90% directly nutritive dry matter. A given weight of dry food provides up to 4.7 times more nutrition than the equal weight of wet food (which is 70 to 80% water), and therefore cost (price per meal of 2 to 3 FF/day for a premium dry food) is as much as three times lower than for canned food, and considerably lower than for homemade preparations.

• **Recommended by experts:** In France, 90% of all breeders recommend dry food, and nearly 85% of sales at veterinary offices are for dry foods.

• **Practicality:** This is a strong argument for dry foods. Once the package is open, it can be stored longer than other types of food. Feeding the proper amount is simple and no preparation is required. Transporting and storing dry food is also simpler.

Available Commercial Foods and Feeding Guidelines

Physiological foods to nourish the animal

• Popular brands

This group includes all foods providing the average nutritional requirements of all cats. This type of food does not take into consideration the age or activity level of individual cats nor necessarily provide special formulas for different needs. Some are adequately digestible (80%) and have a satisfactory taste.

This is the type of food normally found in supermarkets. It is available in canned, semi-moist, and dry formulas.

• Premium brands

These are high-quality, complete foods formulated to meet the specific needs of cats of different ages and activity levels, cats with sensitive digestive systems, or spayed or neutered cats. These highly digestible foods (85 to 87%) provide optimal nutrition and are very appetizing.

Premium brands use excellent quality, hand-picked ingredients. Advanced manufacturing methods are applied and the production process closely monitored. Carefully selected packaging uses natural preservation methods. All of the above guarantees the stability of the ingredients used in the food.

Most premium brands are sold in the form of dry food. They are generally marketed through specialized centers, such as pet stores, veterinary offices, or feed stores.

Prescription Foods

This line of complete foods must be prescribed by a veterinarian. They are used to treat illness such as obesity, diabetes mellitus, chronic diarrhea, or renal failure.

Their taste is enhanced to make them more palatable to animals that typically become finicky eaters due to their health problems.

Digestibility varies depending on the desired results. They may be used to prevent the

---

CREATING A COMMERCIAL FOOD

Bringing a new food to market is a complex process. The first step is to define the specific physiological needs of the animal. Research at this stage is intense. Researchers draw on the many scientific articles published each year that shed new light on our understanding of cats' dietary requirements. This information is used to establish the specifications for the new food. Once the food has been formulated, a small quantity is produced for testing in animal research centers. Digestibility is measured and taste tests are carried out. Cats are given the choice between two types of food, and their preference is determined by weighing the remaining amounts of the two foods. The animals are observed and their stool analyzed. If the food meets the researchers' expectations, it is produced in small quantities at a pilot plant in preparation for the transition to commercial production. The foods are then tested by panels of breeders and veterinarians, then finally by consumers, before the product is released on the market.

occurrence of some clinical disorders and to improve the efficacy of concurrent medical treatment.

Prescription foods are sold exclusively in veterinary offices, which are also authorized to sell other premium brands. In France, more than 84% of all cat food sold by veterinarians is premium brand dry food.

(source Royal Canin)

COMMERCIAL FOODS: ADVANTAGES AND DISADVANTAGES

TYPE	ADVANTAGES	DISADVANTAGES
Dry (kibble)	Does not degrade after being open; more nutrition per pound; more economical than foods containing large quantities of water; easy to serve; practical in terms of serving and storage; stays fresh even when left in the bowl for the cat to feed freely.	Water needs to be made available; quality of food degrades if stored in a damp location.
Semi-moist	Highly appetizing; practical serving-size packaging.	Often must be stored in the refrigerator or freezer; degrades after package is opened; degrades if stored in a damp location; expensive preservation methods; some cats do not digest it well; contains additives.
Canned (wet)	Simple preservation method, durable packaging, highly appetizing.	Expensive (nutrients diluted in water); costs more on a per pound basis; heavy to transport and store; fairly long preparation time; not practical for free feeding; degrades after being opened.

Genetics

Each individual is characterized by a multitude of traits which, taken as a whole, form what is known in genetics as the phenotype. In cats, these traits involve morphology (size, shape of the head and body, eye shape, etc.) and coloring (of the coat and eyes), as well as physiological (frequency of heats, average litter size) and psychological aspects.

All these traits are determined by proteins which are either structural proteins or enzymes. Each protein is manufactured by the cells in an organism, thanks to a gene. All the genes are contained in the nucleus of each cell as long chains of DNA (deoxyribonucleic acid) that form the chromosomes.

In each cell of the so-called "higher" life forms, including the cat, all chromosomes—and therefore all genes—exist in duplicate. Cats have nineteen pairs of identical chromosomes, for a total of thirty-eight chromosomes. Actually, this is completely true only of female cats, since one pair of chromosomes—the sex-determining chromosomes—is special. Female cats have two identical X chromosomes, whereas males have two different sex-determining chromosomes: one X chromosome and one Y chromosome. It is the Y chromosome that causes an embryo to develop as a male.

At puberty, a cat's body manufactures reproductive cells, or gametes (eggs in the female and sperm in the male). Unlike other cells, the gametes contain only one copy of each pair of chromosomes, or one copy of each of the genes that the parent carries in duplicate. In fertilization, the sperm and egg unite to produce one cell, the future kitten, that now contains a full thirty-eight chromosomes: nineteen from the mother and nineteen from the father. In this way, parents transmit half their gene pool to their offspring. The offspring will have a phenotype resulting from the combination of all the genes provided by the two parents, and thus a certain resemblance to their parents.

One of the pleasures and objectives of pure-bred cat breeders is to improve the genetic makeup of their animals.

To this end, breeders must determine which genes are carried by all individuals of a given breed and choose for reproduction the individuals with the most interesting genes. This

Female   Male

process is known as selection. Next, the breeder crosses individuals that complement each other in terms of the genes they carry, in order to obtain offspring that improve upon the aesthetic qualities of the breed. This is known as logical mating. The science that makes this possible is called genetics.

Now, let us look at how breeders work and how genetics works. We have chosen to present these topics in an extremely simplified manner that will be easy for everyone to understand:

• We will confine ourselves to the genes that determine hair length and coat color;

• We will turn the genetics of feline coat color into a card game!

Readers who wish to see how the terms used here correspond to the terms used in genetics may refer to the following table.

How Sex is Determined

As an introduction to how the card game works, let us apply this analogy to the determination of sex in kittens. In each cell of her body, the female cat holds two X cards (with an X chromosome), so each of the eggs her body manufactures will contain one of these two X cards. In each of his cells, the male cat holds one X card and one Y card. He will therefore produce sperm containing either an X card or a Y card. During fertilization, either the egg encounters a sperm with an X card, and the kitten will be female, or the egg encounters a sperm with a Y card, and the kitten will be male. The Punnet square is a simple representation of all the possible crosses between sperm and egg. It indicates that ultimately, half the offspring will be female and half will be male.

Element of the Card Game	Corresponding Term in Genetics
A series of cards	A locus
One card in a series	An allelic gene (or simply an allele)
A strong card	A dominant allele
A weak card	A recessive allele
Two cards of equal strength	Two co-dominant alleles
The card in a series that is most common in cats	The wild-type allele
The card(s) in a series that are fairly rare in cats	The mutant-type allele(s)
The combination of all cards held by a cat	The cat's genotype

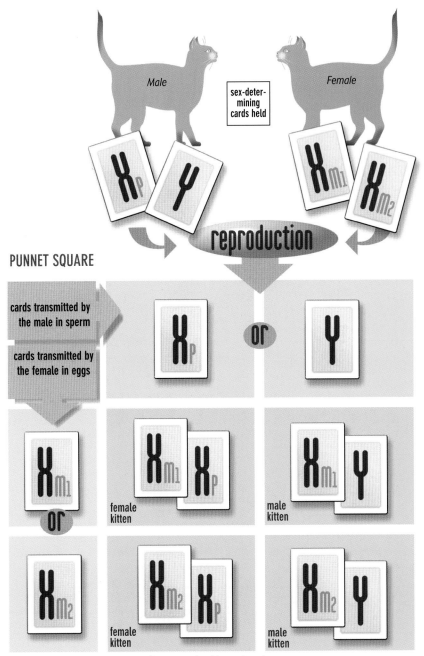

P = paternal   M = maternal

The Card Game and Coat Color

Now let us apply the card game to coat color and hair length in cats. Based on current knowledge in genetics, this game would include twenty-five cards arranged in eleven series.

- eight series of two cards each (A, B, Ch, D, I, L, S, and W series)
- three series of three cards each (C, T, and O series)

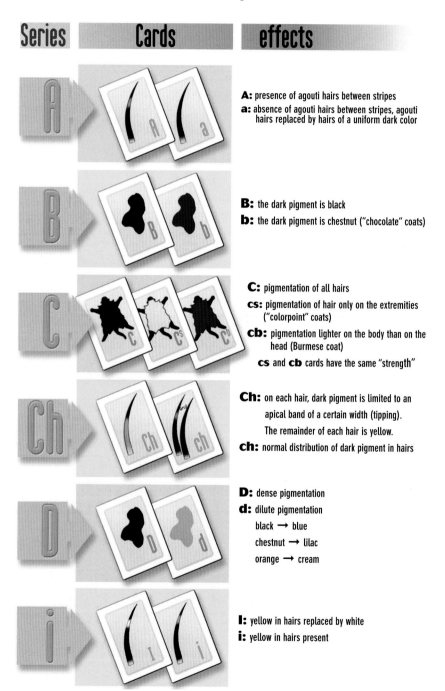

The Card Game of Coat Color and Hair Length in Cats

Series	Cards	effects

A: presence of agouti hairs between stripes
a: absence of agouti hairs between stripes, agouti hairs replaced by hairs of a uniform dark color

B: the dark pigment is black
b: the dark pigment is chestnut ("chocolate" coats)

C: pigmentation of all hairs
cs: pigmentation of hair only on the extremities ("colorpoint" coats)
cb: pigmentation lighter on the body than on the head (Burmese coat)
    cs and **cb** cards have the same "strength"

Ch: on each hair, dark pigment is limited to an apical band of a certain width (tipping). The remainder of each hair is yellow.
ch: normal distribution of dark pigment in hairs

D: dense pigmentation
d: dilute pigmentation
    black → blue
    chestnut → lilac
    orange → cream

I: yellow in hairs replaced by white
i: yellow in hairs present

Note that the O series is a bit special, since it is located on the sex-determining X chromosome. Thus, this series contains the following cards: XO, Xo, and Y. Similarly, the combined effects of the A and T series require some explanation; see the illustrations on the next page.

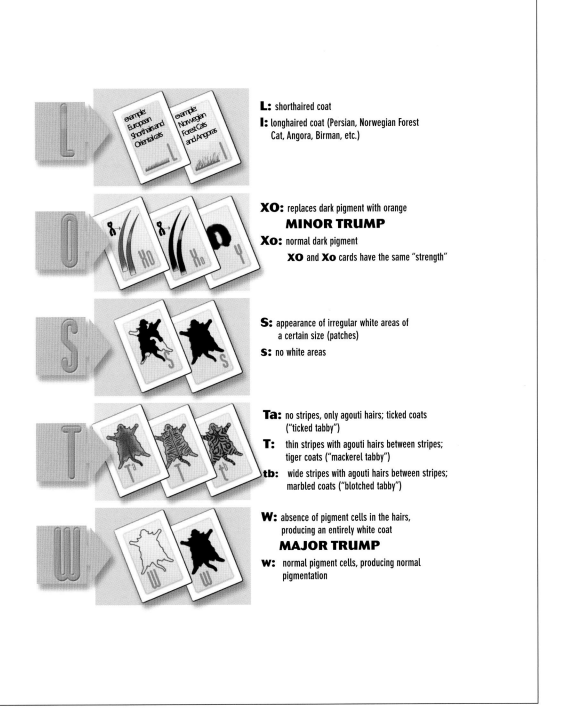

L: shorthaired coat

l: longhaired coat (Persian, Norwegian Forest Cat, Angora, Birman, etc.)

XO: replaces dark pigment with orange
MINOR TRUMP

Xo: normal dark pigment
    XO and **Xo** cards have the same "strength"

S: appearance of irregular white areas of a certain size (patches)

s: no white areas

Ta: no stripes, only agouti hairs; ticked coats ("ticked tabby")

T: thin stripes with agouti hairs between stripes; tiger coats ("mackerel tabby")

tb: wide stripes with agouti hairs between stripes; marbled coats ("blotched tabby")

W: absence of pigment cells in the hairs, producing an entirely white coat
MAJOR TRUMP

w: normal pigment cells, producing normal pigmentation

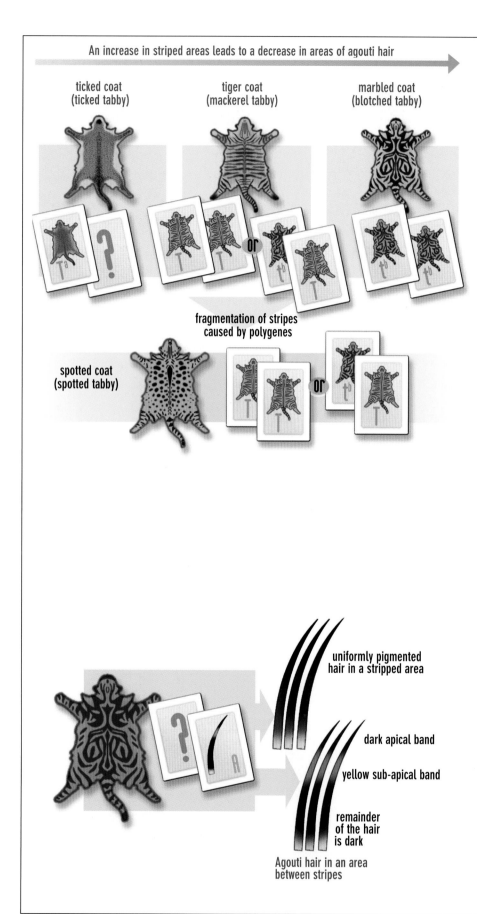

An increase in striped areas leads to a decrease in areas of agouti hair

ticked coat
(ticked tabby)

tiger coat
(mackerel tabby)

marbled coat
(blotched tabby)

fragmentation of stripes
caused by polygenes

spotted coat
(spotted tabby)

uniformly pigmented
hair in a stripped area

dark apical band

yellow sub-apical band

remainder
of the hair
is dark

Agouti hair in an area
between stripes

TABBY AND SELF VARIETIES

The cards in the A and T series determine self-colored coats and the various striped patterns known as tabby coats. Tabby coats correspond to the most common phenotype of mixed breed cats, as well as that of the Eurasian wild cat. Tabby coats contain two types of hair. The hair in the stripes is uniformly colored by dark pigment. The hairs between the stripes are of the "agouti" type, that is, they have a sub-apical band of yellow pigment that interrupts the dark pigment; breeders call this "ticking." The juxtaposition of agouti hairs produces the yellowish-chestnut coloring of areas between stripes that is typical of tabby cats. The A card is what determines the existence of agouti hairs. A mutation in the domestic cat has produced a weak a card that erases the yellow sub-apical band on agouti hairs. Thus, a self-colored black cat actually has a coat consisting of black stripes (uniformly colored "normal" hairs) and areas between stripes that are also black, since they consist of mutant agouti hairs that have lost their yellow band.

Cards in the T series define the shape and coverage of stripes with relation to agouti hairs. The T card, considered "wild," produces the thin striping of so-called tiger coats (mackerel tabby for the British). Two mutations have produced two new T series cards. One, the tb card, is weak and produces the wide stripes of marbled coats (blotched tabby). The other mutant card, Ta, is stronger than the T card and erases the stripes. The resulting coat contains only agouti hairs and is called "ticked" (ticked tabby). This coat is found in the Abyssinian and Singapura. Note that a self-colored cat also holds T cards. This means that its coat actually has one of the three possible types of tabby markings, but we cannot tell which, except by observing what it transmits to its offspring.

400

What are the ground rules of the feline coat color game?

1 – Each cell in a cat's body holds two cards from each series.

2 – To make a gamete, take one card at random from each series in the parent's set of cards.

3 – To make a kitten, randomly select one set of cards for the sperm from among all the sets potentially produced by the male, and combine them with one set of cards for the egg from among all the sets potentially produced by the female. These random combinations are represented in a Punnet square.

4 – In some series, the cards have different "strengths." Place the stronger card on top of the weaker card. The names of stronger cards are in uppercase letters, and the names of weaker cards are in lowercase letters. For example, in the L series, the cat will have short hair if it holds two L cards or one L card and one l card. In the latter case, the stronger L card imposes its effect. The cat will have long hair only if it holds two weak l cards.

In other series, all the cards are equal in strength. The combination of two equal cards produces an effect that is intermediate to the effect of each card taken separately. For example, in the O series, the XO card produces orange pigmentation, while the Xo card produces non-orange pigmentation. The combination XO Xo produces a coat with a juxtaposition of patches of orange hairs and patches of non-orange hairs. This is what breeders call a "tortoiseshell" coat (see Part 1, Section 3). Similarly, in the C series, the combination of a cs card and a cb card produces a special coat corresponding to that of the Tonkinese breed.

5 – Finally, as in many card games, there are trump cards, or cards that are stronger than those in other series. In our game, the O series acts like a minor trump. The XO card in this

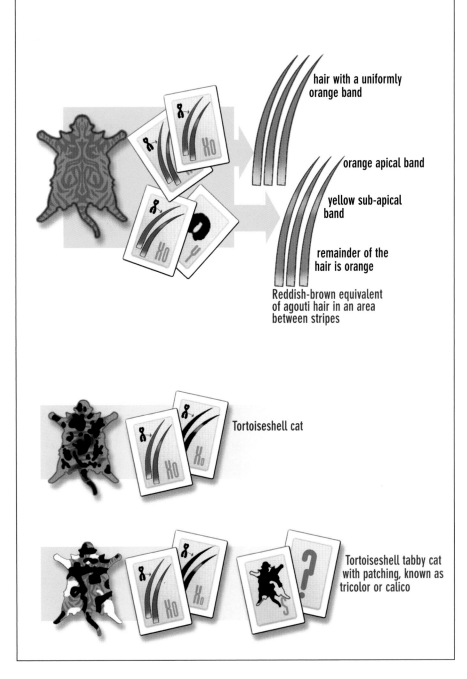

REDDISH BROWN CATS AND TORTOISESHELL CATS

A very special mutation in cats has produced an O card for a gene located on the sex-determining X chromosome. The O card turns all the dark pigment in the hair into an intense orange pigment. Thus, a reddish-brown tabby cat has a coat consisting on the one hand of stripes of entirely orange hairs (the equivalent of uniformly dark-colored hairs in tabby cats that are not reddish-brown), and on the other hand of areas between stripes consisting of orange hairs with a yellow sub-apical band (the equivalent of agouti hairs). This reddish-brown coat is exclusive to XOY males and XOXO females. Females with XOXo cards have a special coat pattern called tortoiseshell tabby (tortie tabby for the British). This coat is a mosaic of patches of the reddish-brown tabby cat type and patches of the "normal" tabby cat type. If the female also holds the S card that produces white patches, then the coat is called tricolor or calico.

hair with a uniformly orange band

orange apical band

yellow sub-apical band

remainder of the hair is orange

Reddish-brown equivalent of agouti hair in an area between stripes

Tortoiseshell cat

Tortoiseshell tabby cat with patching, known as tricolor or calico

series produces orange pigmentation that masks the effect of B series cards. In the W series, the W card is a major trump, since it masks the effects of all the cards in other series except those in the L series.

This major trump card status is easy to understand, to the extent that since the W card erases melanocytes (the cells that synthesize pigment), a cat that holds a W card will be all white due to the absence of pigment. None of the effects of the other cards acting on pigment are visible, given the lack of pigment.

How can you tell which cards potential parents hold?

We will use three examples to illustrate this technique.

Example 1:
The cat's phenotype is solid blue with short hair. For all traits determined by weak cards, the cat must hold two weak cards. Thus, in this case, we can predict that this cat must hold two a cards (since it has no agouti hairs and therefore solid coloring), two ch cards, and two i cards (since the hairs have no tipping or partial decoloration), two d cards (because blue is a dilution of black), two s cards (since there are no white patches), and

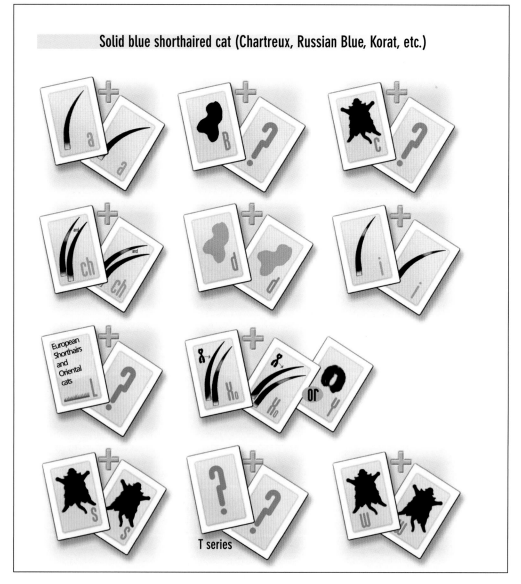

Solid blue shorthaired cat (Chartreux, Russian Blue, Korat, etc.)

two w cards (since melanocytes are present). In terms of the O series, if the cat is male, it must hold one Y card and one Xo card (since it is not reddish-brown), and if it is female, it must hold two Xo cards (since it is neither reddish-brown nor tortoiseshell). For traits determined by strong cards, the cat must hold at least one corresponding strong card, with the other card in the series being unknown, either strong or weak. The cat in our example thus holds at least one L card (since it has short hair), one B card (since its basic pigment is black and not chestnut), and one C card (since it is neither colorpoint nor shaded like a Burmese). Finally, we cannot tell which T series cards the cat holds, since the striped markings are not visible. The various unknowns cannot be ascertained without additional information on the coat color of the cat's parents and/or offspring.

Example 2:
The animal is longhaired, with tortoiseshell and blotched tabby markings (dark stripes are present). Using the same reasoning as above, we can predict that this cat must hold two i, ch, l, s, tb (since the stripes are wide), and w cards. It must also hold at least one A, B, C, and D card. Finally, since it is a tortoiseshell, it must hold one XO card and one Xo card. In passing, we know that this type of coat is specific to females.

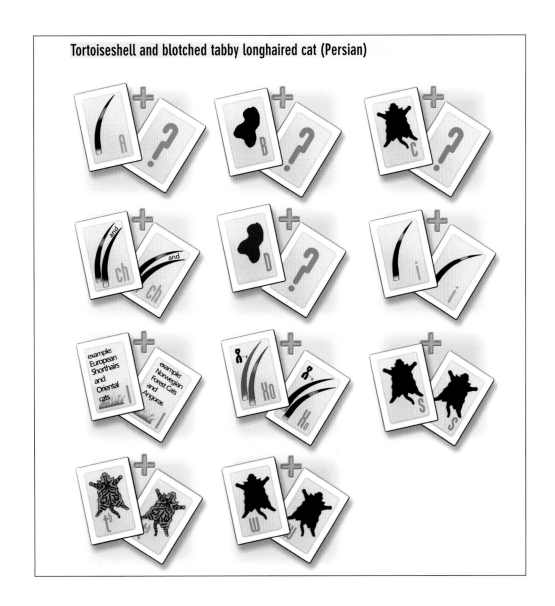

Tortoiseshell and blotched tabby longhaired cat (Persian)

Example 3:

The final example is a shorthaired variety of cat called a "silver blotched tabby." We can tell it is different from the traditional striped cat because the areas between the stripes are light-colored and silvery in appearance, rather than brownish-yellow.

This is because the agouti hairs between the stripes have undergone a partial decoloration affecting the yellow sub-apical band. From this we can deduce that this cat holds at least one strong I card.

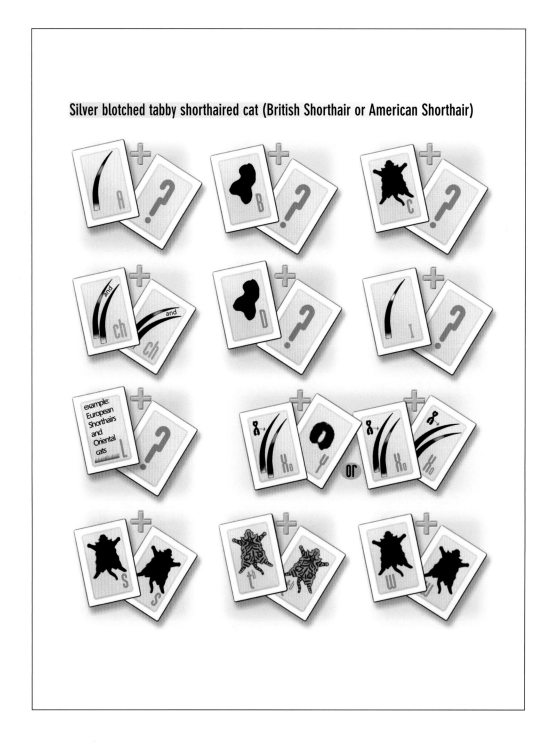

Silver blotched tabby shorthaired cat (British Shorthair or American Shorthair)

How can we predict what types of kittens will be produced from crosses between known parents?

Case 1: What types of kittens will be produced by crossing a reddish-brown tom with a tortoiseshell queen?

To simplify the game and our predictions, it is important that we limit the question to the series of cards that are interesting in this case.

Here, what interests us most are the O series cards held by each parent. These cards are XO and Y for the father, and XO and Xo for the mother. The sperm produced by the father will have either an XO card or a Y card. The eggs produced by the mother will have either an XO card or an Xo card. The various kittens that will result from the random combination of these eggs and sperm appear in the Punnet square below. Note that if a sufficient number of kittens are produced, half of them will be

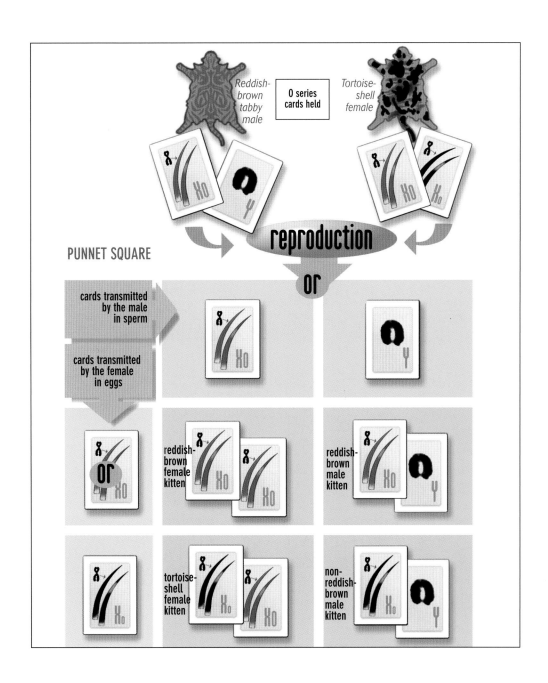

reddish-brown (male and female), one-fourth will be non-reddish-brown males (either tabby or self-colored, depending on the parents' cards in the other series), and one-fourth will be tortoiseshell females. This cross will therefore produce quite a range of offspring!

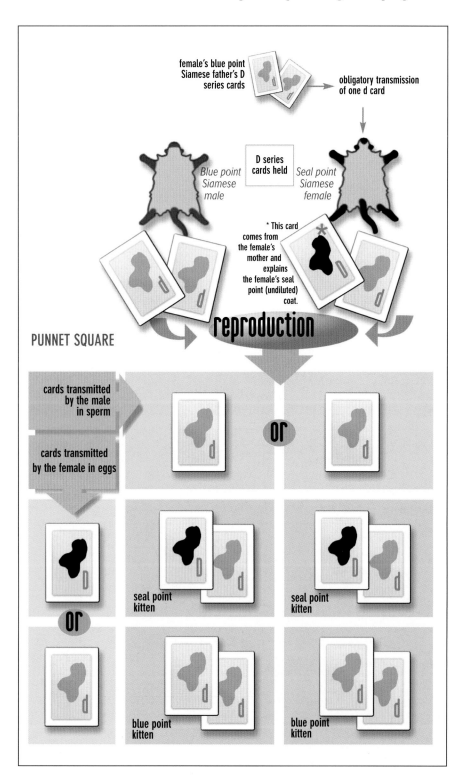

female's blue point Siamese father's D series cards

obligatory transmission of one d card

D series cards held

Blue point Siamese male

Seal point Siamese female

* This card comes from the female's mother and explains the female's seal point (undiluted) coat.

reproduction

PUNNET SQUARE

cards transmitted by the male in sperm

cards transmitted by the female in eggs

or

or

seal point kitten

seal point kitten

blue point kitten

blue point kitten

Case 2: What would be the result of crossing two Siamese cats: a blue point tom and a seal point queen from a blue point father?

In this case, we do not consider the C series, since both parents are Siamese. The Siamese (colorpoint) pattern is determined by the weak cs card, so each parent must hold two cs cards and can therefore transmit only cs cards to its offspring. In other words, all the kittens will be Siamese.

However, the D series is very interesting. The blue coloring of the blue point variety is a dilution of black pigment, and the dilution card d is a weak card. Thus, the tom must hold two d cards. As for the queen, she is black in appearance (or "seal point," to use the accepted term), so she must hold at least one D card (since dilution is absent). However, since her father was blue point and therefore held two d cards, he must have transmitted one d card to her. Thus, we know exactly which two D series cards the queen in this cross must hold. She is said to be a "carrier" of dilution.

The Punnet square reveals the various types of kittens we would obtain: 50% seal point Siamese kittens (with black extremities) and 50% blue point Siamese kittens (with blue extremities).

Both a Conclusion and an Introduction

This brief overview of feline genetics is enough to show how breeders can select (choose) the parents they find interesting in terms of appearance (coat color and hair length) and then cross them in a logical manner to obtain kittens of the varieties they desire.

The breeder might focus on maintaining the range of coat colors that is traditional in a particular breed. But the breeder can also use these techniques to introduce a new coat color that did not exist previously in a breed. For example, beginning in the 1930s, breeders launched breeding programs aimed at introducing the cs card into the Persian breed. The Siamese cat provided this cs card. After extensive efforts focused on recovering the typical Persian morphology, which was significantly modified by the Siamese morphology genes transmitted with the cs card, breeders arrived at the magnificent colorpoint Persians we can now admire in cat shows.

This same technique is used to create new breeds from a spontaneous mutation. A spontaneous mutation is actually a new card that appears in the game. For example, in 1981 a female cat with ears curled back over the head was discovered in the United States. This was a spontaneous mutation determined by a strong card.

In this manner, a new series of cards was added to the game: the Cu series determining ear curl. This series includes a weak cu card that determines "normal" ears and a strong Cu card that determines the new, curled type of ears. Next, through selection and logical mating, breeders produced enough cats with the Cu card that a new breed of cat, the American Curl, was recognized.

Not all spontaneous mutations are harmless to a cat's health. Some cause hereditary genetic diseases. In this case, breeding is aimed at

PRIMARY CONGENITAL AND HEREDITARY CONDITIONS DESCRIBED IN PUREBRED CATS		
(modified based on Ph. Bossé, 1994)		
Breed	**Affected functions or organs**	**Affections**
Abyssinian	Kidneys	Renal amyloidosis
	Eyes	Retinal atrophy
	Nervous system	Lysosomal accumulation neuropathy
	Thyroid	Hypothyroidism
Burmese	Skeleton	Craniofacial deformities, dorsoventral flattening
	Muscles	Periodic muscle weakness
Korat	Nervous system	Lysosomal accumulation neuropathy
Manx	Vertebral skeleton	Sacrococcygeal hyopoplasia, spina bifida, incontinence, locomotor ailments
Persian	Kidneys	Polycystic kidney
	Eyes	Corneal sequestration, photophobia, hypopigmentation, cataracts
	Nervous system	Lysosomal accumulation neuropathy
	Abdomen	Peritoneopericardial defect
Cornish Rex	Abdomen	Umbilical hernia
	Thymus (?)	Wasting syndrome
Devon Rex	Skeleton	Patellar luxation
	Coagulation	Hemorrhagic ailments
	Muscles	Respiratory muscle degeneration
Scottish Fold	Skeleton	Limb and tail defects
Siamese	Skeleton	Craniofacial defects (hydrocephalus, cleft palate), knotted tail
	Nervous system	Lysosomal accumulation neuropathy
	Eyes	Retinal degeneration, strabismus
	Skin	Hypotrichosis

identifying the individuals that carry bad cards and not using them to renew the breed.

To conclude, we must mention that the simple reasoning presented here applies only to traits determined by single genes with a significant effect, or major genes. This is the case for the majority of coat color traits and for a certain number of specific morphological traits (absence of tail, folded ears, short legs, etc.). This is not true for so-called quantitative traits that affect morphology, physiology, and psychology. The current view is that these traits are produced by a combination of many polygenes, or genes that each have a very slight effect. Selective breeding based on polygenic traits is more delicate and complex than that based on traits determined by a single gene. This is why we did not broach the subject in this short presentation. Still, this concept is extremely important in establishing and maintaining many of the features that characterize each feline breed and are recorded in its respective standard. Note that some pigmentation traits, although determined essentially by the major genes described above, are also influenced by polygenes. This is true of irregular white spots (or patches), in particular. This explains why breeders have such difficulty establishing these traits definitively.

COATS WITH WHITE PATCHES

In cats, the irregular white spots called patches are determined by a mutation that has produced a strong card S. However, the extent of white patches is significantly modified by a whole set of polygenes, or genes that each have a slight effect individually. Of course, all intermediate forms (including harlequin and bicolor van varieties) are based on the polygenes carried by each individual. It is very difficult, even impossible, to establish a breed with a specific pattern of white patches. This is true especially of the Birman, whose famous white-gloved paws are actually minimal patches that vary from one animal to the next, based on polygenes. To make matters worse, a "well-gloved" cat will not necessarily produce offspring that are all well-gloved.

Let us mention in passing that the Birman also holds two cs cards that superimpose a color-point coat on its glove markings.

Preventive Medicine

Microscopic ear mites (Otodectes cynotis) responsible for otitis externa in carnivores

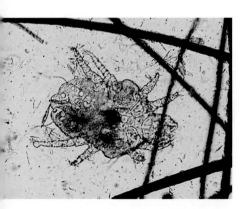

Microscopic mites (Cheyletiella blakei) responsible for cheyletiellosis in cats

Parasites and External Fungi

There are many and varied parasites and fungi responsible for skin disorders in cats. Mites are microscopic animals responsible for mange or itching. Insects such as fleas and lice can be found in a cat's coat. They cause conditions called respectively pulicosis (flea infestation) and pediculosis (louse infestation).

Dermatophytes are microscopic filamentous fungi that subsist on the keratin in hair or on the surface of the skin. They are the agents responsible for ringworm.

Some of the pathogenic agents described here can be transmitted to humans. Cheyletiella mites produce a small scabby rash on the body and pruritis (itching). Itching may be so intense that a visit to a dermatologist is necessary. In this case, based on the lesions, the physician may recommend that the owner take his cat to a veterinarian to treat the cat for parasites.

Fleas found on domestic animals occasionally get the taste for human blood. Finally, dermatophytes, particularly the species common to cats, are easily transmitted to humans. They produce annular lesions, called tinea circinata, on glabrous (smooth and bare) skin, most often on the forearms, face, or neck. Unlike the symptoms observed in the animal, inflammation and itching in humans can be extreme.

Of all feline skin disorders, pulicosis (flea infestation) and ringworm merit particular attention. These disorders are very common and often difficult or impossible to prevent, particularly when we consider that the cat is not an isolated animal, but part of a community of cats.

Flea Infestation (Pulicosis)

Ctenocephalides felis (cat flea) is not finicky. This flea will feed on a wide variety of mammals, including cats, dogs, herbivores, and humans. Many cats are not sensitive to flea bites. However, some cats develop allergic reactions to flea bites and the symptoms of dermatitis appear as a result. This allergic reaction presents in the form of miliary dermatitis, a red, crusty rash on the back and around the neck. The skin takes on a sandy appearance. Since the infected animal scratches incessantly, there is a danger that it might scratch and injure itself.

Some animals respond to the irritation caused by the fleas by constantly cleaning and licking themselves. This may result in hairloss on the abdomen, thighs, flanks, or tail. Fleas also carry diseases. They transmit tapeworms and the bacteria responsible for cat-scratch disease.

Research carried out over the last decade studying the biology of cat fleas has given us insight into their life cycle. Full understanding of this life cycle is required if we are to effectively prevent infestation.

We now know that there are a number of misconceptions regarding cat fleas. The first is that adult fleas do not remain on the cat, but only stop in for a meal. In fact, adult fleas spend their entire life on the same animal. Only a very small number of fleas on a cat will move to other nearby domestic animals. Therefore, the risk of contamination from other animals in the veterinarian's waiting room or at a cat show is almost zero.

Adult fleas reproduce rapidly. Each female is capable of laying up to fifty eggs per day for a period of several weeks. These white, ovoid eggs are 0.5 mm long. They do not attach to the animal, and therefore fall to the floor as the animal moves about. Under favorable temperature and humidity conditions, the eggs hatch in several days, revealing wormlike larvae several millimeters in length. These larvae are not parasites.

They feed on the organic debris found in their surroundings, particularly adult flea feces. Larvae love humidity, but dislike light. At the end of the larval stage (a few days to one month), each larva weaves a cocoon around itself. Adult fleas emerge a few days later, bringing the metamorphosis cycle to a close. If conditions are favorable (if animals are present in the environment), the adult emerges immediately. If no animals are present, the adult fleas are able to survive in their cocoon for several months.
The adult fleas that remain in the cocoon will immediately take advantage of a host if it passes by. Fleas that are still in their protective cocoon are relatively unaffected by insecticides. Once they emerge, the adult fleas actively search for a host.

In conclusion, it is important to remember that adult fleas are parasites, but in their immature forms, they live freely in the environment. The life cycle of fleas is very short (three weeks is often sufficient). Recently emerged fleas pose the greatest risk, not fleas already happily inhabiting another host.

Eliminating Fleas

Effective control requires treating fleas on the body of the cat as well as the physical surroundings. Products used to prevent flea infestation must meet two criteria: They must take effect immediately and be long-acting (residual activity). Fleas must be eliminated before they eat their first meal of blood and most especially before they reproduce and start laying eggs. A flea feeds within minutes after landing on an animal and is capable of laying eggs within one day. Insecticides such as thrinoides, fipronil, or amidacloprid are effective immediately and have satisfactory residual activity. All of these products can be used in formulas that can be applied in just one spot, a method particularly suited to cats. Once a small amount of the product is applied to the skin (typically between the shoulders), it spreads to the rest of the body within one day.

With this type of treatment, a cat is protected for a period of one month. Flea collars currently available on the market only partially control fleas, since they do not prevent infestation in the first place. To eliminate fleas in a cat's environment, it is first necessary to identify all potentially infested areas. Not only should a cat's living area, outside territory and resting areas be considered, but also other animals (other cats, and possibly dogs) with which the cat will come into contact. It is necessary to ensure as much as possible that all animals encountered by the cat are treated on a regular basis. This is, of course, impossible if your cat has the habit of socializing with strays.

Formulations used in living areas typically combine an insecticide with a growth regulator, which interferes with the normal development of immature fleas. Foggers (flea "bombs") treat a large area. Sprays should be used as a supplement to foggers in order to treat hard-

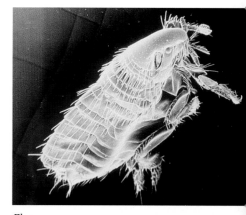

Flea
(Source - Mérial Laboratories)

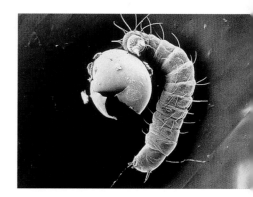

Hatching flea
(Source - Mérial Laboratories)

to-reach areas, such as under furniture. Lufeneron is an insect growth regulator administered orally once a month or injected once every six months. The product enters the bloodstream.

Once an adult flea ingests the chemical, the lufeneron interrupts the development cycle. Eggs do not hatch or larvae die. One of the advantages of this product is that it has a secondary effect of controlling fleas in the environment, though it is only administered to the cat carrying adult fleas.

Ringworm

A common skin disorder in cats is dermatophytosis, or ringworm, caused by the dermatophyte *Microsporum canis*. Hairs infested by this parasite are literally consumed from the inside out. They become very fragile and break off. The typically well-defined bald patches that appear normally start on the head and then spread outward to the rest of the body.

The infection may resolve itself spontaneously within a few weeks, but other bald patches are likely to appear. In longhair breeds, hairloss may be distributed throughout the coat and only a slight thinning in certain areas may be noted. Ringworm is highly contagious. Fragments of infested hairs transmit the parasite to healthy animals.

These infectious agents are present both on animals showing signs of ringworm as well as in the environment. Direct contact is not necessary. A cat can easily contract the parasite in a dirty environment; from a carpet where a contaminated cat lay down several days earlier, a carrier used to transport a contaminated animal, a brush, or a clipper.

The infectious agents are very resistant. It is believed that *Microsporum canis* can survive for several months (perhaps up to a year) in the external environment. Another unique aspect

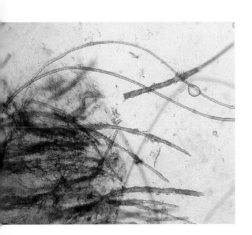

Hairs of a cat infected with ringworm fungi.

of this fungus is its lack of specificity. *Microsporum canis* prefers cats as hosts, but it is also responsible for ringworm in rabbits, dogs, rodents, primates (including humans), and even herbivores. Infected cats are treated with an oral or topical antifungal medication. Treatment must be continued for at least six weeks.

There are few methods for preventing ringworm. A vaccine is currently available in the United States, but its effectiveness remains disputed. Unlike flea treatments, there are no long-acting antifungal treatments that can be applied once a month as a preventive measure. Currently, the best way to protect a cat is to keep her away from infected animals. Though this may appear simple, it is, in fact, quite difficult.

Cats can easily come into contact with strays, which benefit from no health care and often carry dermatophytes. Moreover, it is often difficult to identify cats that may be carrying ringworm fungi, and which are therefore contagious, since some exhibit no symptoms.

Cat shows or any other feline gathering should be considered at-risk areas. To reduce the chances of infection, a topical antifungal treatment should be applied to all cats prior to a show. In a cattery, normal sanitation guidelines should be strictly followed when a new cat is introduced. The newcomer should be quarantined until its health status can be determined. Examination under a Wood's light and a fungal culture will determine if the cat presents a danger to the other residents.

Finally, since ringworm can be transmitted in a dirty environment, carpets, rugs, and upholstery should be vacuumed regularly to eliminate the majority of the dermatophytes. Special solutions and fumigants are also available from veterinarians. These can be used to treat contaminated areas.

Disease	Responsible Agent	Frequency	Transmission	Danger to Humans
Otisis externa	Mites (Otodectes cynotis)	++ (young cats)	Direct (cat to cat)	None
Mange	Mites (Notoedres cati)	Very rare	Direct (cat to cat)	+ (scabies)
Cheyletiellosis	Mites (Cheyletiella blakei)	+	Direct (cat to cat) or from external environment	++ (scabies)
Pulicosis	Fleas (Ctenocephalides felis)	+++	Mostly indirect from a contaminated environment	+ (flea bites)
Pediculosis	Lice (Felicola subrostratus)	+ (young cats)	Direct (cat to cat)	None
Ringworm	Dermatophytes	+++	Direct or indirect from a contaminated environment	++ (ringworm)

Internal Parasites

In addition to external infestations by external parasites such as fleas, lice, and ticks, cats of any age, young and old alike, are susceptible to internal parasitic infestations by worms (helminths) or microbes called protozoa.

It is difficult to determine the frequency of helminths (worms). Studies have produced widely varying results. Cats living in rural areas often have more worms than urban cats. The same is true of indoor/outdoor cats, as compared to indoor cats only. Finally, young cats are more susceptible than adult cats. At-risk cats can be divided into two groups: kittens, from birth to ten months of age; and indoor/outdoor cats living in rural or urban areas (residential areas with yards).

A 1996 study showed that on average one in five cats has worms. This number climbs to one in three in kittens under one year of age.

The primary parasitic worms in cats are ascarids, or roundworms (*Toxocara cati*), anky-lostoma, or hookworms, and some tapeworms, including *Dipylidium*.

Ascarids

Toxocara cati is a roundworm (nematode) 4 to 8 cm in length. It occurs in the small intestine of a cat and forms balls that can cause intestinal irritation or obstruction. Cats can become infected either by ingesting the eggs of the parasites or while nursing in the first ten days following birth.

Infected cats harbor the larvae in their body tissues, including muscle and mammary, their entire lives. For some reason, the larvae become reactivated toward the end of gestation, producing adult intestinal ascarids. Some larvae migrate to the mammary glands where they are carried to the kittens in the milk. Queens also contaminate their environment with the ascarid eggs passed in their feces, another way for the kittens to be infected.

The microscopic eggs, which are passed in large quantities in the cat's feces, are very resis-

Parasite	Epidemiological Information
Ollulanus tricuspis	Strongyloid parasite of the stomach. Rare.
Ackylostoma tubaeformis	Ancylostoma parasite of the duodenum, particularly common in warm climates. Cats become infected by ingesting the larvae or by the larvae penetrating the skin.
Uncimaria stenocephala	Common ancylostoma in dogs. Present in France.
Toxocara cati	Ascarid parasite of the duodenum. Very common in young cats (to the age of one year).
Toxascaris leonina	Ascarid found in adult cats that hunt mice, primarily in rural areas.
Dipylidium caninum	Most frequently observed tenia in cats living in cities or in countryside. Follow the ingestion of fleas.

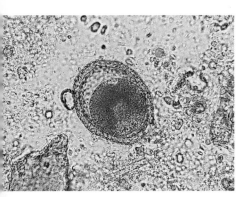

Toxocara cati

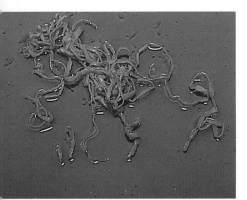

Dipylidium caninum

tant to cold and dry conditions, as well as traditional disinfectants. In fact, they can survive for more than three years on the ground.

After being ingested, the larvae migrate throughout the cat's body, passing through the liver and lungs before returning to the intestine where they develop to adulthood. This cycle lasts approximately six weeks.

Ascarid infections often produce dramatic symptoms. Kittens may have abdominal swelling or experience bouts of diarrhea. Infection may also be associated with poor growth (rickets and dry, dull coat). Adult worms may be found in the vomitus of infected cats. Untreated, it can result in death by peritonitis.

Tapeworms

Dipylidium caninum is a segmented tapeworm (cestode). Fleas carry the larvae of this parasite. Cat's ingest the infected fleas while grooming. Three weeks later, adult worms appear in the intestinal tract. Round or oval shaped segments are expelled with the stool. They can often be seen around the anus or on the cat's fur. These whitish segments are 5 to 6 mm in length and mobile when fresh. After they dry out, they resemble small grains of rice. Owners often think they are seeing pinworms, but this parasite does not exist in cats.

Other worms may also infect cats, appearing after a cat eats prey, particularly mice. These types of worms are most often seen in rural areas.

Worm infestation normally does not cause serious illness in cats, though it can result in malformations or a dull coat, as well as anal pruritis (itching) after segments are expelled.

Preventing Worm Infestation

It is important to limit the risk of infection from the time a kitten is born.

- Queens should be treated with a dewormer fifteen days prior to and one month following delivery.

- Kittens should be treated at the ages of one, three, and six months.

- Cats should then be treated with a dewormer twice per year.

- If toxocarosis is diagnosed within the cattery, kittens should be treated once per month until the age of six months.

Many dewormer treatments are currently on the market. They are available in paste or pill form. The choice is determined by the type of parasite to be eliminated and ease of administration.

In addition to medications, the cat's environment should be thoroughly cleaned to remove eggs. All cats should be monitored and the queens treated with a dewormer.

The risk of Dipylidium infection can be reduced by ridding living areas of fleas. Deworming should only be done if the cat is passing worm segments, is a regular hunter, or is infested with fleas.

Keep in mind that Toxocara cati, like ascarids in dogs (Toxocara canis), can be transmitted to humans and cause serious illness (zoonoses). This may occur if the owner or breeder ingests the larval eggs present in the environment.

Common Protozoa

Even very young cats can be infected with digestive parasites other than worms. Two categories of protozoa are observed in cats: Giardia and coccidia. These protozoa occur as frequently as worms and infect 30 to 60% of all kittens in catteries, compared to 5 to 20% of kittens in private homes.

When the Giardia protozoa multiply, they irritate the intestinal lining (enteritis) and inhibit digestion and absorption, resulting in weight loss and chronic diarrhea. Young and old cats alike are vulnerable to Giardia. Cysts are expelled with fecal matter, the source of contamination of other individuals.

After a confirmed diagnosis, Giardiasis may be treated with drugs such as metronidazole or fenbendazole.

There are many coccidian protozoa found in cats. The most common are Isospora, which cause acute enteritis in young cats between the ages of one and six months. Cat are infected when they ingest the oocysts present on the ground. Another method of infection, though less common, is ingestion of rodents (particularly mice).

Other coccidian protozoa are ingested when cats eat their prey. These include Besnoitia, hammondia, and Toxoplasma gondii. Toxoplasma gondii, the protozoa responsible

DEWORMER TREATMENTS

Active Ingredient	Product Name	Form	Worms Treated
Piperazine	Ascaperazine®	Syrup	Ascarids
Pyrantel	Strongid®	Oral compound	Ascarids, ancylostoma
Oxibendazole + Niclosamide	Vitaminthe®	Oral compound	Ascarids, ancylostoma, *Taeina* and *Dipylidium* (minimal dose required for satisfactory effectiveness on *Dipylidium*)
Flubendazole	Flubenol®	Oral compound	Ascarids, ancylostoma, *Taenia*
Praziquantel	Droncit® Droncit®Pill Plativers®	Tablet (microtablet for Droncit®Pill), or sub-cutaneous injection	Cestodes (including *Dilpilydium*, Mesocestodes, *Taenia*, and *Echinococcus*)
Pyrantel + Praziquantel	Drontal®Chat	Tablet	Ascarids, ancylostoma and cestodes (*Taenia* and *Dipylidium*)

for toxoplasmosis, can infect all mammals, including humans. The cat is the only host that harbors intestinal forms and expels the cysts. Other mammals, including humans, are infected by ingesting cysts eliminated by cats, or, as is more often the case, by consuming other infected animals (mutton, pork, and occasionally beef). Approximately 90% of all adult cats have been infected with Toxoplasma.

Most coccidian protozoa have little effect on cats and infections are typically asymptomatic. Only Isospora are likely to cause serious diarrhea in young kittens.
Coccidian protozoa are treated with trimethoprime-enhanced sulfonamides (sulfa drugs).

The best way to prevent protozoan infection is through good sanitation. The floors of the cattery should be cleaned regularly to reduce the number of cysts in the environment. Testing and treating adult carriers (often queens) is also an important part of an overall prevention plan.

Digestive parasites are common in cats. Fortunately, the frequency and seriousness of infections can be reduced by implementing appropriate treatment, both in catteries and in private homes. Worms are prevented through regular deworming (twice-yearly treatment is recommended). If in doubt, consult your veterinarian, who can test your cat and confirm or rule out parasitic infection.

Vaccinations

Owners who are concerned about the health of their cats must have their pets vaccinated to protect them from serious illness.

The prevalence of several serious cat diseases has declined in recent years, due in large part to the availability of a wide range of effective vaccines. Though the number of cats vaccinated each year is on the rise, in France cats receive less medical attention than dogs and therefore are not as well protected by preventive vaccines.

Certain common cat diseases almost always result in death. Others only rarely threaten the life of the animal, but it is always preferable to avoid potential disease by vaccinating the cat.

Of all vaccines available, some vaccines are essential, others are strongly recommended, and others are recommended in certain situations. Unfortunately, there is not an effective vaccine for every disease that has been identified to date.

Zoonoses (anthropozoonoses) are diseases shared by humans and animals. The primary diseases that can be transmitted from cats to humans or vice versa are: Rabies, toxoplasmosis, tuberculosis, and cat-scratch disease. None currently present a serious threat. Rabies is effectively controlled as the result of mandatory vaccination in certain circumstances (see below).

About Vaccines

A brief review of immunology

The organism's reaction to a foreign substance is to develop a response to counter the invader. This response is referred to as an immunological or immune response. The body mounts its defense with white blood cells called lymphocytes, which create a response specific to each antigen.

Lymphocytes have specialized roles. Some, such as B-cells, produce antibodies to neutralize infectious agents. Others, such as T-cells, directly attach infected cells in an effort to destroy them. In both cases, the lymphocytes "remember" this initial contact with the foreign body, and if they come into contact with this same foreign body again, they can respond immediately and destroy it even before it has a chance to multiply and produce illness (if it is a pathogenic agent).

Therefore, if an animal has had contact with the foreign body, whether through natural contact or vaccination, the animal is generally protected. The level of protection is determined by several factors, the antibodies being the most important mode of defense.

Age and Vaccinations

Kittens

A kitten's immunocompetence, that is, its ability to develop a good immune response, is complete by the second or third week of life. In theory, kitten may be vaccinated after the age of 15 days, though in reality, in most cases, vaccinations given to kittens are cancelled out by interference from immunity passed on from the mother.

Geriatric Cats

Over time, the number of antibodies produced by a cat's immune system decreases and its immune system weakens. Therefore, it is important to administer booster vaccinations to geriatric cats.

Vaccinations for Cats

Nature of vaccines

Indications and contraindications.

In general, it is contraindicated to vaccinate cats that are ill, infected with parasites, or undergoing treatment with an immunodepressant. Kittens as a rule should be treated with a dewormer before any vaccinations are administered. Moreover, modified (attenuated) vaccines are contraindicated for gestating females, since, until evidence to the contrary, it is

believed that they may cause abnormalities in the fetus.

Cats that go outdoors are at higher risk of contracting disease through contact with other cats or other contaminated areas. Therefore, vaccination is all the more important. However, it should not be assumed that a sedentary indoor cat is not at risk and therefore does not require vaccination. Even indoor cats that will never have direct contact with other animals can be exposed. Contaminants from other infected animals can be brought in on the sole of a shoe, for example. It is also important to keep in mind that even a cat that "never goes out" will on occasion leave the house, whether for a trip to the veterinarian, to a kennel, or for travel, when the owners move, for example. If a cat has not been vaccinated and is exposed to contaminated areas, such as waiting rooms, kennels, or the interior of a car, he is at high risk.

One of the difficulties of defining vaccination requirements is that some infections have an asymptomatic stage during which a cat shows no clinical signs of infection, even when examined by a veterinarian, but is still able to contaminate other cats with which he comes into contact. Animals with infections such as rhinitis and chlamydiosis may appear cured, but may in fact be carriers and potentially excrete the pathogenic agent responsible for the disease.

Other infections develop slowly. The infected cat appears to be in good health, but is actually simply in the asymptomatic stage of the disease. Without administering a specialized test to identify the specific disease, the cat cannot be diagnosed and will pose a risk to other cats. All of these possible opportunities for infection demonstrate the interest of ensuring that a cat is vaccinated.

When a cat is vaccinated, the veterinarian will record the type, method, date, and lot number of the vaccination in the cat's vaccination record. Only a veterinarian is authorized to enter this information.

The Age Factor: Kittens

In carnivores, 90 to 95% of the mother's antigens are passed on to her offspring through her first milk, or colostrum. When kittens first nurse, they receive almost all the mother's antibodies, built up throughout her life through contact with infectious agents and vaccinations. Her complete immunologic heritage is passed on to her offspring. The immunity resulting from this process is called passive immunity. During this phase, the kitten is not yet producing his own antibodies.
The intestinal barrier is highly permeable, allowing the antibodies of the colostrum to enter the kitten's circulatory system in the first two days of life.

The concentration of antibodies in the kitten's blood decreases gradually and is undetectable by the age of two and a-half months on average. This period varies from kitten to kitten and is influenced by several factors, the most important being the concentration of antibodies in the mother's milk and the size of the litter.

The positive aspect of this transmission process is that the mother's antigens will protect the kittens during the first weeks of life. However, unfortunately, these same antibodies can interfere with early vaccinations. By combining with the vaccine's antigens, these antibodies cancel out the immunization that would normally result following vaccination.

The critical period is the time between which the kitten becomes vulnerable to natural infection and the moment that he can be effectively vaccinated. This is a dangerous time for kittens, who are surrounded by a multitude of potentially infectious agents. The viruses in their physical surroundings are highly resistant, especially the feline panleukopenia. The solution is to begin vaccinations at the age of six weeks and repeat them every two weeks until the age of twelve to fourteen weeks. This "heavy-handed" approach is particularly suitable for kittens in catteries where disease has been identified. Kittens in private homes are at lesser risk, particularly since they have typically received their first round of shots prior to being sold.

Types of Vaccines

Some vaccines have been around for a long time and are commonly used. Others have been developed only recently, using advanced technologies. These are the wave of the future.

Traditional vaccines include inactivated (dead) and attenuated (modified, live) vaccines.

Inactivated vaccines are prepared using bacterial or viral agents treated by heat or chemicals. When developing a new vaccine, it is necessary to first create an inactive vaccine since the casual agent has not yet been stabilized in a non-virulent form, as is the case with the rabies vaccine, for example.

In live vaccines, the agent is modified so that it no longer produces clinical disease. However, it is still able to multiply. As a result, the vaccinated animal produces a strong immune response. These are considered highly immunogenic (producing immunity) vaccines.

Vaccines prepared using today's **advanced technologies** promise a bright future for vaccinations. In fact, a vaccine of this type for feline leukemia is already available on the market.

Vaccination Calendar

A veterinarian can set up a vaccination calendar that takes into account the various needs of each individual cat, considering lifestyle, age, and environment. However, some general principles apply.

The biggest challenge is vaccinating kittens as soon as possible after passive immunity has waned. In order to do this, two series of injections are required. The first is administered between six and ten weeks of age (typically at eight weeks of age), followed by a second round three to four weeks later, between the ages of twelve and fourteen weeks. Current legislation on rabies vaccination stipulates that kittens are not to be vaccinated until three months of age.

Vaccinated cats require booster shots from time to time in order to maintain effective immunity.

Disease Prevention

Mandatory Vaccination

All cats must be vaccinated against rabies.

Rabies is a form of viral encephalomyelitis common to all warm-blooded animals (including humans). It is one of the most feared zoonoses, because it is always fatal. The illness begins with an incubation period lasting thirty days on average, after which symptoms of nervous disorder appear. Death occurs within three to six days. Rabies is classified as an infectious disease and vaccination is regulated. Outdoor cats are most at risk. However, the prevalence of rabies has decreased dramatically in recent years in France, markedly decreasing risk of infection. All cats entering France from a foreign country must be vaccinated, as must cats travelling from infected departments within France. In addition, rabies vaccination is required if owners wish to bring their cats into a campground or enter their cat in a cat show.

French law stipulates that kittens must not be vaccinated until the age of three months. Since complete protection is not assured until one month following vaccination, requests for access to areas where vaccination is required (campgrounds, cat shows, border crossings) cannot be approved until the cat reaches four months of age.

Recommended Vaccinations

Currently, most cats are vaccinated against rabies, panleukopenia, viral rhinotracheitis, and leukemia (see table on page 421).

In the past, **feline panleukopenia** took the life of many cats. However, the disease is now rare in urban areas, thanks to a widespread vaccination program. Most panleukopenia vaccines available on the French market are modified vaccines. Vaccination of queens during the third trimester and kittens under the age of four weeks is contraindicated.

Feline viral rhinotracheitis (FVR) is an acute infectious disease caused primarily by two different viruses acting alone or in concert. Symptoms cannot be linked to the specific responsible agent. Therefore, all symptoms are grouped under the heading rhinotracheitis. As noted in the introduction to this section, cats are at risk of exposure, and therefore disease, from asymptomatic carriers. One purified subunit vaccine and several modified vaccines are available in France.

Feline leukemia is caused by the FeLV virus, one of two viruses causing immunodeficiency in cats, the other being Feline Immunodeficiency Virus, or FIV. Symptoms of feline leukemia typically appear two years following infection. FIV leads to acquired immunodeficiency syndrome **(Feline AIDS)** eight to ten years following infection.

Both diseases present with generalized symptoms, including weight loss, fever, general decline, and appetite loss, accompanied by a wide array of localized infections.

A vaccine is available only for feline leukemia, not FIV. Cats at risk of exposure to FelV can be protected against this deadly disease by being vaccinated. However, the vaccine is only effective in FeLV-negative cats, though it will not harm cats already infected with the virus. Vaccination does not interfere with blood test results and diagnosis. Diagnosis is based on the presence of viral antigens, not antibodies fighting the virus.

Chlamydiosis is a bacterial disease producing conjunctivitis and sometimes accompanied by runny nose and cough. The bacteria may act alone or in conjunction with the rhinotracheitis virus, aggravating FVR symptoms. Cats that have contracted this disease and appear to be cured carry the virus for an extended period of time and may excrete the virus, with or without symptoms, posing a threat of infection to other cats.

Vaccines are not available for the following diseases in France

Feline Infectious Peritonitis (FIP) is a serious viral infection. In the most common form,

effusive FIP, fluid accumulates in the abdomen, enlarging the abdomen. In France, individuals purchasing kittens are protected by law and are entitled a refund if they purchase a kitten that is later diagnosed with FIP. There is no authorized vaccine available in France for this disease. Until recently, all FIP vaccination trials were unsuccessful. However, an attenuated FIP virus strain was recently isolated. When administered by the intranasal route, its effectiveness seems to be promising. This product has already been approved in the United States and some European countries. In France, additional studies are required before approval can be granted.

There is currently no vaccine available to protect the cat against FIV, which leads to feline AIDS, though much research is currently under way. This feline disease is very similar to AIDS in humans, and as a result, the advantages of such research are two-fold, benefiting the fields of both veterinary and comparative medicine. If an effective vaccine were devel-

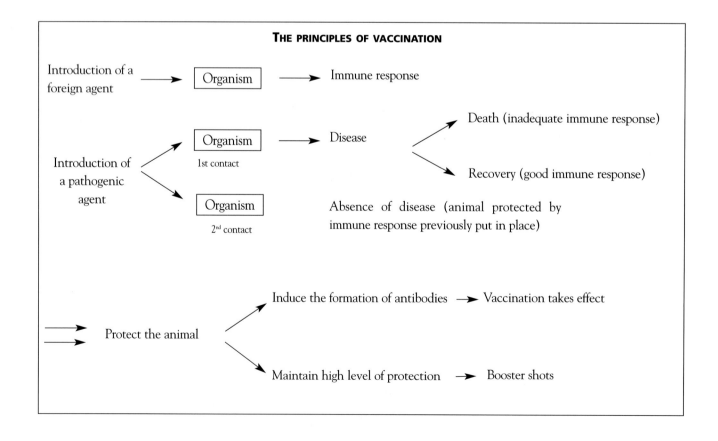

THE PRINCIPLES OF VACCINATION

Introduction of a foreign agent → Organism → Immune response

Introduction of a pathogenic agent → Organism (1st contact) → Disease → Death (inadequate immune response) / Recovery (good immune response)

Organism (2nd contact) → Absence of disease (animal protected by immune response previously put in place)

Protect the animal → Induce the formation of antibodies → Vaccination takes effect / Maintain high level of protection → Booster shots

oped for FIV, this accomplishment would be of great interest to researchers working on a vaccine for humans.

Vaccination is a simple, generally harmless method for protecting cats from serious infectious diseases. In order to protect the health of their beloved companions, all owners must ensure that their cats are vaccinated in accordance with their veterinarian's recommendations.

FELINE VACCINES AVAILABLE IN FRANCE

		Viral Diseases	Bacterial Diseases
Inactivated vaccines	Traditional	Rhinotracheitis (two valences) Leukemia Rabies	Chlamydiosis
Live vaccines	Traditional Nasal route	Panleukopenia Rhinotracheitis (two valences) Infectious Peritonitis*	Chlamydiosis
By intranasal route Subunit vaccines	Portion of the infectious agent obtained through genetic engineering	Herpesvirus valence of rhinotracheitis Leukemia	
*Not yet approved in France at the time of this writing.			

Common Diseases

Owners love their cats and want to keep them healthy and happy. It is important that owners be familiar with the following diseases and the symptoms that should prompt a visit to the veterinarian.

A healthy kitten looks alert and has a full, clean, soft coat. His gait is relaxed. The ears contain only a small quantity of light brown ear wax. The eyes are well open and do not tear. Breathing is not labored, and the mouth and tongue look healthy and smell sweet. The area around the anus is clean. In male cats that have not been neutered, the two testicles have descended normally into the scrotum. Cats exude a distinctive feline odor, but the odor is not disagreeable.

Sick cat

Even the most careful exam will not reveal diseases invisible to the naked eye, so a visit to the veterinarian for a thorough exam and any necessary tests is advisable.

The food a kitten eats has an impact on his health. Commercial foods provide a healthy, balanced diet for cats at all stages of life, and as a result, bone disorders in growing kittens are now rare. However, feeding an all-protein diet or administering vitamins incorrectly (overdose of Vitamin E, for example) can cause osteofibrosis, in which the fragile bones are prone to greenstick or other serious fractures.

At the age of three months, the fully weaned kitten is capable of feeding himself and is well adapted to his environment. It is the owner's responsibility to provide the nourishment and care required for healthy growth.

Viral and Bacterial Infections

Once a kitten is no longer protected by the antibodies provided by his mother during gestation and nursing, he is vulnerable to viral and bacterial infections.

Leukemia and Feline Immunodeficiency

Cats are vulnerable to several infectious agents responsible for frequently fatal diseases. The most serious are three viruses: Feline Leukemia Virus (FeLV), Feline Immunodeficiency Virus (FIV), and Feline Infectious Peritonitis (FIP).

The first two, FeLV and FIV, are caused by a retrovirus.
Since the mode of transmission and susceptibility differs with each disease and each cat, it

is impossible to say that only specific populations are at risk.

FeLV is transmitted through contact, licking, and use of a common litter box. The animals most at risk are kittens or young adults, indoor/outdoor cats, and/or those living in multiple-cat households.

FIV is transmitted primarily through bites. FIV infection is rare in catteries. It is much more common in free-roaming cats. Older, intact, indoor/outdoor males are the most at risk.

If a susceptible cat comes into contact with FeLV, the virus may be immediately eradicated by the body and not result in symptoms. However, if the virus escapes the body's initial immune defenses, it will enter the bloodstream. The presence of the virus in the bloodstream is called viremia.

If the body's immune response is sufficient, the spread of the virus is halted, but the virus may remain in bone marrow cells. If the virus overwhelms the body's immune defenses, it spreads throughout the organism, and the disease develops.

Symptoms vary considerably and follow an asymptomatic phase during which the cat is contagious. Anemia sets in, mucous membranes turn pale, the cat tires easily and is winded quickly. Since the body's immune defenses are weakened, the cat is at risk for a variety of complications, including respiratory viral infections, abscesses, chronic diarrhea, or skin disorders. Any cat with recurring illness or an illness not responding to treatment should be tested for retroviruses. Reproductive disorders are a classic symptom, as are tumors (especially lymphomas).

The clinical progression of FIV infection corresponds to a progressive weakening of the immune system, which can be divided into five stages, as follows:

- primo-infection - low-grade fever and swollen glands
- asymptomatic carrier (seropositive)

- early clinical stage - onset of symptoms, including hairloss and fever (this phase lasts several months)
- consolidation - appearance of major, recurring infections that respond poorly or not at all to treatment (this phase lasts several months)
- terminal - the cat is vulnerable to all germs, even those that are not highly infectious; onset of a wide variety of infections, resulting in death within one to six months

It is not uncommon for a cat infected with FeLV to be infected with FIV as well. These cats typically suffer from extremely serious diseases and die shortly after symptoms first appear.

There is no effective treatment for retroviruses, though several treatments are available that may prolong an infected cat's life, including corticosteroids and antimitotic drugs. Treatment of secondary infections with antibiotics simply postpones death.

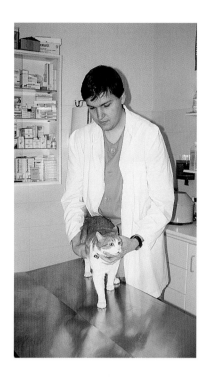

Feline Infectious Peritonitis

Feline Infectious Peritonitis, FIP for short, takes two forms - effusive (wet) and noneffusive (dry). The causal agent is a virus belonging to the family Coronaviridae.

While the incidence of FIP is higher among purebred cats, this seems to be caused by environment (confinement) rather than a genetic predisposition. Nevertheless, some lines seem to be more susceptible than others.

FIP is a serious, deadly concern for breeders, animal shelters, and areas where many cats live together, particularly if kittens are present. Cats of all ages contract FIP, though it is more common in kittens and young cats up to one and a half year of age. The primary route of transmission is oral-fecal. A susceptible cat is infected through licking or through contact with the excreta of an infected cat. It is thought that airborne transmission of the virus is possible, though researchers have not determined whether fleas and other insect bites can spread the disease.

It is likely that some cats that have come into contact with the virus are healthy carriers who excrete the virus on occasion, in times of stress, illness, or during reproduction. The FIP virus is highly resistant and can survive outside the body for several weeks.

There are different strains of feline coronaviruses (FcoV), from very mild (unnoticed infection), to moderately severe (causing enteritis), and the highly virulent strains responsible for clinical FIP. Depending on the strain contracted, the mortality rate ranges from 0% to 100%. Most strains are only moderately virulent. The viruses responsible for clinical FIP are probably mutations of FcoV. Following infection by a feline coronavirus, the following symptoms may appear:

• An asymptomatic infection or moderate intestinal infection; the cat tests positive and is often a healthy carrier

• An isolated abdominal or ocular inflammation

• Full-fledged peritonitis; only 1% to 10% of all cats infected with a feline coronavirus develop FIP symptoms, the most serious form of the disease. FIP is almost always fatal.

Incubation ranges from one to two days up to several years. Two major forms of FIP exist: Effusive, in which fluid builds up in body cavities, and noneffusive. The clinical signs of the noneffusive form vary depending on the organ(s) affected (encephalitis, for example). Symptoms are treated to slow the progression of the disease, but no cure currently exists.

Feline Panleukopenia Virus

This disease, commonly referred to as distemper, is caused by a highly resistant parvovirus capable of surviving outside the body for more than one year. Cats are infected when they come into contact with an infected animal or an area where the virus is present.

TESTING FOR FeLV AND FIV

How are the FeLV and FIV retroviruses detected?

Testing confirms or rules out the presence of a retrovirus. Testing can also identify healthy carriers so that contagious cats are not introduced to healthy environments. FeLV tests analyze a cat's blood to detect presence of the virus. A test can be false-positive in the first few weeks following exposure. The reverse is also true—a cat testing positive can test negative at a later date. Therefore, the test should be administered twice at a three month interval.
The test for FIV looks for the presence of FIV antibodies in the blood. One hundred percent of all cats showing antibodies in the blood are infected with FIV. Therefore, there is no need to repeat this test.
How is FIP diagnosed?
The tests currently available in France detect the antibodies produced by the cat's body in reaction to contact with a feline coronavirus. These tests are effective for diagnosing FIP (in conjunction with other clinical elements). They can also be used to protect a healthy cat population, ensuring that only seronegative cats are introduced to the group.
These tests do have their limitations. False positives can result from vaccinations, maternal antibodies, or other coronaviruses. False negatives are possible in the case of in utero infection, slow spread of the virus, or a temporarily seronegative healthy carrier. In addition, several techniques may be used, and therefore results may differ from one laboratory to the next.

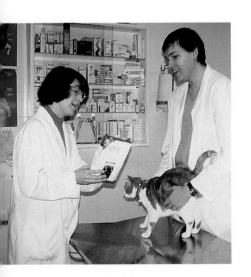

Symptoms vary, depending primarily on the age of the animal. Young cats are typically the most seriously affected.

In the most severe cases, an infected cat may die suddenly, within less than twelve hours following infection.

The acute form of FPV is characterized by a high fever and severe depression. The animal refuses to eat and vomiting and diarrhea occur, resulting in dehydration. Blood tests show a dramatic drop in the white blood count.

The mortality rate varies from 50% to 60%. Animals that recover from FPV sometimes suffer from recurring bouts of diarrhea.

If a gestating queen is infected with a wild virus or vaccinated with a live attenuated virus, the virus is capable of infecting the fetus. If infection occurs in the early stages of gestation, the fetuses will be aborted. During the second trimester, the infection will cause hypoplasia—underdevelopment of the cerebellum. Clinic signs appear when the kittens reach approximately four weeks of age. They begin trembling, lack coordination, and are unable to move about.

There is no treatment for the form of FPV affecting kittens. For older cats, a veterinarian will rehydrate the sick animal using an IV, treat the symptoms, and administer antibiotics to limit complications from secondary infections. Prognosis is guarded and mortality is high.

Rabies

The occurrence of this disease, which reared its ugly head again in France in 1968, is dropping as a result of effective health measures including vaccination of domestic animals and fox, and monitoring of biting animals.

Rabies is a form of encephalitis (inflammation of the brain) caused by a rhabdovirus.

The primary means of rabies virus transmission is the bite of an infected animal. The virus enters through the break in the skin caused by the bite. The length of incubation varies from several weeks to several months. Rabies is always fatal once clinical signs appear. If bitten by an animal showing clinical signs of rabies or suspected of being infected with the rabies virus, treatment with a rabies virus antiserum must begin immediately during the incubation period.

Rabies in cats produces dramatic clinical symptoms, including paralysis and complete prostration. Most often, rabid cats go through a furious stage during which they are wild and aggressive.

Strict laws have been imposed in the attempt to prevent the spread of rabies in humans and animals. Any animal that has bitten or scratched a human must be quarantined and observed by a veterinarian for a period of fifteen days.

Eye and Upper Respiratory Disorders

The most serious of these are caused by three viruses and a chlamydia bacterial agent. All survive no more than 48 hours outside the body, except caliciviruses, which are capable of living up to ten days. As a result, these illnesses are typically not transmitted by simple contact with the virus in the environment, but instead, are passed directly from cat to cat.

Clinical signs are similar to those of a cold in humans. Common symptoms include fever, followed rapidly by conjunctivitis and tearing, sneezing, and sometimes a runny nose and a cough. Some symptoms point to specific agents, but it is not uncommon for multiple infections to occur in the same cat.

Feline viral rhinotracheitis is caused by feline herpesvirus type 1. Symptoms include paroxysmal sneezing, nasal discharge, tearing with corneal ulcers, and lesions on the tongue. Infected pregnant cats frequently abort. Mortality is high among kittens and adults in a weakened condition.

Eighty percent of all cats that recover are carriers. They harbor the dormant virus in their bodies, but show no clinical signs. During times of stress, these cats may excrete the virus.

The symptoms of feline calicivirus vary depending on the particular strain of calicivirus responsible for the illness as well as the health of the infected cat's immune system. In the mildest cases, symptoms are limited to ulcers on the tongue, palate, lips, and nasal septum. Due to the pain caused by the ulcers, the cat refuses to eat. Tearing and runny nose are also common. In more severe cases, onset of pneumonia may lead to death (the mortality rate in kittens is 100%). Less commonly, symptoms include contracture of the toes and stiff gait caused by joint and muscle pain. Once cured, some cats completely eliminate the virus from their body, while others remain carriers.

Reovirus infection is caused by a reovirus. Conjunctivitis is typically the only symptom and complications are rare. No vaccine exists.

Chlamydia psittaci is the causal agent for feline **chlamydiosis**. The first signs of infection are conjunctivitis and chemosis (edema of the ocular conjunctiva) affecting only one eye, then spreading to the other. These symptoms sometimes disappear without treatment. In the most severe cases, these symptoms worsen after ten to twelve days and the cat begins coughing and sneezing. Pregnant queens sometimes abort. Complete recovery takes two to six weeks.

Cats that have recovered from the illness are sometimes asymptomatic carriers that excrete the chlamydial bacteria in times of stress.

A veterinarian will prescribe antibiotics and treat the symptoms. Attentive care is required. Since the cat's air passages are blocked, he will not eat voluntarily nor clean himself. It is imperative that he be made to eat (force fed if necessary). Wet foods and soups or liquid specialty nutritional formulas are appropriate, as prescribed by a veterinarian. Feeding, cleaning, clearing nasal passages, and administering inhalations will speed recovery. Aerosol inhalations can be administered at home or in a veterinarian's office.

Digestive System Disorders

The health of the **digestive tract** depends first and foremost on the health of the teeth. Over the years, tartar builds up on teeth. The mineral salts contained in saliva are deposited on dental plaque present on teeth forming a hard stonelike concretion sealed by bacteria present in the mouth. Tartar buildup pushes on the gingiva (gums) causing inflammation, infection, and eventually resulting in periodontitis. Tartar must be removed. In severe cases, it may be necessary to remove some teeth, which can lead to problems in the future.

Many adult and geriatric cats suffer from osteoclastic or tooth resorption. Initially, areas of depression appear at the neck of the tooth. As resorption progresses, the teeth become fragile and then break. The roots may also be eliminated, but sometimes remain in the gingiva, resulting in the potential for chronic gingivitis. Cats with advanced cases drool continuously and refuse to eat. When food is put down, the cat rushes to the bowl, but refuses to take even one bite or takes a bite, but paws at his mouth as if to remove a foreign body. Early lesions can be treated, but once the dental pulp is involved, extraction of the tooth is normally the only option.

The **esophagus** propels food to the stomach through the cardia, the opening into the stomach. If the cardia does not function properly, food piles up in the lower end of the esophagus and is eventually regurgitated. This can also occur if a tumor in the chest or a vascular arch present at birth compresses the esophagus. Over time, this buildup of food stretches the esophagus, a condition called megaesophagus. Typically, kittens swallow maternal milk easily. The problem appears when they begin eating solid food. Mild cases can be treated with changes to the diet, but generally, the prognosis is grim.

The cat's **stomach** may be the seat of acute and chronic disorders, gastritis, but is also involved in other pathological disorders.
Acute gastritis may follow ingestion of unhealthful, medicated, toxic, or nonfood substances. It may also be a clinical sign of other disorders, including allergies, liver, kidney, or heart disorders, or infectious or parasitic illnesses.

The most benign cases result in a twenty-four hour fast (no more), after which the cat slowly begins eating again. More serious cases require the care of a veterinarian in order to control vomiting and administer treatment appropriate to the causal agent.

Chronic gastritis accompanied by occasional vomiting, weight loss, and food intolerance can also appear alone or in conjunction with other symptoms.

Long-term treatment involves more than the administration of medications. Changes must be made to the diet, such as feeding several small meals per day of concentrated, hypoallergenic food. Additional tests, such as x-rays, barium transit, or exploratory fibroscopy or exploratory laparotomy, are required for accurate diagnosis. Gastric ulcers are uncommon and difficult to identify.

Stomach torsion, a very serious condition in dogs, is extremely rare in cats.

Problems in the **small intestine** can result in diarrhea.

Acute diarrhea can be caused by diet. If a cat's food is suddenly changed, the microbial balance in the digestive tract is upset. Certain bacteria develop at the expense of others, producing toxic waste that irritates the intestinal mucosa.

Several viruses cause acute diarrhea, including FIP, feline panleukopenia virus and coronavirus. Young kittens often suffer severe complications after the onset of acute diarrhea: Intussusception (the prolapse, or telescoping, of one part of the intestine into an immediately adjoining part) may occur, requiring emergency surgery to correct the problem. Equally serious are intestinal occlusion or obstruction, rarely caused by a foreign body, because cats taste their food and almost never swallow small objects. The more common cause is a tumor in or near the digestive tract (lymphosarcomas, for example).

The intestine is a favored site for many parasites, the most common being worms such as *ascaris* or *dipylidium*. These bothersome parasites cause diarrhea, digestive disorders, and weight loss. In cases of severe infestation, they may even completely block the intestinal lumen, resulting in intestinal occlusion.

Chronic enteritis may follow an acute illness or appear spontaneously. A sick animal typically has difficulty absorbing the nutrients in the intestine. Enteritis is also one of the clinical signs of other diseases, including diabetes and chronic kidney failure.

Depending on their cause, some cases of chronic enteritis can be treated or alleviated with medication. An appropriate diet is vital in all cases. Such a diet contains easily-digestible, high-quality proteins, and very limited amounts of saturated fat and lactose. Specially formulated commercial foods are almost always prescribed.

Identifying the cause of chronic enteritis is difficult. Invasive tests, such as a biopsy of the intestinal mucosa, are almost always required. Tumors affecting the small intestine cause chronic diarrhea before other signs appear, such as weight loss, abnormal palpation, or compression of neighboring organs.

Exocrine pancreatic insufficiency is rare in cats. In this disease, insufficient excretion of pancreatic juices impairs digestion of fats, carbohydrates, and, to a lesser extent, proteins. The cat loses weight, though constantly hungry, and passes soft, pale, voluminous stools. Supplementing each meal with digestive enzymes and feeding a special diet typically allows a cat to lead a normal life.

Colitis is the inflammation of the large intestine (colon). In acute or chronic colitis, the cat passes soft, voluminous, slimy stools, sometimes flecked with blood. Many things can cause colitis, including infection, parasites, and stress. Sometimes the cause cannot be determined. Hairballs are sometimes at fault. Treatment varies depending on the origin of the problem

Finally, the **rectum** and the **anus**, the end of the digestive tract, are involved in some diseases. Some kittens are born with an anus with no opening to the outside of the body, a serious condition since the kitten is unable to defecate.
Geriatric, obese, and sedentary cats often suffer from constipation. If left untreated and no adjustment is made to the cat's diet, constipation can lead to a condition called coprostasis (accumulation of fecal matter in the rectum) and intestinal occlusion. Medical treatment including laxatives and enemas generally resolve the problem, but serious cases may require surgical intervention.

Causes of Acute Diarrhea in Cats (Cotard)

• Food: Changes in diet, food allergies, food intolerance, overeating.
• Toxins: Particularly acetaminophen (the ingredient in aspirin).

• Viruses: Panleukopenia , FIP, enteritic coronavirus, FeLV, FIV, rotavirus, astrovirus.

• Bacteria: Salmonella, *Campylobacter*, *Yersinia*, E-coli, *Mycobacterium tuberculosis*.

• Parasites: *Ascaris*, hookworm, whipworm, coccidia, yeast.

• Other: Partial blockage, foreign bodies, such as string, wire, needles.

Causes of Chronic Diarrhea in Cats (Paragon)

• Excess water in the intestines: Overload of the intestines, inadequate digestion, inadequate absorption; pancreatic or biliary insufficiency; lactase deficiency; tumor or inflammation of the intestinal epithelium or intestinal wall.

• Excess secretions from the glands of the intestines: Bacterial toxins, viruses, bacteria, parasites, or toxins (as in acute diarrhea).

• Intestinal motricity (movement): Peristaltic seizing, insufficient fiber, partial obstruction.

Primary Causes of Constipation in Cats (Fayolle)

• Thickened consistency of stools: Ingestion of hair or litter, dehydration.

• Blockage: Obstacle outside the intestine (pelvic fracture, tumor, dry fecal matter around the anus).

• Neuromuscular disorders: Malfunction of the central nervous system or the nerves in the colon (resulting in a condition called megacolon); idiopathic (unknown origin), feline autonomic dysfunction.

• Refusal to defecate: Dirty litter, change in environment, hospitalization, pain when squatting; anal/rectal lesions (anal glands, foreign body, tumor, abscess).

• Some medications

Respiratory System

The respiratory system is the target of specific infectious agents. Rhinitis, tracheitis, bronchitis, and pneumonia are often caused by viral infections.

In serious cases, cats may have difficulty breathing (dyspnea). Certain diseases such as leukemia, in which a lymphoma in the chest may inhibit free movement of the lungs, and FIP, resulting in pleurisy, may also cause breathing difficulty.

If a cat coughs, she may be suffering from one of these infections or feline asthma. A cough is the symptom of a disorder in the airways—larynx, trachea, and bronchi. A cough is typically observed when other organs in the chest are diseased, such as congestive heart failure with pulmonary edema.

An acute cough is caused by irritation in the upper respiratory system (tonsillitis, laryngitis, tracheitis, normally caused by infection, or swallowing difficulties), or, less commonly, by lower respiratory disorders, including infections, acute pulmonary edema, inhalation of irritants, or asthma.

A cough is not always caused by a problem in the respiratory system. An acute cough may also result from cardiovascular disorders.

Chronic upper respiratory disorders are normally caused by acute disorders, as described above, which take hold and become chronic. They may also be caused by problems at the level of the trachea: For example, a foreign object in the trachea, collapse of the trachea, compression of the trachea from an outside source, such as a tumor between the lungs.

The condition of the cardiovascular system should also be considered. Congestive heart failure causes pulmonary edema, which, in combination with the resulting enlargement of the heart, compresses neighboring organs. This compression may lead to a chronic cough.

Asthma in Cats

The term cat asthma refers to recurring episodes of paroxysmal coughing, wheezing, and shortness of breath. This syndrome resembles human asthma in many respects. Feline asthma probably stems from an allergic reaction to allergens inhaled into the lungs, resulting in inflammation of the airways and contraction of the smooth muscles of the airways. Sometimes the coughing fit is so violent that the cat vomits or coughs up digestive juices. Some particularly serious episodes require emergency medical care. A cat suffering from a severe asthma attack lies flat on the ground with elbows held apart and neck extended. The mouth is open with the tongue sticking out. Sometimes, the tongue takes on a blue hue from oxygen deprivation.

The problem is caused by hyper-reactive airways, which contract (bronchospasms) and become inflamed when they come into contact with airborne allergens. Antibiotics have little affect on this type of respiratory disorder, since infectious agents are not the causative factor, though in the case of secondary infections, antibiotics may be appropriate. Anti-inflammatory steroids generally control the attacks and improve the overall health of the cat suffering from asthma.

Cardiovascular Diseases

Cardiovascular disease can afflict cats of all ages, young and old alike. Young cats may be born with deformed hearts, whereas adult and geriatric cats are prone to certain diseases specific to cats. Cats are not likely to experience myocardial infarction due to the positioning of their coronary arteries

My cat is drinking a lot

Polyuria and polidipsia are symptoms that appear in a large number of conditions, including:

• Kidney disorders, such as chronic or acute renal failure, interstitial nephritis, pyelonephritis, or a reaction after a obstruction has cleared;
• Reproductive disorders, such as pyometra or metritis;
• Liver disorders, such as liver failure;
• Endocrine disorders, such as disease of the adrenal glands, diabetes mellitus, diabetes insipidus, hyperthyroid, or acromegaly.
• Electrolyte imbalances, such as hyper- or hypocalcemia, hyponatraemia, or hypokalemia;
• Following medical treatment with corticosteroids, diuretics, and some antibiotics;
• Excessively salty food;
• Psychogenic (potomania).

Congenital heart defects are not common in felines, though when they do appear, they are often very serious, retarding growth, limiting activity, and causing cyanosis (bluish discoloration of the skin and mucous membranes) with even minimal exertion. Cats suffering from a heart defect often die at a young age. The most common deformities include ventricular septal defects, atrial septal defects, aortic stenosis, deformed tricuspid valves and patent ductus arteriosus. Many other abnormalities also exist.

Arrhythmias and conduction disturbances, which are relatively rare in cats, are caused by irregular contraction of the heart. Tachycardia is a faster than normal heart rate. Its opposite, brachycardia, is a slower than normal heart rate. Heart contractions may be irregular, premature, or late. Symptoms vary considerably. Some cats may show almost no outward signs, whereas others may suffer serious respiratory distress. Some antiarrhythmic medications, if carefully administered, may be used to treat these types of disorders in cats.

Cardiomyopathy is a disease of unknown etiology of the heart muscle. It causes hypertrophy (overgrowth) or dilation of the heart. Using an ultrasound, a veterinarian can distinguish between the three types—hypertrophic, dilated, restrictive—of cardiomyopathy by analyzing the changes to the heart muscle and cavities. Similar heart lesions are seen in primary myocardial diseases and other disorders such as taurine deficiency and hyperthyroid.
The different types of cardiomyopathy have similar symptoms. General symptoms include appetite loss, weakness, and sometimes vomiting. Symptoms more specific to cardiomyopathy are those related to left-sided heart failure (labored breathing, wheezing, and cough) or right-sided heart failure (shortness of breath and ascites—accumulation of serous fluid within the abdominal cavity). A cat having difficulty breathing will present exaggerated breathing movements, sometimes assuming the characteristic crouch with front legs

tucked in close to the chest, and breathing through the mouth. If a clot detaches, the cat may suffer an iliac thromboembolism.
In cases where the cause of the cardiomyopathy is known (hyperthyroid, taurine deficiency), the underlying illness is treated. Cardiomyopathies of unknown origin are treated with various classes of medications, including diuretics, vasodilators, more specifically conversion enzyme inhibitors, and sometimes digitalis-like drugs. Rest, stress management, and a reduced-salt diet are also important to treatment.

Hyperthyroidism is a disorder that occurs in older cats. In the long-term, it leads to heart abnormalities, with symptoms including tachycardia (rapid heart rate) with strong contractions of the heart muscle, and sometimes the appearance of a murmur. As the disease progress, arrhythmia and hypertrophic cardiomyopathy may develop. If a cat is not treated early enough, the illness may be irreversible and result in death. Other clinical signs include weight loss, ravenous appetite, hyperactivity or nervousness, sometimes vomiting, excessive drinking and urinating, and hairloss. A blood test analyzing thyroid hormone levels provides a definitive diagnosis. Hyperthyroidism can be treated with medications (antithyroid drugs) or, more commonly, surgically.

The thyroid is not the only endocrine gland susceptible to disease. The pituitary and adrenal glands may also fail or harbor tumors.

Diabetes mellitus is rare in cats, though is probably under-diagnosed. The initial clinical signs are nonspecific, the most common being excessive thirst (polydipsia) and urination (polyuria). Appetite generally increases, though sometimes drops off. The cat suffering from diabetes mellitus is weak and vomits occasionally. He is sometimes obese and is generally more than five years old. Other diseases or endocrine disorders, such as reproductive or urinary infections, may accompany diabetes mellitus. Blood and/or urine tests confirm the diagnosis.

Glycemia (blood sugar level) is controlled by two opposing hormones—insulin and glucagon—secreted by the pancreas. In 80% of all diabetic cats, insufficient insulin is secreted, while the other 20% secrete sufficient insulin, but their body utilizes it poorly.

Treatment of diabetes mellitus must include a dietary element. Food must have a higher fiber content (green vegetables) and contain complex carbohydrates. If a cat is obese, a lower-calorie diet is required in order to achieve gradual weight loss. A veterinarian can suggest an appropriate food to meet the diabetic cat's dietary requirements.

If appropriate, a veterinarian will also prescribe oral hypoglycemic drugs or insulin therapy. It is difficult to determine the appropriate quantity and dose frequency in cats, as requirements may vary over time. Some cats are only temporary diabetic. Diabetic cats must be seen by a veterinarian regularly and closely monitored.

Diabetes Mellitus and Diabetes Insipidus

Though both diseases bear the same first name, the two should not be confused. Diabetes mellitus is a disease characterized by elevated blood sugar levels (hyperglycemia). Diabetes insipidus is a rare disease caused by the kidney's inability to concentrate urine as a result of deficient pituitary secretion of vasopressin (antidiuretic hormone), which controls urine concentration, or the kidney's inability to respond to the vasopressin hormone.

Most of the body's waste is eliminated by the liver and the kidneys, but these organs can fail.

The functions of the **liver** include the manufacture of certain hormones and bile containing bile salts. The liver is also important in the absorption of fats and detoxification, and plays a vital role in the metabolism of sugars (storage and redistribution), as well as the synthesis of certain proteins and fats. The liver stores vita-

mins A, D, and B12 and mineral salts, including iron and copper. It eliminates toxic products after assailing them with an array of complex chemical reactions. One of the classic detoxification pathways is almost nonexistent in cats. For this reason, cats are extremely sensitive to a variety of products, including insecticides such as DDT and lindane, aspirin, and acetaminophen.

Once the liver ceases functioning, the condition is referred to as liver failure.

Acute liver failure can be attributed to several causes, including infection—FIP, pseudotuberculosis, various bacteria, and toxoplasma—toxins, shock, hemolysis, or immune disorders. Symptoms of liver failure are weakness, inappetence, vomiting, diarrhea, and excessive thirst. Jaundice develops rapidly, and nervous disorders set in—unsteady gait, prostration, followed by coma, and sometimes convulsions. Blood tests can be helpful in making a definitive diagnosis. A veterinarian will treat the cause of the disease if it can be identified and will administer medications to treat the symptoms. Rest and a high-carbohydrate, low-fat, low-protein diet are vital.

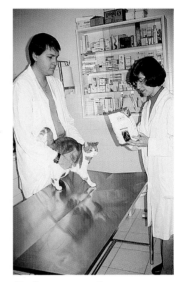

Cat being examined by a veterinarian

The **onset of chronic liver failure** is so subtle that by the time symptoms raise concern, a large portion of the liver has already been destroyed. At this stage, it is almost impossible to determine the cause of the problem.

Possible causes include cholangiohepatitis (inflammation of the biliary tract), infectious diseases such as FIP, endocrine disorders such as diabetes mellitus, as well as cirrhosis of the liver. Cancers of the liver (lymphosarcomas, primary or metastasized carcinomas) produce similar clinical signs.

A cat suffering from liver failure experiences weight loss, has a dull coat, has a reasonable appetite but experiences digestive problems including diarrhea or constipation, and often consumes greater quantities of water than normal. Over time, slight, then more severe jaundice sets in. Blood tests may reveal slight abnormalities.

A special diet regime is the primary treatment method. A diet rich in high-quality proteins and easily digestible carbohydrates should be fed in several small meals per day.

The **kidneys** may be affected by several disorders.

Acute renal failure corresponds to a significant, sudden decrease or total shutdown of kidney functions. The origin of the failure can be broken down into three categories.

1. Pre-renal, such as hemorrhagic shock, digestive disorders, burns, or heart failure;
2. Renal, including acute nephritis, infection, or toxins;
3. Post-renal, such as obstruction of the urinary tract, whether as the result of inflammation, a tumor, or formation of calculi (stones).

A cat suffering from acute renal failure does not urinate, is depressed and weak, and vomits. Blood and/or urine tests confirm diagnosis. Treatment sometimes requires hospitalization, since the patient must be closely monitored and normally requires an IV.

Chronic renal failure is probably the number one non-accidental cause of death in geriatric cats. As the kidney ages, its ability to cleanse the blood diminishes and toxic wastes begin to accumulate in the blood. The cat loses weight, loses interest in food, vomits, suffers from diarrhea and halitosis (urine smell), and eventually presents nervous disorders (coma) resulting in death. Changing the diet early on by restricting phosphorus increases the life expectancy of a cherished companion. Medical treatment is normally provided at times of crisis or when the condition worsens suddenly. A veterinarian will typically prescribe a special diet, since the onset of chronic renal failure can be delayed through appropriate diet.

Urinary tract obstruction is often the cause of acute renal failure. Cats are plagued by lower urinary tract disorders, all grouped under the heading Feline Urologic Syndrome (FUS). The anatomy of male cats makes them particularly vulnerable.

Dry foods (kibble) have often been blamed for this disorder. In the 1970s, some low quality, high-magnesium foods were responsible for creating alkaline urine, which contributed to the formation of crystals and the accumulation of struvites (magnesium ammonium phosphate calculi). These irritating grains caused cystitis in both genders, obstructing the long, narrow, curved urethra of male cats.

Today, veterinarians have a broader view of this syndrome, now referred to as Feline Lower Urinary Tract Disease **(FLUTD)**. This term includes disorders characterized by a variety of clinical signs, including frequent or painful urination or the presence of blood in the urine (hematuria). Urination outside of the litter box can also be a warning sign.

Urinary bacterial infections (rare), tumors, anatomical malformations, urolithiasis (presence of urinary calculi), and idiopathic cystitis may all cause FLUTD.

The urine of a healthy cat contains varying amounts of crystals (struvites, calcium oxalates, etc.). Urinary sediments are not produced by diet, but diet may make a cat more prone to precipitation of these sediments. Cat foods are now formulated to reduce the risk of precipitation of minerals at each stage of an animal's life. Though dry foods are perfectly adapted to the requirements of a healthy cat, wet food or rehydrated dry food should be fed to cats that have previously been diagnosed with a urinary tract stone in order to increase their water intake.

In more than 60% of all cases, a cat suffers from idiopathic cystitis. This involves periods of remission followed by reappearance of symptoms and is the cause of most toilet accidents in cats. Stress plays a major role in the onset of idiopathic cystitis. Stress may be caused by difficulties in the relationship with the owner, a change in food, environmental problems relating to confinement, overcrowding, the litter box, or any number of reasons known only to the cat.

Sometimes an obstruction in male (neutered or intact) cats may not pass due to the size of the obstruction and the accumulation of protein matter. The cat passes only a little urine, or none at all. As a result, the urine accumulates in the bladder. The cat is prostrate and curled up and exhibits signs of intense pain caused by the distention of the bladder. If the bladder is struck, unskillfully palpated, or intervention comes too late, it may rupture. The waste products contained in the urine are resorbed by the body, leading to uremic toxicity. The only option in these cases is surgery.

We greatly appreciate the beauty and softness of the cat's coat. But dermatoses can mar that beauty.

The number one cause of **feline dermatosis** is parasite infestation, notably **flea** infestation.

The cat is susceptible to other more rare skin parasitoses:
including other forms of mange and lice causing miliary dermatitis and itching, cheyletiellosis producing seborrhea sicca, miliary dermatitis lesions, intense itching, and thick dandruff, which are transmissible to humans. The bright orange chigger larvae settle into the folds of the skin, particularly of the cat's ear, in summer. Ticks and demodex (mites) also occasionally feed on cats.

Ringworm invades the skin and the hair. It is caused by a dermatophyte fungus, typically Microsporum canis. These two conditions are discussed in the section on prevention of dermatoses and external fungi.

Miliary Dermatitis

This disease complex is characterized by a crusty rash and flaky skin that feels like fiber-glass. It is typically caused by an allergic reaction to flea bites, but may also be associated with a number of other feline skin conditions. Miliary dermatitis is not actually a disease, per se, but rather the manner in which a cat's skin reacts to various conditions. It is the most common skin disorder in cats. Apart from flea bites, possible causes include:

• Inhalant allergies, such as hypersensitivity to mites in dust; unlike humans, who develop hayfever, the allergic reaction in cats takes the form of itchiness and a scabby rash;
• Food intolerance or hypersensitivity;
• Bacterial folliculitis: bacteria (commonly staphylococcus) accumulate in the hair follicles and cause infection. This is typically the cause of chin acne;
• All skin parasitoses;
• Allergic reaction to medications;
• Malfunctioning of the immune system;
• Contact dermatitis, etc.

Treatment varies depending on the cause of the condition. Common treatments that normally produce satisfactory results include antihistamines, corticosteroids, essential fatty acids, and possibly megestrol acetate.

Cats suffering from **psychogenic alopecia and neurodermatosis** groom themselves incessantly. They lick, clean, and bite at themselves all day long. Some shy cats, or those that have been scolded for constant grooming, often clean themselves only at nighttime or out of view of the owner. All breeds, including strays, are subject to this condition, but Siamese, Orientals, Burmese, and Abyssinians are particularly prone to the disorder. These are also the breeds that commonly suck and eat wool. Once again, this condition is a disease complex, not a single disease. Many believe that it is purely stress-induced (possible stress factors being the introduction of a new cat into the household, loss of a loved one—animal or human—boredom, etc.). Others hold that it is exclusively an allergic reaction, and that the stress factors simply aggravate the condition.

Hormonal causes seem to be rare, though they are often mentioned as a possible explanation. If an underlying cause is uncovered, it is typically (in order of frequency) an allergic reaction to flea bites, an inhalant or food allergy, ringworm, or parasites.

The primary symptom of a **food allergy** is intense itching. This hypersensitivity to one or more elements in food can develop at any age. It is difficult to identify the particular offending substance(s), but without identifying the specific cause, the condition will not improve. In addition to constant itching, a cat suffering from a food allergy may also present milliary dermatitis, scabs on the head and neck, and thickened, irritated patches of skin.

Eosinophilic granuloma complex is a group of skin disorders specific to cats. It produces lesions that develop and spread gradually. Examination of the lesions reveals an abundance of eosinophilic cells.

Eosinophilic granuloma complex can be divided into three different categories. The eosinophilic ulcer, or indolent ulcer, almost always occurs on the upper lip. The eosinophilic plaque is an oozing, often ulcerated, lesion that causes intense itching. It typically occurs on the abdomen and inner thighs. Eosinophilic granuloma lesions appear in relatively straight lines and are firm areas of hair loss, most commonly occurring on the backs of the hindlimbs. The condition may clear up spontaneously in young cats, but older cats typically experience relapses and worsening of the condition. Some medications, including corticosteroids, offer some improvement of the lesions, but a definitive cure is elusive.

A cat's **eyes**, which lend charm and personality, are also subject to several diseases.

Congenital **eyelid disorders** may include the absence of an upper eyelid or entropion—inward turning of the eyelid causing the eyelashes to scratch the cornea and creating lesions. Surgery is required to correct these conditions. Blepharitis, infection of the eyelids, is caused by bacteria or fungi (ringworm).

The eyes are lubricated by **tears**. Insufficient tear production can lead to serious eye conditions, such as keratoconjunctivitis sicca.
Tears drain from the eyes through narrow lacrimal canaliculi (ducts), which sometimes become plugged as the result of infection or a congenital deformity. If tears do not drain properly, they flow down the sides of the nose leaving brownish markings.

Conjunctival diseases are common in cats. They are often one of the symptoms of a more general disease and are one of the early symptoms of chlamydiosis. The herpesvirus of infectious rhinotracheitis is responsible for a mucuslike, pussy discharge as well as keratitis punctata or serious corneal ulcerations, either during the acute stage of the illness or as a chronic condition following the primary infection.

Cat's sometimes develop **corneal lesions** that are unique to the feline species, such as corneal sequestrum, characterized by the formation of a blackish plaque on the corneal surface.

Uveitis causes the coloration of the iris to change. The iris becomes dull and pinkish, and the surface becomes hazy and rough. There are three types of uveitis specific to cats. They are part of the clinical presentation of feline leukemia, feline immunodeficiency virus, and feline infectious peritonitis. Uveitis may also appear in cases of toxoplasmosis, trauma, or eye infections.

Glaucoma, an elevation of intraocular pressure beyond normal levels, increases the volume of the eye and causes extreme pain.
The integrity of the **retina** is essential to good vision. Hemorrhages within the retina and retinal detachment may appear following trauma or serious illness. These two conditions are

also complications of uveitis. Retinal degeneration caused by taurine deficiency is no longer an issue, since commercial foods now contain adequate quantities of this essential amino acid. Dog food does not contain sufficient quantities of taurine, therefore it is not appropriate to feed cats dog food.

Finally, cats may also suffer from four **nervous disorders affecting the eyes**: Strabismus, third eyelid prolapse, Horner's syndrome (contraction of the pupil in one eye and prolapse of the third eyelid), dilated pupil syndrome, and feline dysautonomia.

Prolapse of the third eyelid

The cat has a third eyelid located at the inner corner of the eye. It helps protect the eye and distribute tears to protect the cornea. Sometimes, this third eyelid remains continuously visible for a variety of reasons:

• Mechanical causes related to the condition of the eye - microphthalmos (abnormally small eye) or atrophy of the eyeball, extreme weight loss, tumors, or trauma to retractor muscles caused by a scratch.

• Neurological causes irritating the area or disrupting equilibrium, an overactive parasympathetic system, or following an abdominal condition.

• Lesion of the cervical sympathetic nerves caused by a variety of conditions, including a herniated disc, otitis, a tumor, an abscess, or trauma.

In cats, most cases of prolapsed third eyelid follow an abdominal disorder. This is why the veterinarian is particularly interested in the health of the cat's digestive tract and often prescribes a laxative (for hairballs), a dewormer (undetected *dipylidium* tapeworm infections often produce this type of symptoms), or an intestinal antiseptic.

As the life expectancy of cats has increased, the number of **cancers** diagnosed has also risen. Perhaps cats, like us, are also suffering from the problems, such as pollution or an owner who smokes, associated with modern society.

A tumor—uncontrolled proliferation of cells—may be benign or malignant. A malignant tumor is called cancer. In cats, malignant tumors are six times more common than benign tumors after the age of three. Skin cancer is the most common cancer in the cat population as a whole, followed by mammary tumors, then various cancers of the soft tissues.

The occurrence of glandular tumors and lymphosarcomas is directly related to the feline leukemia infection rate.

Symptoms of cancer vary depending on the organ affected, the rate of growth of the tumor, whether it is localized or has metastasized, and its impact on other parts of the body (for example, a tumor in the endocrine gland).

Nevertheless, there are some general warning signs that warrant a trip to the veterinarian. Cancer produces localized and non-localized effects. Localized effects include a lump or visible or palpable swelling, destruction of the organ, compression of nearby organs or impaired function. Non-localized effects result from excessive or absence of production of a hormone, or production of substances by the tumor itself. Several non-specific signs may indicate cancer and merit further exploration.

These include weight loss, increased thirst or appetite, convulsions, cough, and internal or external bleeding.

If a veterinarian suspects a cancerous tumor, she will typically perform additional tests to confirm her diagnosis or to provide a more precise diagnosis. Some tests for tumors include x-rays, ultrasounds, and other more expensive techniques such as MRI or scanning. Yet another technique involves examining biopsied tissue or effused liquid under a microscope.

In animals, surgery is the primary treatment for cancerous tumors. Chemotherapy is sometimes elected in conjunction with surgery, or as the sole treatment method. Radiation therapy, in conjunction with surgery and/or chemotherapy, and immunotherapy are promising new techniques, but are still in the development stages.

Study of cancer in cats is of interest to comparative pathology. Feline leukemia, caused by infection with the feline leukemia virus, is one of the oldest known diseases for which researchers have been able to demonstrate cause and effect between a viral infection and the development of tumors.

The tumors most commonly associated with feline leukemia are lymphosarcomas. Though FIV (feline immunodeficiency virus) is not recognized as an oncogenic (causing tumor formation) disease, cats infected with FIV have a higher incidence of certain cancers, such as lymphosarcomas, myeloid tumors, and sarcomas.

Ear cancer in white cats

White-eared cats frequently exposed to the sun run a much greater risk of developing a cancerous tumor. Chronic irritation from the sun's rays gradually evolves, eventually resulting in squamous cell carcinoma. This type of tumor generally affects white-eared cats over eight years of age. The cancer first affects only the edge of the ear, then quickly spreads to the surrounding tissues. To protect your white-eared cat against cancer of the ears, keep him indoors in summer and during peak sunlight hours. Before the cancer spreads to the entire earflap, the edges of the ears should be amputated. Owners should be aware that recurrence is not uncommon despite amputation.

Diseases of Older Cats

The life expectancy of cats, at least those that receive medical care and loving attention, is increasing. It is important to recognize the disorders that can affect older cats so that they can be treated effectively.

• Coat and claws: The coat sometimes becomes so matted, particularly on the back and lumbar region, that thick knots form which cannot be brushed out. The claws also need special care since the older cat is not as active as he once was. Older cats require daily brushing and combing, and claws should be trimmed regularly. The older cat will appreciate this loving attention, which will stimulate his own desire to groom and improve his overall state of mind, warding off depression.

• Eyes: The color of the iris changes as a cat ages, and the pupil becomes opaque. This sclerosis of the lens, physiological in origin, has very little effect on eyesight.

• Teeth: Some cats have tartar buildup and begin losing teeth at a relatively young age. Oral hygiene products are available to keep the teeth clean, and a veterinarian can remove tartar buildup, or extract teeth if necessary.

• Sensory organs: The senses tend to diminish with age.

• Heart: Heart failure is rare, except in cases of hyperthyroidism.

• Endocrine glands: These glands are often affected by the aging process. Diabetes is not uncommon and is difficult to control.

• Digestive System: With age, a cat's digestive enzymes become less efficient, and as a result, older cats tend to lose weight. Chronic diarrhea is sometimes a problem.

• Reproduction: Reproduction declines gradually with age. Most mammary tumors are malignant, and therefore prognosis is generally not promising.

• Respiratory system: The health of the respiratory systems depends more on the medical history of the individual cat than age.

• Musculoskeletal system: Unfortunately, arthritis and joint pain is the lot of the older cat.

• Kidneys: Owners should be on the lookout for symptoms of chronic kidney failure.

• Cancer and tumors: The occurrence of cancer increases with age.

Household Dangers

Though indoor/outdoor cats are more likely to contract infectious diseases and fall victim to an accident, indoor cats are not entirely out of harms way. Cats of all ages fall, but young cats run the greatest risk of falling, since they are still exploring the limits of their environment. Therefore, it is wise to place a screen or net around terraces and balconies.

The kitchen is filled with many potential dangers—hot burners, boiling water, hot food, fryers, knives, open bottles, strings tied around meat, etc.

An iron is also a potential hazard, as are electrical cords. Young cats love to chew. If they bite through an electrical cord, they may suffer a severe burn on the mouth in the best case scenario, and death by electrocution in the worst case scenario.

Cats can drown in washing machines, bathtubs, or even in the toilet bowl.

Cats are rarely poisoned by household products because they are finicky about what they eat, but many houseplants cause irritation or are poisonous to cats.

Some toys, such as bells and strings, also pose a threat. Never leave a threaded needle lying around.

The Most Common Types of Poisoning

Cats tend to taste their food before indulging, so poisoning is fairly uncommon. However, some poisons have a taste that the cat likes, or a cat may eat small prey that has consumed toxic products.

Cats lack detoxification mechanisms and are less likely than dogs to regurgitate disagreeable substances. A cat's nervous system is very easily disrupted by a number of poisons.

Dangerous products include:
• Pesticides
- agricultural herbicides
- chlorinated hydrocarbons used to treat wood (sawdust from treated wood should not be used for litter)
- carbamate insecticides
- chloralose, the chemical used to kill rodents and crows. Sadly individuals who have no respect for the law or animals also use this product to kill cats.
- strychnine and crimidine, the two most common convulsants
- metaldehyde, used in gardens to control snails and slugs
- anticoagulants, most commonly ingested by eating a poisoned rodent.

• Medications
- external parasite medications, most often resulting from incorrect application
- aspirin (aspirin is sometimes used for iliac thromboses, but should only be administered in small doses and strictly under the supervision of a veterinarian)
- acetaminophen.

• Plants: Young cats are the most commonly affected after playing with the leaves of plants, particularly houseplants, such as Dieffenbachia.

• Pollutants and various household chemical products, such as white spirits and antifreeze.

Though the conditions described in this chapter are the most common, they by no means represent an exhaustive list of the afflictions that can befall cats. If in doubt, consult your veterinarian immediately. In most cases, early treatment greatly increases the likelihood of complete recovery, ensuring that you and your cat will enjoy a long life together.

THE CAT AND THE LAW

As cat populations grow, countries around the world are creating new laws to regulate cats' place in society.

In general, most countries regulate the legal status, sale, trade, breeding, mandatory registration, insurance, identification, vaccination, and protection of the animal and its environment, and have laws in place with regard to owners responsibilities vis-à-vis society.

For information regarding a specific country, contact the local feline association for that country (see Useful Addresses on p. 448).

The veterinarian and your cat

Though there are more cats in France than dogs, cats are seen less often at veterinary offices than dogs. So why are owners more likely to take their dog to the vet?

Generally, cat owners avoid taking their cat to the vet because they are afraid the trip will not go well. Cats tend to get very upset about visits to the vet. They do not like to leave home, and certainly have no interest in a clinic filled with the smells of other cats. And being independent creatures, they do not appreciate being required to stand immobile on the examination table, to be poked and prodded by a stranger and worse yet, stuck with needles.

The owner's presence during an examination will help calm the cat.

Urban owners tend also to think that their indoor cats are safe from infectious diseases, whereas owners living in rural areas do not feel the need to invest in vaccinations and sterilization, arguing that their cats will probably die young anyway as the result of an accident, possibly being struck by a car or shot by a careless neighbor.

The cat himself is also partly at fault. Cats rarely complain and adapt readily to their handicaps. They often hide their illness well, so owners do not become concerned until the symptoms are very serious. Anemia commonly goes unnoticed for an extended period of time. The cat suffering from anemia is often not taken to see a veterinarian until the terminal stage of the illness, when hemoglobin levels are low and the red blood cell count has plummeted. In anemia, the blood is no longer able to carry sufficient quantities of oxygen, so the cat becomes winded easily. But he adapts by limiting his activity. It is not until the disease is very advanced, when hemoglobin levels are down to 4 or 5 g/dl (normal levels being 10 to 15 g/dl), that the owner finally notices that something is wrong.

Despite all this, cats receive considerably more attention from their owners and veterinarians now than they did in the past. Some basic practices will help your cat "survive" a trip to the vet.

Transporting a cat

Your cat will feel much more secure if he is transported in a cat carrier. Make sure he is in the carrier when you take him out to the car and when he is in the waiting room. (Note that some cats prefer to move about freely in the car, rather than remain in their carrier.) The carrier serves as a hiding place, protecting the cat from humans and other animals, dogs and cats alike. The carrier also provides protection against disease, shielding your cat from the secretions of a sneezing cat suffering from rhinitis. If you take a taxi rather than your own car, chose a watertight plastic carrier that will not allow urine or vomit to escape from the bottom if your cat has an accident. If your cat refuses to get into the carrier, turn him around and put him in backend first. If your cat tends to be aggressive toward the veterinarian, select a carrier that opens from the top (basket type). The vet will have less difficult taking hold of the cat. If instead, you make the trip to the veterinarian on foot, chose a soft carrier with a flat bottom, which is easier to carry. Some very calm cats will walk on a leash and others like to ride on their owner's shoulder, though many become agitated when they arrive in the waiting room since they have nowhere to hide.

The visit

Most veterinarians prefer that the owner remain in the room with the cat to offer reas-

surance. It is important that the cat be able to see or smell his owner at all times. Timid cats like to hide their head under their owner's arm or a piece of clothing.

A cat is generally only minimally restrained during examination. The veterinarian holds the cat on the examination table with one hand placed on the front of the chest. If an injection or painful palpation is required, the veterinarian will hold the cat by the scruff of the neck so that he cannot escape. Though this may look uncomfortable, it causes no pain to the animal.

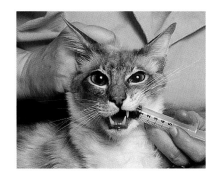

Taking blood or capturing a urine sample may require a veterinary assistant and firmer restraint. The owner must make an effort to remain calm since cats are very sensitive to the moods of their owners. Speed and composure are the keys to success, so the cat does not become impatient or panic.

In rare instances, a veterinarian will be required to take more extreme measures to restrain a particularly aggressive cat. Sometimes a cat becomes so upset that he panics and loses control, turning into a whirling dervish biting and scratching at everything within reach, even his owner, whom he no longer recognizes. In such situations, thick gloves and a large towel are called for to restrain the cat. Though this method may seem cruel upon first consideration, it is actually in the best interest of all concerned, since it prevents the cat from injuring himself and others.

Symptoms

It is difficult to treat cats because their symptoms are often well hidden, and the same symptoms—inappetence, vomiting, reclusion—are common to several diseases. Unlike dogs, which complain when they are in pain, cats simply stop all activity, conserve energy, and hide. Fortunately for veterinarians, owners often notice minor behavioral changes. Therefore, before the veterinarian examines the animal, it is important that the owner describe in detail everything out of the ordinary that he has noticed. This discussion time will also give the cat a chance to relax a bit and feel more at ease.

The clinical examitation

Next, the veterinarian will examine the cat. This important step must be done in such a way that it does not overly stress the animal. The veterinarian will inspect the color of the mucous membranes, smell the cat's breath, and examine the coat. She will use an ophthalmoscope to examine the eyes and an otoscope for the ears. Next, she will palpate the abdomen, which is typically fairly easy since a

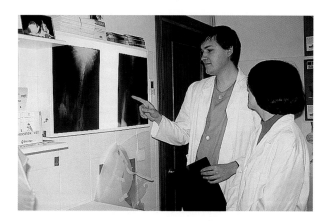

cat is quite small. When palpating, the vet is looking for abnormal masses, such as swollen glands, tumors, or foreign bodies. At the same time, she checks the consistency of the bladder and the intestines. Finally, using a stethoscope, the veterinarian will listen to the cat's lungs and heart. Cats have a rapid heart rate, beating 200 times per minute on average, but reaching as much as 260 beats per minutes when the cat is frightened. It can be difficult to hear the lungs and heart clearly if the cat is purring, often the case with kittens and extremely sick geriatric cats. In geriatric cats, this purring is not a sign of pleasure, but instead a sign that the cat is suffering. Additional tests, such as blood and/or urine analysis, x-rays, ultrasound, or biopsy, are often necessary to make a definitive diagnosis. Since cats show few outward signs, a veterinarian

must apply all her knowledge and insight to diagnose the cat's specific condition.

Fortunately, feline medicine is growing by leaps and bounds, due in large part to demand on the part of cat owners who are increasingly concerned about the health and well-being of their small companions. Cats that visit the veterinarian regularly, beginning at a very young age for vaccinations, become accustomed to being handled.

Feline medicine in France and abroad

Feline medicine has made remarkable advances since the 1960s. It is the field of internal medicine that has developed the most, starting with the identification of viral diseases, then the leukemia virus, immunodeficiency syndrome, and feline infectious peritonitis, followed by urinary tract disorders (such as kidney failure and cystitis, leading to the development of new "urinary tract health" foods), liver disorders (the various forms of hepatitis responsible for jaundice), and most recently, heart disorders which are now easier to identify thanks to advances in ultrasound and Doppler technologies.

The English-speaking world is particularly advanced in this field. Cornell University in New York formed a department devoted exclusively to feline medicine twenty-five years ago. The University of Bristol in the United Kingdom led the way in Europe, creating a feline medicine department in 1993. In France, breeders and veterinarians have formed the Société française de félinotechnie (S.F.F.), which organizes conferences focusing exclusively on cat health issues.

Cat clinics

Veterinary clinics devoted exclusively to cats have appeared in some countries, springing from a passion for cats. The first cat clinic was founded by Dr. Barbara Stein in Chicago in

1975. Many others followed suit, and now more than three hundred cat clinics exist in the United States alone. The first cat clinic in Europe opened in Denmark in October 1987. Similar clinics opened soon after in Great Britain and France. Access to these clinics is reserved exclusively to cats, in order to avoid introducing the smells and noises of other animals, which could disturb the cats.

The field of cat medicine is progressing at a swift pace. Cat owners, breeders, researchers, and veterinarians alike have taken notice. These cat lovers are delighted with all the attention that the object of their affections is receiving!

Hospitalization

When a cat is hospitalized, certain steps are taken to make the cat as comfortable as possible. Cats scare easily and require considerable sleep—18 hours per day on average. Cats are housed away from barking dogs, since if a cat cannot sleep, it becomes irritable. Moreover, cats love comfort, so they should not be placed in a cold, empty cage. A bed and cushion must be provided, and a piece of clothing with familiar smells, such as the owners scarf or sweater, will be a comfort. The area must be heated. Though cats do not like noise, they do enjoy some level of activity, such as watching birds outside a window or the presence or movement of people. This allows the cat to enjoy his favorite activity—watching the world go by as he relaxes. Cats enjoy a visit by their owner, and it is often during such visits that cats begin eating again after undergoing surgery. The visit also gives the cat incentive to get his legs back under him so he can walk over to see his owner. Cats like to keep clean, therefore every attempt should be made to groom them—brushing, cleaning the eyes and the mouth, etc. It's the little things that count. Grooming, petting, the cat's favorite food, sweet talk... all help keep a cat's spirits up. When outside his familiar environment, a cat can easily give up hope, no matter how good the medical attention that he receives.

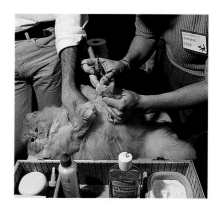

SYMPTOMS THAT WARRANT A VISIT TO THE VET

- Coughing or sneezing
- Runny eyes and/or nose
- Drooling, the cat stops grooming himself (gingivitis and toothache)
- Recurring vomiting and diarrhea
- Labored breathing with exaggerated chest motion (presence of liquid in the chest)
- Yellow skin and mucous membranes: Gums, conjunctiva, earflap (sign of jaundice)
- Any mass or growth on or under the skin or near the mammary glands (possible tumor)
- Vaginal discharge: Pus or blood (sign of metritis or uterine cancer)
- Increased water intake coupled with excessive urination (sign of liver or kidney failure or diabetes)
- The cat crouches by the water bowl, but does not drink
- The cat has "accidents" (urinates or defecates outside of the litter box)
- Frequent trips to the litter box, but the cat is unable to urinate or produces only a few drops of urine (cystitis)
- The cat suddenly becomes aggressive and begins biting (possible toothache)
- A geriatric cat that suddenly begins running into furniture (vision loss caused by hypertension)

U S E F U L   A D R E S S E S

Fédération Internationale Féline
d'Europe (FIFe)
Présidente : Mrs Alva Uddin
Little Dene, Lenham Heath
GB Maidstone – Kent –ME 14 2BS
Angleterre
Tél : 44 16 22 858 510
Fax : 44 16 22 850 908

World Cat Federation (W.C.F.)
Présidente : Mrs Anneliese
Hackmann
280 Hubertstr. D – 45307 Essen
Allemagne
Tél : 49 201 55 07 55
Fax : 49 201 55 27 47

FRANCE

Société Française de
Félinotechnie(SFF)
Ecole Nationale Vétérinaire,
7, avenue du général de Gaulle
94704 - Maison-Alfort
Tél : 02 35 28 11 57

Livre Officiel des Origines Félines
(LOOF)
C/O SCC
5, rue Regnault
935300 Pantin

BELGIUM

Cat Fanciers of Belgium (CFB)
Avenue du Domaine
1190 BRUXELLES
Tél : (0)2 343 44 55

Felin's Fan Cat Club de Belgique
(FCCB)
rue Try des Mâles 39
5190 Jemeppe sur Sambre
Tél : 071 78 43 14

Association Autonome des
Amateurs Félins (AAAF)
rue du château d'eau 43
4680 Oupeye
Tél : 04 264 42 29

Antwerp International Cat Club
(AICC)
Ravelbergstraat 59
2100 Deurne
Tél : 03 366 10 82

UNITED KINGDOM

The Governing Council of the Cat
Fancy (GCCF)
4-6 Penel Orlieu
Bridgewater Somerset TA6 3PG
Tél : 44 1278 427 575

The Cat Association of Britain
(CAB)
Mill House / Letcombe Regis
Oxen – OX12 9 JD
Tél 44 12357 66543

ITALY

Federazione Italiana Associazioni
Feline (FIAF)
Via Carlo Poma, 20
46100 Mantova
Tél : 39 376 224600
Fax : 39 376 224041

Associazione Nazionale Felina
Italiana (ANFI)
Via Principi d'Acaja, 20
10100 Torino
Tél : 39 11 4344627
Fax : 39 11 4332479

SPAIN

Asociacion Felina Espanola
(ASFE)
C/Capitan Haya N°47,
Despacho 402
28520 MADRID
Tél-Fax : 34 1 571 66 65

Club Felino de Madrid (CFM)
C/Baeza, 4,
28002 MADRID
Tél : 91 413 23 59

SWEDEN

SVERAKs KANSLI
Box 55174
504 04 Boras
Tél : 033 10 15 65
Fax : 033 10 08 99

STOCKHOLMS KATTKLUBB
Braviksvägen 29
120 52 Arsta
Tél/Fax : 08 741 05 26

SYDKATTEN
Grastensvägen 5
261 71 Landskrona
Tél : 0418 302 12
NERIKES KATTKLUB
Skottvallavägen 692 36 Kumla
Tél : 019-56 01 25

VASTSVENSKA KATTKLUB-
BEN
Pepparedsäng 25
431 50 Mölndal
Tél : 031 87 87 01

VASTERAS KATTKLUBB
Eddagatan 31
723 55 Vasreras
Tel : 021 224 52

NORWAY

NRR
Postboks 8769 Youngstorget,
00228 Oslo
Tél : 47 22 42 88 89
Fax : 47 22 41 02 48
http://www.nrr.no

DENMARK

LANDES FORENINGEN FELIS
DANICA
Tryggevaeldevej 145
2700 BRONSHOJ
Tél : 45 31 60 49 88

JYRAK
Esbjergparken 5
9220 Aalborg
Tel : 45 981 59348

RACEKATTEN
Egebjersvej 112 ,1tr
4500 Nykobing
Tel : 45 5993182

DARAK
Tryggevealdevej 145
2700 Bronshoj
Tel :45 31604988

PERSEREN
Lyngby 4
9370 Hals
Tel : 45 98750707

NETHERLANDS

FELIKAT
Jol 9
NL-1276 BS Huizen
Tél – Fax : 31 355243270

Nederlandse Vereniging Van
Kattenvrienden (N.V.V.K)
Steendonkstraat 132
B 9140 Temse
België
Tel : 32 37 711 545

Nederlandse Katten Fokkers
Vereniging (N.K.F.V)
Vaartje 6
5156 NB Waspik
Tél – Fax : 0416 313987

NEOCAT
Slochterwaard 19
1824 KR Alkmaar
Tél – Fax : 072 5622821

O.P. : Committee Overleg
Platform van de Nederlandse Cat
Fancy
Ludermarbog 69
9722 WG Groningen
Tél – Fax : 050 5276601

GERMANY

Deutsche Edelkatze e.V
280 Hubertstr.
D – 45307 Essen
Tél : 49 201 55 07 55

RVDE Ev rattaché au WACC
Sprengertteich 10
24220 Flintbek
Tél. : 49 043473916
Fax 49 043479767

Erster Deutscher
Edelkatzenzuchter
Verband(EDEV)
Berliner strasse, 13
Asslar
Tél : 49 64 41 84 79

Berliner Edelkatzen-club e.V

Niederbergischer Katzenverein

Siegerländer Rassenkatzen-
Verband

CANADA

Association féline Candienne
20, advance Blvd
Suite 101
Branpton, Ontario L6T4J5
Tél : 1 905 459 14 81